Feeding the Victorian city

IN MEMORIAM

Roger Scola, April 1987

Plate 1 Manchester from Kersal Moor, *c.* 1840

Feeding the Victorian city

The food supply of Manchester, 1770–1870

ROGER SCOLA

edited by
W. A. Armstrong *and* Pauline Scola

Manchester University Press
Manchester and New York
Distributed exclusively in the USA and Canada by St. Martin's Press

Published by Manchester University Press
Oxford Road, Manchester M13 9PL, England
and Room 400, 175 Fifth Avenue, New York, NY 10010, USA

Distributed exclusively in the USA and Canada
by St. Martin's Press, Inc., 175 Fifth Avenue, New York,
NY 10010, USA

A catalogue record for this book is available from the British Library

Library of Congress cataloging in publication data
Scola, Roger.
    Feeding the Victorian city : the food supply of Manchester,
1770–1870 / Roger Scola.
        p.   cm.
    Includes bibliographical references and index.
    ISBN 0–7190–3088–9
    1. Food supply—England—Manchester—History.   2. Food industry
and trade—England—Manchester—History.   I. Title.
HD9011.8.M36S38   1991
363.8'09427'3309034—dc20   91–15929

ISBN 0 7190 3088 9 *hardback*

Typeset in Great Britain
by Northern Phototypesetting Co. Ltd, Bolton
Printed in Great Britain
by Bell and Bain Ltd., Glasgow

Contents

Contents

Contents

Illustrations

Plates

Line illustrations

Maps

Figures

xi

Tables

Tables

Tables

Abbreviations

Record repositories

HLRO	House of Lords Record Office
JRULM	John Rylands University Library of Manchester
LRO	Lancashire County Record Office
MCL	Manchester Central Library
MCLAD	Manchester Central Library, Archives Department
MTH	Manchester Town Hall, Muniments Room
PRO	Public Record Office

Miscellaneous

Aikin	J. Aikin, *A Description of the Country from Thirty to Forty Miles round Manchester*, London, 1795
Courier	*The Manchester Courier*
Court Leet	*The Court Leet Records of the Manor of Manchester*, J.P. Earwaker (ed.), VIII–XII, 1756–1846, Manchester, 1888–90
EcHR	*Economic History Review*
Guardian	*The Manchester Guardian*
HC	House of Commons
HL	House of Lords
Holt	J. Holt, *General View of the Agriculture of the County of Lancaster*, London, 1795
JRASE	*Journal of the Royal Agricultural Society of England*
JSSL	*Journal of the Statistical Society of London*
MC	Manchester Borough/City Council
Mercury	*The Manchester Mercury*

MPC	Manchester Police Commissioners
PP	*Parliamentary Papers*
Redford	A. Redford and I.S. Russell, *The History of Local Government in Manchester*, 3 vols., London, 1939–40
SC	Salford Borough Council
SPC	Salford Police Commissioners
TLCAS	*Transactions of the Lancashire and Cheshire Antiquarian Society*

Foreword

ROGER SCOLA was born in 1943 and brought up at Hastings and later in London, where he attended the Stationers' Company's School. In October 1961 he opted to go up to the University of Manchester, as a state scholar, to read history. This was a decision he never regretted. Then, as now, the Manchester history department subsumed economic and social history, and he was soon drawn towards this field of specialisation in which he was to make his career.

After taking his degree, he spent the following year pursuing the postgraduate certificate in education, before embarking on a doctoral thesis on the food supply of Manchester, 1770–1870. As it happened, he gave only one year's full-time study to this project because, like others of his generation, he was soon caught up in the heady expansion of the university system, being appointed to a lectureship at the University of Kent from October 1966. However, scarcely had he settled in Canterbury with his wife, Pauline, a fellow Manchester graduate, when, after a serious illness, he was diagnosed as having Hodgkin's disease, a cancer of the lymph system, and only a very limited life expectation. In fact, what turned out to be a twenty-one-year struggle began, punctuated at first by courses of radiotherapy and, from 1971, by increasingly frequent chemotherapy, with debilitating side-effects. In the face of such adversities, the courage he displayed was truly astounding.

Had Roger enjoyed normal health, there is no knowing how far he would have progressed in his chosen career, such were his natural talents. In the circumstances, it was perhaps as a teacher that he made his most important contribution to the life of the University of Kent. With the postgraduate certificate in education behind him, he aspired to be an educator and not simply a purveyor of historical facts, maintaining an abiding interest in the art of teaching to an extent that is unusual in university circles. This was not simply a matter of careful preparation, meticulous though that invariably was; he was a firm advocate of the view that history should not merely be interesting, but should be used to further our understanding of the present. Students often remarked on the uncompromisingly high standards he set, while tempering his candour with wit, good humour, approachability and an ever-ready sympathy and patience whenever this was needful. His standing as a teacher was recognised when he was named as one of only a handful deemed exemplary in a 1985 edition of *Phoenix*, the Kent students' magazine; it was reinforced by tributes in the numerous letters received from former students in 1988–89. One, a handicapped student, remarked on how his life was transformed by 'Kent and Roger Scola'; another recalled his seminars as 'truly inspirational'.

Roger's popularity and esteem among his academic colleagues was just as great. Among those who knew about his situation, there was general admiration for the way he coped with his illness, never using it as an excuse to avoid responsibilities. His contribution to the administration of both the Board of Studies in Economic and Social History and the Social Science Faculty was generous and unstinting; as a valued member of the library committee, he was instrumental in setting up the reserve collection; in addition, he was one of the first secretaries of the Kent Association of University Teachers. Tenacious in argument and shrewd in judgement, his advice was always wise and universally respected. Many more colleagues knew him, rather, as an eminently likeable companion whose humour could invariably lift their spirits. He was, too, an engaging conversationalist and, with the same enthusiasm that he brought to bear on economic history, would discourse upon arcane horticultural matters, or analyse and debate the fortunes of the Labour Party, Arsenal Football Club and county and test cricket.

The effects of his illness were most obvious with regard to his own work, since he was not able to bring to full fruition his extensive and ongoing researches on Manchester. Even so, his chief publications (an article in the inaugural volume of the *Journal of Historical Geography* (1975) and a valuable essay in Johnson and Pooley (eds.), *The Structure of Nineteenth Century Cities* (1982) – for details, see Bibliography) established him as an authority on food history and the much-neglected retail trade. His advice was sought and highly valued by other explorers in these fields, including research students and staff at other universities, both in this country and abroad.

When Roger died, in April 1988, Pauline felt that the most fitting memorial to her husband would be the publication of his researches. The original intention to submit the work for a Ph.D. had been abandoned many years before, and the text that follows is the book that Roger hoped to publish and which he came so close to completing. Although Chapters I–X of his text potentially required only some re-ordering, I decided to revise and expand Chapter II to take account of recent research on Manchester, as Roger would have done, had he been able. It was also necessary to prepare a final chapter, which I hope does justice to the richness of the research findings, and which aims to set out the conclusions that his plan indicated he would have been inclined to draw.

This is the first book-length study to appear on the supply of food to, and its distribution in, a major city and, as such, it should commend itself to a wide audience among historians and social scientists. It has been a privilege to have been associated with its publication, but a far greater one is simply to have known Roger Scola.

Alan Armstrong

Acknowledgements

ROGER would have wished to express his gratitude to those who helped him in various ways in the research and preparation of this work: to Professor A.E. Musson of the University of Manchester, who initially guided him to this subject; to Professor T.C. Barker, who subsequently took a close interest in its development during the years when they were colleagues; to archivists and librarians in Manchester, London and elsewhere; to John Pell of the University of Kent, who drew the graphs, which are pivotal to the argument in several chapters; and to the University of Kent, which granted him occasional periods of study leave.

Since his death, many people have assisted in the preparation of the book for publication: the staff of the library of the University of Kent, and John Goy in particular, have been unfailingly helpful; Margaret De Motte and Jean Ayton of Manchester Central Library have given invaluable assistance both in the compilation of the Bibliography and in locating illustrative material; Jim Styles, photographer of the University of Kent, and his assistant, John West, have coped remarkably with that material to produce the illustrations; Judith Fox of the University of Reading has drawn the maps; and Professor D.J. Oddy, Richard Perren, John Walton and Michael Winstanley have given much-appreciated advice. Thanks are also due to friends who have given generously of their time and expertise, namely, Stewart Miller, Robin Dowie, Theo Barker, John Hatcher, Jim Hughes, Leslie Pressnell, Eunice Flavell and especially Keith Lindley and Sue Horrocks. Sue Macdonald, who had been Roger's secretary for many years, has continued to give support by typing the manuscript; Ray Offord, Juanita Bullough, Jane Carpenter and David Rodgers of Manchester University Press have provided essential counsel throughout the editorial process; and the University of Kent has given a grant to cover the cost of maps and illustrations. All the above-mentioned have contributed to ensure that this book is in every way as Roger would have wished it to be.

Pauline Scola
Alan Armstrong

CHAPTER I

Introduction:
Background, scope and sources

WHEN I began these researches, the neglect of food history was serious enough to provoke the comment: 'It is incredible that economic historians, whose work is concerned so much with standards of living, have done so little to study the history of food'.[1] There was, of course, a good deal of justice in this criticism, although exceptions could be made. Levels of nutrition had featured in the discussion about the reasons for the fall in mortality in the eighteenth and nineteenth centuries,[2] and the debate about the living standards of the working classes during the Industrial Revolution was beginning to direct attention to the question of what people actually ate. Changes in the prices of various foodstuffs had long been an important component of the different cost-of-living indices used,[3] but in the Hobsbawm–Hartwell confrontation of the later 1950s and early 1960s, the consumption of food was given a much more central position. Hobsbawm went so far as to claim that evidence about consumption patterns – and here he seems to have meant mainly food – was the area 'least likely to lead to contestable results',[4] and both authors devoted much space to rehearsing and refuting arguments about whether or not the working-class diet improved, not only in a

---

[1] Quoted in J. Yudkin, 'History and the nutritionist', in T.C. Barker, J.C. McKenzie and J. Yudkin (eds.), *Our Changing Fare*, London, 1966, p. 150.

[2] T. McKeown and R.G. Brown, 'Medical evidence related to English population changes in the eighteenth century', *Population Studies*, IX, 1955, esp. pp. 140–1; T. McKeown and R.G. Record, 'Reasons for the decline of mortality in England and Wales during the nineteenth century', *Population Studies*, XVI, 1962, esp. pp. 114–16.

[3] See particularly T.S. Ashton, 'The standard of life of the workers in England, 1790–1830', in F.A. Hayek (ed.), *Capitalism and the Historians*, London, 1954, pp. 152–6.

[4] E.J. Hobsbawm and R.M. Hartwell, 'The standard of living during the industrial revolution: a discussion', *EcHR*, 2nd ser., XVI, 1963, p. 121.

quantitative sense but also qualitatively. Much of the debate centred around whether such items of food as meat, fish and vegetables appeared on working-class tables in sufficient quantities to indicate a general rise in living standards.[5]

There are two ways of approaching the subject of food consumption: one is through the evidence of diets, and the other is through the study of changes in the supply of food. While the dietary method is obviously more direct, the available documentation is extremely fragmentary. Accounts of what people actually ate are few and far between, and even rarer are those which were compiled systematically over a long enough period of time to enable historians and nutritionists to assess the significance of any changes on more than an impressionistic basis.[6] The alternative approach, by way of the supply of food, appeared to me more promising. Not only would there be less dependence on the chance survival of individual pieces of evidence, but it would be possible to use a wider range of sources to build up a picture of changes in the quantities and sorts of food being supplied to any particular community. Here, it seemed, was an aspect of the problem that could be resolved by a detailed examination. *Per capita* figures of imported goods, such as tea and sugar, were readily accessible, but more intriguing was the supply of home-produced foodstuffs. Surely, for example, it should be feasible to determine whether the supply of vegetables improved in response to the growth of large urban markets, or to assess the extent to which developments in the fishing industry and transport increased the availability of fish in inland towns? Moreover, it was generally acknowledged that, to counterbalance an excessive reliance on London, more information was needed about provincial trends. Here, sound historical reasons and personal motives happily came together to suggest Manchester as the provincial town to be studied.

My topic, then, had become the food supply of Manchester, with as yet only an approximate idea of the period to be covered, except that it would obviously extend over the years of most rapid growth from the

[5] The main points of the discussion were contained in E.J. Hobsbawm, 'The British standard of living, 1790–1850', *EcHR*, 2nd ser., X, 1957, pp. 57–60, 62–8; R.M. Hartwell, 'The rising standard of living in England, 1800–1850', *EcHR*, 2nd ser., XIII, 1961, pp. 406–12; and Hobsbawm and Hartwell, 'Standard of living', pp. 132–4, 143–6.

[6] What can be done in this area is well illustrated by J.C. McKenzie, 'The composition and nutritional value of diets in Manchester and Dukinfield in 1841', *TLCAS*, LXXII, 1962, pp. 123–40; and T.C. Barker, D.J. Oddy and J. Yudkin, *The Dietary Surveys of Dr Edward Smith 1862–3: A New Assessment*, Occasional Paper No. 1, Department of Nutrition, Queen Elizabeth College, London, 1970.

later eighteenth century through the first half of the nineteenth. The first task, however, was to break the subject matter down into a number of component themes. My first inclination was to look at the response of the food producers to the growth of a large urban population; to examine how this produce reached Manchester; and to explore the ways in which the markets of the town distributed it. But very quickly I came up against the problem of a rapidly expanding supply system:

Time was when this market was dependent upon Cheshire and the Lancashire bank of the Mersey for its supplies of fresh vegetables and fruits; but since the abolition of duties, improved steam navigation, and the more complete development of the railway system, no spot upon the earth's surface appears sufficiently remote to deprive the teeming populations of these districts of its productions.[7]

Leaving aside the difficulties of isolating the impact of the growth of Manchester from that of other markets, food reached the town from increasingly distant parts of Britain and other countries, and it would have been quite impossible to examine the response of food producers across an ever-widening area of supply. Even on a more restricted scale, it seemed that such a study would require the detailed examination of estate and farm records and an immersion in the nicer points of agricultural history, which would pull me further away from the objective of looking at how the people of Manchester were fed. It would be more sensible to consider the question of the supply of food from the point of view of the needs of Manchester rather than from that of the response of the producers.

The other end of the chain, the market place, was too constricting. It soon became clear that the markets of a large industrial town could be understood only in the context of the distribution system as a whole, and that I needed to extend my proposed field of study into an examination of food retailing in Manchester in a much broader sense than I had originally intended. These realisations involved a shift in emphasis rather than a redefining of the topic. My concern now was with the marketing of food rather than its production, and with the means by which it was distributed once it reached the town.

Of course, every academic thinks that his or her topic is a much neglected one, but my subject did seem to span an area in which surprisingly little had been written: agricultural historians were being

---

[7] J. Page, 'The sources of supply of the Manchester fruit and vegetable markets', *JRASE*, 2nd ser., XVI, 1880, p. 475.

roundly condemned for having 'lost interest in the produce of the land once it had rumbled off through the farm gate', and for exceptions, the writer was having to cast back to the work of Fussell and Goodman of the previous generation.[8] The force of the criticism might be thought to rest on how neatly one could label both historians and their subject matter; certainly, studies as diverse as those of Skeel and Haldane on aspects of the cattle droving trade and that of Westerfield on the growth of middlemen did contain useful insights into the process by which farm produce became available to the urban consumer.[9] However, it was true that, with the exception of Fussell and Goodman, only Fisher, in his celebrated study of London in the sixteenth and early seventeenth centuries, had looked at the problem directly.[10] For the nineteenth century, Whetham's survey of the milk supply of London had shown the profound impact of the railways, but the work which pointed the way more clearly than any other to the kind of study that I envisaged was Blackman's article on Sheffield.[11] The themes examined there were common to most of the writings on the marketing of foodstuffs, namely, the widening of the area of supply; the impact, often delayed, of transport innovations; and the growth of intermediaries between producer and consumer. But what her work also suggested was the potential for exploring the sequence of developments from the later eighteenth century across a range of foodstuffs that were being supplied to a provincial town, and for relating these to the changing methods of distribution within that town. She was not alone in following food into the market place, but she went a good deal

[8] T.C. Barker, 'Nineteenth century diet; some twentieth century questions', in Barker, McKenzie and Yudkin (eds.), *Our Changing Fare*, p. 18; and see G.E. Fussell and C. Goodman, 'Eighteenth-century traffic in livestock', *Economic History*, III, 1934–37, pp. 214–36; *idem*, 'The eighteenth-century traffic in milk products', *ibid.*, pp. 380–7; *idem*, 'Traffic in farm produce in eighteenth-century England; except livestock and livestock products', *Agricultural History*, XII, 1938, pp. 355–68.

[9] C. Skeel, 'The cattle trade between Wales and England from the fifteenth to the nineteenth centuries', *Transactions of the Royal Historical Society*, 4th ser., IX, 1926, pp. 135–58; A.R.B. Haldane, *The Drove Roads of Scotland*, London, 1952; R.B. Westerfield, *Middlemen in English Business, particularly between 1660 and 1760*, New Haven, Conn., 1915. See also J.H. Smith, 'The cattle trade of Aberdeenshire in the nineteenth century', *Agricultural History Review*, III, 1955, pp. 114–18.

[10] F.J. Fisher, 'The development of the London food market, 1540–1640', *EcHR*, 1st ser., V, 1934–5, pp. 46–64; see also P.V. McGrath, 'The marketing of food, fodder and livestock in the London area in the seventeenth century, with some reference to the sources of supply', University of London, M.A., 1948.

[11] E.H. Whetham, 'The London milk trade, 1860–1900', *EcHR*, 2nd ser., XVII, 1964, pp. 369–80; J. Blackman, 'The food supply of an industrial town: a study of Sheffield's public markets, 1780–1900', *Business History*, V, 1963, pp. 83–97.

further than others in linking what was happening there to changes in the distribution system as a whole.

In this, Blackman touched on another area which had long been overlooked in economic history. Certainly, the tertiary sector of the economy has always tended to come a poor third to the extractive and production industries on the research agenda. In part, as Wilson has said, this may be attributable to the notion that 'the distribution of jam, corned beef and margarine [is] not the most obvious stuff from which to fashion either weighty economic theory or even significant history'.[12] In the mid-1960s, however, it also reflected the feeling that this was an area about which little more needed to be said, in that there existed a book definitive enough to make further research almost unnecessary. This was J.B. Jefferys' *Retail Trading in Britain, 1850–1950*, published in 1954. His starting point was that the distributive sector had been remarkably slow to respond to the growth of urban–industrial society, and, although his interest lay chiefly in the century after 1850, his views set the tone for any discussion of the previous half-century or more. Jefferys saw the retail trades as small-scale, under-capitalised, labour-intensive and run on essentially pre-industrial lines. They did not emerge from this stage of development until after 1850, and it was not until two decades later that the process gathered pace, when economies of scale began to be exploited through the multiple-outlet company or large departmental store.[13] The most obvious link with the question of town food supplies came in the discussion of the role of the market place. Jefferys' view, and one strongly reinforced by Davis in 1966, was that the traditional role of the food market as the last link in the chain of supply and, in many cases, the place where producer and consumer came together in the final transaction, continued well into the nineteenth century; it gave way only slowly to a system which involved more and more inter-mediaries until food retailing passed out of the market place into shops.[14]

It is somewhat surprising that Jefferys' view, based, it has to be said, on slender evidence for the nineteenth century, was so influential. As long ago as the 1920s no less distinguished a historian than Clapham had argued that changes in the system of distribution began well

---

[12] C. Wilson, 'Economy and society in late Victorian Britain', *EcHR*, 2nd ser., XVIII, 1965, p. 190.

[13] J.B. Jefferys, *Retail Trading in Britain, 1850–1950*, Cambridge, 1954, esp. chapter 1.

[14] *Ibid.*, pp. 5–6; D. Davis, *A History of Shopping*, London, 1966, pp. 252–4.

before the nineteenth century and were not far out of line with progress on the industrial front. By the 1820s, at least in large industrial towns, the appearance of increasing numbers of middlemen meant that the producer–retailer was fast conceding his place in the market to the ordinary retailer who traded on a permanent basis from a fixed stall.[15] The effect of Blackman's work on Sheffield was to uphold Clapham's view and, at the same time, to go further by suggesting that, in northern industrial towns, markets and shops should be seen, not as successive steps in the history of retailing, but as evolving together, the one supplying perishable foods and the other everyday groceries.[16] The argument that small shops played a significant part in supplying food to the working classes was also taken up by Burnett, who claimed that they were 'possibly the most important "amenity" of the early industrial town'.[17]

Out of these conflicting views came two points of particular relevance to my study as it developed. First, the markets of a town could not be examined in isolation from the rest of the distribution system. Therefore, the most suitable period to cover could be taken as the hundred years before 1870 when, by general consent, a new phase in retailing history began. Secondly, in any explanation of the role of the market in an urban distribution system, factors other than changes in the pattern of supply of different foodstuffs would have to be taken into account. There was now enough doubt about the role of the market place and its relevance for traders who were not producer–retailers to indicate that numerous influences were at work. Especially suggestive was the idea of a connection between different methods of distribution and the level and pattern of consumption of various foodstuffs.[18]

In the light of what has been said, the plan of this study will be self-evident. The starting point is an outline of the growth of Manchester and Salford, which, for our purposes, are best treated as a single entity, except where a distinction is specifically being drawn; and a sketch of the main agricultural features of the surrounding

[15] J.H. Clapham, *An Economic History of Modern Britain*, Cambridge, 1926, I, chapter VI, esp. pp. 225–6; Cambridge, 1932, II, chapter VIII.
[16] Blackman, 'Food supply', p. 96; *idem*, 'Changing marketing methods and food consumption', in Barker, McKenzie and Yudkin (eds.), *Our Changing Fare*, pp. 38–9.
[17] J. Burnett, *Plenty and Want: A Social History of Diet in England from 1815 to the Present Day*, London, 1966, p. 35.
[18] A.H. John, 'Aspects of English economic growth in the first half of the eighteenth century', *Economica*, new ser., XXVIII, 1961, pp. 185–6.

region, as a background to the main body of the research. I then examine the evolving patterns of supply for a number of foodstuffs over the hundred-year period, 1770–1870, choosing those commodities whose stories best illustrate the differing nature and timing of the developments involved and whose consumption was most sensitive to changes in living standards. It is not possible, of course, to trace the journey of every single morsel of food that passed Mancunian lips: how groceries such as tea, coffee and sugar reached Manchester is one issue that I do not look at in this detailed way, and the other, rather more arbitrarily, is the supply of grain and flour. These omissions require a word or two of justification. Tea, coffee and sugar came from abroad, and they presented few problems of perishability or transportation once they had reached this country. Corn, likewise, kept and travelled well. It came closest of all home-grown foods to having a national market, and most of the trade was conducted between merchants outside the public market and beyond the historian's gaze. Hence, key developments such as a widening market area and the growth of intermediaries between producer and consumer belonged to the years before 1770 rather than after.[19] I was strengthened in this decision by the knowledge that Manchester was not an important centre for the grain and flour trade.[20] Only a small proportion of the town's needs came direct, and most of the transactions conducted by dealers concerned supplies lying in Liverpool or Wakefield, the two great northern corn centres.[21] Of greater significance with regard to groceries, grain and flour was the means by which they were distributed once they had arrived in the town, and this question is addressed in the second part of the book.

A range of different kinds of evidence has been used and, while I do not wish to describe all those listed in the Bibliography, it is worth commenting on some of the more important ones. No-one can proceed very far in eighteenth- and nineteenth-century agricultural history without incurring a considerable debt to the numerous contemporary commentators in the changing rural scene. Their best-known

[19] C.W.J. Granger and C.M. Elliott, 'A fresh look at wheat prices and markets in the eighteenth century', *EcHR*, 2nd ser., XX, 1967, pp. 257–65; Westerfield, *Middlemen*, chapter II.

[20] See *PP* 1820, II, *Select Committee on Petitions complaining of Agricultural Distress*, Appendix A, *A Weekly Account made by the Inspectors to the Receiver of Corn Returns etc.*; and *PP* 1842, XL, *Return of the Quantities of Wheat sold ... in 1836, 1839, and 1842 etc.*, p. 683.

[21] *PP* 1836, VIII–Pt. I, *Second Report from the Select Committee on the State of Agriculture*, Mins. of Evidence, p. 41. Even after the opening of an official Corn Exchange in 1837, the weekly corn market reports in local newspapers gave a clear indication of the pre-eminence of Liverpool

contributions are the county reports to the Board of Agriculture and the prize essays published in the *Journal of the Royal Agricultural Society*, but there are many others.[22] They suffer from the fault of betraying their authors' prejudices against one type of farming or another, and they frequently highlight the exceptional rather than the typical, but, without them, the subject would be much the poorer. These commentaries combine with the mass of descriptive and statistical material contained in the parliamentary papers of the time to provide my basic terms of reference.

The second class of evidence, drawn on heavily in Chapters III to VI, is rather less familiar and relates mainly to the channels by which foodstuffs reached Manchester. It is of two kinds. One is the information generated by parliamentary select committees' examination of private bills seeking permission to build or alter canals, roads and railways. The verbatim evidence begins in 1793 and covers only bills that were opposed, but its great virtue is that part of the arguments for or against concerned itself with details of traffic that was expected to use the proposed means of communication. Naturally enough, it was not unknown for witnesses before these select committees to exaggerate their case, but occasionally I have found the proverbial nugget of gold when surveys of existing traffic were carried out and presented as evidence. The other source of information is the records of the canals and railways, once they had come into existence. In many respects, these have proved disappointing, in that they fail to provide any systematic record of the traffic conveyed. Much of the surviving documentation is concerned with company policy rather than the mundane details of what was actually being carried. Even when it is possible to get down to the level of local traffic committees, all too often one is confronted with the cryptic: 'The traffic return was laid on the table'. Still more elusive, however, is evidence about foodstuffs that went by road. The few records of the turnpikes leading to Manchester that I have been able to trace concerned themselves with the forming of the tolls and legal and administrative matters dealing with

---

and Wakefield. For an interesting account of this exchange, see S.C. Johnson, 'Manchester Corn and Produce Exchange: Memoirs of Persons and Streets in the Eighteen Nineties' (MCLAD, MS. F. 942.73912 J15).

[22] A general survey of these is provided in Lord Ernle, *English Farming, Past and Present*, 6th edn., London, 1961, pp. xci–cxv. For comments on some of the Lancashire writers, see T.W. Fletcher, 'The agrarian revolution in arable Lancashire', *TLCAS*, LXXII, 1962, pp. 99–102, 117–18.

the road itself rather than what passed along it.[23] Fortunately, the omission is not too serious, since cattle droving routes, for example, were often designed to avoid passing along the turnpikes.[24] In any event, the occasional traffic surveys mentioned above are a partial compensation. Yet the fact remains that their absence may well cause the amount of food that came by road, often in small loads, to be underestimated in comparison with the traffic that went by water or rail.

The third category of evidence on the supply side is the weekly market reports printed in the local newspapers. These provide, from 1822, details of quantities and prices for the livestock market and, for a time, descriptions of the origins of cattle and sheep. For other commodities, there is only information on the prices that prevailed in the market, but, from 1826, this covers potatoes and other root vegetables and, from 1850, a wider range of foods, including fish. The data have been analysed in a variety of ways, but my principal aim has been to use the evidence to try to assess the extent to which, in a paraphrase of Fisher's comment on London, Manchester's appetite was developing more quickly than the country's ability to satisfy it.[25]

The second part of the study begins with an examination of the development of the public markets as the authorities struggled to adapt the facilities to the changing needs of Manchester and Salford in the century after 1770. I then look in more detail at the three groups of food traders who initially dominated the market scene, namely, the sellers of fruit and vegetables, meat and fish, and explore the changes in the ways that these commodities were distributed. Next, the stories of the other major food dealers, those in the grocery, provision and bakery trades, are taken up. Finally, there is an attempt to bring together the different sectors of the urban distribution network, including itinerant traders, and to examine their relationship to each other, with special reference to the locational behaviour of six key classes of retailers.

In considering food distribution, the sources of evidence can again be classed into three main types. First, there is a variety of material

---

[23] This seems to be true of most turnpike records. See E. Pawson, *Transport and Economy: The Turnpike Roads of Eighteenth Century Britain*, London, 1977, p. 58. Accordingly, they have been used mainly for administrative issues, for example by W. Albert, *The Turnpike Road System in England, 1663–1840*, Cambridge, 1972, esp. chapters 4, 5 and 7.

[24] Haldane, *Drove Roads*, pp. 52, 178–9, 208–9; K.J. Bonser, *The Drovers*, London, 1970, p. 68.

[25] Fisher, 'London food market', p. 64.

relating to the markets of Manchester and Salford. The markets in Manchester were controlled until 1846 by the lords of the manor, and the records of the Court Leet detail the proceedings of the manorial court that sat twice yearly to appoint various officers and to hear the cases of those who offended against its laws. Since an increasingly large part of the court's time was taken up with cases concerning market offences, its proceedings provide a useful outline of developments in this area of trading. From 1846 the main source of such information is the reports of the Manchester Council's Markets Committee. In Salford, the situation was rather different. The manorial court had long since fallen into disuse by the time a market was opened in 1827.[26] Initially, its running was the responsibility of the local Police Commissioners and, later, of the Markets Committee of the Salford Council. All these records are printed and readily accessible, but they tend to be slanted towards administrative rather than trading arrangements.[27] Naturally, they also represent the official view of what was happening. However, the provision of market facilities frequently brought the authorities into conflict with other groups of citizens. Some saw the continuance of manorial rights as a symbol of the old political order; others opposed the constant congestion of much of the town centre; and there were those who simply resented the lack of freedom to trade how and where they wished that market regulations inevitably implied. Together, the protesting voices offer a useful corrective to the reassuring tones of official pronouncements. One source of this kind of evidence is local newspapers; another is the proceedings of the Manchester Police Commissioners, who often took a rather less sanguine view of matters than the market authorities; but most useful of all is the legal evidence generated when the disputants had recourse to the law. This is particularly valuable for the first half of the period when the different parties were anxious to establish a picture of current, and often past, practices as they existed within the formal market system, and hence provide flashes of insight into the realities of market trading.

The second main body of evidence in this part of the study is that provided by directories and rate books. Commercial directories containing classified lists of tradesmen were published for Manchester

[26] J. Tait (ed.), *The Court Leet or Portmoot Records of Salford, 1735–1738*, Chetham Society Publications, new ser., XCIV, Manchester, 1935, p. 3.
[27] See Redford, I, chapter VI; III, chapter XXXII.

and Salford from 1815.[28] These have been used chiefly to provide the basic framework for studying the wholesale and retail food trades, especially those that operated outside the markets. It should be pointed out that, when using commercial directories, account must be taken of the variability in their coverage. The categories used and the numbers listed fluctuated a good deal, and some groups were frequently omitted altogether. In Manchester's case, it was not until 1840 that these problems were overcome; before then, small shopkeepers and market traders were particularly prone to disappearing from view. The explanation would seem to lie in the priorities of the publishers, who produced these directories principally as guides for wholesalers and manufacturers, often from outside the town, for whom small retailers would hold little interest.[29] Before 1815 some unclassified directories were published, the first of which claimed, in 1772, to comprise an alphabetical list of 'every inhabitant of the least consequence'.[30] These appear to have been compiled partly out of interest and partly for commercial use, and it seems reasonable to assume that most retail traders would have been included, if only as likely purchasers of the completed work. The danger here is that one might be counting private houses as retail outlets, but the risk is not very high. The word 'house' appears often enough to suggest that the compilers were well aware of the few lock-up shops that existed, and of any partnerships.

The obvious way of cross-checking the entries in both types of directory is against the local rate books, but this proved inconclusive. The numbering of buildings was, at best, imprecise; changes in occupancy compound the problem; and, most importantly, it is probable that many small shops operated from a single room and were never declared for rating purposes.[31] Where the rate books have proved extremely useful, however, has been in providing information about

---

[28] For a list of Manchester directories, see G.H. Tupling, *Lancashire Directories, 1684–1957*, revised edn., by S. Horrocks, Manchester, 1968; J.E. Norton, *Guide to the National and Provincial Directories of England and Wales, excluding London, published before 1856*, London, 1950, pp. 130–9.

[29] Norton, *Guide to Directories*, pp. 7–9.

[30] E. Raffald, *The Manchester Directory for the Year 1772*, Introduction. This ambitious claim was never, of course, realised. Although the coverage was widened, the 1811 directory listed only about one in ten inhabitants of the townships of Manchester and Salford.

[31] W.K.D. Davies, J.A. Giggs and D.T. Herbert, 'Directories, rate books and the commercial structure of towns', *Geography*, LIII, 1969, pp. 43–4; R.S. Holmes, 'Ownership and migration from a study of rate books', *Area*, V, 1973, p. 244.

11

the occupancy of the various market sites in Manchester.[32] Entries for the markets begin in 1796 and vary in the amount of detail they contain. Sometimes the assessment was made on the gross estimated rental of the site; at other times it was based on the actual number of stalls occupied, occasionally with details of the stall-holders. The entries tended to become increasingly formal, but for the first half of the nineteenth century they are invaluable additions to the directories and other market records. No doubt some traders still slip through the net, but I am convinced that directories and rate books together offer the best means of systematically examining the basic structure of the wholesale and retail food trades in this period. The only alternatives that might be used to give an indication of the relative importance of different trades would be the different forms of occupational data, but these, too, have their problems. Some are selective, such as lists of freemen or poll books; others are all-embracing, such as parish registers or the census enumerators' books; thus, for purposes of assessing the number and location of retail outlets, they are of little use.[33]

This sort of evidence provides only the bare skeleton and says little about how the different trades were conducted, which brings us to the third type of source used in connection with distribution. At a very general level, an understanding of trading practices can be derived from the trade press, though this did not begin until the latter part of the period considered here. Most of these publications were geared to the upper end of the retail spectrum, but they contain a good deal of wider applicability, and their comments, often in the form of lamentations on current and past developments, have proved useful. Accounts and ledgers of individual traders are, in many ways, more interesting, in that they can give a valuable insight into how the businesses were run. Unfortunately, however, very few such records appear to have survived. Most food traders operated on a small scale and, when their businesses ended, they vanished without trace. In any case, they would have been unlikely to retain, for more than a short time, details of routine transactions with wholesalers or customers. Enquiries to present-day firms that had their origins in this period revealed only

[32] Very few of the Salford rate books have survived for the period before 1870 and, unfortunately, these have not proved of any use.

[33] For examples of the use of this sort of data see: J. Langton and P. Laxton, 'Parish registers and urban structure: the example of late-eighteenth-century Liverpool', *Urban History Yearbook*, 1978, pp. 74–84; P. Borsay, 'The English urban renaissance: the development of provincial urban culture, *c.* 1680–*c.* 1760', *Social History*, II, 1977, pp. 585, 601; S.I. Mitchell, 'Urban markets and retail distribution 1730–1815, with particular reference to Macclesfield, Stockport and Chester', University of Oxford, D.Phil., 1974, p. 246.

that whatever records had not succumbed to the ravages of time had a more spectacular end in the blitz of the Second World War, when the central market area of Manchester was badly bombed.

However, two particularly detailed sets of trading records that have been used are those of the two main co-operatives in the area, the Manchester and Salford Equitable Co-operative Society and the Failsworth Industrial Society, both of which began trading in 1859.[34] It could be argued that the co-operatives were a special case and that evidence from this source would not tell us about more typical trading practices. But it is likely that, in large industrial towns, the co-operatives were in many respects much more akin to ordinary retailers than their special place in the 'self-help' movement might suggest. In towns such as Manchester, they could not rely on a sense of customer loyalty to the same extent as in small communities, nor could they dominate the retail scene in the same way. In Manchester, they had to compete more directly with other retailers for custom, and this was reflected in their pricing policies and other trading practices.[35] As a result, I have chosen to incorporate their evidence rather more closely into the main arguments than might have been expected.

Another potential source of trading records is the impounded accounts of businesses which fell foul of the bankruptcy laws. However, the survival of these records seems to have depended on whether or not their owners reclaimed them after the hearings, and only a small proportion were left in official hands to come down to us in this way. Unfortunately, a lengthy search of the papers of the Court of Bankruptcy, the Chancery Masters' Exhibits and related papers in the Public Record Office failed to unearth any records that had been retained from food traders in the Manchester area.[36] More successful was an examination of the papers of insolvent debtors who appeared before the local Court of Quarter Sessions. Although these contained no trading accounts, they did embrace a 'true schedule or account of

[34] With the exception of one or two short-lived attempts to form other societies in the 1860s, their only rival was the Manchester and Salford Industrial Co-operative Society, which at one time had eight branches, but ran into difficulties in the later 1860s and went into liquidation in 1870 (Manchester and Salford Equitable Co-operative Society Ltd, Mins. of Committee, 13 Aug. 1862; 15, 22 Sept. 1869; 24 Oct., 2 Nov. 1870; *The Co-operator*, 1 Nov. 1866; 28 Jan. 1871; *The Co-operative News*, 9 Mar. 1872).

[35] For contemporary comment along these lines, see Anon., 'The proletariat on a false scent', *The Quarterly Review*, CXXXII, 1872, p. 289; *Co-operative Wholesale Society Limited: Annual for the year 1884*, Manchester, 1884, pp. 48–50.

[36] PRO, Court of Bankruptcy, B. 3, 4, 9, 10; Chancery Masters' Exhibits, C. 103–7; Six Clerks' Office Exhibits, C. 171; Liquidation (Companies) Proceedings, C. 26.

the real estate' of the debtor, which, in some cases, included a list of the people who owed him sums of money. From these, some understanding has been gained of the network of credit relationships that existed in the food trades in the later eighteenth and early nineteenth centuries.[37]

In a study as wide-ranging as this, no individual body of evidence can provide a central core; instead, a multiplicity of sources must be drawn on. Despite its obvious disadvantages, this approach has at least one compensating factor, namely, that deficiencies in a particular area can be made up by using evidence from elsewhere. The childhood memory comes readily to mind of starting to build a Meccano model, only to find that you lack some of the pieces. If it is a wheel that is missing, you can do little about it, but often it is possible to improvise with other bits. At such times, you are especially grateful for those little straight pieces that, by themselves, seem to be of no apparent use. For me, in this study, their equivalents were the numerous contemporary accounts of the often mundane details of eighteenth- and nineteenth-century life. To those whose curiosity was aroused and who went to the trouble of finding out more and recording what they had learned, thanks are due. As pieces of evidence, they lack the aura of the more recondite sources, but, without them, the finished model would have been even less like the picture on the front of the box.

[37] LRO, Court of Quarter Sessions, Debtors' Insolvency Papers, QJB. A similar source for this sort of information is the inventories of traders, usually of those who died intestate, contained in the probate records, but detailed examples became very infrequent in Lancashire and Cheshire by the second half of the eighteenth century, and I could discover none of use for this study. See B.C. Jones, 'Inventories of goods and chattels', *Amateur Historian*, II, 1954–5, esp. p. 79.

CHAPTER II

Manchester and its environs, 1770–1870

M ANCHESTER has figured so prominently in the annals of modern British history that it would scarcely seem to need any introduction. In the early years of Victoria's reign, contemporaries of every political complexion could agree that it had established itself as 'the principal manufacturing town in the world', or was the 'classic type of modern industrial town',[1] and the overwhelming importance of textiles was captured in the fashioning of such pseudonyms as 'Cottonborough' (1851) and 'Cottonopolis' (1853).[2] It is true that the advance was punctuated by marked fluctuations associated with the trade cycle,[3] but the underlying economic vitality of Manchester was never called into question and was the basis for a much-quoted comment by Disraeli, in his novel, *Coningsby* (1844), that 'rightly understood, Manchester is as great a human exploit as Athens'.[4] But if 'the din of machinery' was simply 'the music of economic progress', as a social experiment Manchester seemed to be 'a standing rock of offence to poets, literati and aesthetes'.[5] The accounts by novelists, notably Mrs Gaskell, taken in conjunction with numerous official and unofficial statistical reports of the 1840s, fixed in many minds the idea that Manchester was a social catastrophe, marked out to be the scene of conflict between the classes, and its Janus-headed character has

[1] J.R. McCulloch, *A Dictionary, Geographical, Statistical, and Historical, of . . . the World*, new edn., London, 1852, II, p. 267; F. Engels, *The Condition of the Working Class in England*, translated and edited by W.O. Henderson and W.H. Chaloner, Oxford, 1958, pp. 50–1.

[2] These names are traceable to works published by Ainsworth and Lowe in the 1850s. See D.A. Farnie, *The English Cotton Industry and the World Market, 1815–1896*, Oxford, 1979, p. 63.

[3] A useful overview of these cycles is provided by W.W. Rostow, *British Economy of the Nineteenth Century*, Oxford, 1948, chapters II, V.

[4] B. Disraeli, *Coningsby*, Everyman's Library edn., London, 1911, p. 127.

[5] A. Briggs, *Victorian Cities*, London, 1963, pp. 85–6; Farnie, *Cotton Industry*, p. 41.

lingered in the writings of many twentieth-century historians.[6] Yet there is no doubt that its development on every front – economic, social and political – during the Industrial Revolution has lent itself to caricature, and in recent years historians have begun to correct some of the more heroic over-simplifications. While it would be futile to attempt to rewrite the history of Manchester in a few pages, it is important to provide a context for the subject of this book and, at the same time, to take some account of the more pertinent findings of other researchers.

i. The population growth of Manchester and Salford

Even at the beginning of the eighteenth century, Manchester was considered to be a populous place.[7] However, the first estimate that carries any degree of credibility is the one derived from returns made to the Bishop of Chester about 1717, the *Notitia Cestriensis*, which give the number of families of Churchmen, Dissenters and Papists. If a multiplier of 5 per family is employed, they suggest an aggregate population of some 16,000 for the parish of Manchester.[8] But the parish is not an appropriate unit for our purposes, since it sprawled over some fifty square miles. Within the figure of 16,000, it can be estimated that the townships of Manchester and Salford contained 10,000 and 2,500 souls respectively.[9] These townships, based upon the demesnes of medieval manors,[10] were the units of analysis taken in the first satisfactory attempt at a complete enumeration, made by Thomas Percival, a local doctor and founder of the Manchester Literary and Philosophical Society, who, in 1773, advanced a total population of 29,151.[11] This suggests not only considerable

[6] The best-known short essay on Manchester, and a very fine one, is that of Briggs, *Victorian Cities*, chapter 3.

[7] See, for example, D. Defoe, *A Tour through the Whole Island of Great Britain*, Penguin edn., Harmondsworth, 1971, p. 545.

[8] A.P. Wadsworth and J. de L. Mann, *The Cotton Trade and Industrial Lancashire, 1600–1780*, Manchester, 1931, p. 509.

[9] *Ibid.*; and see the map forming a frontispiece to Redford, I, *Manor and Township*, from which it is apparent that the parish extended from Blackley in the north to Didsbury in the south, and from Stretford and Salford in the west to Haughton in the east. Altogether, the area embraced over a hundred modern parishes (p. 11).

[10] Redford, I, pp. 9–10.

[11] T. Percival, 'Observations on the state of population in Manchester', (1789 edn.), reprinted in *Population and Disease in Early Industrial England*, Pioneers of Demography Series, Farnborough, Hants., 1973, p. 53.

eighteenth-century population growth but also that Manchester now stood in the first rank of British urban settlements.[12]

Subsequently, growth was even faster, carried forward on the basis of both natural increase and immigration. Percival put the crude rate of mortality at 35 per 1,000 at risk, and reckoned that one-half of all children born in Manchester died before reaching the age of five.[13] Despite these high rates, he claimed to discern 'a sensible improvement in the healthiness and longevity of its inhabitants', while the fact that baptisms regularly exceeded burials, from 1754 at least,[14] points to high rates of marriage and procreation. Chalklin has drawn attention to an enormous boom in marriages, which nearly tripled from 567 in 1782 to reach 1,657, their pre-1800 peak, in 1792; and Fleischman has observed that marriage rates in Manchester and Salford were running at about twice the national level through the years 1801–41, and still exceeded it by a large margin thereafter.[15] Rather less can be said about fertility, although it must have been high.[16] It is improbable that brisk procreation can be ascribed, as a 'physician of the first rank in his profession' in the late eighteenth century supposed, to tea, acting as an aphrodisiac. This view was put to Percival, who clearly did not know quite what to make of it,[17] and he was surely on safer ground in claiming that population growth was chiefly attributable to 'the large accession of new settlers . . . as these usually come in the prime of life and must raise the proportion of births and weddings to the burials, higher than they would otherwise be'.[18] The inflow continued into the nineteenth century and throughout the period

[12] According to the comparative figures for 1801, given in B.R. Mitchell and P. Deane, *Abstract of British Historical Statistics*, Cambridge, 1962, pp. 24–6, outside London, Manchester's population was surpassed only by Glasgow, Liverpool and Edinburgh and, if Salford is added in, not even by these.

[13] Percival, 'Observations', pp. 7, 37, 41.

[14] *Ibid.*, pp. 3, 5.

[15] C.W. Chalklin, *The Provincial Towns of Georgian England: A Study of the Building Process, 1740–1820*, London, 1974, p. 276; R.K. Fleischman, *Conditions of Life among the Cotton Workers of Southeastern Lancashire, 1780–1850*, New York and London, 1985, pp. 263–4.

[16] Fleischman, *Conditions of Life*, p. 268. He does not proffer a rate for Manchester, but his high crude fertility rate for Lancashire (46 per 1,000 in 1811–20 against 39 in England as a whole) would certainly have been shared by the town.

[17] Percival, 'Observations', p. 45. The physician imputed 'the amazing population of China . . . to the general use of it'. Percival himself reflected that the Dutch drank much tea and were not remarkable for the number of their children, but acknowledged that 'warm infusions of tea, by relaxing and augmenting the sensibility of the fibres . . . may promote the increase of the human species'.

[18] *Ibid.*, pp. 5–6.

covered in this study. Much of it, as Redford has shown, was short-distance in character and, given the industrialised nature of the country round about, it is unlikely that more than a small proportion was drawn directly off the land.[19] The principal exception to this was, of course, the Irish. At the end of the eighteenth century a sizeable Irish element was already apparent in Manchester; by 1841 the census returns gave a figure of 34,300 Irish-born; those of 1851, following the Great Famine, showed this had risen to 52,504, making Manchester one of the most heavily settled towns in the country.[20] In 1816 Aston remarked on the fact that not one-half (and perhaps not more than one-third) of the adult inhabitants of Manchester were natives of the town.[21] Indeed, the persistent influx of immigrants is considered by some historians to have given it an unusually cosmopolitan character, even to have created 'a town of strangers'.[22]

The results of natural increase and immigration, inextricably interwoven as they are, can be followed more easily from 1801 onwards, using the decennial census returns. The 1851 census is particularly valuable: as well as providing figures for the two townships (and thus giving continuity to Percival's estimate), it came to terms with the parliamentary boroughs of Manchester and Salford, established in 1832,[23] and with the two municipal boroughs, set down in 1838 and 1844 respectively.[24] Moreover, all population

[19] A. Redford, *Labour Migration in England, 1800–1850*, 2nd edn., Manchester, 1964, pp. 183, 185; M. Anderson, *Family Structure in Nineteenth Century Lancashire*, Cambridge, 1971, pp. 34–41; B. Roberts, 'Agrarian organization and urban development', in J.D. Wirth and R.L. Jones (eds.), *Manchester and São Paulo. Problems of Rapid Urban Growth*, Stanford, Calif., 1978, p. 85.

[20] Redford, *Labour Migration*, pp. 134, 155; M.A.G. O'Tuathaigh, 'The Irish in nineteenth-century Britain: problems of integration', *Transactions of the Royal Historical Society*, 5th ser., XXXI, 1981, p. 152. See J.M. Werly, 'The Irish in Manchester, 1832–49', *Irish Historical Studies*, XVIII, 1972–3, pp. 345–58, for a description of the conditions of Irish life in Manchester.

[21] J. Aston, *A Picture of Manchester*, Manchester, 1816, p. 25.

[22] Roberts, 'Agrarian organization', p. 85, who contrasts Manchester in this respect with Oldham and other textile towns; J. Bohstedt, *Riots and Community Politics in England and Wales, 1790–1810*, Cambridge, Mass., 1983, p. 69.

[23] The parliamentary limits of Manchester comprised the townships of Ardwick, Chorlton-on-Medlock, Hulme, Manchester, Bradford, Newton, Beswick, Cheetham and Harpurhey. Those of Salford encompassed the townships of Salford, Broughton and Pendleton, and a small part of the township of Pendlebury (*PP* 1852–3, LXXXVI, *Census of Great Britain, 1851. Population Tables, Pt. I, Numbers of the Inhabitants*, II, North-Western Counties, p. 64).

[24] *Ibid.*, p. 65. The municipal borough of Manchester was smaller than the parliamentary borough, comprising Ardwick, Chorlton-on-Medlock, Hulme, Manchester, Beswick and Cheetham townships. This was likewise true of the municipal limits of Salford, which originally took in only the township of Salford and a small part of Broughton township. However, in this

figures for 1801–41 were reworked according to these boundaries to form a consistent series that continued through 1861 and 1871.[25] From Table 2.1 it is apparent that the peak nineteenth-century rates of expansion occurred in 1811–31 (22.3 per cent and 46.1 per cent,

Table 2.1 *Population growth of Manchester and Salford, 1773–1871*

| | | Numbers enumerated within | |
Year	Townships	Municipal limits	Parliamentary limits
1773	29,151	–	–
1801	84,020	93,806	95,313
1811	98,573	114,506	116,568
1821	133,788	159,713	162,682
1831	182,812	234,322	239,328
1841	217,056	305,394	312,870
1851	250,409	388,490	401,321
1861	256,412	440,760	460,018
1871	257,265	475,990	504,175

Notes

For boundaries, see notes 9, 23 and 24. In the case of Salford, the municipal limits taken here are in accordance with the revised boundary of 1853.

Sources For 1773, T. Percival, 'Observations on the state of population in Manchester' (see text); for 1801–71, Census Population Abstracts, 1851, 1861, 1871 (see Bibliography).

if the parliamentary limits are preferred), and that thereafter they tended to decline. However, it was not until 1841–51 that the greatest decennial increase in absolute numbers was experienced, and the actual increments of population were still very considerable in 1851–61. Between 1801 and 1871 Manchester, with Salford, suc-

case, the parliamentary and municipal boundaries were made conterminous in 1853. N.J. Frangopulo (ed.), *Rich Inheritance*, Manchester, 1962, provides a useful map of the boundaries of Manchester, facing p. 48.

[25] The complexities of boundary-drawing go somewhat further than notes 23 and 24 suggest, in that from 1851, although information is always given for the municipal and parliamentary boroughs, the basic units with which the census authorities operated was the system of registration districts and sub-districts established with the introduction of civil registration in 1837. Manchester (municipal or parliamentary limits) fell into – but did not constitute the whole of – Registration Districts 471 (Chorlton) and 473 (Manchester), each with a number of sub-districts. Salford (municipal or parliamentary limits) fell entirely into R.D. 472 (Salford), which had four sub-districts. In fact, it is not difficult to follow these engaging variations by using the notes in successive census volumes, and it is unnecessary to set out the full details here, since the registration districts and sub-districts have not been used as units of analysis in this book, except to a limited extent in Appendix B.

ceeded in doubling its share of the rising national population and, at the second date, actually exceeded the total number of inhabitants of no fewer than thirty-one individual English counties.[26]

ii. Economy and employment patterns

Research continues to reaffirm the dynamic role of cotton in Manchester's economy.[27] The first cotton mill in Manchester was established by Richard Arkwright in the early 1780s, and their numbers multiplied briskly to reach twenty-six in 1802 and sixty-six by 1821, while cotton manufacturing firms (not necessarily the same thing) are computed as having increased from ninety in 1815 to 128 by 1841.[28] However, it would be erroneous to assume that all of these were large-scale enterprises; likewise, that the cotton trade in Manchester could simply be equated with manufacturing; or, indeed, that the majority of Manchester wage-earners were employed in cotton mills.

In the late 1970s an interesting debate on the size of cotton-manufacturing firms took place, prompted perhaps by the contention of Engels and others that the industry saw an ever-increasing concentration of capital in fewer and fewer hands. According to Gatrell, small and middling firms actually held up well in the second quarter of the nineteenth century, partly because the advantages of scale were far from unequivocal.[29] On the other hand, Lloyd-Jones and Le Roux argue that between 1815 and 1841 small and large firms (in terms of the size of labour force) lost ground relatively to medium-sized ones.[30] For the social historian, the most important point to emerge from the debate is the agreement of the participants that too much attention has

[26] The registration counties concerned were Beds., Berks., Bucks., Cambs., Cornwall, Cumberland, Derbys., Dorset, Essex, Herefs., Herts., Hunts., Leics., Lincs., Mon., Norfolk, Northants., Northumberland, Notts., Oxon., Rutland, Shropshire, Somerset, Suffolk, Surrey, Sussex, Westmorland, Wilts., Worcs., and the East and North Ridings of Yorkshire. See the tables in Mitchell and Deane, *Abstract*, pp. 20, 24, 26.

[27] For example, R. Lloyd-Jones and M.J. Lewis, *Manchester and the Age of the Factory*, London, 1988.

[28] W.H. Chaloner, 'The birth of modern Manchester', in British Association for the Advancement of Science, *Manchester and Its Region*, Manchester, 1962, p. 133; F. Vigier, *Change and Apathy. Liverpool and Manchester during the Industrial Revolution*, Cambridge, Mass., 1970, pp. 127, 129; R. Lloyd-Jones and A.A. Le Roux, 'The size of firms in the cotton industry: Manchester, 1815–41', *EcHR*, 2nd ser., XXXIII, 1980, p. 75.

[29] V.A.C. Gatrell, 'Labour, power, and the size of firms in Lancashire cotton in the second quarter of the nineteenth century', *EcHR*, 2nd ser., XXX, 1977, esp. pp. 95, 105, 107–8, 125.

[30] Lloyd-Jones and Le Roux, 'Size of firms', esp. pp. 74–5.

been paid to the giant firms. While Cobden might write of 'the huge factories of the cotton district, with three thousand hands under one capitalist', or de Tocqueville of 'workmen . . . counted by the thousand, two or three thousand in the factories',[31] it is apparent that enterprises on this scale were rare indeed. Gatrell identifies only three firms with over 1,000 employees in 1833 (M'Connel & Co., Birley & Kirk and Thomas Houldsworth) and puts the average size at 260 in 1841; while Lloyd-Jones and Le Roux give a median figure of 174 employees, with 29 per cent of firms employing 100 people or fewer.[32]

In any event, Manchester and its environs did not account for more than 17.3 per cent of the total number of Lancashire's cotton workers in 1851 (against 22 per cent of the county's total population).[33] Moreover, it has always been apparent to enlightened observers that Manchester's fame as the 'Cottonopolis' rested as much on its commercial function as on manufacturing *per se*. This was well understood by contemporaries such as Faucher, who likened Manchester to a 'diligent spider' in the centre of Lancashire's industrial web; and modern historians are apt to stress that its role was that of a 'commercial hub', or 'not a capital of industry so much as an emporium of commerce . . . a Shanghai of the north'.[34] Indeed, Lloyd-Jones and Lewis go so far as to suggest that in 1815 it was primarily a warehouse town, in that the aggregate rateable value of warehouses at that date was approximately six times as great as that of cotton-spinning factories.[35] Nor was the increase in the number of these warehouses simply a reflection of a shift from secondary (or manufacturing) to tertiary (or service) industries in the way posited by many theories of economic growth and progression. This was a view apparently subscribed to by Roland Smith, who surmised that by the 1820s Manchester was moving on from being a manufacturing to a commercial centre.[36] In fact, warehouses were numerous even before the first

---

[31] Passages quoted in Gatrell, 'Labour, power', p. 125.

[32] *Ibid.*, pp. 100, 125; Lloyd-Jones and Le Roux, 'Size of firms', pp. 74–5.

[33] See the table given in Fleischman, *Conditions of Life*, p. 29. He is taking the registration districts of Manchester, Salford and Chorlton.

[34] L. Faucher, *Manchester in 1844: Its Present Condition and Future Prospects*, London, 1844, p. 15; J.K. Walton, *Lancashire. A Social History, 1558–1939*, Manchester, 1987, p. 112; Farnie, *Cotton Industry*, p. 64.

[35] Lloyd-Jones and Lewis, *Age of the Factory*, pp. 30–2.

[36] R. Smith, 'Manchester as a centre for the manufacture and merchanting of cotton goods, 1820–30', *University of Birmingham Historical Journal*, IV, 1953–4, pp. 61–5; and see Lloyd-Jones and Lewis, *Age of the Factory*, pp. 105–6.

21

factory was set up. Manchester merchants had long employed domestic workers over a wide area, and the advantages of a warehouse, as a place where goods could be stored and displayed to potential customers, were ever more apparent, some manufacturers taking a salesroom exclusively and others sharing.[37] For 1815, Lloyd-Jones and Lewis discern no fewer than 1,577 warehouse units in the Manchester rate books and, although (*pace* Smith) a temporary hiatus was visible over the next ten years, this was followed by indications of a convergence of the activities of the factory and the warehouse into one business unit.[38]

The conclusion to be drawn from these various works, clarifying what might be meant by the term 'Cottonopolis', is that it is easy to exaggerate the extent to which cotton manufacturing was a source of employment in Manchester. Even in 1815, when the industry probably accounted for its highest share (proportionately) of all employment in Lancashire, the estimated number of cotton workers in Manchester cannot have represented more than about 12 per cent of the total population of men, women and children.[39] Sharpless has likewise shown that in 1861 the proportion of the city's industrial workforce engaged in textile production was decidedly lower than in a number of neighbouring towns.[40] From these observations it follows that Manchester had a far more complex and diverse occupational pattern than is sometimes assumed. 'The erection and keeping up of the various and complicated machinery which is constantly at work is itself a source of very great business in and around Manchester', remarked Charles Hulbert in 1825. By that date Manchester could boast a string of iron foundries and general engineering works, mostly along the banks of the Ashton and Rochdale Canals. They included those of Peel & Williams, Ebenezer Smith, Fairbairn, Hewes & Wren and the Ormrods, and employed many artisans with 'craftsmanly skills'.[41]

[37] Wadsworth and Mann, *Cotton Trade*, pp. 250–60; M.M. Edwards, *The Growth of the British Cotton Trade, 1780–1815*, Manchester, 1967, pp. 145, 173–5.

[38] Lloyd-Jones and Lewis, *Age of the Factory*, pp. 34, 115, 120–4.

[39] Farnie, *Cotton Industry*, p. 24, puts the number of cotton employees as a proportion of Lancashire's population at 37 per cent in 1811, falling to 16 per cent by 1871. The figures given for Manchester are from Lloyd-Jones and Lewis, *Age of the Factory*, p. 37.

[40] J.B. Sharpless, 'Intercity development and dependency: Liverpool and Manchester', in Wirth and Jones (eds.), *Manchester and São Paulo*, p. 142, instancing Oldham, Rochdale, Preston, Bolton, Stockport, Blackburn, Bury, Burnley and Ashton-under-Lyne.

[41] Lloyd-Jones and Lewis, *Age of the Factory*, pp. 155–6, 159. See also A.E. Musson and E. Robinson, *Science and Technology in the Industrial Revolution*, Manchester, 1969, p. 454; R. Samuel, 'The workshop of the world: steam power and hand technology in mid-Victorian Britain', *History Workshop*, No. 3, 1977, p. 19.

Moreover, the need to process and finish cloth stimulated the growth of chemical enterprises such as the integrated dyeing and printing works established by Thomas Hoyle at Mayfield (Ardwick) in the 1790s.[42] Likewise, the warehouses dealing in cotton goods offered relatively secure, if far from opulent, employment for growing numbers of clerks and warehousemen.[43] Nor did the occupational complexity of Manchester end with activities such as these. It has been pointed out that, according to the 1841 census, there were more shoemakers and possibly more carpenters in Manchester than male cotton spinners or handloom weavers, which is perhaps less surprising when one considers that there were some 57,000 houses to be maintained and nearly 800 under construction (to say nothing of business property) and 600–700,000 feet to be shod.[44] Finally, it has been suggested that a considerable proportion of the employment offered by Manchester was of a casual nature; its social problems were those of a large commercial city rather than a mill town, and perhaps, in this respect, it had more in common with Liverpool or Hull than with Birmingham or Leeds.[45]

Yet it may be possible to go too far in qualifying the impression that Manchester was predominantly a manufacturing town, certainly with regard to the distribution of employment, as is apparent from Table 2.2, which depicts the pattern of occupations at the close of our period. Manufacturing industry, broadly defined, accounted for one-half of all male employment in 1871, and textiles and the industries usually associated with them for nearly one-third. For females, the range of opportunities was narrow indeed: seven out of ten among those occupied were employed in either textiles or domestic service.

iii. Government and politics

Compared to the rate of economic development, local government

[42] Lloyd-Jones and Lewis, *Age of the Factory*, p. 158.
[43] On clerks, see G. Anderson, *Victorian Clerks*, Manchester, 1976. This book focuses on Liverpool and Manchester, but is concerned primarily with the post-1870 period when they were much more numerous.
[44] Walton, *Lancashire*, p. 148, citing the work of R. Sykes.
[45] A.J. Kidd, 'The middle class in nineteenth-century Manchester', in A.J. Kidd and K.W. Roberts (eds.), *City, Class and Culture: Studies of Social Policy and Cultural Production in Victorian Manchester*, Manchester, 1985, p. 15; *idem*, ' "Outcast Manchester": voluntary charity, poor relief and the casual poor, 1860–1905', *ibid.*, pp. 50–2.

changed only slowly.[46] Manchester was unrepresented in Parliament until 1832 and – unlike Liverpool, with its charter dating from 1208 – was not an incorporated borough. Indeed, the status of the township was essentially that of a mere village, as Defoe remarked.[47] The vestry of the sprawling parish of Manchester was responsible for poor relief, the upkeep of churches and the maintenance of the King's highway; otherwise, the township was governed by the Court Leet of the lords of the manor, the Mosley family. Each year the Court Leet chose unpaid officers, including a boroughreeve (a kind of mayor but without executive power, except that he alone could convene a public meeting), day police, market lookers or inspectors, and scavengers. It met only twice a year and was widely regarded as sluggish and inactive. A third instrument of local government, originating as a result of the pressure of local reformers, was a body of Improvement Commissioners. Two local Acts, of 1765 and 1776, empowered the constables to administer the cleansing of the streets and to arrange for the improvement of some of them, while 1792 saw the setting up of the Manchester and Salford Police Commissioners, with powers to light and cleanse the streets and to maintain a night watch, a move which can be said to have 'marked the first substantial step towards a recognizably modern system of local government'.[48] There matters stood for the next forty years, and opinions are divided as to how far these three separate, but overlapping, agencies added up to an effective system of local government.

For some contemporaries, mindful of the restrictions that were alleged to hamper free enterprise in borough towns, the situation was not unsatisfactory. James Ogden, in 1783, stated of Manchester that 'nothing could be more fatal to its trading interest, if it should be incorporated, and have representatives in Parliament', while Aikin also took the view that the absence of such institutions was 'probably to its advantage'.[49] Among modern historians, Farnie appears to

---

[46] Descriptions of Manchester's system of local government are fairly numerous, ranging from the brief remarks in Chaloner, 'Birth of modern Manchester', through the more detailed account given in Vigier, *Change and Apathy*, chapters 5, 6, 9, to Redford's monumental survey, volume I of which has already been mentioned (see note 9). This and volume II, *Borough and City*, are directly relevant to the present study.

[47] Defoe, *Tour*, p. 544.

[48] Chaloner, 'Birth of modern Manchester', p. 135.

[49] J. Ogden, *A Description of Manchester by a Native of the Town*, Manchester, 1783, p. 93; Aikin, p. 191. For a discussion of a contrary case, whose privileges were said to have contributed to its decline, see A. Armstrong, *Stability and Change in an English County Town: A Social Study of York, 1801–51*, Cambridge, 1974, pp. 20–7.

Table 2.2 *Industrial classification of occupations, Manchester and Salford, 1871*

	Percentage of total population		Percentage of occupied population	
	Male	Female	Male	Female
Agriculture	1.30	0.01	1.95	0.05
Mining	0.79	0.01	1.19	0.02
Building	5.83	0.01	8.75	0.03
Manufacture–aggregate	33.48	23.13	50.27	63.26
(MF 1,2,4,5 –				
machinery, tools, metals	8.77	0.38	13.16	1.03)
(MF 9,22 –				
chemicals, dyeing	2.59	1.68	3.89	0.46)
(MF 18,19,20,21 –				
textiles	10.14	15.97	15.22	43.68)
Transport	7.73	0.14	11.61	0.39
Dealing	8.22	2.06	12.34	5.65
Industrial Service	4.79	0.07	7.19	0.19
Public Service and Professional	3.51	0.86	5.28	2.35
Domestic Service	0.94	10.26	1.41	28.06
Property owning; Indefinite Occupations; Dependants	33.41	63.44	–	–
	100.00	99.99	99.99	100.00

Note

The table utilises the methods and procedures of W.A. Armstrong, 'The use of information about occupation', in E.A. Wrigley (ed.), *Nineteenth-Century Society. Essays in the use of quantitative methods for the study of social data*, Cambridge, 1972, pp. 226–310. The designations MF 1,2 etc. refer to the sub-divisions used by Charles Booth, described therein.

Source Census Occupational Abstract for 1871 (see Bibliography).

agree, suggesting that 'the lack of any communal spirit nurtured an unrestrained and hyperintelligent individualism'.[50] Be that as it may, few historians have anything good to say about the operations of the Court Leet, seen by Redford as 'an absurd anachronism', at least in its last fifty years, and by Shirley as 'flimsy'.[51] Views on the Commis-

---

[50] Farnie, *Cotton Industry*, p. 61.
[51] Redford, I, p. 46; R.W. Shirley, 'Legal institutions and early industrial growth', in Wirth and Jones (eds.), *Manchester and São Paulo*, p. 159.

sioners, however, have differed. From the first decade of the nineteenth century their activities became noticeably more vigorous.
Chaloner points to the building of a municipal gas works and the using
of the profits to pay for paving and refuse disposal.[52] Moreover, it is
primarily on the basis of the Commissioners' work that Sidney and
Beatrice Webb and, more recently, Bohstedt have judged that Manchester was better governed than most provincial towns.[53] On the
other hand, Vigier is less impressed by their work, noting their outlay
on a very expensive Town Hall, and the fact that about one-half of the
streets remained unpaved and unsewered as late as 1844.[54]

Contemporary and modern appraisals of the working of local
government in Manchester, and of the major changes that occurred in
the 1830s, cannot be understood without some reference to the political context of the time. It is clear that Manchester was singularly free
from 'county' influences, and that the voice of the working classes,
being occupationally much sub-divided and usually voteless, could be
only a faint one.[55] Accordingly, as Kidd puts it, local politics were
firmly in the control of the bourgeoisie. He acknowledges, however,
that this bourgeoisie was a complex one, deeply fissured by religion
and party, and Gatrell, in particular, has done much to illuminate the
competitive struggle for power among the Manchester middle class.[56]
It has been suggested that the 1770s and 1780s were decades when
'commercial unity outweighed political differences',[57] but by the end
of that period this was no longer true. Through the years 1790–1832
Manchester's Tories established a stranglehold over the town's institutions, including the vestry, the Court Leet and the Police Commissioners, to say nothing of the magistracy. Their ascendancy drew
strength from the prevailing political climate in the nation at large and
was strongly linked with the High Church and with loyalist causes.

[52] Chaloner, 'Birth of modern Manchester', p. 135.
[53] S. and B. Webb, *English Local Government*, IV, *Statutory Authorities for Special Purposes*,
London, 1922, pp. 256–8; Bohstedt, *Riots*, p. 75.
[54] Vigier, *Change and Apathy*, pp. 142, 152–3, 195. This author sees nothing but failure in the
local government of both Manchester and Liverpool, owing mainly to a lack of communication
between the municipal authorities and the citizenry, and to middle-class apathy. Apparently, the
book was written to enable modern industrial cities to avoid the mistakes of the past.
[55] V.A.C. Gatrell, 'Incorporation and the pursuit of liberal hegemony in Manchester,
1790–1839', in D. Fraser (ed.), *Municipal Reform and the Industrial City*, Leicester, 1982, p. 22.
[56] Kidd, 'Middle class in nineteenth-century Manchester', pp. 4–6; Gatrell, 'Incorporation',
pp. 24–53.
[57] Bohstedt, *Riots*, p. 102.

Among their ranks were men whose fortunes were derived from mercantile or manufacturing activities,including members of the Wanklyn, Fleming, Peel and Birley families.[58] A serious challenge to this Tory dominance made itself apparent only after 1819, in the aftermath of Peterloo. H.H. Birley had led the fateful charge, and it was this event that polarised middle-class opinion for the first time in twenty years.[59] Gatrell has traced the emergence of what was initially only a 'small but determined band' of radical, dissenting Liberal politicians, a group which included notable businessmen and bankers such as the Heywoods, Loyds, Gregs, Potters, James M'Connel and James Kennedy. All were wealthy and well educated; many were closely associated with the Unitarian Chapel at Cross Street. These factors, along with a considerable degree of intermarriage, helped to cement them into a cohesive political force.[60] Meanwhile, as Lloyd-Jones and Lewis point out, the increasing convergence of factory and warehouse had produced by the mid-1820s a much more coherent business strategy, one which called for the diminution of constraints on market forces.[61]

Some preliminary skirmishes were fought over a Tory plan to build churches using ratepayers' money (1820) and to check the allegedly oppressive powers of the Police Commissioners (1826), but the first clear sign of a shift in the political mood came with the election of two Liberals as Members of Parliament for Manchester when the town was enfranchised in 1832.[62] However, the achievement of Liberal hegemony was not finalised until they carried the day with a proposal to incorporate the town in 1838, much to the chagrin of the officers of the Court Leet, whose boroughreeve continued to be elected in competition with the new mayor, and of the churchwardens, who at first refused to produce their rate books, and of the Commissioners, who denied the Corporation access to the Town Hall.[63] The success of the campaign, now spearheaded by Richard Cobden and his associates, who had managed to align small businessmen and prominent members of the 'shopocracy' behind them, was a real one, and a Liberal Manchester proved to be an appropriate base from which to press for

[58] Walton, *Lancashire*, pp. 136–7; Gatrell, 'Incorporation', pp. 23, 29–35.
[59] Gatrell, 'Incorporation', pp. 32, 35.
[60] *Ibid.*, pp. 24–9, 35.
[61] Lloyd-Jones and Lewis, *Age of the Factory*, p. 145.
[62] For details, see Gatrell, 'Incorporation', pp. 35–8.
[63] Vigier, *Change and Apathy*, p. 191.

the repeal of the Corn Laws.[64] In the event, the rate-levying powers of the churchwardens and the responsibilities of the Police Commissioners passed to the Council in 1842 and 1844 respectively, and the Court Leet met its demise in 1846. Nevertheless, it would be a mistake to assume that the cause of Toryism was dead in Manchester. As Walton has observed, the façade of Mancunian unity presented by the Liberal reformers and the Anti-Corn Law League masked the continuity of Church-and-King Tory traditions among the town's professional men and prosperous merchants and manufacturers; Manchester's middle class remained deeply divided, and appearances to the contrary were only superficial.[65] Indeed, the electorate rejected two prominent 'Leaguers' in the 1857 election, preferring a couple of Palmerstonian Liberals, and in 1868 Manchester returned its first Conservative Member of Parliament.[66] The Council itself remained under Liberal control until 1891, although once the leading figures of the 1830s had moved away, in some cases onto the national stage, a meaner, penny-pinching style of Liberalism was the order of the day.[67]

The history of local government and politics in Salford has received far less attention. Perhaps its most surprising feature is the fact that separation from Manchester persisted when the two towns simultaneously entered the era of rapid growth and industrialisation. Things might have been different, for in the local Acts of 1765, 1776 and 1792 the two towns were treated as one. However, the Commissioners chose to form two distinct bodies and to levy their own rates. Improvement Acts were subsequently sought by Manchester in 1828 and by Salford in 1830, and administratively the towns went their separate ways.[68] In Salford, as in Manchester, the Police Commissioners were the most effective form of local government, and here, too, reform was in the air. A prominent local Radical, Joseph Brotherton, took his seat as the first Member of Parliament for the borough in 1832, and from the mid-1830s Radical and Liberal elements succeeded in dominating the Police Commissioners, forming a tight interest group around William Lockett, a retired silk mercer. In

[64] Gatrell, 'Incorporation', pp. 48–50; Briggs, *Victorian Cities*, pp. 114–22.

[65] Walton, *Lancashire*, p. 138.

[66] Briggs, *Victorian Cities*, pp. 125–9. For further indications of the continuing strength of Conservatism in Manchester, particularly among the working classes, see H. Pelling, *Social Geography of British Elections, 1885–1910*, London, 1967, pp. 242–6.

[67] Gatrell, 'Incorporation', pp. 51–3.

[68] R.L. Greenall, 'The making of the borough of Salford, 1830–1853', in S.P. Bell (ed.), *Victorian Lancashire*, Newton Abbot, 1974, pp. 35–58, upon which essay much of this paragraph, except where otherwise noted, depends.

due course, these men were responsible for promoting a campaign for a municipal charter, which was intended to include the whole of the parliamentary borough, as constituted in 1832. This objective was secured in 1844, and thereafter the Council, through its Improvement Committee, discharged the functions of the former Police Commissioners. However, the reformers did not have things all their own way. Within Salford itself, suspicion among Tories and Chartists ran deep, and in the townships of Broughton and Pendleton there was a strong fear that the result of incorporation would be that rates would soar in order to pay for Salford's more urgent problems. These out-townships were brought in only when, with ever-increasing pressure for sanitary reform, they effectively faced the choice of joining Salford or adopting the 1848 Public Health Act, with its overtones of 'London management'. Even then, the terms of the arrangement created by the Salford Extension and Improvement Act of 1853 ensured that the separate identities of Broughton and Pendleton were not submerged, and that they had a combined council representation equal to that of Salford, a much more populous place.[69] To a very large extent, each of the districts was able to continue to manage its own affairs, causing the borough to be labelled 'A Trinity without Unity'.

In the years 1844–53 the new municipal Council initiated various improvement and amenity schemes, including the widening and paving of streets, the suppression of nuisances and the development of gas and water supplies, a public park, a museum and a free library.[70] But this momentum was not fully sustained, even though the Council remained under Liberal control. As Garrard has pointed out, Salford never quite succeeded in developing the urban institutions that might have been expected in a town of this size – it was, after all, the third largest in the north-west in its own right. This was due in a large measure to the proximity of Manchester, where one-third of Salford's resident councillors were in business, and to the separatist instincts of Broughton and Pendleton.[71]

[69] J. Garrard, *Leadership and Power in Victorian Industrial Towns, 1830–80*, Manchester, 1983, p. 39.
[70] Greenall, 'Making of the borough of Salford', pp. 50–1.
[71] Garrard, *Leadership and Power*, pp. 86–7, 89. For comments on the performance of Salford's Markets Committee, see below, pp. 174–5.

iv. Social classes and spatial segregation

The notion that Manchester society could be divided into two classes – whether the bourgeoisie and proletariat of Engels, or simply the middle, as distinct from the working, classes or operatives – is closely bound up with the presumption that social differences found expression in spatial terms. Manchester has often been regarded as one of the first towns to develop well-demarcated districts or zones, apparently foreshadowing the theories of Burgess and Park, which attempted to make sense of American cities, notably Chicago, in the 1920s.[72]

In the main, it was middle-class suburban development that first caught the attention of contemporaries as Manchester expanded. Aikin, in 1795, likened Ardwick Green, once regarded as 'a rural situation', to London's West End for the splendour of its houses; and the writers of guidebooks published around 1815 were also much impressed by developments at The Crescent, on the banks of the River Irwell, to the west of Salford. Manchester could be proud, it was said, of two such 'very beautiful suburbs'.[73] Over the next two or three decades the middle-class exodus from the central districts reached sufficient proportions for James Kay to remark in 1832 that 'the opulent merchants chiefly reside in the country, and even the superior servants of their establishments inhabit the suburban townships'.[74] By the 1830s, facilitated to some extent by the development of horse-omnibus services, Oxford Street, Greenheys, All Saints, Plymouth Grove and Victoria Park could be added to the list of desirable residential areas to the south of Manchester, while their counterparts to the north-west and north of Salford stretched along the roads to Pendleton, Broughton and Cheetham.[75]

For the rest, Manchester was said to be 'chiefly inhabited by shopkeepers and the labouring classes'.[76] Indeed, according to Engels, who spelled this out in more detail than most, the emerging town plan of Manchester was nothing short of a social disaster, albeit one that was only to be expected in an unfettered capitalist system. At the very heart of the town, there had come into existence by the 1840s a

[72] See, for example, R. Dennis, *English Industrial Cities of the Nineteenth Century. A Social Geography*, Cambridge, 1984, pp. 81–4.

[73] Aikin, pp. 205–6; Aston, *Picture of Manchester*, pp. 222–3; Anon., *The New Manchester Guide*, Manchester, 1815, p. 46.

[74] J.P. Kay, *The Moral and Physical Condition of the Working Classes Employed in the Cotton Manufacture in Manchester*, 2nd edn., London, 1832, p. 20.

[75] B. Love, *Manchester As It Is*, Manchester, 1839, p. 181.

[76] Kay, *Moral and Physical Condition*, p. 20.

district, approximately half a mile square, that was 'almost entirely given over to offices and warehouses. Nearly the whole of this district [had] no permanent residents and [was] deserted at night.'[77] That his comments on this point were not far wide of the mark is confirmed by later studies, which, in their discussions of the commercial life of Manchester, have drawn attention to the way houses were converted into shops and offices, or even demolished and replaced by warehouses.[78] Likewise, the driving through of railways, in Manchester as elsewhere, was a factor leading to the destruction of much housing.[79] Significantly, the years 1841–51 saw a 3 per cent decline in the population of the registration sub-district centred on Market Street, and in the following decade this and the Deansgate and London Road sub-districts all showed falls of over 10 per cent.[80]

To some contemporaries, these centrifugal tendencies were a matter for regret, since they were 'driving most of the respectable inhabitants into the suburbs'.[81] But they affected the working classes just as much, if not more so. Engels drew attention to the existence, immediately adjacent to the commercial quarter, of 'a belt of built-up areas on the average one and a half miles in width ... occupied entirely by working-class dwellings'. These included the Old Town or, at least, that part of it which lay between the northern limit of the commercial quarter and the River Irk (a 'hell upon earth'); and the New Town – also known as Irish Town – characterised by single rows of houses and courts of back-to-backs, constructed with scant regard for the health of the inhabitants. This pattern continued to the east, into the Ancoats district, which also contained many of Manchester's largest factories.

---

[77] Engels, *Condition of the Working Class*, p. 54.

[78] Richard Cobden and his neighbours sold their Mosley Street houses in 1832 for this purpose (Lloyd-Jones and Lewis, *Age of the Factory*, p. 35). See also H.B. Rodgers, 'The suburban growth of Victorian Manchester', *Journal of the Manchester Geographical Society*, LVIII, 1961–62, pp. 2, 4; H. Baker, 'On the growth of the commercial centre of Manchester: movement of population and pressure of habitation, 1861–71', *Transactions of the Manchester Statistical Society*, 1871–72, pp. 90–2.

[79] J.R. Kellett, *The Impact of Railways on Victorian Cities*, London, 1969, pp. 290, 325, points out that some 7.3 per cent of the central zone of Manchester was railway-owned by 1900, and instances the case of 255 cottages due for demolition under the 1866 Manchester Central Bill (they housed 1,275 persons). See also the notes attached to the population abstracts of the 1861 and 1871 censuses.

[80] PP 1852–3, LXXXVI, *Census of Great Britain, 1851. Population Tables, Pt. I, Numbers of the inhabitants*, II, North-Western Counties, p. 42; PP 1862, L, *Census of England and Wales, 1861. Population Tables*, I, *Numbers and distribution*, North-Western Counties, p. 573.

[81] B. Love, *The Handbook of Manchester*, Manchester, 1842, quoted in Briggs, *Victorian Cities*, p. 103.

Still moving clockwise, one would encounter depressing working-class districts on either side of the River Medlock, including possibly the very worst neighbourhood in the whole of Manchester, namely, Little Ireland, lying to the south-west of Oxford Street. By the 1840s the spread of working-class areas on this side of the town also extended into the erstwhile suburb of Ardwick and embraced most of Chorlton-on-Medlock and Hulme.[82] The encirclement of the commercial quarter continued with another working-class district centred on Deansgate ('a maze of long narrow lanes, linking the tiny courts and passages'), and was completed, on the other side of the River Irwell, by Salford. This was considered by Engels to be 'really all one large working-class quarter' and, in some parts, even more dirty and dilapidated than Manchester itself.[83] The middle- and working-class areas of Manchester were thus quite distinct. Engels even averred that it would be possible for a Mancunian to travel daily to and from work in the town, or for a visitor to arrive and depart again, without ever seeing a working-class district or a slum.[84]

The pattern that has been described for the 1840s was not a fixed one. Former middle-class suburbs such as Ardwick Green, Greenheys, The Crescent, and the like, might lose their exclusiveness as working-class housing expanded or as industry drew too near; but the only effect was to push the better-off further afield, as far as Didsbury or even Altrincham and Alderley Edge by the close of the period.[85] Such adjustments detract little, if at all, from the proposition that the Manchester of Victoria's day – or even earlier – had evolved a very distinctive layout, with many implications for the texture of class-relations. It is a proposition that has been generally accepted by historians and, in this study, is taken as broadly, though roughly, correct. But, in general, there is considerable scope for debate about the rate at, and extent to, which British towns of the Victorian era came to develop Chicago-style zones.[86] Places such as York and Exeter, argues Cannadine, exhibited no such well-defined characteristics in the nineteenth century, although he and the target of his criticisms, the geographer, Ward, do not appear to have substantial

[82] Engels, *Condition of the Working Class*, pp. 54–73.

[83] *Ibid.*, pp. 73–5.

[84] *Ibid.*, p. 54.

[85] Rodgers, 'Suburban growth', pp. 5, 8–9.

[86] See, for example, D. Ward, 'Victorian cities. How modern?', *Journal of Historical Geography*, I, 1975, pp. 135–51; D. Cannadine, 'Victorian cities. How different?', *Social History*, II, 1977, pp. 457–82.

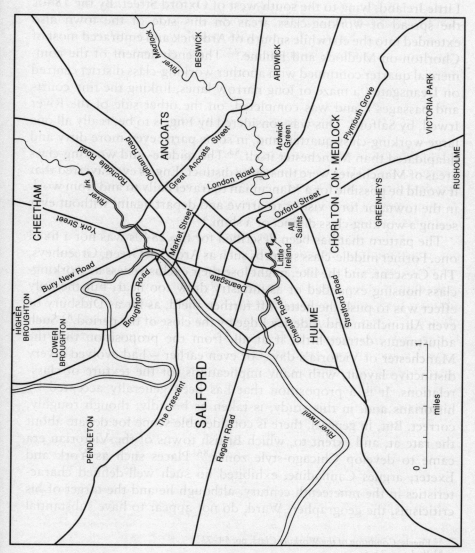

Map 1 Manchester, Salford and their environs

grounds for disagreement about Manchester; it is its typicality, rather, that is in dispute. Ward does make the point, however, that 'we need to know much more about the degree of residential sorting, if any, amongst the less prosperous majority'.[87] Given what has been said about Manchester's occupational complexity and shifting perceptions of class, it is not difficult to agree with this view, although it is clearly impossible to pursue the matter within the context of the present book.

v. Feeding the multitude

In a recent bibliography of works published on the history of nine-teenth-century Manchester, running to 1,200 items altogether, only two deal directly with the question of food supply and distribution.[88] In some ways, this neglect is amazing, bearing in mind the size and economic importance of the market. If we assume, for the sake of argument, that Mancunians (men, women and children) spent 2s each per week on food about 1800, then we are talking of a market approaching £0.5 million, a sum about twice as great as the aggregate expenditure of all English counties in the discharge of their respon-sibilities for bridges, gaols, constables and prosecutions.[89] For 1871, allowing 5s per head, the aggregate would be £6.5 million, a total larger than the income of the Post Office, rather greater than the annual value of coal exports (1869–71), and not very far short of current relief expenditure on the poor for the whole of England and Wales (£7.8 million).[90]

[87] Ward, 'Victorian cities', p. 137.

[88] T.J. Wyke, 'Nineteenth century Manchester: a preliminary bibliography', in Kidd and Roberts (eds.), *City, Class and Culture*, pp. 221–71. [The two exceptions are overtures to the present book, viz., R. Scola, 'Food markets and shops in Manchester, 1770–1870', *Journal of Historical Geography*, I, 1975, pp. 153–67; *idem*, 'Retailing in the nineteenth-century town: some problems and possibilities', in J.H. Johnson and C.G. Pooley (eds.), *The Structure of Nineteenth Century Cities*, London, 1982, pp. 153–69.]

[89] For purely illustrative figures of this nature, very approximate sums will suffice. The estimate of 2s per head per week is based on the expenditure pattern of a Manchester carter, his wife and five children in the 1790s (see F.M. Eden, *The State of the Poor*, London, 1797, II, pp. 358–9). Considered as an average figure for all Mancunians, it may well be a conservative estimate. The comparative figures for county expenditure are from Mitchell and Deane, *Abstract*, p. 411.

[90] Again, the figure of 5s is only broadly indicative. PP 1863, XXV, *Fifth Report of the Medical Officer of the Privy Council*, Appendix V, No. 3, *Report of Dr E. Smith, Economics of Diet*, p. 325, produces illustrations showing how the range of *per capita* food expenditure among Manchester operatives extended from 1s 7¼d to 6s 3d, 'in ordinary times', according to family size and composition. Ten years on, and allowing for the fact that not all Mancunians were

The growth of a market of this size could not fail to have a marked impact on the agricultural areas in closest proximity, that is, the counties of Lancashire and Cheshire, which, on the whole, were not well regarded by late-eighteenth-century observers. Of the two counties, Lancashire tended to come in for the heavier criticism. 'Agriculture', wrote a traveller through the county in 1800, 'though not despised is much neglected'. If he had taken a similar journey half a century later, he would have encountered little to make him change his opinion that he had been passing through an 'ill-drained, badly cultivated and neglected district'.[91] Cheshire, while not subjected to quite such sweeping condemnation, was not exempt from adverse comment. 'Improvements in agriculture', noted Caird, 'have made very slow progress in Cheshire'. The farmers and their families, in his eyes, worked harder than those in most other counties and yet received scant return for their labours.[92] Another mid-nineteenth-century critic remarked of the two counties:

Look at Lancashire and Cheshire: considering the immense breadth of fine arable land, and the unequalled markets for all kinds of produce, what has yet been done for the improvement of the soil? With a few notable exceptions very little. In general, cultivation is slovenly and wasteful, much as it was a century ago.[93]

In the interpretation of comments such as these, it must, of course, be remembered that throughout the period many observers of the agrarian scene were men who hailed from the south or took southern conditions as a desirable norm, and who encountered a very different situation in the north-west. In the first place, Lancashire was noteworthy as a county in which only a small proportion of the population derived its living from agriculture. In the 1821 census, when whole families were simply assigned to broad categories, only 11.2 per cent appeared to rely on agriculture as a means of support, easily the lowest proportion in all England, with the exception of Middlesex. By 1851 a mere 4.1 per cent of all persons aged over twenty and credited with an

---

'operatives', 5s seems a suitable round figure to adopt. The comparisons chosen are from Mitchell and Deane, *Abstract*, pp. 304, 393, 410.

[91] Anon., 'A rural sketch of the county of Lancaster', *The Farmer's Magazine*, I, 1800, p. 246; W.J. Garnett, 'Farming of Lancashire', *JRASE*, 1st ser., X, 1849, p. 1.

[92] J. Caird, *English Agriculture in 1850–51*, London, 1852, p. 253.

[93] J. Roberton, 'Are the laws and customs of England . . . beneficial or injurious to society?', read in 1851, *Manchester Statistical Society Papers, 1837–61*, p. 21 (MCL, 310.6 M2).

occupation appeared in the census agricultural classification.[94] It is true that Cheshire was nowhere near so thoroughly given over to non-agricultural pursuits: the corresponding percentages for that county were 34.8 per cent (close to the national average of 33 per cent), and 16.6 per cent,[95] but here, too, the trend was similar. Secondly, both counties were characterised by comparatively small farm units. The *Agricultural Returns* for 1867 revealed that the average size of farms in Lancashire was 35.1 acres, the lowest figure of all English counties, while in Cheshire it was not a great deal higher, at 43.1 acres.[96] Thirdly, the composition of farm output was decidedly different from that of most of southern and eastern England, inasmuch as the production of grainstuffs played only a minor role. In 1794 Wedge recorded that Cheshire had once been as famous for its corn as for its cheese, but noted that the amount of wheat grown had been declining.[97] As early as the mid eighteenth century, Lancashire was importing oatmeal and wheat from Wales, and even from as far afield as the London area and the Isle of Wight; and by 1795, according to Aikin, it produced only one-quarter of its annual consumption of cereals.[98] McCulloch, in 1852, was merely repeating already commonplace observations when he remarked that Cheshire was noted primarily for its luxuriant pastures, arable husbandry being but 'a secondary object' and one less suited to its mild, damp climate; and in Lancashire, likewise, grazing was 'more attended to than tillage husbandry'.[99]

Of course, these are gross generalisations of a kind that are almost inescapable with agrarian topics.[100] Many farms in both counties were mixed in character, and the precise balance of agricultural activities varied from one district to another and over time, according to the encouragement (or otherwise) provided by variations in prices.

[94] E.A. Wrigley, 'Men on the land and men in the countryside: employment in agriculture in early-nineteenth-century England', in L. Bonfield, R.M. Smith and K. Wrightson (eds.), *The World We Have Gained: Histories of Population and Social Structure*, Oxford, 1986, p. 326; Fleischman, *Conditions of Life*, p. 45.

[95] Wrigley, 'Men on the land', p. 326; PP 1852–3, LXXXVIII–Pt. II, *Census of Great Britain, 1851. Population Tables, Pt. II, Ages, Civil Condition, Occupations, etc.*, II, North-Western Counties, pp. 625, 628.

[96] PP 1867, LXXI, *Agricultural returns for Great Britain . . . for 1867*, p. 10.

[97] T. Wedge, *General View of the Agriculture of the County Palatine of Chester*, London, 1794, p. 14.

[98] Wadsworth and Mann, *Cotton Trade*, p. 356; Aikin, p. 18.

[99] McCulloch, *Dictionary*, I, p. 589; II, p. 135.

[100] W.J. Thomas and R.J. Perkins, 'Land utilization and agriculture in the north-west', in British Association, *Manchester and Its Region*, pp. 160–6, discern six types of farming, but warn that 'innumerable gradations of types exist'.

In the chapters that follow, we shall see that the farmers of Lancashire and Cheshire, far from being so unintelligent and narrow-minded as they were sometimes portrayed, seized the opportunities presented by expanding urban markets and by improvements in transport facilities, particularly with regard to dairy and market-garden produce. But it was clear, even in the 1790s, that the region was no longer capable of feeding its own population,[101] and its reliance on imports in some ways foreshadowed the situation that would develop on a national plane by 1914. Thus, even if we disregard tropical produce, Manchester's demand for foodstuffs increasingly tapped sources of supply lying further and further afield, extending not only to far-flung counties of England, Scotland and Wales, but also to Ireland and, in a smaller measure, to continental Europe and the United States.

[101] These remarks apply more particularly to Lancashire, and to grainstuffs, oats being the largest article of consumption grown locally. See, for example, J. Chamberlaine, 'Account of making Cheshire cheese etc.', *Annals of Agriculture*, XVII, 1792, p. 48; Holt, pp. 185, 210; J.P. Dodd, 'South Lancashire in transition: a study of the crop returns for 1795–1801', *Transactions of the Historic Society of Lancashire and Cheshire*, CXVII, 1965, pp. 90–1.

CHAPTER III

Meat

i. Local supplies

JOHN HOLT, in his survey of agriculture in Lancashire (1795), surmised that very little of the meat consumed within the county was provided by local producers. Sheep and cattle, echoed Aikin, were 'generally driven from a distance'; only veal and pork were derived from local sources. Twenty years on, William Marshall went so far as to claim that it was possible to pass through Lancashire and Cheshire without seeing a single sheep.[1] These impressions of a paucity of local supply were valid up to a point, and remained so. As we shall see, a ready market for dairy products and whatever arable crops could be grown, together with competition from distant livestock producers including the Irish, certainly tended to discourage the small farmers who were typical of the region from diverting their energies or produce to feeding up a few heifers or sheep for the local butchers. However, there is reason to believe that local supplies were not so scanty as contemporaries, prone as they were to rhetorical exaggeration, tended to imply.

In the first place, meat was a by-product of dairy farming. Throughout the period it was the practice of farmers to sell calves to butchers, soon after birth or following a few months' fattening.[2] Moreover, when their milk-yield fell, cows were disposed of for meat. Wedge, in 1794, suggested that this trade was confined chiefly to very elderly beasts, but Holt instanced the case of a dairy farmer, Mr Mayo of

---

[1] Holt, pp. 184–5; Aikin, p. 204; W. Marshall, *The Review and Abstract of the County Reports to the Board of Agriculture*, York, 1818, II, p. 35.

[2] H. Holland, *General View of the Agriculture of Cheshire*, London, 1808, p. 257; R.W. Dickson, *General View of the Agriculture of Lancashire*, London, 1815, p. 544; W. Palin, 'The farming of Cheshire', *JRASE*, 1st ser., V, 1844, p. 75; H.M. Jenkins, 'Report on Cheshire dairy-farming', *JRASE*, 2nd ser., VI, 1870, p. 170.

Hope, near Manchester, who kept his cows for only eighteen months before selling them to butchers, allegedly at a profit.[3] It would surely have needed but a fraction of the number of cows estimated as kept in Cheshire alone (around 92,000 according to Holland in 1808)[4] to be sold each year for a useful proportion of the needs of Manchester and other towns to have been satisfied, at least in the early part of the period.

Secondly, local sources of pork were significant in volume. It is true that the early agricultural writers found few pigs being fattened in Lancashire and Cheshire. Even on dairy farms, where they could be fed on the whey produced by cheese-making, their numbers were surprisingly small.[5] But in the towns, it was quite another matter. No-one can read of the epic struggles to improve their sanitary standards without becoming aware of the omnipresence of the pig. In the mid nineteenth century reformers were quick to blame the Irish migrant who had brought 'his disgusting . . . companion' with him and, as often as not, kept it inside the house.[6] But there were enough cases of offenders appearing before the manorial court in the late eighteenth and early nineteenth centuries, charged with allowing their pigs to run loose or causing a nuisance, to show that pig-keeping was well established in Manchester before the major waves of immigration from Ireland.[7] Nor was this custom confined to individuals keeping pigs for their own use. Herds were sometimes kept by butchers, or by persons known to James Kay as 'porkers', who would rent any suitable piece of land for their piggeries.[8] Gradually, however, the practice of urban pig-keeping became less common in the face of sanitary regulations, rising real incomes and a desire for better housing conditions. While as late as 1866 the sanitary authorities of Salford

[3] T. Wedge, *General View of the Agriculture of the County Palatine of Chester*, London, 1794, p. 64; Holt, pp. 149–50.

[4] Holland, *General View . . . of Cheshire*, p. 252.

[5] Holt, p. 174; Dickson, *General View . . . of Lancashire*, p. 588; Holland, *General View . . . of Cheshire*, p. 263.

[6] For example, P. Gaskell, *Artisans and Machinery*, London, 1836, p. 83; F. Engels, *The Condition of the Working Class in England*, translated and edited by W.O. Henderson and W.H. Chaloner, Oxford, 1958, p. 106.

[7] For example, *Court Leet*, VIII, pp. 149–50, 28 Apr. 1773; p. 172, 11 Oct. 1775; p. 180, 16 Oct. 1776; p. 247, 13 Apr. 1785; IX, pp. 133–4, 27 Oct. 1797; X, p. 21, 20 Apr. 1807; p. 34, 19 Oct. 1807; pp. 81–2, 8 May 1811.

[8] J.P. Kay, *The Moral and Physical Condition of the Working Classes Employed in the Cotton Manufacture in Manchester*, 2nd edn., London, 1832, p. 41. For examples of butchers keeping pigs see: LRO, QJB 43/6 (Ralph White, 1776); *Court Leet*, XI, pp. 41–2, 15 Oct. 1821, case of James Jackson. For other instances of pig-keeping clearly undertaken on a commercial scale, see *Court Leet*, X, p. 71, 14 May 1810; XII, p. 26, 14 Oct. 1833.

remarked on the persistence of 'a passion or infatuation amongst very many of the working classes for pig breeding and pig fattening', only ten years on they were able to report that they were meeting with less resistance in their efforts to clear away the pigs, even from the poorest areas.[9] On the other hand, it appears that increasing attention was given to pig-keeping by local farmers. By the mid-century pigs were being kept in much larger numbers, especially in the countryside close to Manchester and other south Lancashire towns.[10] On dairy farms, too, pig fattening became an integral part of the farm economy, particularly on smaller establishments where the feeding of cattle for the butcher was not feasible.[11]

Lancashire hog

Thirdly, there are indications that local supplies of mutton were by no means so negligible as Holt, Aikin and others implied. When Arthur Young made his northern tour in 1768, he noted that most

---

[9] SC, *Proceedings*, 30 Oct. 1866; 30 Oct. 1876.
[10] Palin, 'Farming of Cheshire', pp. 73–4; W.J. Garnett, 'Farming of Lancashire', *JRASE*, 1st ser., X, 1849, p. 41; J. Binns, *Notes on the Agriculture of Lancashire with Suggestions for its Improvement*, Preston, 1851, p. 76.
[11] Jenkins, 'Cheshire dairy-farming', p. 171; J.C. Morton, 'Report on the Liverpool prize-farm competition, 1877 – dairy and stock farms', *JRASE*, 2nd ser., XIII, 1877, pp. 502, 506, 518–19, 525.

farms visited in south-west Lancashire grazed small flocks of twenty to forty sheep, and in one case, near Ormskirk, up to a hundred. In Cheshire, too, small flocks were fattened on a number of farms around Knutsford and Altrincham.[12] Over the next thirty years the practice became more common. Sheep from the Welsh borders were brought into Cheshire and, on one farm in the heart of the dairying area, about a hundred of these were being fattened for sale in Manchester.[13] Consequently, even by the time of the second round of the *General Views*, writers were noticeably more enthusiastic about this aspect of the region's farming. Holland, in 1808, observed that the number of sheep in Cheshire had increased over the previous twenty years, and some could now be found on many farms. The Lancashire fattening business had likewise grown in importance to the point where the established custom of farmers having to travel north to make their purchases was transformed into one whereby graziers from Westmorland came south to the local fairs. This was a profitable business, and on some of the richer pastures two lots of sheep were fattened each year. By 1815, even what Holt had called the 'half-starved creatures' of the eastern hill districts of Lancashire were deemed worthy of attention, for Dickson described in detail how they were brought down to more sheltered pastures in the winter and finally sold when three or four years old to be fattened in lowland areas.[14] Palin, too, remarked in the 1840s on the number of sheep purchased by Cheshire farmers in the autumn to be fattened along with their lambs born in the following spring, or bought in the early summer and kept for a few months only.[15]

The fattening of cattle was never so widespread, but it was not so unimportant as contemporary writers implied. In 1768 Young encountered farmers in the districts to the south of Ormskirk, and at Altrincham and Knutsford in Cheshire, keeping some beasts specifically designated for fattening.[16] At that time, the Bridgewater estate at Worsley was involved in this activity. Day books of the 1770s record the Duke as buying in Scottish bullocks at Garstang and

[12] A. Young, *A Six Months Tour Through the North of England*, 2nd edn., London, 1771, III, pp. 166, 171–4, 184–5, 246.

[13] W. Redhead, R. Laing and W. Marshall, *Observations on the Different Breeds of Sheep and the State of Sheep Farming in Some of the Principal Counties of England*, Edinburgh, 1792, p. 13.

[14] Holland, *General View . . . of Cheshire*, p. 288; Dickson, *General View . . . of Lancashire*, pp. 542, 575, 577–8; Holt, p. 166.

[15] Palin, 'Farming of Cheshire', pp. 71–2.

[16] Young, *Tour*, III, pp. 173–4, 184–5, 246.

Bolton, and by the 1790s from fairs at Preston, Ormskirk and Wigan. The usual practice was to keep them for a year or two, but sometimes it was only a matter of months before they were disposed of in small lots at the Manchester or Warrington markets.[17] Other examples of farmers buying in stores for fattening include Samuel Oldknow's stepfather at Marple in Cheshire in the 1780s, and the holder of a large dairy farm at Middlewich about 1790, where no fewer than eighty beasts were fattened every year.[18]

Lancashire cow

All these considerations suggest that local sources of supply were by no means negligible, and that around the beginning of the nineteenth century farming for meat production was poised to develop considerably, in the face of what one contemporary described as 'the extraordinary growth of the town population, and the consequent increase of demand ... especially for butcher's meat'.[19] At the national level, the nineteenth century did indeed see marked progress

[17] LRO, NCBw 1/2, 25 Feb., 30 Sept., 10, 24 Nov., 1 Dec. 1775; 26 Jan., 16 Feb., 1 Apr., 1 July, 10 Aug., 7, 13 Sept., 9 Dec. 1776; NCBw 2/2, 10 Sept., 29 Oct., 9, 24 Nov. 1789; 14 May, 11 Aug., 11 Sept. 1790; 13 Sept., 23 Nov. 1791; 13 Nov. 1792; NCBw 2/3, 10, 31 May, 29 June, 13 Aug. 1793.

[18] G. Unwin, *Samuel Oldknow and the Arkwrights*, Manchester, 1924, pp. 142–3; Redhead, Laing and Marshall, *Sheep Farming*, pp. 12–13.

[19] *The Edinburgh Review*, CXX, 1834, p. 392, quoted in E.L. Jones and G.E. Mingay (eds.), *Land, Labour and Population in the Industrial Revolution*, London, 1967, p. 39.

in the integration of meat production with other types of farming. Locally, however, while by no means so inflexible and unenterprising as writers such as Holt tended to suggest, the farmers' response could be only a limited one. The small scale of many farms in the region precluded a major shift in the direction of grazing for meat production, and cattle fattening, in particular, tended to remain confined to larger-scale enterprises.[20] But if, as has been suggested, some contemporaries were reluctant to acknowledge local signs of progress in this sphere, they were surely correct to attach great importance to long-distance sources of supply.

ii. Mainland sources of supply and overland droving

The movement of livestock over considerable distances in order to satisfy the demands of the urban population was already a long-established traffic.[21] Inevitably, the main market was London, and much of the trade was geared to driving cattle and sheep from their breeding grounds to grazing areas closer to the capital, and then to their final destination at the capital's Smithfield Market. In the late eighteenth and early nineteenth centuries, however, some important changes could be detected in the north of England. Areas that had been obliged by their relative isolation to concentrate on providing lean stock for the southern graziers were given the opportunity, with the growth of the industrial population, to develop the fattening side of the business. Farmers in Northumberland, Durham and Westmorland not only found growing markets for fatstock on their own doorstep, but were also looking further afield to the towns of south Lancashire and the West Riding,[22] while it was natural for Manchester to turn to a grazing area that lay somewhat closer, namely, the Craven district of Yorkshire.

[20] See G. Beesley, *A Report of the State of Agriculture in Lancashire*, Preston, 1849, pp. 23–4, 48–9; Morton, 'Liverpool prize-farm competition', *passim*; S.D. Shirriff, 'Report upon the Liverpool prize-farm competition in Lancashire, Cheshire and North Wales, 1877 – arable farms', *JRASE*, 2nd ser., XIII, 1877, pp. 476, 480–1.

[21] See, *inter alia*, A.R.B. Haldane, *The Drove Roads of Scotland*, London, 1952; K.J. Bonser, *The Drovers*, London, 1970; C. Skeel, 'The cattle trade between Wales and England from the fifteenth to the nineteenth centuries', *Transactions of the Royal Historical Society*, 4th ser., IX, 1926.

[22] A. Pringle, *General View of the Agriculture of Westmoreland*, London, 1794, p. 317; J. Bailey and G. Culley, *General View of the Agriculture of the Counties of Northumberland, Cumberland and Westmoreland*, 3rd edn., London, 1813, pp. 174–5.

The Craven had long been noted for the breeding of longhorn cattle, but its importance for Manchester lay in a strategic position on a number of ancient drove roads from Scotland. There were two main streams of livestock moving south towards London from the Scottish borders, one passing through Northumberland and Durham, to the east of the Pennines, and the other through Westmorland and Cumberland, to the west. These then diverged into a host of different droving routes, but many came together again in the Craven, as livestock from the west crossed over into Yorkshire before continuing south.[23] However, increasing numbers of lean livestock from Scotland and other parts of the north were purchased and retained by the local farmers with a view to fattening them for the towns of the West Riding and south Lancashire. 'The graziers in Craven', observed Aikin, 'are very large dealers in this branch of business'.[24]

The movement of sheep over such long distances was a less pronounced feature of the trade. Even so, there was a sizeable traffic moving down both sides of the Pennines from Scotland and the north of England to be grazed on richer lowland pastures. Again, it was via the Craven that some of this flow was tapped, as farmers bought the sheep coming south with the purpose of fattening them for Lancashire markets.[25] Supplies of sheep were also taken into Lancashire from south Yorkshire. There, the customary practice had been for farmers to buy ewes in lamb in the autumn at Penistone, and to bring them on during the next spring and summer for the local market. By the end of the eighteenth century, however, this was rivalled by a growing trade in sheep and, to a lesser extent, cattle already fattened in Lincolnshire and the neighbouring counties, and then sent to Wakefield or the newly-established Rotherham market, where William Marshall noticed that most of the buyers came from the manufacturing towns on the other side of the Pennines.[26]

The other direction from which Manchester might have been

[23] Haldane, *Drove Roads*, pp. 178–80; Bonser, *Drovers*, pp. 162–3.

[24] Aikin, p. 96; G.B. Rennie, R. Brown and J. Shirreff, *General View of the Agriculture of the West Riding of Yorkshire*, London, 1794, p. 31; J. Tuke, *General View of the Agriculture of the North Riding of Yorkshire*, London, 1800, p. 259.

[25] J.H. Campbell, 'Answers to queries relating to the agriculture of Lancashire', *Annals of Agriculture*, XX, 1793, p. 122; A. Young, 'Excursion to Yorkshire', *ibid.*, XXVII, 1796, p. 295; also G.E. Fussell and C. Goodman, 'Eighteenth-century traffic in livestock', *Economic History*, III, 1934–37, pp. 226–7; Haldane, *Drove Roads*, p. 187.

[26] Rennie, Brown and Shirreff, *General View . . . of the West Riding*, pp. 96, 122; Aikin, p. 553; A. Young, *General View of the Agriculture of Lincolnshire*, 2nd edn., London, 1813, p. 454; W. Marshall, *The Rural Economy of the Midland Counties*, London, 1790, I, p. 230.

expected to draw supplies of cattle and especially sheep was from north Wales and the Welsh borders. This was the starting point of another of the ancient drove routes to London, and it might be assumed that the growth of Manchester and other industrial towns of south Lancashire would have been sufficient to divert some part of this flow northwards, or even to have encouraged Welsh farmers to develop the fattening side of the trade. However, this seems to have occurred to only a very limited extent. Welsh cattle farmers, in particular, saw little reason to be deflected from their traditional role of providing lean stock for fattening in the Midlands or south of England, and whatever went up into Lancashire was exceptional.[27] This was probably less true of sheep than of cattle, for there is at least some evidence that Welsh and Shropshire ewes were grazed on Cheshire farms prior to being sold in Manchester.[28]

iii. Overseas sources of supply

(a) *Ireland*

From what has been said so far, it is clear that at the beginning of the nineteenth century Manchester and other towns of south Lancashire and the West Riding were increasingly able to benefit from the surplus of lean and fat livestock in the north country. Quite how long they would continue to be so favourably placed was another question. London remained a powerful competitor for such supplies, and improved communications would buttress its influence. Without doubt, the demands of a rapidly rising urban population would soon have begun to press hard on the increase in production that was possible without major structural changes being made in the pattern of farming. Blackman has pointed to the decades following the Napoleonic Wars as the time when these pressures intensified,[29] and it was precisely then that greater quantities of livestock started to arrive from Ireland.

The importation of Irish livestock had been banned under the Cattle

[27] Skeel, 'Cattle trade', p. 149.
[28] Redhead, Laing and Marshall, *Sheep Farming*, p. 13; J. Plymley, *General View of the Agriculture of Shropshire*, London, 1803, p. 261; Holland, *General View . . . of Cheshire*, p. 288.
[29] J. Blackman, 'The cattle trade and agrarian change on the eve of the railway age', *Agricultural History Review*, XXIII, 1975, pp. 48–50.

Acts of the seventeenth century. Although this prohibition was lifted in 1759, the trade grew only slowly. The pace quickened towards the end of the century, but involved almost entirely the sending of lean stock into the west of Scotland, where the imports were incorporated into the pattern of feeding and migration southwards that has been described.[30] It was not until after 1815 that the shipping of livestock already fattened took on major significance. Two circumstances brought this about. Traditionally, most of the Irish cattle fed at home had been absorbed by a flourishing provision industry geared largely to colonial markets and the armed forces, but for a number of reasons this branch of the trade went into rapid decline at the end of the Napoleonic Wars.[31] This recession coincided with the beginning of steam navigation across the Irish Sea. A passenger steamer service began in 1816, and in 1824 a regular run was established between Dublin and Liverpool 'for the purposes of trade'.[32] This transformed the Irish traffic in livestock. Previously the voyage had taken seven days or more, but now the Dublin–Liverpool run, a notoriously rough crossing, was reduced to fourteen hours. As a result, the trade in lean cattle to be fattened in England or Scotland was soon overshadowed by the shipping to Liverpool of cattle fattened in Ireland and ready for sale to the butchers. Table 3.1 sums up the recorded figures of importations of Irish livestock into Liverpool in the years 1829–52, showing, for example, that the number of pigs alone arriving in 1829 easily exceeded the entire Irish export trade of only ten years before.[33]

Imports of this magnitude induced some gloom among local farmers[34] and certainly could not fail to have a major impact on the supply of livestock to Manchester. Already, in the late 1830s, the market reports from Cross Lane in Salford, which, in 1837, had replaced Manchester's Smithfield as the town's main livestock market, indicated their prime importance: comments such as 'chiefly Irish', 'chiefly from Ireland' and 'large part from Ireland' appeared

[30] J. O'Donovan, *The Economic History of Live Stock in Ireland*, Dublin, 1940, pp. 110–12, 148; L.M. Cullen, *Anglo–Irish Trade, 1660–1800*, Manchester, 1968, p. 73.

[31] O'Donovan, *Live Stock in Ireland*, pp. 150–2, 158.

[32] PP 1833, VI, *Select Committee on Manufactures, Commerce and Shipping*, Mins. of Evidence, p. 531.

[33] The average annual export of livestock, both lean and fat, from Ireland for 1816–20 was: 45,299 cattle, 26,595 sheep, 58,642 pigs (O'Donovan, *Live Stock in Ireland*, pp. 193, 196, 212).

[34] PP 1833, V, *Select Committee on Agriculture*, Mins. of Evidence, pp. 175–6, 178–80, 182, 276.

Meat

Table 3.1 *Imports of livestock from Ireland into Liverpool, 1829–52*

Year	Cattle	Calves	Sheep	Lambs	Pigs
1829	53,158	43,671	99,768	29,877	178,178
1830	24,113	19,600	107,625	29,536	166,854
1831	90,715	1,196	134,762	25,725	156,001
1832	68,728	1,755	73,622	12,854	145,917
1833	50,999	2,237	54,636	19,439	225,353
1834	62,009	3,974	54,349	24,995	288,699
1835	60,240	5,353	60,423	32,005	261,345
1838	102,337	–	201,371		216,443
1839	104,897	–	214,908		284,833
1840	87,217	–	221,796		182,016
1841	91,992	–	170,846		147,511
1842	84,441	–	147,675		189,233
1843	78,363	–	134,444		254,710
1844	83,765	–	137,370		243,650
1845	92,663	–	160,399		306,275
1848	151,364	1,322	161,432	64,335	73,278
1849	166,023	2,036	181,431	39,770	59,757
1850	163,440	1,518	192,855	35,614	95,019
1851	148,013	1,732	90,705	21,116	103,998
1852	167,584	996	113,762	21,992	116,504

Sources Figures for 1829–35, PP 1837, V, *Select Committee on the State of Agriculture in England and Wales*, Mins. of Evidence, p. 229; for 1838–45, J. MacGregor, *Commercial Statistics*, London, 1850, V, Supplement II, p. 169; for 1848–52, B. Poole, *The Commerce of Liverpool*, London, 1854, p. 180.

commonly for cattle, if less frequently for sheep.[35] By the 1850s somewhat fuller market reports point to the conclusion that 80–90 per cent of the cattle came either direct from Ireland – an increasing tendency – or via Stanley Market in Liverpool, in which case they were highly likely to be of Irish origin.[36] Fewer details are available of the origins of sheep marketed there, but for a short period in 1860 figures were given of the numbers coming from Ireland (either direct or

[35] For example, *Guardian*, market reports for 14, 21 Oct. 1838; 31 Mar., 7 Apr., 5 May, 25 Aug. 1841; 15, 29 Nov. 1843; 21 July 1847; 30 Aug. 1848; 21 Feb., 8, 22 Aug. 1849.

[36] *Ibid.*, market reports, 1850–57 and 1860. Information obtained by summing weekly totals according to stated places of origin. N.B. a reliable estimate of sources of supply to Liverpool itself in 1866 indicated that over 85 per cent of cattle were from Ireland (PP 1866, XVI, *Select Committee on Trade in Animals*, Mins. of Evidence, p. 27 – the witness was the treasurer of the Liverpool cattle market).

through the Liverpool market) and from mainland sources ('the north'), suggesting that, at least in October–November, they were contributing 52 per cent and 45 per cent respectively of the total supply.[37]

A graphic illustration of the pre-eminence of the Irish trade at this time can be seen in the controversy surrounding a proposal to change the market day at Cross Lane from Wednesday to Tuesday. The proponents of the change suggested that an earlier market day would bestow benefits on butchers by giving them a longer period in which to rest their purchases before the weekend slaughtering. It soon became evident, however, that the true reason for the proposal was that it would enable Irish dealers to attend both the Liverpool and Manchester markets, and then to return home in time for the Irish markets on Thursday, ready for the shipping of the following week's consignment on Friday and Saturday. They suggested that, although a day's gap between the markets at Liverpool and Manchester might have been justifiable when livestock moved by road, it was now quite unnecessary.[38] Opposition to the change was very fierce. Local butchers argued strongly for the *status quo*; representations were sent from sheep farmers in Yorkshire and Lincolnshire stating that a Tuesday market would necessitate working on the Sabbath; some opponents pointed out that the new day would clash with a number of local markets in the north of Lancashire and Westmorland; others that it would prevent Yorkshire dealers from being able to gauge the strength of the Irish supply in Liverpool before deciding what to send to Salford.[39] Seemingly, the majority of opinion was firmly against any change, and the butchers were able to present a petition of over 900 signatures to this effect. The Salford Council dutifully took cognisance of this and rejected the proposal. They were then faced with an ultimatum that the Irish dealers would boycott the Salford market and open their own. This threat caused council members to reconsider their verdict, with the result that the Irishmen emerged triumphant, and the day was changed to Tuesday in March 1861.[40]

Ten years on, the evidence indicates that the pattern had changed little. Irish cattle, it was claimed, had the markets at Manchester and

---

[37] *Guardian*, market reports for 10 Oct.–21 Nov. 1860. A cattle salesman at Salford made a similar observation to the Select Committee on the Cattle Plague and Importation of Livestock (*PP* 1877, IX, Mins. of Evidence, p. 192).

[38] SC, *Proceedings*, 18 July 1860.

[39] *Ibid.*; *Guardian*, 22 Feb. 1860, and letters to editor, 18, 23 Feb. 1860.

[40] SC, *Proceedings*, 18 July, 5 Dec. 1860; 3 Feb. 1862.

Liverpool 'pretty nearly to themselves'.[41] At particular times in the year, this must have been so. A leading salesman at Salford's Cross Lane Market pointed out that, although in the first three months of the year the Irish contribution fell to one-half, in the summer it would be almost five-sixths.[42] This suggests that, over the year as a whole, Irish cattle still accounted for about 70–75 per cent of the total, a proportion only slightly lower than in the 1850s.

(b) *Foreign sources of livestock*

Quantitatively, these were of much smaller significance, but gained in importance, especially where sheep were concerned, towards the end of the period. The first foreign sheep appeared at Salford market in May 1851. The market report for that week hailed their arrival by recording that their coarse appearance created a prejudice against them and that many were left unsold. With such inauspicious beginnings, the trade grew only slowly.[43] Table 3.2 shows, however, that by the 1860s they had passed beyond the novelty stage, had established a regular presence in the market and were contributing a growing proportion of the total supply. Most were described as coming from Hamburg, but Dutch sheep were also being sent to Manchester via Hull and Harwich, on the east coast.[44] Since very few foreign sheep entered the country by way of Liverpool at this time, the alternative route for northern supplies, particularly those from the German states, was through Newcastle and the other ports of the north-east. By the beginning of the 1870s, at certain times in the spring, foreign sheep constituted one-third of the total at the market and, on occasions, it was claimed, one-half.[45] However, even the considerable numbers that these proportions represented amounted to less than one-tenth of the annual total; nine out of ten sheep sold at Salford still came from within the United Kingdom.[46]

[41] *PP* 1870, LXI, *Report from the Committee . . . on the Transit of Animals by Sea and Land*, Mins. of Evidence, p. 34.

[42] *PP* 1873, XI, *Select Committee on Contagious Diseases (Animals)*, Mins. of Evidence, p. 541.

[43] *Guardian*, report for 14 May 1851; they were not mentioned again until the report for 27 Apr. 1853.

[44] *PP* 1866, XVI, *Select Committee on Trade in Animals*, Mins. of Evidence, pp. 17, 77, 267.

[45] *PP* 1873, XI, *Select Committee on Contagious Diseases (Animals)*, Mins. of Evidence, p. 541.

[46] *PP* 1877, IX, *Select Committee on the Cattle Plague and Importation of Livestock*, Mins. of Evidence, p. 189. The observations were made in 1871.

Table 3.2 *Foreign sheep as a percentage of total at Salford market, 1860–64*

Year	Number of weeks recorded	As a % of total in weeks when recorded	As a % of annual total
1860	8	10	2
1863	23	7	4
1864	23	10	6

Sources *Courier* and *Guardian*, market reports.

Table 3.3 *Foreign cattle as a percentage of total at Salford market, 1860–64*

Year	Number of weeks recorded	As a % of total in weeks when recorded	As a % of annual total
1860	6	5	0.4
1862	7	11	1
1863	7	9	1
1864	17	7	2

Sources *Courier* and *Guardian*, market reports.

Importations of foreign cattle were of less consequence. A few appeared at Cross Lane shortly after import restrictions on foreign livestock were lifted in 1842, presumably forwarded from the Liverpool market; but it was another ten years before the market reports recorded the arrival of the first foreign cattle sent direct to Manchester. Initially, the reception was as cautious as that given to foreign sheep, and many could not find a buyer.[47] Over the next few years they warranted few mentions by the compiler of the weekly reports, and as late as 1860 the numbers involved were small. However, as Table 3.3 demonstrates, within a further three years the trade had grown to the extent that they represented about one-tenth of the supply in those weeks when they were on sale at the market, although their contribution to the annual total remained inconsiderable. Foreign cattle reached northern towns from two directions: there was a modest trade in Portuguese and Spanish beasts through Liverpool, and a more significant one from Hamburg and Holland via Hull. According to the descriptions in the market reports, it was from the

[47] *Guardian*, market reports for 15 Mar., 25 Oct. 1843; 8 Sept. 1852.

latter direction that most of Manchester's supplies originated.[48] During the last few years of the period, foreign imports were hampered by the restrictions imposed in consequence of the recurrent outbreaks of cattle plague. As a result, there was little chance for the trade to develop further at this time.[49]

iv. The role of railways

Historians have accorded great importance to the advent of the railway in the development of the livestock trade, seeing it particularly as marking the beginning of the end of long-distance droving.[50] In fact, the picture is more complex than at first sight appears. There was no immediate transformation of existing supply lines as far as meat was concerned, and the effects of the railways were gradual on account of the incremental nature of railway building itself. Nor is it easy to isolate the impact of any individual line because of the complications associated with amalgamations and the way in which this process was reflected in the published railway traffic returns. It is clear, however, that their early involvement was marked by many uncertainties, which are particularly well illustrated by the experience of the Liverpool and Manchester Railway (Plate 2) in relation to livestock imported into Liverpool.

Urged on by Joseph Sandars, one of the instigators of the rail link between the two towns, the company was already, in the late 1820s, investing heavily in preparation for the anticipated traffic. Cattle and sheep waggons were built, land was acquired and a cattle station developed at Broad Green, Liverpool, and a siding constructed for unloading at Oldfield Road in Salford.[51] In fact, the fortunes of the company in capturing livestock traffic over the ensuing years were mixed, to say the least. The earliest successes were with the transport

[48] PP 1866, XVI, *Select Committee on Trade in Animals*, Mins. of Evidence, pp. 21, 32, 77, 267; PP 1866, XXII, *First Report . . . into the Origin and Nature etc. of the Cattle Plague*, Appendix D, pp. 175–7; *Guardian*, market reports, 1861–64.

[49] See R. Perren, *The Meat Trade in Britain, 1840–1914*, London, 1978, pp. 109–10.

[50] C.S. Orwin and E.H. Whetham, *History of British Agriculture, 1846–1914*, London, 1964, pp. 27, 97–9; J.D. Chambers and G.E. Mingay, *The Agricultural Revolution, 1750–1880*, London, 1966, p. 171. But see G.R. Hawke, *Railways and Economic Growth in England and Wales, 1840–1870*, Oxford, 1970, chapter V, for a sceptical account of the importance of the railway in the livestock trade, measured in terms of 'social saving'.

[51] PRO, RAIL 371/1, 22 Mar. 1830; RAIL 371/2, 20 Dec. 1830; 30 May, 6 June 1831; RAIL 371/9, 20 Aug. 1831.

of pigs, which were notoriously slow walkers and liable to lose weight at a disproportionate rate.[52] In this instance, the main competition was with waterways, and in the mid-1830s the number of pigs conveyed to Manchester from Liverpool was evenly divided between rail and water.[53] A shrewd reduction of the rate from 30s to 25s per waggon, effected by the company in 1834, engendered a notable increase in its share of the traffic, and in 1843 separate pig stations, soon to be extended, were constructed at Liverpool and at Charles Street, near the Liverpool Road Station, in Manchester.[54] According to Graham, the line was carrying an annual average of around 80,000 pigs in 1840–43 and was one of the three most important railways in the country for the pig trade.[55] Not all these animals remained in Manchester, of course, but it seems clear that the line had captured the bulk of the Irish pig traffic by the mid-century. Less success was achieved with sheep, which were cheaper to move on the drove roads.[56] The special carriages built for sheep were in a state of neglect in 1834, and the company was obliged to introduce a series of reductions of rates in the late 1830s and early 1840s.[57] Even so, in 1845–46 the total number of sheep carried on the Grand Junction Railway – into which the Liverpool and Manchester Company had just been absorbed – remained but a fraction of that of pigs.[58] With cattle, the position was different again, since they lost less weight proportionately *en route*.[59] Despite improvements in the early 1840s at the Broad Green Station and a reduction of carriage rates by as much as one-third, the line continued to experience difficulty in capturing the cattle trade.[60] As late as 1850, a correspondent to the

[52] PP 1846, XIII, *Select Committee . . . on the best means of enforcing one uniform system of Management of Railroads*, Mins. of Evidence, p. 166, where pigs are described as 'bad travellers'. Hence, the Irishman, it was said, put his pigs on the railway as soon as he could. I am grateful to Dr G.L. Turnbull for drawing my attention to this source.

[53] PRO, RAIL 371/3, 23 Sept. 1833.

[54] PRO, RAIL 371/3, 13 Oct. 1834; RAIL 371/5, 18 Oct., 1 Nov. 1841; RAIL 371/6, 23 Jan., 20 Feb. 1843; RAIL 371/11, 9 Mar., 7 Sept. 1843.

[55] W.A. Graham, 'Adaptation of official returns of railway traffic to the general purposes of statistical inquiry', *JSSL*, VIII, 1845, p. 221.

[56] J.B. Williams, 'On the principles of railway management', *JSSL*, IX, 1846, p. 112.

[57] PRO, RAIL 371/10, 7 Aug. 1834; 7 July 1836; RAIL 371/5, 25 Feb. 1839; PP 1845, XXXIX, *Railway Tolls: Return of the Various Charges*, p. 13.

[58] From July 1845 to June 1846, the Grand Junction Company carried c. 46,000 sheep and c. 336,000 pigs (PP 1847–8, LXIII, *Railway Commission: Return of the Passenger and Goods Traffic on each Railway . . . for the Two Years ending 30 June 1846 and 30 June 1847*, pp. 31–2).

[59] Williams, 'Railway management', pp. 111–17; W. Harding, 'Facts bearing on the progress of the railway system', *JSSL*, XI, 1848, pp. 333–4.

[60] PRO, RAIL 371/6, 27 Dec. 1842. The rates for cattle were reduced from 25s per waggon in 1840 to 16s by 1845 (PP 1840, XIII, *Fifth Report from the Select Committee on Railway*

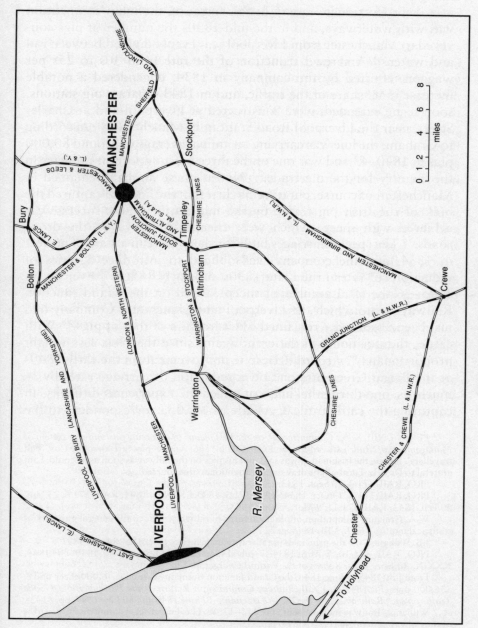

Map 2 Railways of the region

Guardian could assert that three-quarters of the cattle arriving from Liverpool still travelled by road, this being, by droving standards, a relatively short journey.[61]

It is significant that in the mid-1840s a far greater proportion of the imported cattle and sheep being carried out of Liverpool by rail were going south towards Birmingham than were travelling east in the direction of Manchester.[62] Clearly, the greater the distances involved, the stronger was the railways' competitive position, *vis-à-vis* traditional droving methods. Moreover, the intensification of competition between the various companies, as railways proliferated and time passed, affected the supply lines of livestock reaching Manchester both from Ireland and from mainland sources. By 1846 the Grand Junction Railway, incorporating the Liverpool–Manchester line, had itself been absorbed into the London and North Western Company, and the new grouping was to lose its monopoly of rail traffic between the two towns the following year. This came about as a result of the fusion of the Manchester and Leeds (1836), the Manchester, Bolton, and Bury (1835) and the Liverpool and Bury (1845) Railway Companies to form the Lancashire and Yorkshire.[63] From 1849 this company came to hold a two-thirds share in the Preston and Wyre Railway (1835), giving access to the port of Fleetwood and to that portion – not hitherto a large one – of the Irish livestock traffic which was routed through Belfast.[64] Accordingly, in order to meet this perceived threat and to mitigate competition at Liverpool itself, the London and North Western sought, after its acquisition of the Chester and Holyhead Railway in 1858, to develop Holyhead and, subsequently,

---

Communication, Mins. of Evidence, p. 371; *PP* 1845, XXXIX, *Railway Tolls: Return of the Various Charges*, p. 13).

[61] *Guardian*, 9 Jan. 1850. This was disputed in a letter in reply (*ibid.*, 12 Jan. 1850).

[62] This point is inferred from a comparison of returns for the Grand Junction Company, incorporating the Liverpool and Manchester (*PP* 1847–8, LXIII, *Railway Commission: Return of the Passenger and Goods Traffic etc.*, pp. 31–3) with figures given for the number of cattle and sheep carried on the Grand Junction's original line out of Liverpool for 1839–46, provided by S. Salt, *Facts and Figures, principally relating to Railways and Commerce*, London, 1848, p. 57.

[63] The dates given for these railways, here and subsequently, are those of the authorising Acts. In most cases, construction took place over several years. It is not necessary to give more than a skeletal indication of the major developments here, and readers looking for more detail may be referred to an abundant literature on railway history, notably to W.L. Steel, *The History of the London and North Western Railway*, London, 1914; T.R. Gourvish, *Mark Huish and the London and North Western Railway*, Leicester, 1972; J. Marshall, *The Lancashire and Yorkshire Railway*, I, Newton Abbot, 1969; G. Dow, *Great Central*, I, London, 1959; G.O. Holt, *A Regional History of the Railways of Great Britain*, X, *The North West*, Newton Abbot, 1978.

[64] Marshall, *Lancashire and Yorkshire Railway*, I, pp. 85–6.

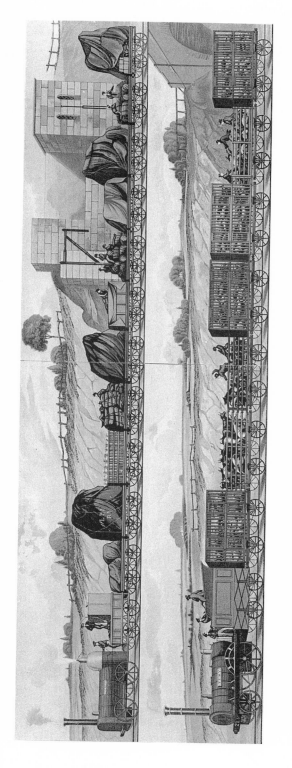

Plate 2 The Liverpool and Manchester Railway, 1831

Plate 3 The Bridgewater Canal passing over the River Irwell at the Barton Aqueduct, 1794

Morecambe, from where cattle could be despatched direct to Manchester and places further afield.[65] In these ways, the central role of Liverpool in the Irish livestock trade was somewhat diminished. As far as Manchester was concerned, however, the effect should not be exaggerated; most traffic destined for this city continued to pass through the Mersey port in the 1860s. Moreover, beleaguered though it saw itself, the London and North Western still carried approximately three-quarters of the supply of Irish cattle reaching Manchester.[66]

With regard to long-distance mainland supplies, the railways helped the movement of fattened cattle from the north to develop into a traffic of major importance. The 1850s and 1860s were to see some celebrated and elaborate traffic-sharing agreements whereby cattle traffic from Scotland and the north was apportioned between the west- and east-coast routes, with the London and North Western as a major partner in the former.[67] The Newcastle market, one that had come into being as recently as 1836 as a more suitable venue than Morpeth, appears to have grown particularly rapidly into the largest cattle market in the north of England and the border counties.[68] As early as 1846, it was claimed that as many as 700–800 head were despatched from there in a day to Manchester and to other towns in Lancashire and the West Riding.[69] Similarly, the unloading of cattle from Cumberland and Westmorland was a familiar sight at the railway station close to Salford market.[70] Evidence from the market reports shows that, taken together, cattle from the four northernmost English counties, with Berwickshire, made up the largest share of supply other than Ireland. It is not surprising, therefore, that when a local livestock dealer was asked in 1866 about the origin of the cattle on sale at

[65] For Holyhead, see Steel, *London and North Western Railway*, pp. 212, 225; for Morecambe, see Holt, *Regional History*, p. 228; *PP* 1867, XXXVIII, *Royal Commission on Railways*, I, Mins. of Evidence, p. 16.

[66] Calculated from the numbers of cattle carried by the London and North Western from Holyhead and Liverpool to Manchester in the twelve months ending 31 Aug. 1865, as a proportion of the numbers at Salford market in that period, and assuming that 75 per cent of these were Irish (*PP* 1866, XXII, *Second Report . . . into the Origin and Nature etc. of the Cattle Plague*, Tables Nos. 6, 7 and 8, pp. 65–6; *Guardian*, market reports).

[67] PRO, RAIL 410/140, 8 Apr. 1853; G. Channon, 'The Aberdeenshire beef trade with London: a study in steamship and railway competition, 1850–69', *Transport History*, II, 1969, pp. 2–3.

[68] Perren, *Meat Trade*, pp. 30–1.

[69] HLRO, Mins. of Evidence, HC, 1846, LXX, Liverpool, Manchester and Newcastle upon Tyne Junction Railway and Lancashire and North Yorkshire Railway Bill, 6 May, pp. 56–7, 116–17.

[70] *Guardian*, 9 Jan. 1850.

Salford, the first sources mentioned, after Ireland, were the north of England and Scotland.[71]

Looking eastwards, the competition engendered by Irish imports and railway development had some interesting implications for the Craven district of Yorkshire, once a prominent supplier of Manchester. In the late 1840s many cattle and sheep were still being driven there in the time-honoured manner, but graziers were rightly apprehensive about the future of their links with Manchester.[72] As it happened, rail traffic in livestock from this district was made possible from 1849 when the East Lancashire Railway extended its line to Colne in order to form a link with a Midland Railway branch from Skipton.[73] However, the railway system that developed in this vicinity was better orientated towards the West Riding, and Craven graziers came to look increasingly to Wakefield and Leeds for their main markets.[74] Some sheep and cattle still reached Manchester, but, especially with cattle, the trade became more a matter of seizing opportunities offered by anticipated shortages from other sources.[75] On the other hand, the position of Rotherham, in south Yorkshire, in regard to Manchester was somewhat strengthened by railway development. The Rotherham market drew in livestock from the Midlands and Lincolnshire, and the advent of the Manchester and Sheffield Railway, authorised in 1837 but not completed until 1845, cut out an exceptionally arduous trans-Pennine road journey. Railway returns covering the first six months of the operation of this line show that it carried almost 37,000 head of livestock.[76] However, by the early 1860s Rotherham, in turn, faced a challenger, as what had by then become the Manchester, Sheffield, and Lincolnshire Railway sought, in alliance with the Great Northern Railway, to build up Retford, in Nottinghamshire, as a market for livestock from the

[71] *Ibid.*, market reports, 1850–57 and 1860 (see above, note 36); *PP* 1866, XVI, *Select Committee on Trade in Animals*, Mins. of Evidence, p. 266.

[72] HLRO, Mins. of Evidence, HC, 1846, LXX, Liverpool, Manchester and Newcastle upon Tyne Junction Railway and Lancashire and North Yorkshire Railway Bill, 6 May, pp. 123–5, 151–2, 181–5; Mins. of Evidence, HC, 1846, LXX, Clitheroe Junction Railway Bill, 13 May, p. 231; 14 May, pp. 31, 79–80, 115–16.

[73] Marshall, *Lancashire and Yorkshire Railway*, I, p. 115.

[74] *PP* 1866, XXII, *First Report . . . into the Origin and Nature etc. of the Cattle Plague*, Mins. of Evidence, p. 120.

[75] *Guardian*, 23 Feb. 1860.

[76] S. Sidney, *Railways and Agriculture in North Lincolnshire*, London, 1848, pp. 94–6; *PP* 1847–8, LXIII, *Railway Commission: Return of the Passenger and Goods Traffic etc.*, p. 77. The period was 1 Jan.–30 June 1846.

eastern counties *en route* to Lancashire and the West Riding.[77]

The ramifications of railway construction and competition were thus considerable; indeed, as time passed, there was a discernible tendency for the movement of livestock to Manchester to adapt itself to the map of railway development. On the other hand, unlike steamships, the railways did not open up any entirely new sources of supply, and the point has now been reached where it is necessary to draw together the various strands so far discussed, to try to quantify the aggregate amount of meat available in Manchester.

v. Long-term changes in meat availability: the quantitative evidence

Among the various foodstuffs examined in this study, meat is by far the best documented, although there remain many pitfalls in attempting to reach a quantitative assessment of the total supply.

(a) *Hides and skins*

There exists an account of the number of hides and skins inspected at Manchester for excise purposes in 1801–20. This series can be supplemented by an estimate of the number of hides and skins collected by tanners and fellmongers in 1836, a survey undertaken with a view to gauging the amount of meat eaten in Manchester; and by a third set of figures, gathered by Braithwaite Poole, showing the number of cattle and sheep slaughtered in Manchester in 1848–50, according to returns from the abattoirs and market inspectors.[78] On the face of things, it is plausible to link these various quantities together and to compare the changes with the increase in the population of Manchester. When this is done, the conclusion emerges that the supply of livestock did not keep pace with population growth in 1801–20,[79] but

---

[77] PRO, RAIL 463/5, 25 Nov., 9 Dec. 1859; RAIL 463/7, 11 Mar., 19 Aug. 1864.

[78] *PP* 1821, IX, *Select Committee on Agriculture*, Mins. of Evidence, pp. 265–7; W. McConnel, 'An attempt to ascertain the quantity of butchers' meat consumed in Manchester in 1836', read in 1837, *Manchester Statistical Society Papers, 1837–61*, p. 51 (MCL, 310.6 M2); B. Poole, *Statistics of British Commerce*, London, 1852, p. 60.

[79] This conclusion is at odds with that of E.J. Hobsbawm, who used the same data to infer, or perhaps one should say concede, 'a probable rise' in Manchester's *per capita* consumption of meat (see his article, 'The British standard of living, 1790–1850', *EcHR*, 2nd ser., X, 1957, pp. 66–7). However, he used population figures relating to Manchester Township, which, as was pointed out in Chapter II, made up a decreasing proportion of the built-up area as time passed.

by 1836 had run ahead of it, and continued to do so. However, these comparisons bristle with problems, the chief of which are:

(i) The statistics of hides and skins are not necessarily an accurate guide to the amount of meat available, since the weight of animals varied according to their place of origin and over time.[80]
(ii) Some of the animals slaughtered locally, and thus leaving their skins behind, were destined for butchers in towns other than Manchester.
(iii) Some skins may have belonged to animals slaughtered elsewhere, and then brought to Manchester for processing.

In view of these difficulties, which might be discussed at great length, but only inconclusively, it seems preferable to turn to local market reports relating to the number of animals on sale.

(b) *The evidence of the market reports: cattle, sheep and lambs*

There are weekly reports giving the number of cattle, sheep and lambs on sale at the local market, located first at Smithfield and, later, at Cross Lane. The series begins in 1822 and, except for a short period in the 1840s, runs through to the end of the period considered here. The annual averages of the weekly number of livestock supplied to the market from 1822 to 1870 have been obtained from these reports and are presented in Figure 3.1, in index form, on the base 1830–32 = 100; the figure also shows the decade-by-decade growth of the population of the municipal boroughs of Manchester and Salford, on the base 1831 = 100. We can see from the figure that, with some year-to-year fluctuations, the supply of cattle and sheep was roughly keeping pace with population growth through the 1820s, and in the mid-1830s was showing signs of out-running it. By the end of the 1830s, however, both cattle and sheep began to arrive in significantly reduced numbers. Following the break in the figures, the series for sheep and cattle show some interesting differences. When numbers began to be reported again in 1846, those of sheep and lambs started from a point below the

---

[80] Some commentators in the standard of living debate have assumed that the weights of British cattle improved, for example R.M. Hartwell, 'The rising standard of living in England, 1800–1850', *EcHR*, 2nd ser., XIII, 1961, p. 410. On the other hand, Irish cattle, which constituted an increasing proportion of supply from the 1820s, were generally reckoned to be lighter than home-produced animals, as were foreign beasts (see R. Herbert, 'Statistics of live stock and dead meat for consumption in the metropolis', *JRASE*, 1st ser., XX, 1859, pp. 475–6; Perren, *Meat Trade*, pp. 2, 77).

earlier peak level of the mid-1830s and, though rising thereafter, did not do so at rates which exceeded population growth until the mid-1860s. By contrast, the rates of increase in the number of cattle on sale were running well ahead of population growth. There are clear signs of a dip in the mid-1850s, no doubt attributable to the greater involvement of the railways and, in particular, the development of Holyhead, which opened up a wider range of markets for Irish cattle,

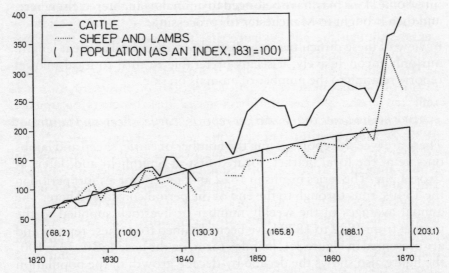

Fig. 3.1 Indices of the number of cattle, sheep and lambs on sale at Manchester markets, 1822–70 (1830–32 = 100)

Sources Weekly returns from market reports in *Courier* and *Guardian*, reworked to determine annual averages. For the population of Manchester and Salford (municipal boroughs), see Table 2.1.

so reducing the supply reaching Manchester. Nevertheless, on the whole, the *per capita* consumption of beef, according to these indications, must have exceeded anything known before 1840. The evidence also appears to reflect a shift in taste, in the direction of beef, after the mid-century. These statistics, and the figure based on them, are undoubtedly the best source for gauging Manchester's meat supply. However, before any firm conclusions can be drawn, it is necessary to discuss the contribution made by pigs and calves, as well as that of preserved meat supplies.

(c) *Pigs and calves*

Here, the evidence is of a much more fragmentary nature. According to the market reports, the number of pigs sold at Smithfield was rising appreciably from 1822 to reach 30,000 by 1837. At this point, they disappeared from the record at both Smithfield and Cross Lane. The main body of the trade moved to railway premises, first in Salford, and then to the purpose-built pig station in Charles Street, where buying and selling developed informally around the facilities provided by the Liverpool and Manchester Company. Curiously, this arrangement appears to have gone unchallenged by the market authorities for many years, although there is evidence that they were seeking to recover some of the pig trade for Cross Lane in the 1860s.[81]

The trade in pigs at Manchester was recognised as being quite distinct from that in other livestock.[82] Moreover, this distinction was reflected in the butchery business itself. Pork butchers occupied a special section of the Bridge Street Shambles, and in the period 1830–70 they constituted about 8 per cent of all meat traders.[83] It is noteworthy, too, that it was in this branch of the trade that the wholesaling of meat first became established, for butchers who bought and slaughtered their own cattle and sheep seem to have been content to rely on specialists for their pork.[84] This may have reflected the fact that in Manchester, as in Lancashire generally, pork was never so popular as other meats.[85] According to Baines, writing in 1867, the main source of supply was Ireland.[86] However, some account must also be taken of the growing trade in pigs, either live or already slaughtered, going direct to butchers from local suppliers. It is difficult, to say the least, to draw up a convincing aggregative picture, but it does not appear that fresh pork came near to rivalling mutton and beef in its share of the total meat trade. During the 1820s and 1830s over five times as many sheep as pigs passed through Smithfield

[81] SC, *Proceedings*, 24 Oct. 1867.

[82] *PP* 1866, XVI, *Select Committee on Trade in Animals*, Mins. of Evidence, p. 33.

[83] From directories listed in the Bibliography, pork butchers as a percentage of all butchers were: 1833, 53/421 (8%); 1840, 40/418 (10%); 1850, 80/641 (8%); 1861, 72/571 (8%); 1871, 81/709 (8%).

[84] See, for example, Manchester and Salford Equitable Co-operative Society Ltd, Butchery Department Accounts, from 30 Aug. 1873. Pork was the only meat always purchased per lb by the department.

[85] Holt, p. 174; Dickson, *General View . . . of Lancashire*, p. 259; *The Meat Trades Journal*, 19 May 1888.

[86] T. Baines, *Lancashire and Cheshire, Past and Present*, London, 1867, I, p. 73.

Market. Similarly, Poole's statistics purporting to show the number of animals slaughtered in Manchester in 1848–50 indicate that twice as many cattle and eight times as many sheep as pigs were killed, though the figures were prepared at a time when Irish pig supplies were much depleted after the failure of the potato crop.[87] In a twelve-month period in 1864–65 the London and North Western Railway conveyed to Manchester just under 66,000 pigs,[88] which must have included the bulk of the Irish supplies. Even if we add 50 per cent to allow for unrecorded local contributions, the total would still be less than one-quarter of the number of sheep and lambs arriving in the town at that time, although rather more, of course, if measured by weight.[89]

The marketing of calves was somewhat simpler, in that they either passed through the official market at Smithfield or, later, Cross Lane, or were killed on the farm and brought into the town already dressed, which Aikin suggested was the usual practice in the 1790s.[90] In 1836 a detailed survey of the calf trade estimated that three-quarters of the veal consumed in Manchester reached the town already prepared, and that the number brought there, either as carcases or still alive, was less than 12,000 a year.[91] According to the market returns, the annual average on sale in the 1860s was 9,265, compared to 2,622 in 1830–39. If the (unrecorded) number of carcases reaching Manchester remained in about the same proportion to that of live animals, it is possible to infer a considerable improvement in supply by the 1860s, but one that still only amounted to the equivalent of about 40,000 calves at that time.

(d) Dead and preserved meat

The fact that some local pork and much of the veal consumed in Manchester arrived already prepared prompts the question whether there existed a more extensive dead-meat trade to supplement that which arrived on the hoof and passed through the markets to be

[87] *Guardian*, market reports; for 1848–50, see Poole, *Statistics*, p. 60. His figures for cattle and sheep are from the market returns, although it should be noted that he had no way of knowing the number of pigs available other than at the Charles Street Pig Station and a smaller carcase market at Bridge Street.

[88] PP 1866, XXII, *Second Report . . . into the Origin and Nature etc. of the Cattle Plague*, Appendix D, Table No. 3, p. 64.

[89] The average number of sheep and lambs at market in these years was 406,108 (*Guardian*, market reports for 1864–65).

[90] Aikin, p. 204.

[91] McConnel, 'Butchers' meat consumed in Manchester', p. 51.

counted in Figure 3.1. In London, dead meat appears to have constituted an important part of the total supply, allegedly feeding 36 per
cent of the population in the 1850s and 1860s, and this is one reason
why the use of the number of beasts passing through the capital's
Smithfield Market, as an index of meat consumption, has been questioned.[92] Such a trade, however, had no counterpart in Manchester.
Some jumped to the conclusion that the beginning of the steamboat
service across the Irish Sea and the advent of the railway were
sufficient to encourage the development of a dead-meat trade to the
town.[93] But it was a false assumption. When asked about a traffic in
dead meat to Manchester, the managing director of the steamboat
company plying between Dublin and Liverpool confidently asserted
before a parliamentary select committee: 'There is a great mistake
upon that subject; there is none'.[94] Nor does one seem to have grown
up subsequently. Figures of the traffic carried by the Liverpool and
Manchester Railway in 1844 show that no dead meat was being
conveyed, in contrast to a small tonnage going to the south on the
Grand Junction line.[95] Two decades later, when outbreaks of cattle
plague necessitated restrictions being placed on the movement of live
animals, the matter came under further review. Once again, it was
clear that Manchester was receiving negligible amounts, if any, of its
meat supply in this form. To institute a dead-meat traffic from
Liverpool would require six months' preparation, it was argued; from
the east coast, it was 'utterly impracticable'.[96]

There were sound economic reasons why the live trade was preferred by railway companies and traders alike. On the whole, it was
cheaper to send the same quantity of meat live rather than dead, for the
simple reason, as the cattle traffic manager of the London and North
Western pointed out, that it 'loads and unloads itself'.[97] But the main
barrier to any dead-meat trade developing in Manchester was a reluctance on the part of local butchers to give up their customary practice
of doing their own buying and slaughtering. As we shall see, it was for
the same reason that a wholesale trade in meat was slow to develop in

[92] Perren, *Meat Trade*, p. 43; Hartwell, 'Rising standard of living', p. 410; Channon, 'Aberdeenshire beef trade with London', pp. 10–11.
[93] PP 1833, V, *Select Committee on Agriculture*, Mins. of Evidence, p. 270.
[94] PP 1833, VI, *Select Committee on Manufactures, Commerce and Shipping*, Mins. of Evidence, p. 535; see also, PP 1833, V, *Select Committee on Agriculture*, Mins. of Evidence, pp. 45, 200–1.
[95] Salt, *Facts and Figures*, p. 90.
[96] PP 1866, XVI, *Select Committee on Trade in Animals*, Mins. of Evidence, pp. 20, 266.
[97] *Ibid.*, p. 40.

Manchester, and such traditionally-minded butchers were even more wary of accepting meat that came from a distance in slaughtered form. They were, in this respect, quite unlike their fellows in the capital.[98] With the imposition of restrictions on cattle movements in the later 1860s, the trade in dead meat did become more important, but its growth was slow, and only small tonnages were involved even in the 1870s.[99] It was not until the arrival of chilled and, later, frozen meat at the end of that decade that the position began to change; but there long persisted a marked reluctance on the part of butchers to incorporate this sort of meat into their normal stock.[100]

There remains the important question of the supply of preserved meat, the most important forms of which were bacon and, to a lesser extent, ham. During the eighteenth century Manchester's supplies of these products derived chiefly from Cumberland and Westmorland,[101] though there are no statistics whatsoever on the scale of the trade. The first half of the nineteenth century saw a marked increase in importations of Irish bacon and ham, amounting to 4,000–5,000 tons into Liverpool alone by the early 1840s, prior to the onset of the potato famine, which cut this back to 700–900 tons in 1848–50. By this date imports of 'foreign' – largely a euphemism for 'American' before the 1880s – bacon and ham into Liverpool were running at around 9,000 tons.[102] At the national level, imports fluctuated wildly from year to year but reached 1.9 million cwt in 1863, owing partly to the Civil War, which artificially diverted supplies to the British market.[103] Unfortunately, it is virtually impossible to gauge what proportion of national, or even Liverpool, imports of bacon and ham were destined for consumption in Manchester, since they were not treated as separate items of carriage in the various waterway and railway traffic accounts that have been examined. All that can be said

---

[98] *Ibid.*, pp. 24, 32, 34.

[99] *PP* 1873, XI, *Select Committee on Contagious Diseases (Animals)*, Mins. of Evidence, p. 540; *PP* 1877, IX, *Select Committee on the Cattle Plague and Importation of Livestock*, Mins. of Evidence, pp. 197–8. There is a vivid illustration of the difference between London and Manchester in quantities of dead meat carried by the London and North Western in 1880: to London, 39,502 tons; to Manchester, 1,809 tons (*PP* 1881, XIV, *Select Committee on Railways*, II, Appendix No. 73, p. 318).

[100] See the comments in R. Roberts, *The Classic Slum*, Manchester, 1971, p. 88.

[101] Fussell and Goodman, 'Eighteenth-century traffic in livestock', pp. 232–3; Bailey and Culley, *General View . . . of Northumberland, Cumberland and Westmoreland*, p. 261; W. Cobbett, *Rural Rides*, G.D.H. and M. Cole (eds.), London, 1930, III, p. 865.

[102] J. MacGregor, *Commercial Statistics*, London, 1850, V, Supplement II, p. 169; Poole, *Statistics*, p. 16.

[103] Perren, *Meat Trade*, p. 73.

is that imported bacon and ham was an addition to that available from British sources – itself an unknown quantity – although in so far as some of the pigs imported live were subsequently cured and consumed in this way, part of the increase in supply has already been accounted for in the previous section.

Evidence of contemporary commentators strongly suggests that in Manchester in the 1840s the lower-paid workers, at any rate, took much of their meat in the form of bacon. Likewise, in 1863 Edward Smith thought that among factory hands bacon was quite as commonly consumed as fresh meat.[104] Moreover, it was at this social level that salted or pickled pork was most likely to find a sale. In England, there was a general distaste for food preserved by such methods, and it accounted for but a small part of total domestic consumption.[105] American pig-meat, in particular, tended to be excessively fatty and salty and, says Perren, 'naturally . . . found its largest sale among the poorer classes of consumer'.[106]

(e) *Conclusions as to aggregate supply*

Clearly, there are some aspects of meat supply which cannot be measured satisfactorily, and the best of the evidence so far considered is that based on the numbers of live cattle, sheep and lambs reaching Manchester's markets. Ideally, one would wish to compare the aggregate quantity of meat sold, both in and outside the markets, with the growth of population. But, even if the supply figures were perfectly comprehensive and completely accurate, we should still have to face a major problem arising from uncertainty about the size of the catchment area that the town's markets were expected to supply. The Smithfield and Cross Lane Markets were catering increasingly for satellite towns, in addition to Manchester and Salford. At the beginning of the nineteenth century, places such as Bolton and Rochdale received their supplies of livestock independently of Manchester.[107] However, the growth of Smithfield and Cross Lane and the natural

---

[104] See Engels, *Condition of the Working Class*, p. 85; W. Neild, 'Comparative statement of the income and expenditure of certain families of the working classes in Manchester and Dukinfield in the years 1836 and 1841', *JSSL*, IV, 1841–2, pp. 327–8; *PP* 1863, XXV, *Fifth Report of the Medical Officer of the Privy Council*, Appendix V, No. 3, *Report of Dr E. Smith, Economics of Diet*, p. 351.

[105] P. Mathias, *Retailing Revolution*, London, 1967, p. 18; Poole, *Statistics*, p. 26; Cullen, *Anglo–Irish Trade*, pp. 72–3.

[106] Perren, *Meat Trade*, p. 71.

[107] Aikin, pp. 248, 261.

channelling of traffic – especially from Ireland – towards these markets, a process reinforced by the railways, meant that smaller towns within a widening radius came to look to Manchester for their supply. By the mid-century it furnished the needs of those in the immediate vicinity, such as Oldham, Ashton and Stockport, as well as Bolton and Rochdale; twenty years on, Burnley, Blackburn and Preston had also come within its orbit.[108] In this situation, where the size of the potential market is both unknown and changing, the relative success or failure of the supply to keep pace with the level of demand is better shown by analysing the price information given in the weekly market reports published in the *Guardian* and *Courier* newspapers.

vi. Price data and their social implications, 1822–70

The weekly market reports provide a range of prices for the different grades of cattle, sheep, lambs, calves and, for a few years, pigs on sale at the Smithfield and Cross Lane Markets. Figure 3.2 presents the annual averages of the weekly minimum prices quoted for cattle and sheep over the years 1822–70, in index form, on the base 1851–56 = 100; the seven-year moving averages of these indices; and year-to-year variations in the (national) Rousseaux price index of animal products, also on the base 1851–56 = 100, included for comparative purposes.[109] From these graphs, it appears that the movement of prices in Manchester passed through four distinguishable phases.

1825–33

The prices of cattle and, to a lesser extent, sheep showed a tendency to drift downwards until the early 1830s, giving some confirmation of the view expressed above, that this was a time when supplies of livestock were growing faster than the level of demand(compare Figures 3.1 and 3.2). For cattle prices, the extent of the fall was rather greater than that exhibited by the Rousseaux index.

---

[108] *Guardian*, 12 Jan. 1850; Poole, *Statistics*, p. 60; PP 1873, XI, *Select Committee on Contagious Diseases (Animals)*, Mins. of Evidence, p. 542.

[109] The Rousseaux index of animal product prices is given in B.R. Mitchell and P. Deane, *Abstract of British Historical Statistics*, Cambridge, 1962, pp. 471–2.

1834–41

Both sheep and cattle prices rose significantly in these years, and at a rate exceeding that of the Rousseaux index. For sheep, this was a time when the numbers recorded at Cross Lane were declining from their 1835 peak (Figure 3.1), and hence prices were likely to rise. For cattle, price increases were even more marked, although the numbers recorded at the market did not reach their highest point until 1838–39 (Figure 3.1). Thus, in contrast to the previous period, the data suggest that increasing consumption and, perhaps, a widening market for livestock sold at Salford were also playing a part in pushing demand ahead of supply.

1842–50

This was another period in which prices showed a tendency to fall, although not without interruptions. Initially, the declining prices were almost certainly precipitated by a decrease in demand at a time of economic depression. As early as August 1840, local newspapers had decided to discontinue publishing details of the exact quantities of livestock at the market 'for reasons that the public and especially the graziers will feel no difficulty in understanding';[110] and over the ensuing years the weekly reports were recording comments such as 'the dullest market ever remembered'; 'the supply larger than the demand'; and 'hundreds were turned out unsold'.[111] Prices staged something of a recovery during the cyclical upswing of 1844–45, but were fading again by the later 1840s, probably owing to another cyclical downswing in the face of increases in supply (Figure 3.1).

1851–70

Price fluctuations continued. The simultaneous dips that occurred in 1858 for cattle and sheep no doubt reflected another cyclical trough and short-term reductions in demand. Overall, however, the indications are that demand was tending to run ahead of supply. During these years the number of sheep reaching the Manchester market kept pace with the growth of population and rose very sharply

---

[110] *Guardian*, 1 Aug. 1840.
[111] *The Manchester and Salford Advertiser*, reports for the markets of 8 June, 23 Nov. 1842; 22 Mar. 1843.

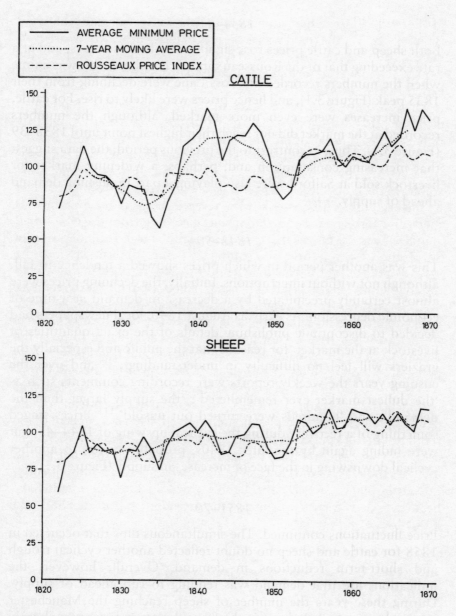

Fig. 3.2 Indices of cattle and sheep prices in Manchester, 1822–70 (1851–56 = 100)

Sources Minimum prices quoted weekly in market reports in *Courier* and *Guardian*, reworked to determine annual averages. For the Rousseaux index, see Chapter III, note 109.

in the mid-1860s, while supplies of cattle were even more buoyant (Figure 3.1). Yet the trend was for prices to move upwards. Moreover, in the 1860s cattle prices showed a clear tendency to outpace the Rousseaux index, confirming an increased propensity to consume beef rather than mutton.

There are limits to the efficacy of using simple price trends as a criterion for assessing social gains, since they were obviously influenced by a range of factors operating on both the supply and the demand sides. However, there is another way of approaching this issue, namely, by measuring the degree to which prices became more stable. In the first place, short-term deficiencies in supply might be met by the bringing in of livestock from 'reserve' areas. A good example is the year 1860, when a shortfall in cattle coming from the traditional sources was compensated by unusually large numbers from Shropshire, Norfolk and 'the south'.[112] Before the railway and the spread of the telegraph system, it was difficult to respond in this way to the changing needs of different markets, since opportunities to redirect established flows from one area to another were severely limited by the time and effort required. Wakefield and Leeds were obvious markets to turn to when Irish or northern supplies were unable to meet the demand, but by the end of the period Edinburgh and London were also being drawn on in times of shortage.[113] As a result of these developments, fluctuations in prices were markedly reduced. If two ten-year periods, 1825–34 and 1858–67, are compared, the mean annual deviation for cattle was approximately halved, from 8.3 per cent of the trend price to 4.3 per cent; for sheep, it fell from 7.7 per cent to 3.7 per cent.[114] The reduction is all the more striking in that the later period includes the years of the Lancashire Cotton Famine and, subsequently, the cattle plague, when considerable price fluctuations might have been expected in consequence of the attendant fall in demand and difficulties of supply.[115]

[112] *Courier* and *Guardian*, market reports.

[113] PP 1866, XVI, *Select Committee on Trade in Animals*, Mins. of Evidence, pp. 33, 35; PP 1873, XI, *Select Committee on Contagious Diseases (Animals)*, Mins. of Evidence, p. 542.

[114] Calculations follow the method described in R.G.D. Allen, *Statistics for Economists*, 2nd edn., London, 1951, pp. 143–4.

[115] See T.C. Barker, D.J. Oddy and J. Yudkin, *The Dietary Surveys of Dr Edward Smith 1862–3: A New Assessment*, Occasional Paper No. 1, Department of Nutrition, Queen Elizabeth College, London, 1970, pp. 40–1. Although Ireland did not fall victim to the cattle plague of 1865–66 (O'Donovan, *Live Stock in Ireland*, p. 257), and Scotland and the north of England escaped relatively lightly, Cheshire was particularly badly affected (PP 1867–8, XVIII, *Report on the Cattle Plague in Great Britain during the years 1865, 1866, and 1867*, Appendix No. 1, pp. 22, 25–6, 29–38).

Meat

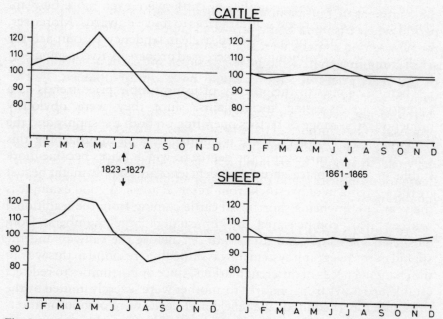

Fig. 3.3 Seasonal variations in cattle and sheep prices in Manchester, 1823–27 and 1861–65

Sources Minimum prices quoted weekly in market reports in *Courier* and *Guardian*, reworked to determine monthly averages. Monthly variations are given as ratios to the trend values (= 100) ruling across the two sub-periods chosen for comparison.

Secondly, there are clear signs of stabilisation in prices over the seasons of the year. This can be seen in Figure 3.3, which compares the average variation in prices of cattle and sheep over the different months for two groups of years, one at the beginning and the other towards the end of the period for which data are available.[116] There were two major factors operating to produce a more even supply and a greater stability in prices. With regard to cattle, the main influence was probably the enhanced flexibility given by the increasing use over these years of yard- and stall-feeding. This enabled producers to choose the time to send livestock to market, and worked to even out the seasonal peaks.[117] With regard to sheep, growing numbers were arriving from

[116] Following the method of Allen, *Statistics for Economists*, pp. 144–51.
[117] See E.L. Jones, 'The changing basis of English agricultural prosperity, 1853–73', *Agricultural History Review*, X, 1962, pp. 112–13.

the continent of Europe in the spring and early summer, during the period when Irish and home-produced supplies tended to decline as the new season's lambs were being fattened. It was claimed before a select committee that, without foreign sheep and cattle at certain times of the year, prices at Salford would have almost doubled.[118] The witness was deeply involved in this branch of the livestock trade and therefore not averse to exaggerating its influence in the face of a proposal to ban imports. His general point, however, was obviously valid. The wider Manchester could cast the net for supplies of food, the easier it would be to minimise exceptional annual or seasonal fluctuations in prices, and that was not an inconsiderable gain for its inhabitants.

[118] *PP* 1873, XI, *Select Committee on Contagious Diseases (Animals)*, Mins. of Evidence, p. 543. Evidence of Septimus Lambert, a Manchester cattle salesman.

CHAPTER IV
Dairy products

i. Milk

A CONTROVERSY about the milk supply of London in the later nineteenth century may seem an unlikely starting point, but it provides a useful background for comparison. It is generally acknowledged that before the mid-1860s London derived the bulk of its supply either from town dairies or from its immediate environs, and the point at issue is the importance of milk brought to the capital by rail before the cattle plague of 1865–66. No-one disputes that railway milk had started before then, but it is usually assumed that the ravages of the town dairies by the cattle plague, and the attendant shock caused by sanitary inspectors' revelations of the conditions in which many cows were kept, gave a substantial boost to the carriage of milk from outside the city.[1] Certainly, contemporaries laid particular stress on the role of the cattle plague in transforming the metropolitan milk supply.[2] However, in an article in 1971, Taylor mounted a sharp attack on this orthodoxy, arguing that railway milk had been an important part of the total supply even before 1865, and that the swing away from town dairies was part of longer-term trends in which milk displaced butter and cheese as the major article of production among British dairy farmers.[3] Since then, Atkins has subjected Taylor's evidence to close scrutiny and concludes that he underestimated the yield of town dairies and overestimated the total of

[1] E.H. Whetham, 'The London milk trade, 1860–1900', *EcHR*, 2nd ser., XVII, 1964, p. 372; G.E. Fussell, 'The early days of railway milk transport – I, *Dairy Engineering*, LXXIII, 1956, pp. 207–11; *idem, The English Dairy Farmer, 1500–1900*, London, 1966, pp. 307, 309.

[2] J.P. Sheldon, *Dairy Farming*, London, 1881, p. v; J.C. Morton, 'Town milk', *JRASE*, 2nd ser., IV, 1868, pp. 95–7.

[3] D. Taylor, 'London's milk supply, 1850–1900: a reinterpretation', *Agricultural History*, XLV, 1971, pp. 33–8; *idem*, 'The English dairy industry, 1860–1930', *EcHR*, 2nd ser., XXIX, 1976, esp. pp. 589–90.

railway milk, thus exaggerating the extent of the changes before 1870.[4] The two authors agree, however, that the cattle plague itself was only one factor among several influencing the structure of London's milk supply, and that it did not have the dramatic effect once thought. Atkins argues that the town dairies recovered from the events of 1865–66, and that it was only after the mid-1870s that they went into permanent decline.[5] As in so much economic history, London is the centre of attention, and the difficulty is knowing the degree to which provincial towns underwent similar processes of change. In fact, Manchester was quite different.

Town dairies had never been important in Manchester. In 1795 Holt noted that there were not more than six cows within the whole of the town,[6] and this observation is confirmed by the early directories. The compilers distinguished between 'cowkeepers' and 'milk sellers' or proprietors of 'milk houses', and Table 4.1 lists the numbers recorded. While the comprehensiveness of the directories can be called into question, the relative importance of the two sources of supply seems clear enough.[7]

Table 4.1 *Number of cowkeepers and milk sellers in Manchester and Salford, 1772–1811*

Year	Cowkeepers	Milk houses, Milk sellers
1772	6	–
1788	–	–
1800	4	20
1811	2	49

Source Directories (see Bibliography).

The contrast with London is striking, as it is with nearby Liverpool, where, according to Holt, 500–600 cows were being kept for this

[4] P.J. Atkins, 'The milk trade of London, *c.* 1790–1914', University of Cambridge, Ph.D., 1977, pp. 145–8.

[5] *Ibid.*, pp. 59–87; Taylor, 'London's milk supply', pp. 36–8; P.J. Atkins, 'The growth of London's railway milk trade, *c.* 1845–1914', *Journal of Transport History*, new ser., IV, 1978, pp. 223–4; *idem*, 'London's intra-urban milk supply, *circa* 1790–1914', *Transactions of the Institute of British Geographers*, new ser., II, 1977, pp. 386–7.

[6] Holt, p. 149.

[7] The 1800 and 1811 directories interchange the terms 'milk sellers' and 'milk houses'. The latter were clearly not town dairies. See Aikin, p. 204; also Samuel Bamford describing his daily chore as a boy of going to the local milk house and waiting for the milk to arrive, in S. Bamford, *Early Days*, new edn., W.H. Chaloner (ed.), London, 1967, pp. 101–2.

purpose in the late eighteenth century.[8] The situation seems to have changed little throughout the period. In 1866 it was reported to Salford Council that there were approximately fifty cattle within the city of Manchester and about 350 within Salford.[9] Not all of these were necessarily kept for milking, and many could not strictly be called town cows, since the Salford municipal limits then included a good deal of open countryside. In any event, all 400 cattle could have provided only a very small proportion – approximately 7 per cent – of the milk consumption of Manchester and Salford. This again marked a contrast with London, which relied on town cows for 72 per cent of its supply in 1861, and with Liverpool, where town dairies remained important until well into the present century.[10] Moreover, evidence from the activities of various sanitary inspectors over the period bears out the unimportance of town milk. Among countless reports of insanitary slaughterhouses and piggeries, rarely were dairies even mentioned. The Court Leet records, for example, show twenty-two irregularities between 1770 and 1846 involving retailers selling milk, but only one case of a nuisance caused by a cowhouse; and the Manchester and Salford Sanitary Association noted only two cases involving shippons in 1853–54.[11]

In place of town milk, Manchester was supplied from the surrounding countryside. The local newspaper of the late eighteenth century carried numbers of advertisements for milk farms emphasising proximity to Manchester and accessibility to main roads.[12] The most desirable were within two or three miles of the town, but milk was coming from further afield than that. Manchester was particularly well placed in this respect because, with the exception of the area to the

[8] Holt, p. 149; and see Atkins, 'London's intra-urban milk supply', p. 387.

[9] *Guardian*, 9 Mar. 1866; see also *PP* 1877, IX, *Select Committee on the Cattle Plague and Importation of Livestock*, Mins. of Evidence, p. 191, for the comment: 'There are no dairies in Manchester in the town'.

[10] For London, see Taylor, 'London's milk supply', p. 35; for Liverpool, see R. Lawton and C.G. Pooley, 'David Brindley's Liverpool: an aspect of urban society in the 1880s', *Transactions of the Historic Society of Lancashire and Cheshire*, CXXV, 1974, pp. 151, 165. My figure for Manchester is based on Smith's estimate for cotton workers in 1861–62 of 1.4 pints *per capita* weekly consumption (T.C. Barker, D.J. Oddy and J. Yudkin, *The Dietary Surveys of Dr Edward Smith 1862–3: A New Assessment*, Occasional Paper No. 1, Department of Nutrition, Queen Elizabeth College, London, 1970, p. 40), multiplied by the population of Manchester and Salford, and set against a likely yield of 750 gallons a year (Taylor, 'London's milk supply', p. 34) × 400.

[11] *Court Leet*, X, pp. 32–3, 19 Oct. 1807; MCLAD, M126/2/2/1, Manchester and Salford Sanitary Association, Visiting Committee's Reports, Chorlton District, 27 Jan. 1853; M126/2/4/8, *ibid.*, London Road District, 18 Aug. 1854.

[12] For example, *Mercury*, 7 Nov. 1780; 9 Jan. 1781; 1, 29 Oct. 1782; 24 Nov., 16 Dec. 1795.

south-west, the town was surrounded by regions given over to dairy farming of one sort or another. In the late eighteenth and early nineteenth centuries, traditional cheese-making had not yet been seriously challenged by liquid-milk production as the natural focus of the Cheshire dairy farmer.[13] Consequently, most of Manchester's milk in that period came from Lancashire. Even so, within the ten-mile radius that is generally thought to have been the limit that milk could travel at that time,[14] Manchester was able to draw on many more potential suppliers than most other towns. Liverpool, for example, was faced with extensive regions of arable farming, once the supplies from surrounding districts had been exhausted; in these circumstances, town dairies, even with their higher costs, would prove profitable.

The existence of town dairies, however, was not only a function of the difficulty of bringing enough milk from outside towns to meet the needs of urban populations, but also reflected a preference for a product that was deemed superior to that carried from more distant parts. Certainly, country milk could not compete for freshness with that drawn straight from a cow and brought to the front door, as was available to the rich, and it was prone to deterioration caused by being shaken about on its journey of several miles over uneven roads from outside the town. In London, spring-carts which went 'at a rapid trot' were bringing milk from as far as twenty miles away, yet inevitably the quality on arrival would be poor.[15] Here again, Manchester was particularly fortunate, for there was little need to go so far in search of supply; in any case, it was not by road but by canal that such milk could be brought.

Originally, milk had been carried in by pack-horse; that had given way to the horse and cart, which, in turn, began to be rivalled by water transport.[16] It is impossible even to guess at how much was conveyed in this way, but evidently it was an important traffic. Holt mentioned

[13] H. Holland, *General View of the Agriculture of Cheshire*, London, 1808, pp. 249–86, discusses Cheshire dairy farming purely in terms of cheese and, to a much lesser degree, butter production.

[14] G.E. Fussell and C. Goodman, 'The eighteenth-century traffic in milk products', *Economic History*, III, 1934–37, p. 380; R. Trow-Smith, *English Husbandry: From the Earliest Times to the Present Day*, London, 1951, p. 210.

[15] J.H. Clapham, *An Economic History of Modern Britain*, Cambridge, 1926, I, p. 228.

[16] R.N. Salaman, 'The Oxnoble potato: a study in public house nomenclature', *TLCAS*, LXIV, 1954, p. 76; Holt, p. 149; R.W. Dickson, *General View of the Agriculture of Lancashire*, London, 1815, p. 545.

'a quantity' of milk arriving daily by canal, and in 1825 an anonymous, but well-informed, authority wrote of 'a vast quantity . . . delivered twice a day by the Duke's canal'.[17] No doubt most of this milk came down the northern part of the canal from around Worsley where, in 1836, Wheeler noticed great improvements over the previous years in the production of milk and butter for the Manchester market.[18] The small milk producers further to the east were served by the Manchester, Bolton, and Bury Canal, whose canal committee began negotiations in 1825 to run a special milk boat toManchester.[19] During the next twenty years, however, Manchester increasingly began to attract milk from the north of Cheshire. Although cheese remained the major dairy product, a new market had been opened up for farmers close to the Cheshire branch of the Bridgewater Canal. 'There are', wrote one of Palin's correspondents from this area in 1844, 'no dairies here, the milk being sold to the dealers for the supply of Manchester and the surrounding neighbourhood'.[20]

A number of factors could influence the decision to switch from cheese or butter production to milk, but a major one would be ease of access to the urban market. There the canal played a crucial role. Not only did it allow milk to be transported to Manchester from outside the limits normally imposed by the difficulties of road transport, but it also enabled it to arrive in good condition. The Bridgewater Canal authorities were not slow to appreciate the importance of cultivating the traffic, and they, too, began a special milk boat along the Cheshire branch.[21] 'Hundreds of milk cans' were commonly to be seen stacked on the canal wharves in Manchester.[22] Lacking any hard quantitative evidence, we can only surmise at the relative importance of this water-borne traffic. It could well be that it was only a modest proportion of the total. Most of the milk producers operated on a very

[17] Holt, p. 149; Anon., *A Treatise on Milk*, 1825, quoted in *The Farmer's Magazine*, XXVI, 1825, p. 330.

[18] J. Wheeler, *Manchester: Its Political, Social and Commercial History, Ancient and Modern*, London, 1836, p. 433.

[19] V.I. Tomlinson, 'The Manchester, Bolton, and Bury Canal Navigation and Railway Company, 1790–1845, I, the canal', *TLCAS*, LXXV–LXXVI, 1965–6, p. 279.

[20] W. Palin, 'The farming of Cheshire', *JRASE*, 1st ser., V, 1844, p. 66; see also R.E. Porter, 'The marketing of agricultural produce in Cheshire during the nineteenth century', *Transactions of the Historic Society of Lancashire and Cheshire*, CXXVI, 1977, pp. 143–4, for evidence from tithe records of the spread of milk production in north Cheshire.

[21] F.C. Mather, *After the Canal Duke: A Study of the Industrial Estates administered by the Trustees of the Third Duke of Bridgewater in the Age of Railway Building, 1825–1872*, Oxford, 1970, p. 5.

[22] Quoted by V.I. Tomlinson in 'Salford activities connected with the Bridgewater Canal', *TLCAS*, LXVI, 1956, p. 81.

small scale; many were still within easy carting distance of Manchester;[23] hence, there would be little incentive to switch to the canal. On the other hand, the early establishment and the subsequent growth of canal milk did enable Manchester to escape the straitjacket imposed by road transport. Clearly, there were limitations on the distance that canals could carry milk, and it would be an uneven competition once the railways entered the scene. However, against this background, we can view the beginnings of railway milk, not as the dramatic event it is often seen to be elsewhere, but rather as just another step in a gradually widening pattern of supply.

After an abortive trial as early as 1832, the carriage of railway milk to Manchester began in earnest in 1844. In that year the Manchester and Birmingham Railway started bringing milk to Manchester from farmers close to the Manchester–Crewe part of the line.[24] By 1846 the traffic amounted to 100–150 cans a day, and already represented something like one-tenth of the total consumed in Manchester. Even allowing for the element of exaggeration to which many early railway estimates were prone, this seems to have been over twice the proportion contributed by railway milk to London even a decade later.[25] The trade grew rapidly. Within a further two years the railway revenue had quadrupled, and in 1849 Beesley was writing of the large quantities being forwarded daily by rail to Manchester, Liverpool and Bolton.[26] By this time the trade had advanced well beyond its tentative beginnings. The London and North Western Railway decided that twice-daily goods trains would stop at the various stations on the Crewe line, specifically to pick up the milk cans for Manchester. Special loading stages were later built at these stations to facilitate their handling.[27] On the northern side of Manchester, the company was meeting competition from the Lancashire and Yorkshire Railway, which, in conjunction with the East Lancashire line, was also seeking to build up a milk traffic. This, too, had initially been run on a rather *ad hoc* basis, with farmers having to load and unload their own milk

[23] See G. Beesley, *A Report of the State of Agriculture in Lancashire*, Preston, 1849, pp. 6–7.

[24] S. Salt, *Facts and Figures, principally relating to Railways and Commerce*, London, 1848, p. 27.

[25] Deduced from Salt's figures. The capacity of the cans varied between 9 and 18 gallons, but the carriage rate seems to have been calculated on the basis of 3*d* for 4.5 gallons for any distance. If we assume a weekly consumption level of 1.4 pints *per capita* (above, note 10), the traffic amounted to 11 per cent of the total consumed by Manchester and Salford in 1846. For details of the London traffic, see Atkins, thesis, pp. 145, 392.

[26] Salt, *Facts and Figures*, p. 27; Beesley, *Agriculture in Lancashire*, p. 8.

[27] PRO, RAIL 410/153, 1 July 1850; RAIL 410/155, 16 Dec. 1852.

cans, but in 1852 the company decided that it was time to standardise the rates and working arrangements.[28] However, it was undoubtedly from the south that Manchester came to derive most benefit from the railways' intervention. To the north, competition came from other industrial towns to which the small farmer tended to turn as the nearest markets.[29] The dairy farms of Cheshire had fewer options open to them, and Manchester drew an increasing proportion of its supplies from this direction. Thus, by the end of the century Cheshire accounted for the bulk of the supply rather than the farms of Lancashire as in times past.[30]

The railway transport of milk was not, of course, without its own problems. The agitation of the train had an effect similar to that of the horse and cart, and milk carried for any distance was particularly prone to souring. Cooling and filling the cans to the brim to stop slopping helped, but, before the adoption of more efficient methods of cooling in the 1870s, it often arrived in poor condition, especially in the summer.[31] Beesley suggested that the wholesale price of railway milk in Manchester and other towns was several pence per gallon lower than that brought in by road or produced in the town.[32] While there is little doubt that top-quality town milk could command a premium, such supplies were negligible in Manchester. The real competition was from milk brought in by road or canal, and there the railway was at much less of a disadvantage. Indeed, the actual wholesale price of railway milk, quoted by Beesley, of 6d–8d per gallon, was almost identical to that quoted by another writer for milk taken by road to Manchester.[33] A key factor in the railway's favour in the transport of milk to Manchester was that most of it had to travel relatively few miles; hence, many of the difficulties associated with railway milk could be avoided. Some was brought from as far as thirty to forty miles away, but the usual limit was only half that, or less.[34]

---

[28] PRO, RAIL 410/159, 7 June 1850; RAIL 343/497, 7 Jan., 31 Mar. 1852.

[29] W.J. Garnett, 'Farming of Lancashire', *JRASE*, 1st ser., X, 1849, p. 9; W.E. Bear, 'The food supply of Manchester, II, animal produce', *JRASE*, 3rd ser., VIII, 1897, p. 506.

[30] S. Delépine, 'The Manchester milk supply from a public health point of view', *Transactions of the Manchester Statistical Society*, 1909–10, pp. 10–12.

[31] Morton, 'Town milk', pp. 77–8; Fussell, *English Dairy Farmer*, pp. 312–13; Whetham, 'London milk trade', p. 374; Atkins, 'Railway milk trade', p. 222.

[32] Beesley, *Agriculture in Lancashire*, p. 9.

[33] *Ibid.*; J. Binns, *Notes on the Agriculture of Lancashire with Suggestions for its Improvement*, Preston, 1851, p. 134.

[34] HLRO, Mins. of Evidence, HC, 1851, XXVII, Warrington and Altrincham Junction Railway Bill, 11 Apr., p. 58; Beesley, *Agriculture in Lancashire*, p. 8; Binns, *Notes on Agriculture*, p.134; J. Caird, *English Agriculture in 1850–51*, London, 1852, p. 228.

There would have been little need to go further since, within a radius of fifteen to twenty miles, Manchester's 'milk-shed' extended deep into the heart of Cheshire dairy farming where the competition came, not from other urban centres, but from the traditional cheese manufacture.

It was not only the more distant farmers who gained from rail transport. For those already within reach of Manchester by road or canal, the railway offered the advantages of speed and regularity, so that two consignments of milk could be sent to town each day, instead of one.[35] Not surprisingly, the Manchester, South Junction, and Altrincham Railway also began to take an interest in developing a local milk traffic into Manchester, using passenger trains.[36] To contemporaries, the quantities of milk carried by rail to Manchester and its satellite towns seemed extraordinarily large, amounting to 'many hundred thousand gallons' annually, and developments in the supply of milk by rail do seem to have been two or three decades ahead of London.[37] Significantly, in 1865, when the London and North Western Railway undertook a special review of its traffic in perishable foodstuffs to the major cities on its line, it drew particular attention to the small quantity of milk being transported to the capital.[38] For Manchester, the story is of a commitment to further expansion, leading, in 1869, to the building of special accommodation for the trade at the goods depot at Ordsall Lane.[39] By this time, according to one observer, most of the town's milk supply was coming by rail.[40]

It is doubtful whether the changes had gone quite so far as this, since it is easy to underestimate the extent of local supplies brought in by cart. As late as 1897 a more systematic survey suggested that milk from this source still accounted for 29 per cent of Manchester's total supply, a figure comfortably above a comparable calculation for London,[41] and one that might reasonably be interpreted as the

[35] HLRO, Mins. of Evidence, HC, 1851, XXVII, Warrington and Altrincham Junction Railway Bill, 11 Apr., pp. 59–60.

[36] PRO, RAIL 465/3, 16 Oct. 1855; RAIL 463/5, 13 Jan. 1860.

[37] Binns, *Notes on Agriculture*, pp. 137–8; for London, see Atkins, thesis, p. 156; *idem*, 'Railway milk trade', pp. 212–13.

[38] PRO, RAIL 410/87, 20 Oct. 1865.

[39] PRO, RAIL 410/175, 17 Sept. 1868; 18 Nov. 1869. The fish traffic was to share the building.

[40] *The Co-operator*, 6 June 1868, in which the writer urged the co-operatives to enter the milk trade.

[41] The figure for Manchester is calculated from Bear, 'Animal produce', p. 506; for London, see Taylor, 'London's milk supply', p. 35. Road and town milk accounted for 16.9 per cent of London's supply in 1891.

remnant of a considerably larger proportion of thirty years before. But that might not be so. In London, road traffic went into sharp decline in the 1860s in the face of the expansion of railway milk. In Manchester, however, whereas water-borne milk seems to have succumbed to railway competition, the milk brought in by road was a good deal more resilient. Certainly, the cattle plague of 1865–66 played little part in the process of boosting the railways' role, because the milk farmers near Manchester – though not those of Cheshire – appear to have escaped relatively lightly from the disease.[42] Even so, the railways' early success with this traffic meant that most of the increase in Manchester's needs had passed into their hands rather than encouraging a proliferation of small producers close to, or even within, the town. Elsewhere, these were the very dairies that were vulnerable to the ravages of disease and the attentions of sanitary inspectors, as well as to the mounting costs involved in small-scale, intensive milk production. Manchester's local suppliers, however, were soundly based,[43] and hence able to retain an important share of the trade until at least the turn of the century.

ii. Butter

The proximity of urban markets and the importance of railway milk meant that Lancashire and parts of Cheshire were well ahead of the national trend in the dairy industry towards concentrating on the production of liquid milk, which became much more pronounced after the 1870s. At a time when about one-third of the total national output took the form of liquid milk and the rest was butter and cheese, Lancashire had already reversed these proportions.[44] As we have seen, the dairy farms in parts of northern Cheshire had probably gone even further in that direction. The implications of such changes for the supply of local butter and cheese to Manchester and the other industrial towns of the region are not hard to envisage. Butter production was particularly badly affected. Like milk, fresh butter did not travel

[42] PP 1867–8, XVIII, *Report on the Cattle Plague in Great Britain during the years 1865, 1866, and 1867*, Appendix No. 1, pp. 22–3; *Guardian*, 13, 16 Oct., 10, 18 Nov. 1865; 9 Jan 1866.

[43] See, for example, MCLAD, M10/23/6/7, Township of Rusholme, Local Board of Health, 3 Dec. 1873, for a sanitary inspector's favourable report on the state of various milk farms in Rusholme, then a semi-rural area, just outside the city.

[44] Taylor, 'English dairy industry', p. 590; T.W. Fletcher, 'Lancashire livestock farming during the great depression', *Agricultural History Review*, IX, 1961, p. 24.

well, and it tended to be made on farms that were close to their market.[45] In fact, milk and butter were very often produced together, with the increase in the milk yield and its improvement in quality in the summer being the basis of the butter production. In this sort of system, skim milk, left when the cream had been removed for butter-making, and butter-milk, the residue after the churning, were important by-products. Holt, in 1795, gave an example of just such a dairy farm near Liverpool where butter contributed slightly more than milk to its total income.[46] However, given the paucity of town dairies and the expanding market for liquid milk, it is not surprising that butter production went into decline. The larger dairy farms near towns, as Dickson pointed out in 1815, were concentrating almost exclusively on milk sales, with most of the butter being made on the smaller farms.[47] Increasingly, even there, butter became the minor partner. Farms actually specialising in butter production became a rarity, and by the mid-century even the small farmers had shifted their emphasis to liquid milk.[48]

It is against the background of a decline in the relative importance of local butter that we have to view the arrival in Manchester of supplies from further afield. Some came from the dairies of Cumberland. London was the main market for this butter, but in 1780 limited quantities were already reaching Manchester, and by the 1820s sales there had assumed a greater importance for Cumbrian farmers.[49] Most, however, came from Ireland. The eighteenth century had witnessed the expansion of the Irish provision trade and, after the lifting of import restrictions in 1764, there had been a rapid increase in the export of butter to Britain, reaching 203,447 cwt in 1800.[50] Although most of these exports were sent to London in the eighteenth

[45] Holt, p. 145; Beesley, *Agriculture in Lancashire*, p. 6; W. Rothwell, *Report of the Agriculture of the County of Lancaster*, London, 1850, pp. 98–9; J.C. Morton, 'Report on the Liverpool prize-farm competition, 1877 – dairy and stock farms', *JRASE*, 2nd ser., XIII, 1877, p. 504.

[46] Holt, p. 152.

[47] Dickson, *General View . . . of Lancashire*, p. 418.

[48] *PP* 1833, V, *Select Committee on Agriculture*, Mins. of Evidence, p. 182; Garnett, 'Farming of Lancashire', p. 9.

[49] J. Bailey and G. Culley, *General View of the Agriculture of the Counties of Northumberland, Cumberland and Westmoreland*, 3rd edn., London, 1813, pp. 244–5, 261; *Mercury*, 8 Feb. 1780, advertisement for 'good Cumberland butter'; W. Cobbett, *Rural Rides*, G.D.H. and M. Cole (eds.), London, 1930, III, p. 865.

[50] J. O'Donovan, *The Economic History of Live Stock in Ireland*, Dublin, 1940, chapter V and esp. p. 115.

century, large quantities also reached Liverpool.[51] From there, they were taken inland to Manchester by the Bridgewater Canal or the Mersey and Irwell Navigation.[52] That a Manchester tea dealer should go to the trouble, in 1774, of advertising his stocks of the 'best Ross butter, by himself imported from Cork, Newry and Belfast' suggests that the trade was one of individual enterprise at that time, though by 1795, according to Aikin, Ireland had become a regular source of the town's supplies.[53] The early directories began to list a few traders who specialised in it,[54] but much more significant were those who had no special label and yet were handling this butter as a matter of course. All the large suppliers of butter to James Bentley, a small general shopkeeper at the turn of the century, dealt in the Irish product, but none are described in the directories as having this as a particular speciality.[55]

The attraction of Liverpool as an importing centre for Irish butter was much enhanced by the improvements in communications across the Irish Sea, and by the 1820s it had ousted London from its prime position in the marketing of this commodity.[56] We can see from Table 4.2 that this was a very considerable traffic, and one which, though subject to reversals in years of bad trade, grew rapidly in the 1830s.

Most of these imports were then forwarded inland. In 1844 the Grand Junction and the Liverpool and Manchester railways were carrying out of Liverpool amounts equivalent to almost two-thirds of the total imported.[57] The waterways were also transporting considerable tonnages of butter at this time. During the early 1840s the Liverpool and Manchester Railway was twice obliged to reduce its rates for the carriage of butter to meet the competition from the Bridgewater Canal and the Mersey and Irwell Navigation, and to

[51] L.M. Cullen, *Anglo-Irish Trade, 1660–1800*, Manchester, 1968, pp. 71–2; for Liverpool imports, see announcements of ship arrivals and their cargoes, *Mercury*, 9 Mar., 10 Aug. 1790; 27 Sept. 1791; 17 Nov. 1795; 4 Sept. 1804.
[52] LRO, NCBw 2/1, 22 Aug. 1778; NCBw 2/2, 21 Jan. 1790; Mersey and Irwell Navigation Company, Mins. of Committee, 1 Mar. 1797.
[53] *Mercury*, 19 July 1774, advertisement of John Currie; Aikin, p. 204.
[54] For example, *Bancks' Manchester and Salford Directory*, 1800, entry for Isiah Lomax; *Pigot's Manchester and Salford Directory*, 1811, entries for S. and J. Briddon and Thomas Read. See also JRULM, Hibbert–Ware Papers, English MS. 1024, Tradesmen's Bills, 1802–15, bill-head (1809) of J. Hodkinson.
[55] Below, pp. 218–19.
[56] PP 1826, V, *Select Committee on the Butter Trade of Ireland*, Mins. of Evidence, p. 100.
[57] Salt, *Facts and Figures*, p. 90; B. Poole, *The Commerce of Liverpool*, London, 1854, p. 174. Not all was necessarily Irish, since small amounts of American butter (3,340 cwt in 1847) were imported into Liverpool (B. Poole, *Statistics of British Commerce*, London, 1852, p. 43), and some could have been of local origin.

Table 4.2 *Imports of butter from Ireland into Liverpool, 1824–50*
(figures in cwts)

Year	Quantity	Year	Quantity
1824–25	154,708	1842	195,289
1825–26	159,358	1843	250,499
		1844	249,259
1831	138,133	1845	262,677
1832	158,141		
		1847	230,500
1838	243,040	1848	223,040
1839	247,499	1849	280,200
1840	226,213	1850	251,800
1841	198,490		

Sources Figures for 1824–25 and 1825–26, *PP* 1826, V, *Select Committee on the Butter Trade of Ireland*, Mins. of Evidence, p. 100, taking one firkin to equal 56 lb net weight; for 1831–32, *PP* 1833, V, *Select Committee on Agriculture*, Appendix No. 4, p. 630, including small quantities of 'cools' taken here to equal ¾ cwt; for 1838–45, J. MacGregor, *Commercial Statistics*, London, 1850, V, Supplement II, p. 169; for 1847–50, B. Poole, *Statistics of British Commerce*, London, 1852, p. 43.

maintain its agreed share of the Liverpool to Manchester traffic.[58] The railway's grip on the trade strengthened during that decade, and by the early 1850s nearly all the Irish butter imported into Liverpool was being taken inland by the London and North Western Railway.[59] A large proportion of this was bound for Manchester. In 1844, for example, almost 90 per cent of the butter leaving Liverpool by rail was on the Liverpool to Manchester line.[60] In addition to whatever came from that direction, smaller quantities were sent to Manchester from ports in northern Lancashire as they tried to build up their own Irish trade.[61] During the last twenty years of the period considered here, Manchester's butter trade was increasingly dominated by the Irish

[58] PRO, RAIL 371/11, 16 Feb. 1842; Mather, *After the Canal Duke*, pp. 161–2.

[59] PRO, RAIL 410/719, Reports on the Merchandise Traffic of the Town and Port of Liverpool, 1853, p. 29.

[60] Salt, *Facts and Figures*, p. 90.

[61] *PP* 1867, XXXVIII – Pt. I, *Royal Commission on Railways*, Mins. of Evidence, p. 16 (Morecambe). Irish butter also came through Fleetwood (HLRO, Mins. of Evidence, HC, 1846, LXX, Fleetwood, Preston and West Riding Junction Railway Bill, 11 May, pp. 3, 122; PRO, RAIL 410/151, 17 Mar. 1854).

product, for which it eventually became the major distribution centre in the country.[62]

Against this background, it was natural that the early co-operatives should look westwards for their main supplies. Even before the formation of the Co-operative Wholesale Society in Manchester, the link with Ireland was being forged as *The Co-operator* urged individual retail societies to deal direct with a recommended wholesaler in Dublin.[63] In the summer of 1866 the Co-operative Wholesale Society itself decided to become directly involved by opening an office in Tipperary and appointing its own resident Irish butter buyer.[64] It was, as the Society's historian points out, a particularly enterprising and happy decision, for its Irish butter trade grew rapidly.[65] By 1870 two more buyers had been appointed, and they were soon to report back substantial increases in business.[66]

The Society's reliance on Ireland arose naturally from the long-established importance of Irish butter in the north of England, but it was also anxious to develop connections with the continent of Europe, and this was a relatively new trade for Manchester.[67] Forty years earlier, Joseph Sandars, as part of his advocacy of a Liverpool to Manchester railway link, had conjured up a picture of the Lancashire market succumbing to floods of Danish butter being carried up the Aire and Calder Navigation, unless the Irish supplies could be transported more cheaply to Manchester from Liverpool than by the existing waterways.[68] In the event, his fears proved groundless. Very little foreign butter came through the Humber ports before 1870, and the continental butter that reached Manchester usually came via London.[69] Salted Irish butter was becoming less acceptable to London palates, and continental imports, particularly the increasing quantities arriving from France, made substantial inroads into this market in the

---

[62] H.B. Wilkinson, *Old Hanging Ditch: Its Trades, Its Traders and Its Renaissance*, London, 1910, pp. 49–55, 83–9; Bear, 'Animal produce', pp. 510–12.

[63] *The Co-operator*, Nov. 1862.

[64] North of England Co-operative Wholesale Society Ltd, Mins. of Committee, 17 Mar., 23 Apr., 12 May, 16 June 1866.

[65] P. Redfern, *The New History of the C.W.S.*, London, 1938, p. 52.

[66] North of England C.W.S. Ltd, Mins. of Committee, 19 Mar. 1870; letters from Irish buyers to Secretary, 6, 13 Oct. 1870, contained in Minute Book.

[67] North of England C.W.S. Ltd, Mins. of Committee, 25 Feb. 1865; *The Co-operative News*, 24 Feb. 1872.

[68] J. Sandars, *A Letter on the Subject of the Projected Railroad between Liverpool and Manchester*, 5th edn., Liverpool, 1825, pp. 24–5.

[69] J.M. Bellamy, 'Some aspects of the economy of Hull in the nineteenth century with special reference to business history', University of Hull, Ph.D., 1965, II, Appendix B, p. 21; Wilkinson, *Old Hanging Ditch*, p. 49.

1860s.[70] The north of England, meanwhile, remained relatively loyal to the Irish product, which was seriously challenged only in the last thirty years of the century, when Danish imports rose dramatically.[71] The future transformation was nicely captured by one commentator, looking back from 1910, when he reminisced that in 1870 it was the Irish butter prices that Manchester dealers anxiously awaited each week; by 1910 it was the price from Denmark.[72]

Local butter, however, was never entirely replaced by produce from further afield. On the supply side, although the proportion of milk devoted to butter production declined, this was partially compensated by an increase in the number of dairy cows and, perhaps, in average yields.[73] Moreover, even dairy farms that specialised heavily in milk or cheese usually made enough butter at some point in their production process to warrant its being sent to Manchester.[74] On the demand side, local butter always had a qualitative edge over that from Ireland. The trouble with Irish supplies was that they tended to be heavily salted and of variable quality. At the Irish end, from the eighteenth century onwards, there were many attempts to regulate the trade, but they met with little success.[75] When proposals were made to free the Irish producers from some of these regulations, the Manchester dealers were quick to hold protest meetings and to petition against any such relaxation of quality control.[76] Despite efforts to improve matters,

[70] O'Donovan, *Live Stock in Ireland*, pp. 304–5; *The Grocer*, 8 Dec. 1866; 26 Oct. 1867; *The Dairyman*, 16 Mar. 1878. For the increase in imports of foreign butter, see J.R. McCulloch, *A Dictionary, Practical, Theoretical, and Historical, of Commerce and Commercial Navigation*, new edn., London, 1852, p. 204; new edn., London, 1869, p. 213.

[71] C. Ó Gráda, 'The beginnings of the Irish creamery system, 1880–1914', *EcHR*, 2nd ser., XXX, 1977, p. 286.

[72] Wilkinson, *Old Hanging Ditch*, p. 89.

[73] In 1870, according to the *Agricultural Returns*, the number of cows and heifers in milk or in calf was put at 91,326 in Cheshire and 116,371 in Lancashire (*PP* 1870, LXVIII, *Agricultural Returns of Great Britain . . . for 1870*, p. 58). The Lancashire figure is significantly higher than an 1803 estimate (84,527) for the total number of cows (see E. Baines, *History, Directory and Gazetteer of the County Palatine of Lancaster*, Liverpool, 1824, I, p. 85); while the Cheshire figure is about equal to the total number of *all* cattle (*c.* 92,000) put forward by Holland, *General View . . . of Cheshire*, p. 252, for 1808. Holderness has suggested that yields may have increased by one-third between 1750–70 and 1850–70 as a result of improvements in breeds, forage and dairy management, while poor-quality cows were taken out of production. See B.A. Holderness, 'Prices, productivity and output', in G.E. Mingay (ed.), *The Agrarian History of England and Wales*, VI, *1750–1850*, Cambridge, 1989, pp. 159, 162–3.

[74] H. White, 'A detailed account of the making of Cheshire cheese', *JRASE*, 1st ser., VI, 1845, p. 104; *PP* 1882, XV, *Royal Commission on Agriculture. Reports of Assistant Commissioners* (J. Coleman), pp. 54–6.

[75] *The Grocer*, 30 Nov., 14 Dec. 1867; 15 Feb. 1868; O'Donovan, *Live Stock in Ireland*, pp. 132–9, 155–6, 309–19.

[76] *PP* 1826, V, *Select Committee on the Butter Trade of Ireland*, Mins. of Evidence, pp. 167–9.

Irish butter never entirely overcame these problems until the introduction of the creamery system at the end of the century.[77]

As a result, fresh butter was always able to fetch a few pence more
per lb in Manchester, though marginal improvements in the quality of
the Irish product helped to narrow the gap over time, at least until the
last three or four years of the period. This can be seen more clearly in
Figure 4.1, which presents in graph form the movement of the retail
prices in Manchester of fresh and salted butter in the years after
1850.[78] The curious reversal of the trend in 1867–70 seems to have
been partly a reaction to the inflated prices of the Irish product during
the cattle plague, when local butter would have been in short supply.[79]
But it also reflected the fact that Irish butter must have been particularly plentiful in the north as a result of being squeezed out of the
London market by foreign competition.[80] By all accounts, the trend
towards reducing the differential did not reassert itself, and in the last
quarter of the century the gap was maintained, and possibly widened,
at least in Lancashire.[81] Hence, the local producer was always pro-
tected from direct competition at the upper end of the market. Quite
how important this niche was can be gauged from the agitation among
local small farmers when the improved steamship service between
Dublin and Liverpool opened up a prospect in the 1820s of a substantial Irish trade in fresh, as opposed to salted, butter. Fortunately for the
local suppliers, however, the traffic does not seem to have prospered.[82]

When these prices are transformed into indices (Figure 4.2), it can
be seen that, although the production of butter had become less
important in the dairying economy of the region, those of the fresh
variety moved very much in line with the general curve, represented by
the (national) Rousseaux animal products' index,[83] suggesting that
the forces of supply and demand were in reasonable equilibrium until
the last few years of the period. That was not so for salted butter.

[77] Ó Gráda, 'Irish creamery system', esp. pp. 285–7; O'Donovan, *Live Stock in Ireland*, pp.
319–25.

[78] These prices are taken from 'Housewife's Corner', a feature appearing in the *Courier* for the
first time on 26 Oct. 1850, and continuing through the rest of the period. The source gives details
of the maximum and minimum prices ruling in retail markets for a variety of products on the
preceding Saturday. The series affords a most useful adjunct to the main series of market reports,
and the weekly entries may be aggregated to obtain average annual prices, as here.

[79] Ireland escaped the effects of the cattle plague of 1865–66 (O'Donovan, *Live Stock in
Ireland*, p. 257).

[80] Above, note 70.

[81] Fletcher, 'Lancashire livestock farming', pp. 24–6.

[82] PP 1833, V, *Select Committee on Agriculture*, Mins. of Evidence, p. 175.

[83] See Chapter III, note 109.

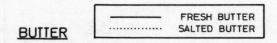

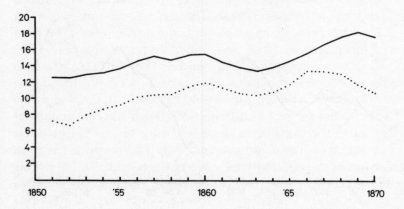

Fig. 4.1 Fresh and salted butter prices in Manchester, 1850–70 (pence per lb)

Source Minimum retail market prices quoted weekly in 'Housewife's Corner' report in *Courier* (see Chapter IV, note 78), reworked to determine annual averages.

Despite all the evidence of the large quantities of Irish imports reaching Manchester, the level of demand for cheaper butter was pushing its price well ahead of the Rousseaux index from the early 1850s onwards, indicating a very significant enlargement of the social range of its market.

iii. Cheese

In the face of the expansion of the liquid-milk trade around Manchester, local butter-making declined relatively quickly. This was much less true of cheese production. There were a number of reasons for this. The dairy farms that concentrated on cheese tended to be those furthest from the market, obliged by distance, even after the advent of the railway, to make the product that kept and travelled best. Lancashire provided a classic illustration of this pattern. As the urban population grew, and access to it improved, widespread local

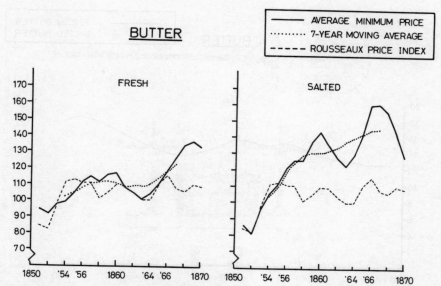

Fig. 4.2 Indices of fresh and salted butter prices in Manchester, 1850–70 (1851–56 = 100)

Source Minimum retail market prices quoted weekly in 'Housewife's Corner' report in *Courier* (see Chapter IV, note 78), reworked to determine annual averages. For the Rousseaux index, see Chapter III, note 109.

cheese-making retreated before the initial advance of liquid-milk production. With the notable exception of Leigh, it became increasingly concentrated in the more remote northern and north-eastern parts of the county.[84] The commitment to cheese-making was also more deep-rooted than that to butter. The equipment needed, the expertise acquired over time, the degree of family involvement and often, in later years, the combination with the rearing of pigs fed on the whey meant that it was a well-integrated system, not lightly abandoned. Here, Cheshire was the prime example, where cheese-making was an ancient tradition, still carried on in 1870 in a way not very different from that of a hundred years before, and where factory production was slow to be established.[85]

[84] Dickson, *General View . . . of Lancashire*, p. 565; Beesley, *Agriculture in Lancashire*, pp. 7, 9; Binns, *Notes on Agriculture*, pp. 81–2.
[85] See Fussell, *English Dairy Farmer*, pp. 235–40; C.S. Davies, 'The agricultural history of Cheshire, 1750–1850', University of Manchester, Ph.D., 1953, p. 278; *PP* 1882, XV, *Royal Commission on Agriculture. Reports of Assistant Commissioners* (J. Coleman), p. 54.

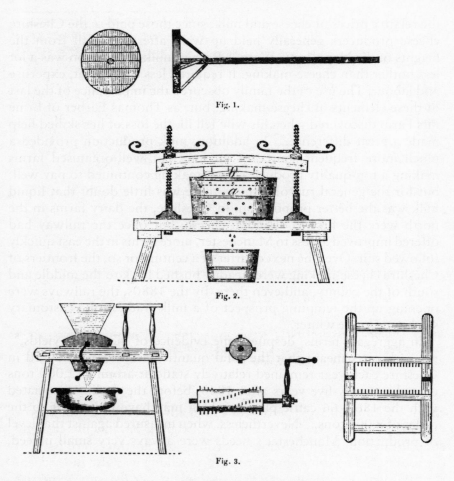

Equipment used in the traditional making of Cheshire cheese

Fig. 1   The curd-breaker, made of wire-work, in an oval form, with a tin rim, about one and a half inches broad.

Fig. 2   The thrusting-tub, where the extraction of the whey from the curd was effected by the application of the screw. The tub (a) was perforated at the sides and bottom, and had a strong, circular board (b) which fitted inside it.

Fig. 3   The curd-mill, which crumbled the salted curd before it was put into the vat for the final pressings. The well-crumbled curd fell into a pan (a), made of brass or tin, about twenty inches in diameter and eight inches deep, which was also used initially for warming the milk.

Over the years, however, a switch to liquid-milk production became increasingly attractive. This was not primarily because of a change in the relative prices of cheese and milk, since those paid to the Cheshire cheese producers generally held up well, after their fall from the heights of the Napoleonic Wars.[86] Rather, milk production was a lot less bother than cheese-making. It required less equipment, expertise and labour. The use of the family obscured the importance of the last of these elements in cheese-making, but, as Thomas Furber of Brine Pits Farm discovered when his wife fell ill, the loss of her skilled help made a great difference.[87] In addition, milk production provided a much more frequent source of income. For well-organised farms making a top-quality product, cheese-making continued to pay well, but for the general run of farmers there was little doubt that liquid milk was the better proposition. In Cheshire, the dairy farms in the north were the first to abandon cheese, but once the railway had offered improved access to Manchester, more farms in the east quickly followed suit. Over the next quarter of a century or so, the frontiers of Cheshire cheese-making were steadily pushed back to the middle and south of the county, and even there, by the 1880s, the railways were opening up the tempting prospect of a milk trade in the customary slack time in the winter.[88]

In aggregate terms, despite some evidence of increasing yields,[89] these changes meant that the total quantity of cheese produced in Cheshire each year remained relatively static at around 12,000 tons over the twenty-five years after 1840, before the decline associated with the 1865–66 cattle plague, which may have reduced it to the order of 9,000 tons.[90] Nevertheless, when measured against that level of production, Manchester's needs were always very small indeed,

[86] W.B. Mercer, 'Two centuries of Cheshire cheese farming', *JRASE*, XCVIII, 1937, pp. 82, 85–6; R.E. Porter, 'The value of farm notebooks: a new example from Cheshire', *The Local Historian*, XIII, 1979, p. 273.

[87] Mercer, 'Cheese farming', pp. 85–6.

[88] PP 1881, XVII, *Royal Commission on Agriculture*, II, Mins. of Evidence, pp. 918–19; PP 1882, XV, *Royal Commission on Agriculture. Reports of Assistant Commissioners* (J. Coleman), pp. 54–6, 68, 71–2; Morton, 'Liverpool prize-farm competition', p. 523.

[89] Holland, *General View . . . of Cheshire*, p. 252 and W. Marshall, *The Review and Abstract of the County Reports to the Board of Agriculture*, York, 1818, II, p. 160, assume an average yield per cow of 2.5 cwt of cheese, and White, 'Making of Cheshire cheese', p. 104, puts it at *c*. 3 cwt.

[90] Holland, *General View . . . of Cheshire*, p. 252; White, 'Making of Cheshire cheese', p. 102; J.R. McCulloch, *A Descriptive and Statistical Account of the British Empire*, 3rd edn., London, 1847, I, p. 154; *The Dairyman*, 16 Apr. 1879, reporting a paper read to the Cheshire Chamber of Commerce.

amounting to no more than about 900 tons even in 1871.[91] Accordingly, the London market long dominated the Cheshire cheese trade. During the eighteenth century most of the large producers from the south and middle of the county, having sold their cheese to the factors off the farm, delivered it to Frodsham, Warrington or Chester, to be taken by sea to the capital.[92] Smaller quantities also went in the other direction, initially by land to the River Trent, but later by the Grand Trunk Canal.[93] In the early nineteenth century the cheese that went to Manchester tended to come from the smaller farmers, especially those in north and north-eastern Cheshire, often via Stockport, in Aikin's opinion, 'the best market for cheese in the county'.[94]

The presence of the London market continued to be felt throughout the period. Farmers producing top-quality cheese still preferred to send the best part of their produce to the capital,[95] but its influence became noticeably weaker. By the 1830s and 1840s, many Cheshire cheese producers had discovered that the fluctuations of trade in Manchester and other industrial towns, rather than events in London, were governing their fortunes.[96] For the farmer, the northern markets had the added attraction of displaying a preference for quicker-ripening cheeses. This enabled him to make a number of sales through the year, and hence receive more frequent influxes of cash than the yearly or twice-yearly payments experienced before.[97] The London and North Western Railway also did its best to encourage the break-up of the old pattern by making concerted efforts in the mid-1840s and early 1850s, not the least important of which were to provide financial support for the cheese fair at Crewe and to build a new cheese hall

[91] This assumes a 1.3 oz *per capita* weekly consumption (J.C. McKenzie, 'The composition and nutritional value of diets in Manchester and Dukinfield in 1841', *TLCAS*, LXXII, 1962, pp. 134–5), multiplied by the 1871 population, though there are obviously large margins of potential error in the calculation.

[92] D. Defoe, *A Tour through the Whole Island of Great Britain*, Penguin edn., Harmondsworth, 1971, pp. 394–5; Aikin, pp. 47, 391; Holland, *General View . . . of Cheshire*, pp. 315–16; see also G.E. Fussell, 'The London cheesemongers of the eighteenth century', *Economic History*, I, 1926–29, pp. 395–6.

[93] Anon., *The History of Inland Navigations*, London, 1766, pp. 66–7; Defoe, *Tour*, p. 394; Holland, *General View . . . of Cheshire*, p. 316; see also A. Henstock, 'Cheese manufacture and marketing in Derbyshire and north Staffordshire, 1670–1870, *Derbyshire Archaeological Journal*, LXXXIX, 1969, pp. 40–1.

[94] Holland, *General View . . . of Cheshire*, p. 316; Aikin, p. 446.

[95] H.M. Jenkins, 'Report on Cheshire dairy-farming', *JRASE*, 2nd ser., VI, 1870, p. 172; *PP* 1881, XIII, *Select Committee on Railways*, I, Mins. of Evidence, p. 342.

[96] *PP* 1833, V, *Select Committee on Agriculture*, Mins. of Evidence, p. 288; W. Cooke Taylor, *Notes of a Tour in the Manufacturing Districts of Lancashire*, 2nd edn., London, 1842, pp. 87–8.

[97] See the example of John Byram in Porter, 'Value of farm notebooks', p. 274.

there, adjacent to its line, all with the aim of redirecting the traffic away from its traditional water-borne routes onto the railway.[98] Perhaps the final factor in the process of re-orientating the trade was the growing significance of imported cheese in the London market over the next twenty years.[99] As a result, after the mid-century more of Cheshire's cheese was consumed in the north of England, with Manchester emerging as the major distribution centre.[100] In that sense, the Cheshire cheese trade was a minor chord of a major theme in nineteenth-century economic history of the shifting balance of influence between London and the provinces.

With these enormous tonnages of cheese available on its doorstep, Manchester had little need of supplies from elsewhere, especially since Lancashire itself made some contribution. Fletcher has claimed that Lancashire cheese did not come onto the Manchester market until the 1890s,[101] but this seems unduly pessimistic. Close to Manchester, the district around Leigh maintained a reputation for cheese-making throughout the period, and by the mid-century even the more distant parts of the county were receiving visits from cheese merchants driven north in the search for fresh sources of supply by the spread of liquid-milk production in Cheshire.[102] In all, Poole estimated in 1852 that Lancashire cheese production amounted to 2,000 tons a year.[103] To that could be added small quantities from Ireland. Indeed, a Cheshire land agent, appearing as a witness before the 1833 Select Committee on Agriculture, included cheese in a catalogue of all things Irish that were affecting local farmers' livelihoods. Before the twentieth century, however, cheese production was only a very minor partner in the Irish dairy industry, and the amounts exported were, in fact, inconsiderable.[104]

In truth, local cheese producers had little to fear until almost the end of the period. A fall in prices after the Napoleonic Wars made them

[98] PRO, RAIL 410/140, 12 Mar. 1852; RAIL 410/150, 19 Mar., 2 Apr., 3 Sept., 1 Oct. 1852; RAIL 410/152, 3 Aug., 1 Sept. 1854; Mather, *After the Canal Duke*, p. 5.

[99] For the national figures, see G.R. Porter, *The Progress of the Nation*, revised edn., by F.W. Hirst, London, 1912, p. 443; for London's importance, see Poole, *Statistics*, p. 64.

[100] *The Dairyman*, 16 Apr. 1879; Bear, 'Animal produce', p. 513; Porter, 'Marketing of agricultural produce', pp. 141–2.

[101] Fletcher, 'Lancashire livestock farming', p. 25.

[102] Holt, p. 145; T. Baines, *Lancashire and Cheshire, Past and Present*, London, 1867, I, p. 192; Garnett, 'Farming of Lancashire', p. 47.

[103] Poole, *Statistics*, p. 63.

[104] PP 1833, V, *Select Committee on Agriculture*, Mins. of Evidence, pp. 271, 276, 278; O'Donovan, *Live Stock in Ireland*, pp. 326, 334, 336; P. Mathias, *Retailing Revolution*, London, 1967, p. 27.

apprehensive about the impact of Dutch imports,[105] but, if the absence of further comment in the evidence given to the many parliamentary enquiries on agriculture is any guide, this threat never materialised. Most European cheese went to the London market, and of more significance was the arrival of supplies from the United States in the 1840s, with Liverpool acting as a major importing centre.[106] For these imports, Manchester was an obvious market. However, American cheese was dogged, like Irish butter, by a reputation for indifferent quality and for some years made little headway. When this improved, in the later 1860s, it became a more serious worry for the Cheshire farmers, especially in the wake of the fall in production after the cattle plague.[107] Not surprisingly, the Co-operative Wholesale Society's first direct entry into the cheese trade was to appoint a Cheshire cheese buyer; but, significantly, once that area had been well established, he was sent to New York as their first resident buyer in the United States.[108] Undoubtedly, American cheese went on to make a bigger impact on the Manchester market than any other from outside the region and, by the end of the century, had clearly become the second favourite.[109] But it would never be able to displace the local product, with its distinctive taste and open, friable texture, so beloved of Mancunians and all, it is tempting to suggest, of a discriminating palate.

[105] Board of Agriculture, *Agricultural State of the Kingdom*, London, 1816, pp. 47–8.
[106] PP 1842, XXXIX, *An Account of the Quantities of Cheese Imported into the Several Ports of Great Britain for the years 1840 and 1841*, p. 421; PP 1843, LII, *An Account . . . of Cheese Imported . . . for the year 1842*, p. 21; PP 1844, XLV, *An Account . . . of Cheese Imported . . . for the year 1843*, p. 13; Poole, *Statistics*, p. 64; see also J. Potter, 'Atlantic economy, 1815–60: the U.S.A. and the industrial revolution in Britain', in L.S. Pressnell (ed.), *Studies in the Industrial Revolution*, London, 1960, pp. 250–1.
[107] *The Grocer*, 5 Oct., 2 Nov. 1867; *The Dairyman*, 16 July 1878.
[108] North of England C.W.S. Ltd, Mins. of Grocery and Provisions Sub-Committee, 9 Sept. 1874; 3 Nov. 1875.
[109] PP 1882, XV, *Royal Commission on Agriculture. Reports of Assistant Commissioners* (J. Coleman), p. 64; Bear, 'Animal produce', p. 513.

CHAPTER V

Vegetables and fruit

i. Local supplies of vegetables

THE CULTIVATION of potatoes was a distinctive feature of the agriculture of Lancashire and Cheshire; indeed, for some agrarian commentators, this was one of its few redeeming aspects.[1] When Arthur Young made his northern tour in 1768, his journey took him down the western side of Lancashire from Burton, in the north, to Garstang and Ormskirk, and then through north Cheshire to Altrincham and Knutsford. In all these areas, potatoes were an established part of the farming scene. Marl was the principal fertiliser used on the light sandy soils, but in one case, that of Altrincham, town manure was already playing an important part in their cultivation.[2] By the turn of the century, there had been significant advances both in the extent of potato growing and in the intensity with which it was undertaken. The latter involved potato sets being planted out into heavily manured ground, having first been induced to sprout by being kept inside, in warm conditions. The early harvesting of the crop was often followed by the planting of a second one later in the season. This method had originally been developed in the Wirral, but it was also practised around Ormskirk.[3] It was a specialised form of cultivation, sufficiently novel to attract the epithet 'remarkable', and the final

[1] See, for example, J. Chamberlaine, 'Account of making Cheshire cheese etc.', *Annals of Agriculture*, XVII, 1792, p. 48; J.H. Campbell, 'Answers to queries relating to the agriculture of Lancashire', *ibid.*, XX, 1793, pp. 134–5; G. Wilbraham, 'System in which potatoes are rendered beneficial to the poor in Cheshire', *ibid.*, XXXV, 1800, p. 14.
[2] A. Young, *A Six Months Tour Through the North of England*, 2nd edn., London, 1771, III, pp. 142–3, 158–9, 171, 180–1, 243.
[3] T. Wedge, *General View of the Agriculture of the County Palatine of Chester*, London, 1794, p. 18; Holt, pp. 61–2.

product was inevitably costly.[4] From both the Wirral and Ormskirk, supplies of early potatoes were sent to Manchester, though apparently only as a secondary market to Liverpool.[5] In fact, for the bulk of its early potatoes, Manchester looked closer to home, to the district around Altrincham. Here, the method of cultivation was more conventional, in that the tubers were planted without any prior forcing; but any disadvantage at which the growers were placed in terms of the earliness of the crop was offset by their proximity to the market.[6]

More significant for the people of Manchester than the niceties of the different forms of intensive production for the early market was the extent of potato cultivation as a main crop. Again, the districts around Altrincham and Ormskirk were important, but it was natural that the latter should look to Liverpool as the major outlet for its produce.[7] In this area, north of the Mersey, we have to go as far east as Warrington before the pull of Manchester could fully exert itself. Here, by the 1790s, farmers were beginning to look in that direction as the main market for their potatoes and other vegetables, and Aikin estimated that 30,000–40,000 bushels of potatoes (*c.* 1,200–1,600 tons) were being shipped from Warrington's quay in a year.[8] But on the other side of the Mersey potato growing was even more extensive. 'Potatoes are cultivated', observed Aikin, 'in the parish of Frodsham, with as much success, and probably to as great an extent, as in any other parish in the kingdom.' According to Wedge, the average crop amounted to at least 100,000 bushels (*c.* 4,000 tons), an estimate repeated by Holland, but increased to 120,000 (*c.* 4,800 tons) by Cooke in 1810.[9]

To contemporaries, this was potato growing on a grand scale, but it needs to be set against an estimate of Manchester's needs. The easiest way of producing one is to take the figures suggested by Salaman for average *per capita* consumption and to multiply them by the

[4] T. Eccleston, 'Remarkable culture of potatoes', *Annals of Agriculture*, XXXVII, 1801, pp. 87–9; H. Kirkpatrick, *An Account of the Manner in which Potatoes are cultivated and preserved and the uses to which they are applied in the counties of Lancaster and Chester*, Warrington, 1796, pp. 17–18; Holt, p. 60.

[5] H. Holland, *General View of the Agriculture of Cheshire*, London, 1808, pp. 147–8; Aikin, p. 316; Holt, p. 60.

[6] Aikin, p. 204; Holland, *General View . . . of Cheshire*, p. 149.

[7] Holt, pp. 61, 65; Aikin, pp. 19, 362; Holland, *General View . . . of Cheshire*, p. 140.

[8] Holt, p. 61; Aikin, pp. 204, 306.

[9] Aikin, p. 46; Wedge, *General View . . . of Chester*, p. 19; Holland, *General View . . . of Cheshire*, p. 140; G.A. Cooke, *Topographical and Statistical Description of the County of Chester*, London, 1810, p. 117.

population of the town.[10] This is not entirely satisfactory, since Salaman's national average almost certainly underestimates the amount of potatoes eaten in Lancashire.[11] However, the calculation produces a plausible figure of 6,000–8,500 tons, representing the likely demand for potatoes at the time when Wedge and Holland were writing. Not all the potatoes produced around Frodsham were going to Manchester. Some went to Liverpool and some even to Ireland, while in times of particular abundance they were also fed to livestock.[12] But even when these factors are taken into consideration, it is clear that the emphasis given by contemporaries to the importance of north Cheshire for Manchester's potato supply was well placed.

Similar calculations for the 1840s, using the *per capita* consumption figures of either Salaman or Neild, and taking account of the enormous increase in the population, suggest that by then Manchester's requirement for potatoes would have risen to 40,000–45,000 tons.[13] Love's *Handbook* of 1842 supports this figure with an estimate that 50,000 tons of potatoes were brought to Manchester each year to be sold there, although not all of these would have been destined for local consumption.[14] By this time transport links with the potato-growing areas of south-west Lancashire had been improved.[15] Nevertheless, the rise in demand must have put heavy pressure on the main body of the town's suppliers in Cheshire. There were a number of ways in which they could respond. First, more of the crop could be diverted to feeding the population of south Lancashire rather than exported. This feature was noted across the Mersey at Warrington where, by 1836, a thriving export trade to the Mediterranean had been superseded by a concern for more local markets.[16] Secondly, average yields could be improved. However, the art of potato cultivation was already well

[10] R.N. Salaman, *The History and Social Influence of the Potato*, Cambridge, 1949, p. 613, who suggests a daily *per capita* consumption of 0.4 lb and 0.47 lb in 1795 and 1814 respectively. These figures have been multiplied by the population within the municipal area of Manchester and Salford in 1801 and 1811.

[11] Salaman's estimate for 1838 of a weekly *per capita* consumption of 4.34 lb (*ibid.*), may be compared to Neild's figure of 5.2 lb for the Manchester district. See J.C. McKenzie, 'The composition and nutritional value of diets in Manchester and Dukinfield in 1841', *TLCAS*, LXXII, 1962, p. 129.

[12] Aikin, pp. 19, 46; G.E. Fussell and C. Goodman, 'Traffic in farm produce in eighteenth-century England; except livestock and livestock products', *Agricultural History*, XII, 1938, p. 365; Holt, pp. 63, 175.

[13] Above, notes 10 and 11.

[14] B. Love, *The Handbook of Manchester*, Manchester, 1842, p. 243.

[15] Below, p. 100.

[16] E. Baines, *History of the County Palatine and Duchy of Lancaster*, London, 1836, III, p. 686.

developed by the later eighteenth century; any change in this respect
was effected, not so much by innovatory methods of cultivation, or a
noticeable improvement in the yield of potatoes from land already in a
high state of cultivation,[17] as by the raising of the average level of crop
from land that had not previously had the benefit of heavy manuring.
By the mid-century town manure, particularly productive in potato
growing, was being transported along the waterways in ever-
increasing quantities, not only for adjoining fields, but also to be
carried to farms at some distance from the canal or river banks.[18] The
third possible response was that the acreage devoted to potato growing could be increased. In south-west Lancashire there was a shift
towards arable farming in which the potato played an important part,
but in Cheshire the process involved a change of emphasis in conventional rotations, rather than an increase in the overall arable acreage.
Palin's report of 1844 gives a number of examples of correspondents
writing from as far south as Nantwich proclaiming the place of
potatoes in their farming regimes.[19] Manchester was no longer so
heavily reliant for potatoes on the northern parts of Cheshire; supplies
were now arriving from much further south.

Other vegetables figure much less prominently in contemporary
accounts. It was generally agreed that green vegetables such as
cabbages, peas and beans were not widely cultivated, and turnips
scarcely more so. Where any of them were grown, it was usually as
livestock fodder.[20] However, certain districts around Warrington and
Altrincham had begun to emerge as market-gardening centres by the
1780s. From the former, Manchester was receiving supplies of
cabbages, and from the latter, peas, beans, onions and carrots, in
addition to new potatoes. It was also common for farmers to grow
these vegetables, as well as turnips, as garden crops, and some of this

[17] For methods of cultivation, cf. Holt's 1795 account (pp. 61–2) with those of W.J. Garnett
('Farming of Lancashire', *JRASE*, 1st ser., X, 1849, pp. 20–1) and W. Rothwell (*Report of the
Agriculture of the County of Lancaster*, London, 1850, p. 43) in 1849–50. The yields from land
in a high state of cultivation quoted by Holt (p. 60) and even Young, suitably adjusted to the
statute acre (*Tour*, III, pp. 80, 243), are comparable with those of the mid nineteenth century (G.
Beesley, *A Report of the State of Agriculture in Lancashire*, Preston, 1849, p. 16; J. Caird,
English Agriculture in 1850–51, London, 1852, p. 269).

[18] Garnett, 'Farming of Lancashire', p. 42; Caird, *English Agriculture*, pp. 262, 269–70.

[19] W. Palin, 'The farming of Cheshire', *JRASE*, 1st ser., V, 1844, pp. 64–8; Caird, *English
Agriculture*, p. 255.

[20] Holt, p. 64; Aikin, p. 45; Holland, *General View . . . of Cheshire*, pp. 154ff; R.W.Dickson,
General View of the Agriculture of Lancashire, London, 1815, pp. 232–3, 334ff.

produce was brought to market along with their main cash crop.[21] Cucumbers and asparagus were also grown commercially, but it is particularly difficult with this sort of contemporary evidence to assess the quantities involved, though it is quite clear that they were small.[22] Even with the more conventional vegetables, there is evidence to suggest that the supply of greenstuffs was less plentiful than that of roots. At the end of the eighteenth century, in a number of legal cases concerned with the market rights in Manchester, witnesses swore affidavits describing the customary practices operating at that time. In this evidence, a distinction was drawn between farmers who brought in potatoes, carrots, onions and turnips by the load (of 240 lb or 252 lb) and those who came with 'small quantities'; it was in relation to the latter group that cabbages, the only green vegetable referred to by name, were mentioned.[23] By the time Dickson was writing, in 1815, the situation appears to have improved, but there is no doubt that even then, potatoes apart, onions and particularly carrots were grown for human consumption more extensively than any other vegetable. Yet for Marshall, onion growing around Altrincham could be dismissed as 'still only gardening'.[24]

The pattern established early in the period had changed little by the mid-century. The districts around Warrington and Altrincham had continued to develop as recognised market-gardening centres.[25] Indeed, according to one observer, in 1836, vegetable growing in the area to the north of Altrincham, around Stretford, had been raised to a level second to none in the whole country; another claimed that this district was the 'garden of Lancashire'. While other agricultural writers were not moved to such superlatives, it is clear from their comments that the first half of the century had seen a considerable expansion of vegetable growing for the Manchester market along the route of the Bridgewater Canal.[26] Even so, much of this still revolved

---

[21] Aikin, p. 204; Holland, *General View . . . of Cheshire*, pp. 164–6, 194; Holt, pp. 64, 80.

[22] Aikin, p. 204; Holt, p. 80; Dickson, *General View . . . of Lancashire*, pp. 425–6. See also F. Beavington, 'Early market gardening in Bedfordshire', *Transactions of the Institute of British Geographers*, XXXVII, 1965, pp. 96–7, for a good example of contemporary exaggeration.

[23] Below, pp. 150–1, for market rights; also Mr Barnes' Book relating to the Tolls, 1787, and evidence of Benjamin and Peter Oldham (MTH, M1/24/132, M1/24/3).

[24] Dickson, *General View . . . of Lancashire*, pp. 363–4, 388–9; W. Marshall, *The Review and Abstract of the County Reports to the Board of Agriculture*, York, 1818, II, p. 154.

[25] E. Baines, *History, Directory and Gazetteer of the County Palatine of Lancaster*, Liverpool, 1824, I, p. 84.

[26] J. Wheeler, *Manchester: Its Political, Social and Commercial History, Ancient and Modern*, London, 1836, p. 435; Rothwell, *Agriculture . . . of Lancaster*, pp. 49–50; Palin, 'Farming of Cheshire', pp. 65–6; Caird, *English Agriculture*, pp. 261–2.

around the growing of potatoes and other root crops, with cabbages sometimes being introduced into the rotations, planted in November to be sold the following spring. The cultivation of other varieties of green vegetables was restricted to small-scale market gardening, and there is little indication of a major increase in the local acreage given over to such produce in the two decades before 1870. Descriptions of the agriculture in the districts around Warrington and Altrincham remained strikingly similar to those of thirty years before. For example, large areas near Warrington, such as Risley Moss, that were potentially suitable for market gardening were still mainly uncultivated.[27] By and large, the most commonly grown vegetables, other than potatoes, were still carrots, turnips and, to a lesser extent, onions. It is not surprising that the market reports for vegetables, which were first regularly published in 1826, continued to confine themselves chiefly to these products down to 1870.

ii. The role of waterways

One of the factors which drew north Cheshire into greater prominence as a source of supply was the construction of the Bridgewater Canal (Plate 3). Once the stretch from Worsley to Manchester had been completed, the Duke began to extend the canal from Stretford towards Runcorn and the River Mersey. The extension reached Altrincham in 1766, Lymm in 1769 and Stockton Heath in 1771. The link with the Trent and Mersey Canal at Preston Brook was made in 1775, and the complete length was opened the following year.[28] The traffic was two-way. Out of Manchester came large amounts of town manure. The surviving records of the canal reveal that, from the very beginning of the period, there was a regular and substantial traffic in this freight from Castlefield Quay in Manchester.[29] Into Manchester went what were labelled 'market goods', and the canal seems to have gone out of its way to encourage such traffic. There was a special market boat, an open 40-ton barge, catering for this trade. It was advertised as leaving

[27] T. Baines, *Lancashire and Cheshire, Past and Present*, London, 1867, I, p. 65; HLRO, Mins. of Evidence, HC, 1865, XL, Manchester, Sheffield, and Lincolnshire Railway (Extensions) Bill, 30 May, pp. 176–7.

[28] C. Hadfield and G. Biddle, *The Canals of North West England*, Newton Abbot, 1970, I, pp. 31–3.

[29] The Book of General Accounts, 1764–90 (LRO, NCBw 6/1) has an annual entry for this traffic. See also the Day Book of Matthias Shelvoke, 1769–70 (LRO, NCBw 1/1), entries for 11 Oct. 1769; 14 Apr., 22 May, 15 Aug., 11 Sept. 1770.

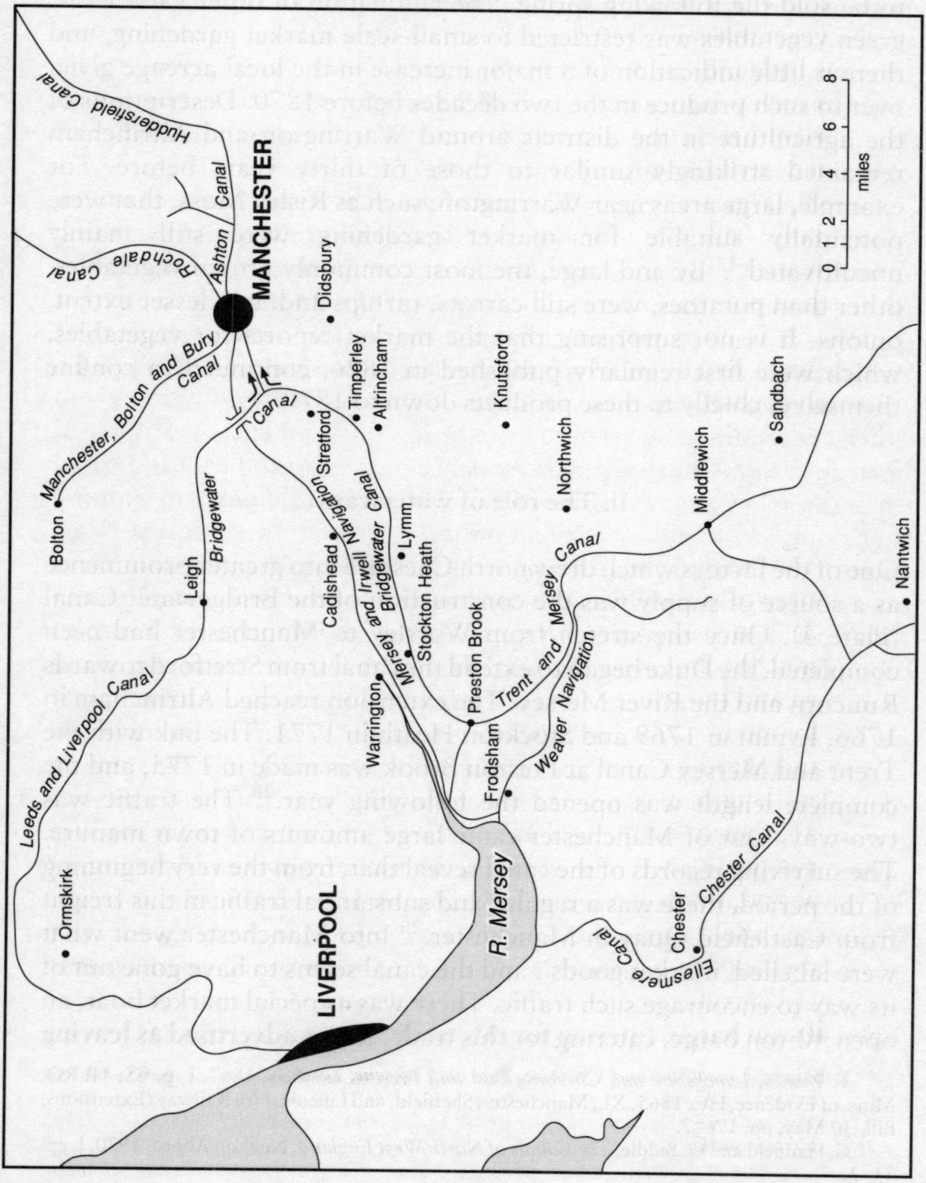
Huddersfield Canal
MANCHESTER
Rochdale Canal
Ashton Canal
Didsbury
Manchester, Bolton and Bury Canal
Canal
Timperley
Altrincham
Stretford
Knutsford
Sandbach
Bolton
Bridgewater
Leigh
Mersey and Irwell Navigation
Cadishead
Bridgewater Canal
Lymm
Stockton Heath
Northwich
Middlewich
Trent and Mersey Canal
Nantwich
Warrington
Preston Brook
Leeds and Liverpool Canal
Frodsham
Weaver Navigation
Ormskirk
LIVERPOOL
R. Mersey
Chester
Chester Canal
Ellesmere Canal
0 1 2 4 6 8
miles

Map 3 Canals of the region

Altrincham on Tuesday, Thursday and Saturday mornings (Manchester's main market days at that time), returning at one o'clock.[30] Initially, the intention must have been to convey farmers and their produce to market together, but before long this arrangement was proving inadequate. Provision was then made for produce to be transported at night, and a special passenger boat started to run to Manchester market on Saturdays, arriving at the more civilised hour of ten o'clock, departing at four o'clock.[31]

Contemporaries frequently stressed the importance of the canal for Manchester's supplies of potatoes and other vegetables, and the traffic in agricultural produce must have been considerable. Some indication of its size can be gained from a calculation of the tonnages of 'market goods' sent to Manchester from two of the canal stations, at Altrincham and Lymm, in the early years of its operation (Table 5.1).

Of course, not all these tonnages would have been potatoes and other vegetables; some would have been grain and cheese. However, bearing in mind the descriptive evidence of the sort of farming carried on in the area traversed by the canal, it is not unreasonable to suppose that potatoes would have predominated. Since farmers in the Warrington and Frodsham districts would also have been sending large quantities of potatoes from the stations at Stockton Heath and Preston Brook, it is not surprising to come across an initiative, in 1804, to move the Manchester potato market a short distance from the centre of the town to Campfield, nearer the Bridgewater Canal wharf.[32] As it happened, this experiment was short-lived, the decision being reversed in 1809; though not without leaving a lasting reminder in the naming of a nearby public house as the Oxnoble Inn, after a variety of potato.[33] But the position of the Bridgewater Canal in the trade was unimpaired; indeed, it was enhanced by the long-awaited opening, in 1821, of a branch of the Leeds and Liverpool Canal to join it at Leigh. This gave Manchester a more direct connection with the district around Ormskirk. Although a potential increase in the potato traffic

[30] LRO, NCBw 1/1, 15 Feb. 1770; E. Raffald, *The Manchester Directory for the Year 1772*, Manchester, 1772, p. 59.

[31] LRO, NCBw 2/1, 29 Nov. 1778; E. Raffald, *Manchester and Salford Directory for 1781*, Manchester, 1781, p. 97.

[32] *Mercury*, 24 Jan., 27 Mar. 1804; J. Aston, *The Manchester Guide*, Manchester, 1804, pp. 266–7.

[33] MTH, M1/56/2, Broadside, 29 July 1809; R.N. Salaman, 'The Oxnoble potato: a study in public house nomenclature', *TLCAS*, LXIV, 1954, p. 75.

Table 5.1 *Tonnages of 'market goods' sent to Manchester from selected stations on the Bridgewater Canal, 1770–86*
(to nearest ton)

Year	Altrincham	Lymm
1770	2,730	589
1771	2,629	777
1772	2,929	682
1773	2,565	712
1774	2,201	859
1775	2,211	940
1776	2,350	890
1777	2,320	1,289
1778	1,785	1,355
1779	1,364	1,126
1780	1,441	1,350
1781	1,413	1,389
1782	1,629	1,446
1783	1,320	1,343
1784	1,239	1,504
1785	1,228	1,349
1786	1,403	1,559

Source Calculated from cash receipts in the Bridgewater Canal Company's Book of General Accounts, 1764–90 (LRO, NCBw 6/1). For details of the assumptions used, see Appendix A.

did not form part of the reasoning behind the proposals,[34] the Manchester market had always been able to attract some produce from this area, and the canal link obviously facilitated such a trade.

While the Bridgewater Canal was active in the carriage of produce from its inception, its position did not go entirely uncontested. The Weaver Navigation (1790) and the Ellesmere Canal (1793) both fed into the Mersey and thereby gave access to the Mersey and Irwell Navigation, itself dating from 1720. However, for many years the Mersey and Irwell showed little interest in the conveyance of farm produce and began to run a special market boat comparable with that of the Bridgewater Company only in 1813.[35] Yet by the 1830s the two

[34] The general context of the proposal was concern for the prosperity of the Leeds and Liverpool Canal's coal trade and, in particular, the desirability of forging a link between Leigh and Liverpool (PRO, RAIL 846/9, 17 June, 17 Sept. 1818).
[35] Mersey and Irwell Navigation Company, Mins. of Committee, 3 Mar. 1813.

waterways were engaged in vigorous competition. At the beginning of 1839 the Mersey and Irwell proposed, 'as an object of importance', to establish a wholesale market for 'potatoes, other roots and vegetables' on one of its wharves in Salford in an attempt to increase its share of this trade. Negotiations with the Salford market authorities for the right to hold a public market in the town proved extremely protracted, and a final agreement was not reached until January 1841.[36] Not surprisingly, the Bridgewater Company was alerted by the proposal and stole an advantage by designating part of the Castlefield Quay as a potato wharf, rather than a market. It thus avoided the need for similar negotiations with the Manchester authorities and was able to proceed forthwith to develop facilities there.[37] The Mersey and Irwell may have had doubts about its own proposal from the start, since it began to explore the possibility of establishing a market on its more centrally situated land in Water Street in Manchester while still negotiating with the Salford authorities.[38] When the continuing success of its rival's activities at Castlefield confirmed its fears, it moved quickly in March 1841 to initiate the development of the alternative site in Water Street alongside the recently constructed Manchester and Salford Junction Canal, which had been opened in 1839 to provide a link between the Irwell and the Rochdale Canal. The company had high hopes that this canal would revive its flagging financial position by providing an improved link to the south and east. However, its plan to attract potato and other vegetable traffic off the Bridgewater Canal through several locks to the new market proved unrealistic, and the market agreement with Sir Oswald Mosley was not renewed.[39] In fact, the Bridgewater always had the upper hand in the competition. This is confirmed by the preferred locations of the wholesale potato merchants listed in the commercial directories of the 1840s. In 1843, when they were included for the first time, eight out of thirteen were to be found at the Castlefield wharf, by the Bridgewater Canal; in 1845 all but one of the sixteen recorded were operating from there; even in 1850, by which time the railways had begun to take a

---

[36] *Ibid.*, 16 Jan., 6 Feb., 17 June, 4 July, 2 Oct., 6 Nov., 12 Dec. 1839; 24 Oct. 1840; 6 Jan. 1841.

[37] F.C. Mather, *After the Canal Duke: A Study of the Industrial Estates administered by the Trustees of the Third Duke of Bridgewater in the Age of Railway Building, 1825–1872*, Oxford, 1970, p. 153; LRO, NCBw 2/9, 22 Sept., 14 Oct., 6 Nov. 1841; NCBw 2/11, 26 Feb., 26 Mar. 1842.

[38] Mersey and Irwell Navigation Company, Mins. of Committee, 6 Nov., 12 Dec. 1839.

[39] *Ibid.*, 3 Mar., 4 Aug. 1841; MTH, M1/41/1A, which includes a schedule of the properties and incomes accruing from the markets of Manchester.

more active interest in the trade, thirteen out of the thirty listed were located by the canal.[40]

It is not possible to ascertain precisely the tonnages of produce reaching Manchester by waterway in the late 1840s, but a starting point for approximation is afforded by figures existing for the Bridgewater Canal and the Mersey and Irwell Navigation, which was taken over by the former in 1844. In addition to Lymm and Altrincham, already used to illustrate the position in the late eighteenth century (Table 5.1), we may take into consideration two further stations, Stretford and Cadishead, for which figures are available and from which the traffic would also have been mainly agricultural, with potatoes looming large (Table 5.2). Of course, the tonnages forwarded from these places would have comprised goods other than vegetables. However, as a compensating factor, we know that other stations were also sending sizeable quantities of agricultural produce to Manchester with their other traffic. Most of the freight despatched from Leigh would have been coal, but it must have included potatoes carried down the Leeds and Liverpool Canal link. Preston Brook remained an important access point for traffic coming up the Trent and Mersey Canal from the Midlands, but it was also a station at which potatoes from southern and mid-Cheshire joined the waterway. Over an eighteen-month period in 1844–45, independent carriers on that route alone brought almost 2,000 tons of potatoes to Manchester.[41] Similarly, the tonnages conveyed from Warrington included substantial cargoes of vegetables, as well as coal from the St Helens coalfield. An estimate in 1851 suggested that an average of 50 tons of vegetables per week were being shipped from there to Manchester, and amounts twice as large as this were not unknown.[42] All in all, it would not be unreasonable to conclude that quantities of vegetables at least equal to, and probably in excess of, those going from the places listed in Table 5.2 were coming from these other stations, and that, together, they could constitute a total of over 20,000 tons sent by water to Manchester in the late 1840s.

[40] *Pigot and Slater's Directory of Manchester and Salford*, 1843; *Slater's Directory of Manchester and Salford*, 1845; *Slater's Directory of Manchester and Salford*, 1850.

[41] S. Salt, *Facts and Figures, principally relating to Railways and Commerce*, London, 1848, pp. 102–3.

[42] HLRO, Mins. of Evidence, HC, 1851, XXVII, Warrington and Altrincham Junction Railway Bill, 11 Apr., pp. 124–5.

Table 5.2 *Tonnages of goods sent from selected stations on the Bridgewater Canal and the Mersey and Irwell Navigation in 1849 and 1850*
(to nearest ton)

Year	Lymm		Altrincham		Stretford		Cadishead		Total
	(a)	(b)	(a)	(b)	(a)	(b)	(a)	(b)	
1849	2,569	469	2,970	4,090	275	598	481	56	11,508
1850	3,348	521	3,951	2,658	544	1,237	620	103	12,982

Notes
(a) Carried by company's own boats.
(b) Carried by independent operators.

Source LRO, NCBw 6/3, Bridgewater Trust General Accounts, 1844–50. See Appendix A.

Speculative calculations of this kind are the privilege of the historian; for those involved in the trade at the time, the degree of accuracy mattered rather more. When, in 1842, the Mersey and Irwell was obliged to come to the rescue of the Manchester and Salford Junction Canal, it first re-examined the various traffic forecasts. Some were reduced, but others were increased, none more so than that for potatoes. The company felt confident that 31,200 tons could represent the annual quantity of 'potatoes and other articles' (presumably root vegetables) that might pass through part of the Junction Canal to market.[43] The subsequent history of the Mersey and Irwell might not inspire too much confidence in these calculations, but, even if somewhat over-optimistic, they must have borne some resemblance to reality. Again, the figures would tend to suggest that about half of Manchester's potatoes came by water in the 1840s.

The role of waterways in facilitating the transport of vegetables to Manchester was thus considerable, although two important qualifications should be made. First, they did not radically transform the geographical range from which Manchester drew the bulk of its supplies. The opening of the Rochdale Canal in 1804 gave Manchester access, by its link with the Calder and Hebble Navigation, to important potato-growing areas around Goole and Selby. Yet such a traffic does not seem to have formed part of the reasoning behind the building of the canal,[44] nor did it materialise in any measurable form

[43] Mersey and Irwell Navigation Company, Mins. of Committee, 12 Aug. 1841. Report by T.O. Lingard (dated 28 Apr. 1841).
[44] Hadfield and Biddle, *Canals*, II, pp. 263–70.

afterwards. Moreover, in April 1836 – admittedly, not a month in which potato traffic was likely to be heavy – when a survey of goods carried on the Rochdale and Huddersfield Canals was made, not a single boat out of over 300 examined was so loaded.[45] As far as this trade was concerned, the connection with Yorkshire remained undeveloped. Secondly, it follows that in the 1830s, and through much of the 1840s, something like one-half of Manchester's supply of potatoes and a much higher proportion of other vegetables arrived by land carriage. 'Truly astonishing' was how Wheeler described the number of carts reaching Manchester's markets early one Saturday morning in 1836. Even ten years later, when a controversial new central market was proposed, one of the few uncontested aspects of the plans was that its site needed to be convenient for the carts and waggons coming up from Cheshire.[46] In actuality, the roles of water and road transport were complementary rather than competitive; the greater the distance from Manchester, the more obvious were the advantages of water transport. Some farmers continued to send their potatoes and other produce by cart from as far away as Nantwich, Sandbach and Northwich, in southern and mid-Cheshire, but the amounts involved were small and only a fraction of those going by water.[47] Closer to Manchester, the balance was more even. A survey undertaken in 1845 showed that traffic from Altrincham, eight miles from Manchester, was split almost equally, with the Bridgewater Canal having a slight edge over road transport; at Stretford, only four miles from Manchester, the advantage was firmly held by land carriage, with over 500 tons of farm produce being brought by road from there each week.[48]

iii. The role of railways

Before the late 1840s this was limited to the carriage of supplies of

[45] HLRO, Mins. of Evidence, HC, 1836, XXIV, Manchester and Leeds Railway Bill, 2 May, pp. 187–8.

[46] Wheeler, *Manchester*, pp. 347–8; HLRO, Mins. of Evidence, HL, 1846, XVIII, Manchester Markets Bill, 23 June, pp. 44–5; *Guardian*, 31 Jan. 1846.

[47] MCL, *Tracts on Railways*, 385.81 M1, *Extracts from the Minutes of Evidence given in support of the Cheshire Junction Railway Bill before the Committee of the House of Lords in the session of 1836*, Manchester, 1836, pp. 31, 79–80.

[48] HLRO, Mins. of Evidence, HC, 1845, Manchester, South Junction, and Altrincham Railway Bill, 9 June, p. 11. The survey recorded 1,082 tons on this road over fourteen days, and another 460 tons passing between Altrincham, Timperley, Sale and Manchester.

greengroceries from Covent Garden in London. Captain Laws of the Manchester and Leeds Railway claimed that 'immense quantities' were involved in this traffic.[49] Laws, however, was one of the formidable breed of early railway managers with an almost evangelical zeal to demonstrate the beneficial effects of railways upon the general well-being; a tendency to exaggerate and to confuse the exceptional with the typical was not unknown. A more detailed appraisal reveals that the contribution made by Covent Garden to Manchester's food supply was a modest affair, consisting of watercress, cauliflowers, rhubarb and 'things of that kind which are produced much earlier in the south'.[50] In 1844 Laws spoke of his line carrying 8–10 tons daily in the spring; in 1846 he estimated that some days, at the height of the season, as much as 13–14 tons of watercress was transported to Manchester for distribution in the north.[51] It was an increasing traffic and one that brought to Manchester produce that was not grown in any quantity in the immediate vicinity. Manchester's supply of watercress, for example, had previously consisted of one or two hampers gathered from Cheshire ditches.[52] Even so, at this point in time railways in general appear to have played only a minor role in the conveyance of vegetables.[53] In the case of Manchester, it is easy to see why. The more likely of the early lines to claim some share of this trade, the Liverpool and Manchester and the Manchester and Birmingham, were badly positioned, passing to the north and east respectively of the important growing areas. Hence, this traffic was not something that would fall easily into the railways' hands, even if they had wished to engage in direct competition. In fact, the companies showed little expectation of so doing. The carriage of vegetables had not formed part of the case put before the House of Commons committee that considered the Liverpool and Manchester Railway Bill, and even so ardent a supporter of the line as Joseph Sandars dealt very perfunctorily with this aspect.[54] The problem with such traffic

[49] PP 1846, XIII, *Select Committee on the best means of enforcing one uniform system of Management of Railroads*, Mins. of Evidence, p. 165.

[50] HLRO, Mins. of Evidence, HC, 1844, XXVII, Manchester, Bury, and Rossendale and Manchester and Leeds Railway (Bury Branch) Bill, 28 Mar., pp. 11–12.

[51] *Ibid.*, p. 11; *PP 1846, XIII, Select Committee on . . . Management of Railroads*, Mins. of Evidence, p. 165.

[52] J. Page, 'The sources of supply of the Manchester fruit and vegetable markets', *JRASE*, 2nd ser., XVI, 1880, p. 476.

[53] PP 1846, XIII, *Select Committee on . . . Management of Railroads*, Mins. of Evidence, p. 166.

[54] MCL, Parl. f. 385.0942 L1, *Proceedings of the Committee of the House of Commons on the Liverpool and Manchester Railroad Bill*, 1825. The discussion about the carriage of food

was to dislodge it once it had settled into a well-established pattern, and it is easy to appreciate that the early railways into Manchester would think the effort required was excessive.

Nevertheless, by the end of the 1840s there were signs of impending changes in this respect, most noticeably at the Oldham Road Goods Station of the Manchester and Leeds Railway. The company had already received one warning from the Town Clerk about the practice of allowing vegetables to be sold at the station in contravention of the market regulations, and by 1849 the potato traffic had increased to the extent that it was thought worthwhile to try to put matters on a more formal basis. A special potato siding was built, and negotiations were begun with Manchester Council for the holding of a covered market there. An agreement was reached whereby the railway company paid £325 *per annum* 'in lieu of and compensation for potato tolls receivable at their station in Oldham Road'.[55] By this date the Manchester and Leeds had been absorbed into the Lancashire and Yorkshire Railway, as had the Wakefield, Pontefract, and Goole, which could tap the potato-growing districts of south Yorkshire and the Vale of York. During the 1850s the amalgamated company went to considerable lengths to develop the traffic. Additional trains were laid on to cater specially for it; preferential ticket rates were offered to potato dealers; and at the height of the season extra porters were employed. It was, in the company's words, 'a very profitable traffic'.[56] The farmers' response was such that the expansion of potato growing was picked out in 1861 by a correspondent to the Royal Agricultural Society as one of the noteworthy developments in Yorkshire's agriculture during the previous decade.[57]

In addition, the Lancashire and Yorkshire Railway was well placed to bring vegetables from the other direction, from the Ormskirk area and the district around Poulton in the Fylde. Although Ormskirk was not a new source of supply, the Lancashire and Yorkshire greatly improved its communications with Manchester by developing working arrangements with other lines and eventually assimilating the

---

concerned itself largely with corn. See also J. Sandars, *A Letter on the Subject of the Projected Railroad between Liverpool and Manchester*, 5th edn., Liverpool, 1825, pp. 20ff.

[55] PRO, RAIL 343/493, 22 June, 14 Sept. 1849; MC, *Proceedings*, 5 Dec. 1849.

[56] PRO, RAIL 343/484, 31 Aug. 1852; RAIL 343/497, 6 Oct. 1852; RAIL 343/499, 21 Sept. 1853; 28 June 1854; RAIL 343/503, 27 June 1855.

[57] W. Wright, 'On the improvements in the farming of Yorkshire since the date of the last reports in this journal', *JRASE*, 1st ser., XXII, 1861, p. 113.

East Lancashire Railway in 1858.[58] Meanwhile, the area around Poulton had seen a considerable expansion of early vegetable growing, largely in response to the construction of the North Western Railway, which afforded easy access to the towns of the West Riding. However, an agreement between the Lancashire and Yorkshire and the London and North Western in 1849 to manage jointly the Preston–Wyre line gave the Lancashire and Yorkshire a chance to carry at least some of this produce to Manchester.[59] Supplies from these districts, combined with those from Yorkshire, helped to establish the Lancashire and Yorkshire Company as a major force in this trade. An estimate of the potato traffic on its system, for a six-month period in 1852, put it as high as 'say, 25,000 tons'.[60] At the Oldham Road Station, market facilities soon came under pressure to expand, and the payments in lieu of tolls, under a new agreement with Manchester Council, began to increase until they had more than doubled to reach £750 *per annum* in 1857.[61]

The example set by the Lancashire and Yorkshire Railway was not lost on other companies. A number of developments encouraged the London and North Western to take a greater interest in the potato trade. In 1850 the northern goods manager, Braithwaite Poole, reported that the traffic in potatoes at Liverpool had grown to such an extent that it seemed worthwhile to provide special facilities for it.[62] The sources of the increase in supply were Scotland and other parts of the north, such as Penrith in Cumberland, some arriving by rail and some by coastal steamer. This traffic built up very rapidly. By 1854 Poole was claiming that about 50,000 tons were reaching Liverpool from these districts and the northern parts of Lancashire and Yorkshire, in addition to 50,000 tons from what he called 'neighbouring agricultural districts'.[63] The arrival of amounts of that magnitude must have meant that Liverpool was acting as a major distribution centre for Scottish and Cumbrian potatoes. To judge from the

[58] See J. Marshall, *The Lancashire and Yorkshire Railway*, Newton Abbot, 1969, I, chapters 7 and 8.

[59] E.F. Carter, *An Historical Geography of the Railways of the British Isles*, London, 1959, p. 132; Marshall, *Lancashire and Yorkshire Railway*, I, pp. 85–6; J. Binns, *Notes on the Agriculture of Lancashire with Suggestions for its Improvement*, Preston, 1851, p. 120; E.F. Manby, 'Cultivation of early potatoes', *JRASE*, 1st ser., XVIII, 1857, p. 101.

[60] PRO, RAIL 343/484, 26 Oct. 1852.

[61] PRO, RAIL 343/495, 1 Apr. 1851; RAIL 343/501, 5 Sept. 1854; MC, *Proceedings*, 17 Dec. 1851; 14 Oct. 1857.

[62] PRO, RAIL 410/159, 15 Nov., 6 Dec. 1850.

[63] PRO, RAIL 410/159, 6 Dec. 1850; B. Poole, *The Commerce of Liverpool*, London, 1854, p. 178.

market reports, where 'Scotch potatoes' took their place from 1868 as a regular listing, supplies from north of the border became increasingly important for Manchester. Thus, in the 1850s, either through Liverpool or more directly via the improved rail connection up the west-coast route, the London and North Western could hope to play a considerably enhanced role in the potato trade. In 1852 the company even considered developing its Liverpool Road Station in Manchester as another potato market, but it ran into technical difficulties and eventually had to abandon the project.[64]

Yet another new source of supply for Manchester was Lincolnshire. The links with south Yorkshire and beyond were the last to be developed for the town. Not till 1845 was the route to Sheffield opened in its entirety, and Gainsborough and Lincoln were not reached until 1849. Lincolnshire featured a very extensive potato- and root-vegetable-growing area, stretching south from the Humber along the Trent and extending westwards to the Isle of Axholme. The traditional markets were either the nearby south Yorkshire towns of Sheffield and Doncaster or London.[65] The circuitous journey had always limited the attraction of Manchester, but once the Manchester, Sheffield, and Lincolnshire Railway had offered a direct rail link, a potato traffic quickly developed to the point where the railway company took the familiar step of seeking to establish a potato market at the Manchester end of the line, on part of its London Road Station.[66] After some delay, caused partly by legal skirmishings over the right of the Corporation to impose a toll charge, the market opened early in 1853.[67] Unlike the agreement with the Lancashire and Yorkshire, which was restricted to the sale of potatoes, this one included the right to sell carrots and turnips.[68] Even so, despite early signs of promise, the traffic turned out to be something of a disappointment. The arrangement began badly, with details of the initial agreement proving difficult to operate. The terms were then re-negotiated, with tolls being paid at a flat rate of £50 in the first year, rising to £100, and then to £150. In 1857, however, the Council's Markets Committee was obliged to report that the tolls had remained at £100, since 'no

[64] PRO, RAIL 410/150, 3 Dec. 1852; MC, *Proceedings*, 14 Oct. 1857.
[65] Carter, *Railways of the British Isles*, pp. 72, 155; J.A. Clarke, 'Farming of Lincolnshire', *JRASE*, 1st ser., XII, 1851, pp. 362–7.
[66] PRO, RAIL 463/1, 10, 17 Jan. 1851.
[67] PRO, RAIL 463/2, 23 Jan., 7 May 1852. The traffic ledger had its first entry under *Corporation Tolls Account* on 28 Feb. 1853 (PRO, RAIL 463/288).
[68] MC, *Proceedings*, 5 Dec. 1849; 14 Dec. 1853.

increase in business appears to have taken place'; and in 1860 the agreement was renewed on the same terms for another three years.[69] Discussion of the traffic expected on this line had tended to concentrate very much on grain and flour, and with good reason. The railway's unusually detailed annual reports of the period show that the vegetable traffic was but a small fraction of the tonnages of·grain and flour forwarded to Manchester from this region.[70] Lincolnshire vegetables were destined to become a more important part of Manchester's supplies in the future, but in this period they seem to have made a relatively small contribution.

Most of the railways so far discussed were concerned with the carriage of produce from areas outside Manchester's traditional sources of supply. From Cheshire, on the other hand, water and road transport were able to maintain central positions in this traffic until the mid-century. As we have seen, the Bridgewater Canal and the Mersey and Irwell Navigation were not required to meet direct competition from the early railways, but this happy state was soon to change. In July 1849 a line opened from Manchester to Altrincham (the Manchester, South Junction, and Altrincham). It was one of the first provincial commuter lines, but it is clear that its eyes were also firmly fixed on the traffic in farm produce.[71] The canal authorities were right to feel apprehensive about the new line, though they were no doubt comforted by the railway's proposal to charge twice as much as the waterway for the carriage of farm produce.[72] Even so, as a comparison of Tables 5.2 and 5.3 shows, the tonnages sent by canal from Altrincham and Stretford fell significantly during the early 1850s.

Worse was to follow with the plan to build a line from the Manchester, South Junction, and Altrincham near Timperley to Warrington via Lymm, through the middle of the arable district of north Cheshire. Farmers from these parts were already tempted to carry

[69] *Ibid.*, 25 Oct. 1854; 14 Oct. 1857; 23 Oct. 1860.

[70] The initial agreement with Manchester Council was at 2s 6d per waggon, usually taken to have a capacity of 3–4 tons. At that rate, the annual tolls at London Road Station represented approx. 3,000 tons in the late 1850s and early 1860s. By contrast, at that time the railway often brought to Manchester over 60,000 tons of flour and grain each year (PRO, RAIL 463/4, 11 Aug. 1858; 26 Jan. 1859; RAIL 463/5, 20 July 1859; 25 Jan., 25 July 1860).

[71] HLRO, Mins. of Evidence, HC, 1845, LXIII, Manchester, South Junction, and Altrincham Railway Bill, 9 June, pp. 5–6.

[72] *Ibid.*, p. 11 (the proposed rail rate between Altrincham and Manchester was 1s 4d per ton); LRO, NCBw 6/3, Bridgewater Trust General Accounts for 1849 (where the charge was 8d per ton). For the canal authorities' attitude to the new railway, see Mather, *After the Canal Duke*, pp. 171–4.

their produce to the railway at Altrincham rather than to the canal,[73] and this line (initially called the Warrington and Altrincham Junction, later the Warrington and Stockport) would obviously pose a direct challenge to the Bridgewater Trustees' place in the vegetable trade, which had seemed so secure only a few years before. The railway was opened in 1854, and within a couple of years the company began a concerted effort to capture this traffic, hoping to be able to use the

Table 5.3 *Tonnages of goods sent from selected stations on the Bridgewater Canal and the Mersey and Irwell Navigation in 1855 and 1860*
(to nearest ton)

Year	Lymm		Altrincham		Stretford		Cadishead		Total
	(a)	(b)	(a)	(b)	(a)	(b)	(a)	(b)	
1855	3,563	13	4,050	299	143	96	537	–	8,701
1860	1,761	416	1,197	1,451	43	227	552	409	6,056

Notes
(a) Carried by company's own boats.
(b) Carried by independent operators.

Source Bridgewater Trust Papers, General Account Books, 1855 and 1860. See Appendix A.

market that the London and North Western was intending to develop at the Liverpool Road Station.[74] That particular plan was abortive, but there is no doubt that over the next few years the railway succeeded in prising much trade away from the canal and the Mersey and Irwell Navigation. Despite desperate efforts by the Bridgewater Trustees to fight off the competition with drastic reductions of freight and toll charges, the decline in the traffic from Altrincham and Stretford, noted in the first half of the 1850s, continued. Table 5.3 also shows that by 1860 it had spread to Lymm, and that the total tonnage sent from these four stations was by then only half of what it had been in 1850, in a period when the overall quantity of goods carried by the Bridgewater Canal increased by one-third.[75]

During the 1860s further extensions were built from the Manchester, South Junction, and Altrincham line into the heart of Cheshire, connecting with many of the areas that had previously sent

[73] HLRO, Mins of Evidence, HC, 1851, XXVII, Warrington and Altrincham Junction Railway Bill, 11 Apr., pp. 5–6, 49.
[74] PRO, RAIL 465/3, 20 May 1856.
[75] Mather, *After the Canal Duke*, pp. 292, 362.

potatoes northwards by water.[76] Knutsford is a good example. The line reached there in 1862, and before long farmers were regularly sending truckloads of potatoes and even cabbages by rail. The previous route to Manchester had been roundabout, and the attraction of a more direct link must have been strong. But the decisive factor in the capture of this traffic was the willingness of the railway to collect produce from the grower, take it to the station at Knutsford, and deliver it to Smithfield Market in Manchester.[77] It was generally acknowledged that much of the earlier success of the waterways had been based on the excellent facilities they offered to this trade, but increasingly the Cheshire railways were prepared to match and even surpass them.[78] Perhaps the clearest indication of the declining importance of water transport in the vegetable trade to Manchester is provided by the locations of the wholesale potato merchants. In 1850 thirteen out of the thirty listed in the commercial directory had been situated by the Bridgewater Canal at the Castlefield wharf; by 1871 only one out of the fifty-seven recorded was trading from there.[79]

More resilient to railway competition was the land carriage of vegetables. There were a number of reasons for this. Much of the traffic in new potatoes and green vegetables arose from within a few miles of Manchester, and farmers from nearby villages, such as Timperley and Carrington, saw little advantage in carting produce several miles to the nearest railway station when the Manchester markets were only two or three miles further away. Most market gardeners in these districts operated on a small scale, and however strongly the case was argued in terms of potential savings in time and money, they were reluctant to pay the extra costs of rail transport, especially if they could employ members of their own families to drive their carts to market.[80] It is not surprising, therefore, that the carriage of vegetables to Manchester by horse and cart remained important

[76] See Carter, *Railways of the British Isles*, pp. 269–70. In 1865, these lines were amalgamated under the Cheshire Lines Committee.

[77] HLRO, Mins. of Evidence, HC, 1865, XL, Manchester, Sheffield, and Lincolnshire Railway (Extensions) Bill, 29 May, pp. 156, 164.

[78] HLRO, Mins. of Evidence, HC, 1851, XXVII, Warrington and Altrincham Junction Railway Bill, 11 Apr., pp. 9–10; *PP* 1881, XIII, *Select Committee on Railways*, I, Mins. of Evidence, p. 764. Evidence of the Manchester, Sheffield, and Lincolnshire Railway's goods manager.

[79] *Slater's Directory of Manchester and Salford*, 1850; *Slater's Directory of Manchester and Salford*, 1871–2.

[80] HLRO, Mins. of Evidence, HC, 1865, XL, Manchester, Sheffield, and Lincolnshire Railway (Extensions) Bill, 30 May, pp. 100, 112, 160, 168, 189–93; *PP* 1882, XV, *Royal Commission on Agriculture. Reports of Assistant Commissioners* (J. Coleman), pp. 33–4, 64.

well beyond the end of the period. One night in August 1879, 230 waggons were counted arriving at Manchester's Smithfield Market before six o'clock in the morning, perhaps only one-third fewer than in the 1840s. The market superintendent estimated these as furnishing about one-eighth of the market's total supply, but in terms of market-garden produce the proportion would have been a good deal higher.[81]

iv. Vegetable price data and their social implications, 1827–70

From October 1826 the wholesale prices of potatoes, carrots, onions and turnips on sale in the Manchester potato market were reported each week in the local newspapers; from these we can derive an indication of relative price movements over the period. Figure 5.1 shows the annual averages of the weekly minimum prices quoted for each of the four vegetables over the years 1827–70, in index form, on the base 1851–56 = 100; the seven-year moving averages of these indices; and year-to-year variations in the (national) Rousseaux price index of vegetable products, also on the base 1851–56 = 100, included for comparative purposes.[82] From these graphs, it appears that the movement of prices in Manchester passed through three distinguishable phases.

1827–42

Notwithstanding annual fluctuations, the long-term price of potatoes was comparatively stable, and the moving average shows no tendency to climb steadily upwards, as it might have done if supply had consistently lagged behind rising demand. Moreover, the level of prices ruling in 1827–42 was decidedly lower, on the whole, than that which obtained in the years after 1850. The same applied, though to a lesser extent, to carrots. On the other hand, the prices of onions and turnips were much higher in these years than in the benchmark years, 1851–56. It can also be seen that potatoes and carrots were markedly

[81] Page, 'Fruit and vegetable markets', p. 475. See also W.E. Bear, 'The food supply of Manchester, I, vegetable produce', *JRASE*, 3rd ser., VIII, 1897, pp. 222–3.

[82] The Rousseaux index of vegetable products, originally published in 1938, may be consulted in B.R. Mitchell and P. Deane, *Abstract of British Historical Statistics*, Cambridge, 1962, pp. 471–3. It is essentially an index of farinaceous products – English and American wheat, flour, barley, oats, maize, potatoes and rice – taking the average of 1865 and 1885 prices as 100. Here, the data have been reworked on the base 1851–56 = 100.

cheaper in Manchester than the general range of agricultural produce, represented by the Rousseaux index, again in contrast to the prices of onions and turnips. Either way, the evidence points firmly to the conclusion that Manchester was much better supplied with carrots and particularly potatoes than with the other vegetables. In the early 1840s the prices of all four were tending to fall locally, mirroring the national trend, captured in the Rousseaux index, and no doubt reflecting the economic depression of the early 1840s.

1843–50

The picture now changed and became more complex, turning especially on the situation with regard to potato cultivation. By 1843 there had been five successive annual falls in potato prices, and Palin, in 1844, remarked that there had been no expansion in the acreage devoted to them for some years, with turnips finding increasing favour.[83] The most striking feature of the mid-1840s, however, was the potato blight of 1845–46. The impact of the disease began to be felt locally in the autumn of 1845, but its worst ravages affected the main crop of the following year. Of course, for potatoes reaching market in sound condition in the winter of 1846–47, prices rocketed, but potato growing became an extremely risky undertaking, with sporadic outbreaks of disease in Lancashire and Cheshire for the next two years.[84] Combined with the fall in potato prices from the late 1830s, this was enough to encourage farmers to look more enthusiastically at the alternative vegetables. As a result, during the late 1840s their prices came tumbling down to reach a nadir about 1850.

1851–70

These years saw an enormous extension in the area from which Manchester could draw its supplies of vegetables and some improvement in the range of choice. For example, the railways could claim credit for tapping supplies of peas from Evesham, Yorkshire and Nottinghamshire. These were not grown in any quantity locally, and yet they were the only new vegetable for which a market report was

[83] Palin, 'Farming of Cheshire', pp. 67–8, 102–3.
[84] *Guardian*, 30 Aug., 22 Oct., 8 Nov. 1845; 2 May, 19 Aug. 1846; 21, 24 July, 21, 25 Aug., 8 Sept. 1847; 19 July, 16, 23 Aug. 1848.

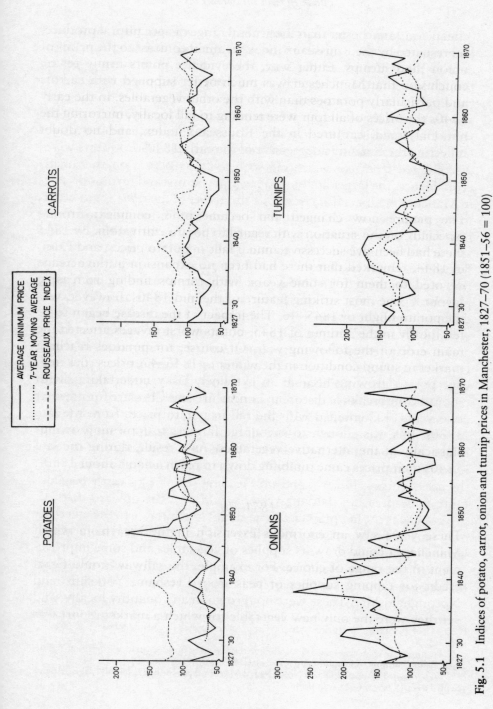

Fig. 5.1 Indices of potato, carrot, onion and turnip prices in Manchester, 1827–70 (1851–56 = 100)

Sources Minimum prices quoted weekly in market reports in *Courier* and *Guardian*, reworked to determine annual averages. For the Rousseaux index, see Chapter V, note 82.

quoted regularly in the years after 1850.[85] It was potatoes, however, that remained the central article of vegetable consumption, and, despite the widening of the sources of supply, their average price, though lower in the 1860s than in the early 1850s, never returned to the level of the years before 1845. It is at this point that the true significance of the tonnages of potatoes carried by the railways can be seen. The increasing quantities of potatoes being brought from outside Cheshire and south-west Lancashire meant that local producers were discouraged from concentrating so heavily as before on this main crop. Hence, the larger amounts of carrots, onions and turnips on sale in Manchester, apart from reflecting the ability of the railways to bring in extra supplies, were a consequence of the much firmer position these now held in local rotations. As a result, the price of onions, in particular, never climbed back to the general level of the 1830s and fluctuated for the last fifteen years of the period only just above what they were fetching in 1852–53. Carrots gained even more from supplies brought by the railways; their average price was actually lower during those fifteen years than in the early 1850s. Rising real wages would have tended to encourage the consumption of such vegetables, and for that reason the improvement in supply, mirrored in these favourable price trends, may be understated. Turnips were the one vegetable of the four that did not follow this pattern; their price continued to rise past the point in time at which those of potatoes, carrots and onions began to decline or, at least, stabilise at a new level. At first sight, this seems curious, since an increase in turnip growing might be thought to have been the natural consequence of any reduction in the potato acreage.[86] It was in these years, however, that the use of turnips in yard- and stall-feeding regimes for cattle became more widespread in dairying regions.[87] Hence, the upward drift of prices in Manchester market was no doubt attributable to the fact that only part of the increased production was being sold off the farm for human consumption.

So far, price movements have been employed to throw further light on long-term changes in the pattern of supply. However, the data may

[85] Page, 'Fruit and vegetable markets', p. 477; Wright, 'Farming of Yorkshire', p. 113; R.E. Porter, 'Agricultural change in Cheshire during the nineteenth century', University of Liverpool, Ph.D., 1974, p. 229. For pea prices in Manchester, see 'Housewife's Corner' (above, Chapter IV, note 78).

[86] Turnips were sometimes used as alternative root crops to potatoes in local rotations (Palin, 'Farming of Cheshire', pp. 63–4, 66, 69; Garnett, 'Farming of Lancashire', pp. 11, 14–15).

[87] E.L. Jones, 'The changing basis of English agricultural prosperity, 1853–73', *Agricultural History Review*, X, 1962, esp. p. 112.

also be used to bring out some interesting social implications, affecting the people of Manchester as consumers. One aspect of this is the extent to which price variations might have been reduced over time. From Figure 5.1 it is not obvious that year-to-year fluctuations were less marked in the 1850s and 1860s than earlier, and this is confirmed by statistical analysis: except for onions, the amplitude of variations was actually rather greater after 1849 than before.[88] The price of rail-borne peas, available after 1850, likewise showed considerable variations on an annual basis.[89] It might be argued that, as real incomes rose, vegetables became a more central part of the average diet; hence, demand was less likely to fall in years of shortage. But there is another, simpler, explanation. For natural reasons, vegetable harvests generally and potato harvests in particular remained notorious for their fluctuations from year to year.[90] Thus, so long as the major supplies came from within this country and were subject to similar weather conditions or pests and diseases to those which afflicted Lancashire and Cheshire, this would remain so. Produce that came from abroad was at the top of the price range, and therefore had only a limited impact on these annual price variations.

However, there was a detectable change in the degree to which the widening circle of supply resulted in an improved availability of vegetables through the seasons. In the years before the mid-century, when local supplies were paramount, it was common (with the exception of potatoes) for vegetables to be unavailable for three to four months during the interval between the last of the old crop and the first of the new. This is demonstrated in Figure 5.2, which indicates the weeks when no prices were quoted for three different vegetables in the market reports. The figure shows that the gap began to close after 1850 as the new season's produce appeared earlier in Manchester than hitherto. Local farmers no doubt played some part in this process by putting more effort into raising early or late varieties, but the main

---

[88] A calculation of the mean deviation from the trend, following the method of R.G.D. Allen, *Statistics for Economists*, 2nd edn., London, 1951, pp. 143–4, gives the following results:

Mean annual deviation from the trend (as a percentage)

	1830–48	1849–67
Potatoes	16.4	19.4
Carrots	6.5	10.6
Onions	21.5	17.7
Turnips	13.6	16.4

[89] The mean annual deviation from the trend, 1854–67, was 21.6 per cent.

[90] See, for example, J.R. McCulloch, *A Descriptive and Statistical Account of the British Empire*, 3rd edn., London, 1847, I, pp. 443–4; Holland, *General View . . . of Cheshire*, p. 143.

explanation lies in the arrival of supplies from growing areas more forward than the north-west. The availability of onions throughout the year by the 1860s is particularly striking and can only be explained by continental imports. Not surprisingly, in the light of the interest already being shown in their intensive cultivation in the late eighteenth and early nineteenth centuries, new potatoes were an exception to this development; the dates when they appeared in Manchester in the 1850s and 1860s varied little from those of thirty years before. Only in the last two years of the period, when continental supplies began to be quoted, was there a significant forward movement in the date when they came on sale.[91]

How far improvements of this kind were translated into real gains for the bulk of the population of Manchester is debatable. Figure 5.3 shows the extent to which this increased availability was mirrored in reduced seasonal price fluctuations by comparing the monthly prices at the beginning and end of the period for which there were market reports.[92] For carrots and turnips, seasonal price variations were actually rather greater in the late 1860s than in 1828–32; for potatoes, they remained much the same. The apparent incongruity with the evidence of enhanced seasonal availability is, in fact, easily explained. The early arrivals were expensive. For example, new potatoes from Cornwall were priced at ten to twenty times the average for the expiring crop from Cheshire, and would have been well beyond the means of most Mancunians.[93] For onions, however, there was a limited reduction in seasonal price variations. This was doubtless facilitated by imports, which, though still expensive, reached the country in increasing quantities in the 1850s and Manchester by the 1860s.[94] Thus, while the 'availability gap' was being reduced, vegetable prices in the difficult weeks tended to range as high as ever, approximately 50–100 per cent above those ruling during the winter months.

[91] In 1869 Maltese potatoes were on sale at the market of 23 Mar., and in 1870 the first new potatoes from Portugal appeared, but not till 30 Apr. (*Guardian*, 24 Mar. 1869; 2 May 1870).

[92] Following the method of Allen, *Statistics for Economists*, pp. 144–51.

[93] See, for example, *Guardian*, market reports for 7 Apr. 1869; 23 May 1870.

[94] R.J. Battersby, 'The development of market gardening in England, 1850–1914', University of London, Ph.D., 1960, p. 57; F. Beavington, 'The development of market gardening in Bedfordshire, 1799–1939', *Agricultural History Review*, XXIII, 1975, pp. 39, 41; Page, 'Fruit and vegetable markets', p. 480.

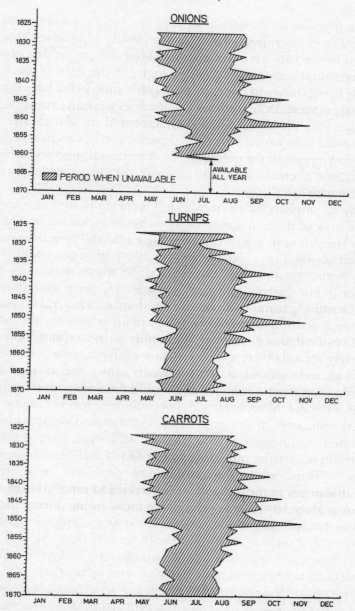

Fig. 5.2   Seasonal availability of onions, turnips and carrots in Manchester, 1827–70

Sources   Weekly market reports in *Courier* and *Guardian*. Unavailability is inferred from the absence of a quotation in the reports. Note that potatoes were available all year.

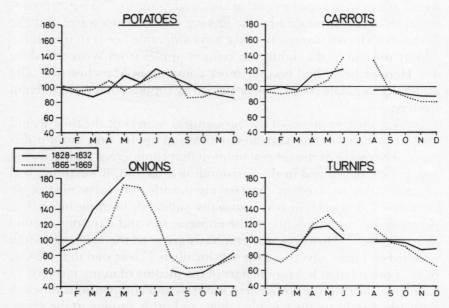

Fig. 5.3 Seasonal variations in potato, carrot, onion and turnip prices in Manchester, 1828–32 and 1865–69

Sources Minimum prices quoted weekly in market reports in *Courier* and *Guardian*, reworked to determine monthly averages. Monthly variations are given as ratios to the trend values (= 100) ruling across the two sub-periods chosen for comparison.

v. Fruit availability

Much in the way that potatoes dominated the vegetable trade, apples arrived in Manchester in far greater quantities than any other fruit. The fruit market was traditionally known as the apple market, and even in the first quarter of the nineteenth century the name still struck one commentator as particularly appropriate.[95] Apples have the advantage of keeping and travelling well. It is not entirely surprising, therefore, to find the readers of the *Mercury* being tempted early in the period with the delights of apples and pears from Worcestershire and

[95] Anon., 'Recollections of Manchester, 1808–30', in J. Harland (ed.), *Collectanea relating to Manchester and its neighbourhood, at various periods – II*, Chetham Society Publications, 1st ser., LXXII, Manchester, 1867, p. 245.

Kent, along with more exotic grapes and walnuts.[96] The improvements in access produced by the linking of the Bridgewater and the Trent and Mersey waterways gave a considerable boost to this trade, and by the end of the eighteenth century apples from Worcestershire and Herefordshire had become more common in Manchester.[97] The middle-class palate could even be tickled by supplies that were arriving from America.[98]

Indeed, the comments of the agricultural writers of the time would lead us to believe that Manchester received apples only from a distance. They were of the general opinion that commercial fruit growing was poorly developed in the surrounding area and, if anything, had actually been reduced in the late eighteenth and early nineteenth centuries.[99] Even Aikin was unusually subdued, limiting himself to pointing out the excellence of the gooseberries and damsons around Warrington.[100] However, the emphasis given to the existence of an orchard on farms advertised for sale locally is a clear sign that the sale of fruit provided at least some part of the income of many farmers.[101] Likewise, the thriving gooseberry societies and competitions of south Lancashire indicate the trouble taken, and pride shown, in the growing of that fruit.[102] The Woods of Didsbury provide a good example of such small-scale fruit growing. This family ran a public house, a small mixed farm and, for a time, a shop in Didsbury, then a village to the south of Manchester. Their accounts between 1794 and 1812 show them taking apples, pears, plums and damsons to sell in Manchester or sometimes Stockport. On two occasions, in the October of 1809 and that of 1812, they also took some nuts. The quantities involved were not large. Some years they did not go at all; usually they went once or twice; often three or four times; in good years, even more frequently. Generally they sold less than two pounds' worth, but in 1795 their

---

[96] *Mercury*, 14 Nov. 1780, advertisement of Thomas Revett.

[97] See W.T. Pomeroy, *General View of the Agriculture of the County of Worcester*, London, 1794, pp. 29–30; Holt, p. 83; Aikin, p. 204; 'Recollections of Manchester', p. 245.

[98] *Mercury*, 6 Jan. 1801, advertisement of Middlewoods; see also Holt, p. 83.

[99] Wedge, *General View . . . of Chester*, p. 13; Holt, p. 79; Holland, *General View . . . of Cheshire*, pp. 195–6; Marshall, *Reports to the Board of Agriculture*, II, p. 35; Dickson, *General View . . . of Lancashire*, pp. 431–2.

[100] Aikin, p. 306.

[101] For example, advertisements in *Mercury*, 13 Feb., 31 July 1781; 19 Jan. 1790; 24 Nov., 16 Dec. 1795.

[102] See, MCL, Broadside f. 1812/18; Holt, p. 81; Dickson, *General View . . . of Lancashire*, p. 429.

sales in Manchester amounted to £6 1s 10d.[103] To the Woods, these sales would have been only a small addition to their regular income, but it must have been supplies brought to market in just this way that provided the main source of fruit, other than apples, for the people of Manchester at that time. This picture changed very little through the rest of the period. Most agricultural commentators said nothing or made but a fleeting mention of local fruit growing; those who dwelled on the subject did so in order to lament its parlous state. In the market-gardening districts around Warrington and Stretford it was treated on a rather less casual basis, but even there pollution was taking its toll.[104] As a major commercial undertaking, fruit growing for the Manchester market was almost non-existent.

The one curious exception to this was rhubarb. Rhubarb had traditionally been prized for its medicinal qualities, but during the first half of the nineteenth century it became an increasingly popular item of general consumption. The story of its commercial cultivation for Manchester is surprisingly well documented, beginning with John Osbaldeston from Baguley, near Altrincham, who sent his first cartload to market in 1833. Of course, the fact that this piece of horticultural enterprise assumed almost legendary proportions indicates how unusual it was; indeed, for a long time the Osbaldestons were almost the sole suppliers of rhubarb to Manchester market.[105] In the mid-1840s the railways started to bring some from Covent Garden, but local production responded to the challenge to the extent that these distant supplies became less and less necessary.[106] It seems to have been a rare exception. The same Osbaldeston family also pioneered the growing of strawberries on a commercial scale, but it was not until the 1880s that these began to be mentioned as a regular part of local market gardening.[107]

Looking for potential sources of supply outside Lancashire and Cheshire, it is difficult to find branches of the fruit trade that were not

[103] These records comprise three ledgers, covering the various activities of the family (MCLAD, M62/1/1–3). They are at their most useful for 1786–1812, giving details of 'Produce Sold' on various pages scattered through the volumes.

[104] J.C. Loudon, *An Encyclopaedia of Agriculture*, 5th edn., London, 1844, pp. 1163–4; Binns, *Agriculture of Lancashire*, p. 136; Baines, *Lancashire and Cheshire*, I, p. 65; II, pp. 341, 343–4; Page, 'Fruit and vegetable markets', p. 480.

[105] *Guardian*, 23 Apr. 1859; Page, 'Fruit and vegetable markets', p. 479.

[106] Above, p. 106; and *Guardian*, 23 Apr. 1859.

[107] Page, 'Fruit and vegetable markets', p. 479; PP 1881, XVII, *Royal Commission on Agriculture*, II, Mins. of Evidence, p. 919; PP 1881, XIII, *Select Committee on Railways*, I, Mins. of Evidence, p. 347.

dominated by London. Although this is not entirely surprising, considering the stimulus exerted by a centre of high purchasing power over a long period, nevertheless it continued well into the nineteenth century. The Select Committee on the Fresh Fruit Trade, reporting in 1839, was preoccupied with the metropolis and its suppliers.[108] Clearly, it would be difficult for Manchester and other industrial towns to break into such well-established supply patterns. As we have seen, apples from Worcestershire and Herefordshire were the one commodity that Manchester had been successful in attracting in large quantities in the eighteenth century, and this traffic continued, along with supplies of pears, for a long time by water, but increasingly by rail.[109] Otherwise, it is difficult to find examples of fruit where it was customary for distant growers to look to Manchester and other northern towns for their main markets. The Vale of Evesham had originally been obliged to confine its soft-fruit trade to local markets in the Midlands, but was able, with the advent of the railway, to widen its range considerably. Even so, Manchester was but one of many industrial towns vying for its share.[110] In the second half of the century, Covent Garden increasingly acted as a distribution centre for the more northerly towns for soft fruits from Kent and other parts of the south, and even from France; but the cost of transit inevitably made them so expensive that they were beyond the reach of most of the population. 'Raspberries', observed John Page, the Manchester market superintendent, revealingly, 'always command a good price'.[111]

From abroad, the only fruits that reached Manchester in any quantity were apples and oranges. At the end of the eighteenth century, most of the European apples imported into the country went to London, but Manchester's well-to-do were able to purchase American varieties arriving in limited amounts in the north of England. After the lifting of import duties in 1846, much greater quantities from America were shipped into Liverpool and, from there, found their way on to the Manchester market.[112] Oranges were the only other fresh fruit imported on a large scale before the last decades of the century, and the

[108] *PP* 1839, VIII. None of the witnesses who gave evidence came from the north.

[109] PRO, RAIL 410/167, 3 Nov. 1861; C. Whitehead, 'The cultivation of hops, fruit, and vegetables', *JRASE*, 2nd ser., XIV, 1878, pp. 739–40.

[110] Page, 'Fruit and vegetable markets', p. 476; Whitehead, 'Cultivation of hops', p. 746.

[111] B. Poole, *Statistics of British Commerce*, London, 1852, pp. 64, 166; G. Dodd, *The Food of London*, London, 1856, p. 394; Page, 'Fruit and vegetable markets', p. 483.

[112] Poole, *Statistics*, p. 11; J.R. McCulloch, *A Dictionary, Practical, Theoretical, and Historical, of Commerce and Commercial Navigation*, new edn., London, 1869, p. 64; Page, 'Fruit and vegetable markets', p. 482.

Liverpool and Manchester Railway was bringing sufficient quantities to Manchester in 1831–32 for the company to think it worthwhile to adopt special precautions against persistent pilferage.[113] Strangely, this appears to have been a particular problem with consignments of oranges,[114] and does seem to indicate that the individual orange was reckoned a prize worth stealing. Yet a witness to the 1839 Select Committee argued that they could no longer be considered luxuries, and they were widely sold on the streets of London.[115] On the other hand, in 1869 the economist, McCulloch, rated them slightly above 'superior' domestic fruit; and, if the novels of Mrs Gaskell are any guide, they were not consumed in the 1840s and 1850s in Manchester in anything like the same quantities as in the capital. In *Mary Barton*, oranges had the status of being a special treat; for a self-made man like John Thornton, in *North and South*, to have 'a basket piled with oranges and American apples' represented the epitome of genteel living.[116]

Even today, fruit growing forms only a very minor part of the agriculture of Lancashire and Cheshire, and therefore the years before 1870 should not be judged too uncharitably. However, the paucity of local supplies would be felt more acutely if so little was arriving from elsewhere. Nor were farmers slow to recognise that, in these circumstances, consumers would be especially appreciative of any fruit brought in on a casual basis. Most farms had a few fruit trees attached to them; damsons were particularly common and formed 'an article of profit to cottagers as well as to small farmers'.[117] Even for the winner of the 1877 Liverpool Prize Competition for dairy and stock farms, the income from fruit was a welcome bonus.[118] Individually, the amounts

---

[113] G.R. Porter, *The Progress of the Nation*, revised edn., by F.W. Hirst, London, 1912, p. 452; Poole, *Statistics*, p. 237; A. Torode, 'Trends in fruit consumption', in T.C. Barker, J.C. McKenzie and J. Yudkin (eds.), *Our Changing Fare*, London, 1966, p. 125; PRO, RAIL 371/8, 21 Dec. 1831; 25 Jan. 1832.

[114] Poole, *Statistics*, p. 237.

[115] *PP* 1839, VIII, *Select Committee on the Fresh Fruit Trade*, Mins. of Evidence, p. 158; Dodd, *Food of London*, pp. 389–92; H. Mayhew, *London Labour and the London Poor*, London, 1861, I, pp. 87–8.

[116] McCulloch, *Dictionary . . . of Commerce*, p. 984; E.C. Gaskell, *Mary Barton*, Everyman's Library edn., London, 1965, p. 72; *idem*, *North and South*, Everyman's Library edn., London, 1967, p. 73.

[117] Baines, *Lancashire and Cheshire*, I, p. 65; W.B. Mercer, *A Survey of the Agriculture of Cheshire*, London, 1963, p. 122.

[118] J.C. Morton, 'Report on the Liverpool prize-farm competition, 1877 – dairy and stock farms', *JRASE*, 2nd ser., XIII, 1877, p. 506; see also S.D. Shirriff, 'Report upon the Liverpool prize-farm competition in Lancashire, Cheshire and North Wales, 1877 – arable farms', *ibid.*, p. 495.

involved could not have been large, but, when added together and brought to market within the space of a few weeks, the total supply would not have been neglible. In that respect, little indeed seems to have changed since the turn of the century.

CHAPTER VI

Fish

i. The supply of fish in the pre-railway era

IN NOVEMBER 1765 a Manchester Fish Society gave notice that within the next few days the 'machines' would begin to load again at Scarborough. The following week it was announced that the first of the season had arrived with a delivery of cod, haddock and lobsters, and that it was hoped to receive regular supplies twice weekly.[1] These machines were specially designed conveyances – well-ventilated, box-like structures, with suspended bodies to reduce jolting – which originated in a competition organised in 1761 by John Blake of London, under the patronage of the Society for the Encouragement of Arts, Manufacture and Commerce, to find an improved method of carrying fish overland.[2] However, despite the encouragement of the *Mercury*, nothing more is recorded of the scheme. A more traditional – but slow and expensive – mode of operation was to carry the fish live on carts in butts filled with water, and an interesting variant of this was tried at Manchester in 1771 when '160 fine large codfish', caught four days earlier off Holyhead and presumably kept alive in a container of sea water, were brought to the town via the Mersey and Irwell Navigation.[3] Experiments of this nature were always likely to founder on the heavy cost of transport and attendant high prices to consumers. Even in London, where there were more potential customers with deep purses, Blake, who was a businessman as well as a champion of

[1] *Mercury*, 5, 12 Nov. 1765.
[2] Anon., *An Account of the Land-Carriage Fish-Undertaking continued by Grant and Company*, London, 1768, pp. 3ff. See also W.M. Stern, 'Fish supplies for London in the 1760s: an experiment in overland transport – I', *Journal of the Royal Society of Arts*, May, 1970; *idem*, 'Fish supplies for London in the 1760s: an experiment in overland transport – II', *ibid.*, June, 1970.
[3] Anon., *A Brief Detail of the Home Fishery from Early Times*, London, 1763, pp. 122–3; Stern, 'Fish supplies for London', Pt. I, p. 361; *Mercury*, 16 Apr. 1771.

technical progress, soon ran into difficulties. Notwithstanding assistance received in the form of a substantial subsidy from the Society of Arts, he was unable, it was claimed, to sell his fish at less than 1s per lb and cover his costs. Significantly, his successor in the business addressed himself explicitly to the custom of 'the nobility and gentry'.[4]

Although such ambitious schemes were apt to be short-lived, it would be a mistake to infer that Manchester was largely bereft of fish supplies until the advent of the railways. Indeed, in 1795 Aikin prefaced his remarks on this subject with the observation that the town was 'better provided than might be expected from its inland situation'.[5] The Fish Society's efforts were not wasted, for it had demonstrated the technical possibility of supplying Manchester from the east coast, and the example was not lost. By the end of the century fish was arriving from that direction on a more regular basis. Furthermore, it was the main source of 'prime' fish, such as cod and turbot, as well as lobsters. At this period and for many decades to come, Yarmouth was preoccupied almost entirely with the smoked-herring trade, geared to London and to export markets, but stretching along the Yorkshire coast was a host of small fishing villages; from Filey, in the south, up to Staithes, fish was regularly sent to Manchester before the railway era.[6] John Walker, probably the largest fishmonger in the town in the 1820s, advertised that he received his supplies from Staithes and from Hartlepool, even further to the north. The fish was speeded on its way in vans or carried by 'men with good horses'; even so, the shortest journey would have taken two days.[7] It must have been a risky business, and one that inevitably imposed restrictions on both the range and the quantity of fish that could be brought to Manchester in this way. As ever, the central problem was that of preservation. Natural ice was first used to preserve Scottish salmon destined for the London market in the 1780s. This was a high-class trade which justified the building of special ice-houses, heavily insulated with

[4] Stern, 'Fish supplies for London', Pt. II, pp. 431, 433, 435; *A Brief Detail*, p. 73; *Land-Carriage Fish-Undertaking*, pp. 3, 18.

[5] Aikin, p. 204.

[6] *Ibid.*; PP 1866, XVIII, *Report of the Commissioners appointed to inquire into the Sea Fisheries of the United Kingdom*, II, Mins. of Evidence, pp. 122, 132. For Yarmouth at this period, see PP 1833, XIV, *Select Committee on British Channel Fisheries*, Mins. of Evidence, p. 132.

[7] *Guardian*, 4, 11 Jan. 1823; PP 1866, XVIII, *Report . . . into the Sea Fisheries*, II, Mins. of Evidence, pp. 122, 146.

straw and well drained.[8] In general, ice was an expensive commodity to be used sparingly, since it was scarcest when most needed, as can be inferred from the willingness of Manchester fishmongers to pay as much as 22s per ton for thirty cartloads of snow in April 1846.[9] At sea, it was not commonly used for preservation purposes until the mid nineteenth century. Before this, it was often the case that three-quarters of the catch would be thrown overboard, comprising most of the plaice, haddock, whiting and ling that the fishermen saw as 'offal'; only the 'prime' fish, cod, sole, turbot and halibut, and the best of the 'offal' would be worth keeping.[10]

It might seem rather surprising that the Lancashire coast played a subordinate role in the supply of fish to Manchester in view of its closer proximity. However, poor communications with the more northerly parts, coupled with the unsuitability of much of the southern reaches for fishing, meant that the sources of supply open to Manchester from this direction were limited to Liverpool and, to a lesser extent, Southport. In Aikin's day, fishing in the vicinity of Southport was simply by hook and line from the beach. But at some point early in the nineteenth century trawling became established there, and for a number of years, before the boats moved to Fleetwood, fish was sent to Manchester by horse and cart. Even so, it was not uncommon for it to spoil before reaching its destination.[11] At Liverpool, fishing was an altogether larger undertaking, but it was geared to the catching of herrings for smoking and salting; indeed, in the 1770s and 1780s the town ranked second only to Yarmouth in the importance of its herring trade. The supply of fresh fish, on the other hand, even to its own market, was 'less abundant than might be expected', apparently to the point where intermittent overflows of turbot from Manchester were welcomed. All that Manchester could expect in return, apart from salted and smoked fish, seems to have been occasional consignments of fresh herrings, presumably when the catch had been particularly large.[12] The trouble was that these were highly seasonal and tended to

[8] *Sixth Report from the Select Committee on the State of the British Herring Fisheries*, 30 June 1800, Appendix B. 6, in *Reports from Committees of the House of Commons*, X, 1803, p. 369; C.L. Cutting, *Fish Saving*, London, 1955, pp. 214–16.

[9] W.E.A. Axon (ed.), *The Annals of Manchester*, Manchester, 1886, p. 236.

[10] *PP 1866*, XVIII, *Report . . . into the Sea Fisheries*, II, Mins. of Evidence, p. 157; Cutting, *Fish Saving*, pp. 221, 223.

[11] Aikin, pp. 327, 362–3; *PP 1866*, XVIII, *Report . . . into the Sea Fisheries*, II, Mins. of Evidence, p. 1219. For Fleetwood, see below, p. 136 and notes 54, 55.

[12] *Third Report from the Select Committee on the State of the British Fisheries*, 14 July 1785, Appendix No. 1, in *Reports from Committees of the House of Commons*, X, 1803, pp. 54–5;

come in a glut. In August 1795 a Committee appointed for the Relief of the Poor offered cash premiums of 5s for every cartload of fresh herrings brought to Manchester market. The quantities arriving fluctuated enormously. In the first week the citizens were confronted with twenty-eight such loads, and it may well be that some harsh lessons in the economic facts of life were learned about what happens to prices when supply overwhelms demand, because several weeks elapsed before any more appeared. After that, over the next three weeks thirty-one loads qualified for the premium, but subsequently only one more reached the town before the scheme ended in December.[13]

A third source of fish, and one that might easily be overlooked, was from fresh water. Aikin remarked on the many local ponds and marl-pits that were 'well stored with carp and tench', and on the eels and pike sold in the market, as well as the trout and salmon that might have been expected.[14] It is difficult to assess the quantities involved, and articles in the *Annals of Agriculture* at the turn of the century give the impression that the farming of freshwater fish on a commercial scale was a practice that had gone into decline from the time of the Reformation and was limited to a handful of landed estates.[15] On the other hand, the catching of an occasional fish such as a large pike, or the more systematic trapping of eels for sale to local fishmongers, would have offered a welcome addition to many rural incomes. In a twelve-month period in 1818–19 the Worsley farm, part of the Bridgewater estates, sold to Thomas Wynne, one of Manchester's fishmongers, 'and others' 160 lb of eels for a total of £3 13s 8d.[16] They must have added variety to the fishmongers' rather limited range, but they were certainly not a cheap alternative to sea fish. At that time Walker was selling eels at 10d per lb and pike at a little more, some two or three times the price of cod and haddock.[17] Trout and salmon were the other freshwater fish that appeared in Manchester. Locally, pollution and over-fishing had taken their toll early, but the marketing of

Second Report from the Select Committee on the State of the British Herring Fisheries, 27 June 1798, Pt. III, *ibid.*, p. 250; Aikin, pp. 204–5, 362.

[13] See *Mercury*, 11 Aug. 1795–12 Jan. 1796.

[14] Aikin, p. 205.

[15] Anon., 'Some notes on poultry and fish', *Annals of Agriculture*, XXXIX, 1803, esp. p. 524; Anon., 'Fishponds', *ibid.*, XXXIII, 1799, p. 638; R. North, 'A discourse on fish and fish ponds', *ibid.*, XXXVIII, 1802, p. 378; J. Bankes, 'On fish ponds', *ibid.*, XL, 1804, p. 108.

[16] LRO, NCBw 2/6, 7 Aug. 1819.

[17] MCLAD, Misc. 41, Three bills for fish etc. bought from John Walker, fishmonger, Market Place, Manchester, 1821. In 1825 Walker was selling cod at 3d–5d per lb and haddock at 5d per lb (MTH, M1/50/8, *Sir Oswald Mosley v. John Walker*, Brief for Plaintiff, 1826. Evidence of William Atkinson).

salmon, especially, was conducted on a national, or even international, scale.[18] At Manchester, in Aikin's time, the Ribble, in north Lancashire, was the main source of supply, but the use of ice considerably extended this range. By the 1820s salmon was arriving from Cumberland and also from Ireland.[19] For supplies from the latter, this was not necessarily the end of the journey, since some was sent to Manchester for distribution to other towns. Inevitably, the cost of transport and ice kept prices high. In 1821 Walker was selling salmon at about 1s per lb; trout was even more expensive at 1s 6d.[20]

Finally, some mention should be made of the contribution of shellfish. Newspaper advertisements of the late eighteenth and early nineteenth centuries drew attention to the arrival of fresh deliveries of oysters from London, though their wording leaves little doubt that these were regarded as delicacies for the well-to-do.[21] Certainly, consumption in Manchester cannot have been anything like so widespread as in the capital, where they were brought up the Thames and kept in the holds of special smacks at Billingsgate.[22] In the round, and by comparison with what came later, the total amount of fish consumed in Manchester cannot have been large, and supply must have been erratic. The advent of a more rapid means of transport was of particular significance for so perishable a commodity as fish, and those who lived through the ensuing changes tended to accord the railways pride of place in heralding a new era in the trade, at least in so far as the supply of inland towns was concerned.[23]

ii. Railways and the fishing industry

As early as December 1831 there is a record of oysters being sent by

---

[18] Aikin, pp. 205, 305–6; W.M. Stern, 'The fish supply to Billingsgate from the nineteenth century to the Second World War', in T.C. Barker and J. Yudkin (eds.), *Fish in Britain*, Occasional Paper No. 2, Department of Nutrition, Queen Elizabeth College, London, 1971, pp. 34–5.

[19] *Guardian*, 1 Mar. 1823, advertisement of William Foster; MTH, M1/50/8, *Mosley* v. *Walker*, Supplemental Observations to Plaintiff's Brief, 1826. Evidence relating to Mr Little.

[20] MCLAD, Misc. 41, Three bills for fish . . . from John Walker.

[21] *Mercury*, 4 Jan., 14 Nov. 1780; 6 Mar. 1804.

[22] On supplies of oysters to, and consumption in, London, see H. Mayhew, *London Labour and the London Poor*, London, 1861, I, pp. 75–6; Cutting, *Fish Saving*, p. 29; and especially Stern, 'Fish supply to Billingsgate', pp. 42–3.

[23] See, for example, *The Fish Trades Gazette*, 1 Mar. 1884; PP 1866, XVII, *Report . . . into the Sea Fisheries*, I, Report, p. xii.

rail from Liverpool to Manchester,[24] but initially the impact of railways on the fish trade was minimal. In fact, there was a noticeable lack of enthusiasm on the part of railway companies to become involved in the traffic. Suggestions that it was an awkward cargo, liable to give offence to the second- or third-class passengers who were obliged to occupy the same carriage, are not convincing,[25] for such comments made sense only if the railways did not think it worthwhile to lay on special facilities. Eventually, attitudes changed and, not for the first time, it was Captain Laws of the Manchester and Leeds Company who, in 1844, took the initiative in trying to increase the traffic to more worthwhile proportions. There are two contemporary versions of the story. According to one, Laws not only greatly lowered railway charges, but also arranged for fishermen on the east coast to stabilise their prices, regardless of the size of catches, and for a stand to be opened in Manchester at which cod could be retailed more cheaply.[26] An alternative version limits the railway company's role to a reduction of their rates of carriage, emphasising particularly the importance of Hull in the traffic.[27] There was agreement, however, on the general effect of Laws's intervention. The price of cod in Manchester, it was claimed, fell from somewhere between 6d and 1s per lb to 1½d–2d per lb; naturally, consumption rose, and the amount of fish carried by the railway jumped from 3½ tons to 80 tons a week.

This was just the sort of prodigious tale of a railway's impact that enthusiasts required as ammunition in their cause, but there are some curious features in the story. In the first place, the pre-railway price of cod was almost certainly overstated; in 1825, for example, it was on sale at 3d–5d per lb. Moreover, prices are unlikely to have fallen to the level suggested; in the late 1840s and early 1850s cod was being sold at 2½d–3d per lb.[28] Likewise, the claim that 80 tons of fish were carried each week is at odds with figures provided several years later. In a three-month period in 1848 the Lancashire and Yorkshire Railway, as the Manchester and Leeds had now become, received an average of 182 'parcels' of fish each working day at the Victoria Station in Manchester. The size of these 'parcels' or packages varied a good deal,

[24] PRO, RAIL 371/8, 21 Dec. 1831; 25 Jan. 1832. Special precautions had to be taken against theft, a status that oysters shared with oranges (above, pp. 123–4).

[25] J.B. Williams, 'On the principles of railway management', *JSSL*, IX, 1846, p. 132.

[26] Hansard, *Parliamentary Debates*, 3rd ser., LXXVIII, col. 1214, 20 Mar. 1845 (J. Morrison). The story also appears in S. Salt, *Statistics and Calculations essentially necessary to Persons connected with Railways or Canals*, Manchester, 1845, p. 97.

[27] Williams, 'Railway management', p. 132.

[28] Above, note 17; *Guardian*, 24 Apr. 1847, letter to editor on 'The price of fish'.

but seems to have ranged from about 40 lb to 1 cwt, in which case the Lancashire and Yorkshire's traffic could not have amounted to more than 55 tons a week, and probably less.[29] Laws himself was uncharacteristically reticent about the subject when interrogated by a select committee on another railway line in which his company had an interest. There was a detectable hint of embarrassment about the way the story had grown in his one-word answer, 'Yes', when clearly rather more had been expected in reply to the leading question whether he had made 'such arrangements as to bring fish down to 2*d* a pound in Manchester and the places around'.[30] Perhaps the exaggerations are explained by the fact that the railway company was connected for a short time with a Flamborough Head and Filey Bay Fish Company that folk memory could recall being established some time in the 1840s with the intention of supplying 'the middling and poorer classes . . . at a cheap rate', and which met with some brief success before commercial pressures took their toll.[31]

That experiment was not one which the railway company was anxious to repeat. A few years later, in 1848, a suggestion that it should actively participate in building up the fishing industry at Fleetwood was declined. Every facility would be offered in the transport of fish, but there was to be no financial commitment.[32] Yet the Lancashire and Yorkshire never lost its faith that the fish traffic was worth developing, and in 1855 it responded in such a spirit to soundings from Manchester Council about the possibility of providing facilities at the Victoria Station for fish wholesalers. The company's motives were not totally altruistic, since it was hoped that, for a modest outlay, a competitive edge could be secured in the carriage of fish to and from the new market. For the Council, the railway's offer provided a welcome solution to the problem of having to provide its own facilities for fish salesmen. Thus, amid self-congratulation on both sides at the favourable terms of the agreement, the first wholesale

[29] PRO, RAIL 343/493, 30 Sept. 1848. S. Salt suggests an average of *c.* 40 lb (*Facts and Figures, principally relating to Railways and Commerce*, London, 1848, p. 101), but this seems to be on the low side (see Stern, 'Fish supply to Billingsgate', p. 46).

[30] HLRO, Mins. of Evidence, HC, 1844, XXVII, Manchester, Bury, and Rossendale and Manchester and Leeds Railway (Bury Branch) Bill, 28 Mar., pp. 83–4.

[31] *Guardian*, 24 Apr. 1847. The writer of a letter on 'The price of fish' remembered it as 'The Robin Hood's Bay and Filey Fish Company'; see also H.G. Duffield, *The Stranger's Guide to Manchester*, Manchester, 1850, pp. 59–60.

[32] PRO, RAIL 343/493, 30 Aug. 1848.

fish market was opened on railway property in 1856.[33]

At that time, it was said, most of Manchester's fish supply came to the Victoria Station,[34] and the bulk of it was brought by the Lancashire and Yorkshire Railway. The prominence of this company in the fish trade might seem curious, since it had no direct access to the north-east coast, from which Manchester derived the greater part of its supplies. However, this was not so great a disadvantage as it might seem. The coast of north Yorkshire and south Durham was well served by early railways, and a traffic in fish soon developed. By 1840–41 lines that were later to form the North Eastern Railway were transporting fish from Whitby and Hartlepool, and arrangements were made to carry it westwards to Leeds and Manchester.[35] The link with the Lancashire and Yorkshire network was a convenient one, and in 1852 fish transferred on to the line from the north-east accounted for almost half the company's total receipts from this traffic.[36] Thus, the first impact of the railway was to reinforce Manchester's links with this coast. Admittedly, villages like Staithes, which did not have a direct rail link, struggled to maintain their former position, but at ports such as Filey and Scarborough the fishing industry prospered.[37] However, the 1850s and 1860s were to witness important changes in the traditional relationship.

The advent of the railway enormously extended the range of markets open to these fishing ports. Places such as Nottingham, Derby, Birmingham and even London were now within reach and able to compete with northern towns for supplies.[38] On the other hand, the railways gave northern towns access to alternative sources of supply. In the first place, the 1850s saw the growth of Hull as a fishing port. Trawling had become established there in the middle of the previous decade, soon after the discovery of new fishing grounds, known as the

[33] PRO, RAIL 343/503, 4 Sept. 1855; RAIL 343/505, 23 Jan. 1856; MC, *Proceedings*, 22 Oct. 1856.

[34] MC, *Proceedings*, 26 Oct. 1870, report in which the background to the decision of 1855–56 was described.

[35] See W.W. Tomlinson, *The North-Eastern Railway*, 2nd edn., Newton Abbot, 1967, pp. 301, 363–4, 461, 473; also K. Hoole, *A Regional History of the Railways of Great Britain*, IV, *North East England*, Dawlish, 1965, pp. 16–17, 24, 56, 58, 66, 149–51.

[36] The main junction between the two systems was at Normanton, and receipts for the carriage of fish from Normanton and 'stations beyond' amounted to 48 per cent of the total (PRO, RAIL 343/497, 2 Nov. 1852). A small amount of this would have come from Hull (see Table 6.2).

[37] PP 1866, XVIII, *Report . . . into the Sea Fisheries*, II, Mins. of Evidence, pp. 122, 132, 146, 1344, 1348–9.

[38] *Ibid.*, pp. 104, 127, 132–3, 146.

Great Silver Pits, at the south-western end of the Dogger Bank, but until the early 1850s the amounts landed remained relatively small.[39] From then on, however, the volume increased rapidly, reaching over 4,600 tons by 1855 and establishing Hull as the major fishing port on the north-east coast. Within ten years the tonnage landed had doubled, and the quantities transported to inland towns – to Manchester, mainly via the North Eastern Railway's connection with the Lancashire and Yorkshire network – were beginning to approach the combined contributions of all the other ports on the north-east coast.[40]

Hull was one new source of supply; of even greater significance was Grimsby. In time, Grimsby would become Manchester's largest single supplier of fish, and this implied a direct challenge to the Lancashire and Yorkshire Company's supremacy in the town's fish traffic. While the Manchester, Sheffield, and Lincolnshire Company was also involved in the carriage of fish from Hull,[41] in due course it became more interested in developing the fishing industry at the rival port of Grimsby. In 1852 this company undertook to build a special fish dock there and, even before construction began, made a further decision to become still more actively involved. Accordingly, it established and provided most of the capital for a Deep Sea Fishing Company, to be run in conjunction with the other two railway companies which used the port as minor partners.[42] In 1854 the fishing company started operations, beginning with nine boats, and in 1856 the fish dock was completed.[43] In the meantime, shareholders were confidently informed that the company was hoping to derive 'a new and important source of traffic' from this initiative.[44] Success, however, was not immediate. In 1858 Edward Watkin, the general manager of the Manchester, Sheffield, and Lincolnshire, was obliged to reaffirm his faith that their heavy investment in the Grimsby fishing industry would pay off 'ultimately'.[45] His optimism, as it turned out, was

[39] W.H. Chaloner, 'Trends in fish consumption', in T.C. Barker, J.C. McKenzie and J. Yudkin (eds.), *Our Changing Fare*, London, 1966, p. 106; J.M. Bellamy, 'Some aspects of the economy of Hull in the nineteenth century with special reference to business history', University of Hull, Ph.D., 1965, II, Appendix IV, p. 1.

[40] *PP* 1866, XVII, *Report . . . into the Sea Fisheries*, I, Report, Appendix No. 6, p. 12; *PP* 1866, XVIII, *Report . . . into the Sea Fisheries*, II, Mins. of Evidence, pp. 157, 177.

[41] *PP* 1866, XVII, *Report . . . into the Sea Fisheries*, I, Report, Appendix No. 7, p. 12.

[42] PRO, RAIL 463/2, 18 Mar. 1852; 28 Apr., 21 June, 10 Nov. 1854.

[43] G. Dow, *Great Central*, London, 1959, I, pp. 175–6.

[44] PRO, RAIL 463/2, 2 Feb. 1855.

[45] HLRO, Mins. of Evidence, HL, 1858, VI, Manchester, Sheffield, and Lincolnshire and Great Northern Railway Companies Bill, 5 July, p. 272.

justified. In 1860, for the first time, over 1,000 tons of fish were forwarded from Grimsby via the Manchester, Sheffield, and Lincolnshire, and from that point onwards the growth of its traffic was rapid, with a fivefold increase by 1864. As a result, the existing facilities came under pressure, and the railway company was constantly being urged to extend the accommodation at the fish dock.[46]

The East Anglian ports of Yarmouth and Lowestoft were two further sources of supply that the Manchester, Sheffield, and Lincolnshire Railway was instrumental in opening up for Manchester. There, the mainstay of fishing was traditionally herrings and, to a lesser extent, mackerel; most of the former were still sold for curing, and the established market for both was London.[47] In 1847 over seven times as much fish was being sent to London from Yarmouth as to the rest of the country altogether, and in the early 1850s the great bulk of the catches was still destined for the fish curers.[48] Even with the spread of the railway system, the circuitous route from these ports to Lancashire meant that it was not feasible to send fresh fish in quantity, and the only traffic of any size in that direction was one in salted herrings to Liverpool, where they were cured for the export market.[49] In 1857, however, the Manchester, Sheffield, and Lincolnshire entered into a close working alliance with the Great Northern Railway and, through that company's earlier links with the Eastern Counties line, was able to offer a much improved service to the north-west.[50] As Watkin pointed out, the length of the journey would always be a problem and, in his view, Manchester was the limit as far as fresh fish was concerned. Nevertheless, the company clearly saw this as a traffic worth developing. Special trains were despatched overnight from Yarmouth to the manufacturing districts, and the fish was delivered there by eight o'clock the next morning.[51] As a result, the 1860s saw a

[46] PP 1866, XVII, *Report . . . into the Sea Fisheries*, I, Report, Appendix No. 7, p. 12; PRO, RAIL 463/7, 23 Sept. 1864; RAIL 463/8, 27 Oct., 24 Nov. 1865; RAIL 463/9, 25 July 1866.

[47] PP 1833, XIV, *Select Committee on British Channel Fisheries*, Mins. of Evidence, p. 132; G. Dodd, *The Food of London*, London, 1856, pp. 343–4.

[48] Salt, *Facts and Figures*, p. 101; B. Poole, *Statistics of British Commerce*, London, 1852, p. 185.

[49] HLRO, Mins. of Evidence, HC, 1858, XLIV, Manchester, Sheffield, and Lincolnshire and Great Northern Railway Companies Bill, 22 Apr., p. 81; Mins. of Evidence, HL, 1858, VI, Manchester, Sheffield, and Lincolnshire and Great Northern Railway Companies Bill, 5 July, pp. 87, 89–90; 7 July, p. 209.

[50] C.H. Grinling, *The History of the Great Northern Railway, 1845–1922*, revised edn., London, 1966, pp. 161–4, 109–10.

[51] HLRO, Mins. of Evidence, HL, 1858, VI, Manchester, Sheffield, and Lincolnshire and Great Northern Railway Companies Bill, 5 July, pp. 88, 272; Mins. of Evidence, HC, 1858,

considerable expansion in the conveyance of fresh mackerel and herrings from these east-coast ports to markets other than London. In
1866 'vast quantities' of fresh herrings, when in season, were reported
as being distributed from Lowestoft to the manufacturing towns, with
Birmingham and Manchester taking the largest share.[52]

In comparison with the east coast, supplies from the north-west
were still of comparatively minor importance. Ironically, the position
of the Lancashire and Yorkshire Company was potentially stronger
here, for it had a number of direct links with the sea. In 1852 the most
lucrative traffic was that from Liverpool[53] and, although it was a
rather specialised one, consisting largely of herrings and salmon, it
was sufficiently profitable to attract the attention of competitors.
Further north, the company was well placed, by virtue of amalgamations and working arrangements, to take advantage of the establishment of Fleetwood. This town was the brainchild of Peter Hesketh
Fleetwood and building only began in 1836. The founding fathers
concentrated on developing its function as a port for the Irish traffic,
and fishing seemed of little consequence.[54] However, the early provision of a rail link had been enough to seduce a number of trawlers
away from Southport, and by the mid-1840s fish was being sent south,
some of it to Manchester.[55] The great days of Fleetwood as the leading
fishing port on the west coast lay some years in the future, for it was
not until the 1890s, with the advent of steam-trawlers, that fishing
became a major industry in the town.[56] Even so, by 1864 it was able to
send inland almost 1,000 tons of fish. Not all of this was directed to
Manchester, but Fleetwood was contributing more than any other
port on that coastline. The white fish that was landed at
Blackpool,Lytham and Southport was little more than was consumed
locally by the growing number of residents and visitors, and only a

---

XLIV, Manchester, Sheffield, and Lincolnshire and Great Northern Railway Companies Bill, 22
Apr., p. 86.

[52] PP 1866, XVII, *Report . . . into the Sea Fisheries*, I, Report, pp. xi–xii.

[53] PRO, RAIL 343/497, 2 Nov. 1852.

[54] For the growth of Fleetwood, see J. Marshall, *The Lancashire and Yorkshire Railway*,
Newton Abbot, 1969, I, pp. 81–3; also J.H. Sutton, 'Early Fleetwood, 1835–1847', University of
Lancaster, M.Litt., 1968, esp. pp. 60–4.

[55] PP 1866, XVIII, *Report . . . into the Sea Fisheries*, II, Mins. of Evidence, p. 1219. Sutton,
thesis, p. 273; PRO, RAIL 458/15, 20 Aug. 1846, item 13; 12 Jan. 1847, item 17; Williams,
'Railway management', p. 132.

[56] Sutton, thesis, pp. 273–4; W.E. Bear, 'The food supply of Manchester, II, animal produce',
JRASE, 3rd ser., VIII, 1897, p. 514.

small amount was left over to be despatched by rail.[57]

A more important commodity from the Lancashire coast was shellfish. Shrimps and other shellfish abounded in the shallow waters of the Mersey estuary and off the shore of south-west Lancashire, and ready supplies of these were a more feasible proposition as transport facilities improved. Moreover, once Manchester had been linked by rail with Morecambe, by the late 1840s, the town gained improved access to some of the richest shellfish grounds in the country.[58] At the point of consumption, a distinction was drawn between the lobsters and crabs supplied for the better-off, and the cockles, winkles and mussels, described by the *Guardian* as 'vulgar but not unwholesome dainties', with oysters and shrimps perhaps occupying the middle ground.[59] That this trade was increasingly buoyant is suggested by the fact that the number of boats employed in shrimp fishing alone in Morecambe Bay rose from eight or nine in 1820 to 150 by the close of the period.[60] Most of the shellfish caught was sent inland by rail to Manchester and other Lancashire towns and, though subject to considerable fluctuations, in good years in the 1850s and 1860s amounted to over 1,500 tons.[61]

This traffic, it should be noted, was one in which the London and North Western Railway played a significant role by virtue of its connection with Morecambe, and the company's challenge to the dominance of the Lancashire and Yorkshire was destined to grow. With its far-flung tentacles, it was able to bring to Manchester a not inconsiderable tonnage, albeit rather limited in variety. In addition to shellfish and herrings from the Lancashire coast, it conveyed salmon from both Ireland and Scotland.[62] Even at the height of a period of self-doubt in the mid-1860s, the London and North Western appears to have handled annually over 3,000 tons of fish and poultry at the Victoria Station in Manchester. Furthermore, its efforts to increase this traffic must have met with some success, for it was encouraged to

[57] PP 1866, XVII, *Report . . . into the Sea Fisheries*, I, Report, Appendix No. 25, p. 19; T. Baines, *Lancashire and Cheshire, Past and Present*, London, 1867, I, p. 30.

[58] See E.F. Carter, *An Historical Geography of the Railways of the British Isles*, London, 1959, pp. 74, 132; G.O. Holt, *A Regional History of the Railways of Great Britain*, X, *The North West*, Newton Abbot, 1978, p. 231.

[59] *Guardian*, 26 Jan. 1850. See also advertisements of John Walker (*ibid.*, 4, 11 Jan. 1823); Mayhew, *London Labour*, I, pp. 63, 78.

[60] Baines, *Lancashire and Cheshire*, I, p. 28.

[61] Poole, *Statistics*, p. 75; PP 1866, XVII, *Report . . . into the Sea Fisheries*, I, Report, Appendix No. 23, p. 19.

[62] PRO, RAIL 410/172, 14 Apr. 1864; RAIL 410/516, 3 Apr. 1867; RAIL 410/175, 18 Mar. 1869.

invest over £2,000 in building special accommodation for the fish trade at its goods depot at Ordsall Lane in Salford.[63] By the late 1870s its immediate objective of competing more effectively for the Liverpool traffic had certainly been achieved, in that it was carrying five times as much fish out of that port as its chief rival, the Lancashire and Yorkshire line.[64]

A symbolic, if somewhat belated, recognition of the end of the Lancashire and Yorkshire's reign as Manchester's main supplier of fish came in 1870 with the decision to move the wholesale fish market away from the Victoria Station. The original argument that a close link with the Lancashire and Yorkshire would be advantageous to the trade was no longer valid, and a central site in the main market area was thought to be more convenient for all parties concerned. This company's former position of pre-eminence had clearly waned. On the west coast it had to meet the competition of the London and North Western, but on the east coast it had suffered even more. There, the focus of the supply of fish to Manchester had, in effect, moved southwards, and in so doing had enabled the Manchester, Sheffield, and Lincolnshire to become the town's major carrier of this commodity. By 1870 it was estimated that this line was bringing all the Yarmouth and Lowestoft traffic and half the rest of Manchester's fish supply to the town.[65]

The shifting configuration of Manchester's sources of fish supply in these years can best be appreciated with the aid of Tables 6.1 and 6.2. These bring together, in a systematic way, all available figures relating to, respectively, the tonnages of fish forwarded by rail from certain ports of special relevance to Manchester, and those carried by the different companies. Obviously, the evidence is imperfect and not very well adapted to our purposes. In the first place, the early returns from the ports (Table 6.1) are suspiciously incomplete. For example, the suggestion that no fish whatsoever was conveyed by rail from Liverpool prior to the 1870s is erroneous.[66] Secondly, Table 6.2 gives a misleading impression of the importance of particular railway companies in supplying Manchester. The series for the Manchester, Sheffield, and Lincolnshire does not include tonnages originating from

[63] PRO, RAIL 410/173, 19 Oct. 1865; RAIL 410/175, 18 Nov. 1869.

[64] PP 1882, LXIV, *Return of the Quantity of Fish conveyed inland by Railway from each of the principal Fishing Ports of England and Wales, Scotland and Ireland, for each year since 1878*, pp. 3–4.

[65] MC, *Proceedings*, 26 Oct. 1870.

[66] Above, p. 136, and note 53.

Table 6.1 Quantities of fish forwarded by railway from selected fishing ports, 1852–81
(figures in tons)

Year	(1) Morecambe(a)	(2) Blackpool, Lytham	(3) Fleetwood	(4) Liverpool	(5) Filey, Scarborough, Whitby, Hartlepool	(6) Hull	(7) Grimsby(b) (i)	(ii)	Total 2–7(i)
1852	–	–	–	–	–	612(c)	–	–	612
1853	–	–	–	–	1,832	1,213(c)	–	–	3,045
1854	567	–	–	–	3,189	1,586	–	–	4,775
1855	1,541	–	–	–	3,869	4,049	–	188	7,918
1856	1,322	–	–	–	3,515	4,717	1,514	152	9,746
1857	1,198	–	–	–	4,495	5,035	3,435	346	12,965
1858	1,087	–	–	–	6,089	4,945	4,344	594	15,378
1859	825	80	–	–	9,108	5,162	4,742	955	19,092
1860	814	30	–	–	7,285	7,270	4,842	1,247	19,427
1861	576	125	–	–	12,164	7,268	5,371	1,907	24,928
1862	1,993	66	604	–	12,523	7,579	8,521	3,251	29,293
1863	1,764	49	837	–	11,363	7,039	9,408	4,187	28,696
1864	1,531	20	983	–	11,360	8,876	11,198	5,855	32,437
1878	–	–	–	–	–	26,938	69,407	44,782	–
1879	1,577	55	2,225	5,265	15,168	26,100	–	48,924	–
1880	702	185	2,177	5,304	15,821	20,562	–	42,730	–
1881	1,382	56	2,086	5,453	14,826	22,071	–	49,583	–

Notes
(a) Largely shellfish.
(b) (i) Total (ii) Tonnages carried by the Manchester, Sheffield, and Lincolnshire.
(c) 1852–53 figures for Hull are tonnages landed within docks.

Sources PP 1866, XVII, *Report of the Commissioners . . . into the Sea Fisheries of the United Kingdom*, I, Report, Appendices Nos. 4, 6, 7, 8, 23, 25, pp. 11–19; PP 1878–9, LXV, *Return of the Quantity of Fish conveyed inland by Railway from each of the principal Fishing Ports of England and Wales in the year 1878*, pp. 1–2; PP 1882, LXIV, *Return of the Quantity of Fish conveyed inland by Railway from each of the principal Fishing Ports of England and Wales, Scotland and Ireland, for each year since 1878*, pp. 3–7.

Table 6.2 *Quantities of fish carried by selected railways, 1856–81*
(figures in tons)

Year	North Eastern[a]	Great Northern[b]	Manchester, Sheffield, and Lincolnshire[c]	London and North Western[d]	Lancashire and Yorkshire[e]
1856	8,153	1,362	947	–	–
1857	9,704	3,089	1,300	–	–
1858	14,272	3,750	1,936	–	–
1859	18,887	3,787	2,375	–	–
1860	18,715	3,595	2,982	–	–
1861	23,405	3,464	3,511	–	–
1862	23,017	5,270	5,430	–	–
1863	23,510	5,221	6,300	–	–
1864	23,470	5,343	8,494	–	–
1878	47,458	14,625	46,820	–	2,214
1879	50,837	–	51,075	15,286	1,242
1880	46,855	–	44,991	14,934	2,078
1881	48,870	–	51,509	12,764	1,582

Notes

(a) Serving north-east coast and Hull.

(b) Serving Grimsby.

(c) Serving mainly Grimsby but also Hull.

(d) Serving mainly Lancashire and north Wales coast.

(e) Serving Liverpool, Southport and Formby.

Sources As Table 6.1.

Yarmouth and Lowestoft, which started their journeys on other lines. Similarly, the nil returns for the Lancashire and Yorkshire in 1856–64 reflect the fact that it had no direct access to the east coast and could not, therefore, be the initial consignor – this was, of course, the North Eastern, which does feature strongly in Table 6.2. Thirdly, and most importantly, supplies despatched from these ports or carried by these railways were not necessarily destined for Manchester.

Despite this formidable catalogue of difficulties, the tables in no way contradict and, at some points, actually confirm what has been said so far. For example, Table 6.1 underscores the early importance of the north-east coast. When supplies from that quarter are combined with those from Hull from the mid-1850s, the tonnages involved dwarf not only the amounts recorded in the table as forwarded from the north-west, but anything that could reasonably have been expected only a few years before. Both tables also reflect the rapid growth of Grimsby in the late 1850s. However, it was not until the 1860s that the full impact of this port was felt in Manchester; for it was from 1862 that the Manchester, Sheffield, and Lincolnshire Company began to capture an increasing share of the traffic. By the late 1870s both the port and the railway were moving ahead of their rivals. Indeed, the significance of the Humber ports in the round would be difficult to overestimate in any assessment of the fish supply to Manchester, or perhaps to any northern town. In 1852 negligible amounts were landed there; within a decade, the tonnages sent inland represented over half the total quantity of fish carried by these northern railways; within a generation, to judge from the 1879 figures, the proportion had risen to three-quarters.

One further point can be made from Table 6.1. While it is evident that the fish trade made a noticeable surge forward after 1850, and although the rates of growth in those early years might seem impressive, when we remember that Manchester was but one of many towns deriving fish from these sources, the absolute tonnages remained quite small. Moreover, it follows that the real trans-formation, at least in quantitative terms, occurred in the last ten to fifteen years of the period considered here. And if it is correct to lay special emphasis on the late 1850s and the 1860s in this way, then it appears that neither the advent of the railways nor the discovery of new fishing grounds were sufficient in themselves to produce a great increase in the supply of fish to provincial towns. Of course, the changes could not have taken place without them, but there must have been other contributory factors. Apart from the likely impact of rising real incomes, two developments on the supply side appear to have been particularly important. One was a marked improvement in the distribution systems of the supplies at their inland destinations. The comment that 'the most abundant supply [of fish] may to a great extent be rendered useless so far as the internal provision of the country is concerned unless proper means are employed to regulate its distribution and arrangement', was as true in the 1850s and 1860s as when it was made in 1800,[67] and this matter will be taken up in Chapter VIII. The other factor was the increased use of ice.

As we have seen, ice had long been used to preserve fish once landed, but it was not until about 1860 that it became commonly used on

[67] PP 1801, II, *Second Report from the Select Committee appointed to consider of the Present High Price of Provisions*, p. 7. The committee reported in 1800.

boats at sea. There had been no technological breakthrough in the manufacture of ice, and the industry was still dependent on supplies from the British winter, stored in ice-houses, or those imported from colder climates.[68] Hence, its increased use in these decades makes sense only when considered alongside the factors already discussed. Quite simply, it became more worthwhile to expend effort and money on keeping fish in good condition. It was, however, a particularly important development because so much of the expansion of the fishing industry took the form of the spread of trawling, with its consequent catches of dead fish. Increasingly, fast cutters were collecting the catches from the trawlers and packing them in ice for the journey back to port.[69] Once landed, the dead fish could be rushed inland by railway, but it was crucial that they should at least begin their journey from the ports in good condition. Thus, the provision of ice for this purpose became a key part of the fishing industry. One of the basic facilities provided by the Manchester, Sheffield, and Lincolnshire Company at Grimsby had been an ice-house, but it soon proved inadequate, and various ways of extending its capacity had to be explored.[70] At Hull, the expansion of trawling in the 1860s went hand in hand with the formation of ice companies.[71] Cutting has even gone so far as to contend: 'The phenomenal increase in the landings of white fish in the third quarter of the century consequent upon the use of ice, completely altered its status from that of a food for the rich to that of a food for the poor.'[72]

iii. Price data and their social implications, 1850–70

Whether the impact was quite so dramatic as Cutting believes is something that can be explored through the study of price movements in the closing decades of the period. Certainly, there was a considerable widening in the range of varieties available, as is evident from the retail price information quoted in the 'Housewife's Corner' report, which appeared from 1850 onwards in the *Courier*.[73] As well as

[68] Writers in the trade, looking back at its history, emphasised these years for this aspect (*The Fish Trades Gazette*, 15 Mar. 1884; 16 Oct. 1920). See also J.H. Clapham, *An Economic History of Modern Britain*, Cambridge, 1932, II, pp. 73, 90–1.

[69] Dodd, *Food of London*, p. 354; Baines, *Lancashire and Cheshire*, I, p. 29.

[70] Dow, *Great Central*, I, p. 176; PRO, RAIL 463/6, 13 Dec. 1861; 7 Nov. 1862.

[71] Bellamy, thesis, I, p. 297.

[72] Cutting, *Fish Saving*, p. 238.

[73] See Chapter IV, note 78.

salmon, trout and one or two other freshwater fish, the report often listed a dozen different varieties of sea fish, over twice the number mentioned by Aikin half a century before. Three price series have been chosen for detailed study: cod, as an example of 'prime' fish, somewhere in the middle ranges; plaice, as probably the most important sort of 'offal', the bulk of which had been thrown overboard before the 1840s; and, in the absence of any prices for fresh herrings, mackerel, as an example of shoal fish, which tended to be caught in large quantities at particular times of the year. Unfortunately, there are only a few price references for mackerel before 1856. Figure 6.1 follows the pattern established in earlier chapters and expresses the annual averages of the weekly minimum prices quoted for each of the three fish over the years 1850–70, in index form, on the base 1851–56 = 100; the seven-year moving averages of these indices; and year-to-year variations in the (national) Rousseaux price index of animal products, also on the base 1851–56 = 100, included for comparative purposes.[74]

At the outset, it can be seen that the general movement of prices of the different fish, as expressed by the seven-year moving averages, did not follow a uniform pattern. From 1851 the price of plaice was moving upwards, initially in line with the Rousseaux index, but leaving that far behind after the mid-1850s as it rose to a peak in 1861. Cod prices were at first relatively stable, but they, too, moved upwards after the mid-1850s to reach a peak in 1860-61, a trend mirrored by movements in the price of mackerel. Clearly, demand was outstripping even the substantial increases in supply in these years, and the signs of quickening activity on the part of those involved in the industry are understandable as a response to the growing market for fish among Mancunians. During the early 1860s, however, the paths of the different prices diverged. Both plaice and mackerel fell relatively in price; for plaice, the fall was to a level similar to that of twenty years before, and below the yardstick provided by the Rousseaux index. The price of cod, on the other hand, after a temporary halt, began to rise again, so that at the end of the decade it was over 50 per cent more expensive than in the early 1850s.

That the prices of different fish should move in such contrary ways in the 1860s belies the impression given by the report of the 1866 parliamentary enquiry into the fishing industry that prices in inland

[74] See Chapter III, note 109.

143

towns had remained generally stable over the previous ten years, in contrast to their doubling in seaside towns as the railways opened up new markets in the interior.[75] In fact, the enquiry's own evidence presented to support the argument and based, as it happens, on prices in Manchester over the years 1856–65 shows that cod was not the only fish to become more expensive: sole, haddock, ray and halibut also cost more at the end of the ten-year period than they did at the beginning. However, the optimism of the official report was not entirely misplaced; as it pointed out, the real gains had been made in the supply of 'the coarser kinds of fish'.[76] No doubt the depression in the cotton industry in the early 1860s played some part in pulling down the prices of those fish most likely to be bought by the working class, but the main part of the explanation seems to lie in the factors on the supply side. For it was precisely in the supplies of fish such as plaice, formerly regarded as 'offal', that Manchester had gained so much from the growth of Hull and especially Grimsby, and the introduction into Manchester market of large quantities of these in the 1860s was reflected in their price levels. Likewise, the improvement in links with Yarmouth and Lowestoft made by the Manchester, Sheffield, and Lincolnshire substantially increased the available quantities of mackerel. On the other hand, 'prime' fish, such as cod, a large proportion of which was still caught live by hook and line, did not benefit from the general expansion of the industry in anything like the same way. Once the demand for fish began to rise, the inelasticity of cod supply, relative to other varieties, would exert an upward pressure on prices through to the end of the period.

The information in the market reports also sheds light on two further aspects of the supply of fish. On the whole, as Figure 6.1 suggests, annual fluctuations in prices were only moderate; indeed, they varied considerably less on average from year to year than those of vegetables over a comparable period.[77] Admittedly, the prices of fish listed in the *Courier* were retail rather than wholesale, and this might have helped smooth out some of the observed variations. But the main factors influencing fluctuations were the relative elasticities of both supply and demand. While we have too little direct evidence on

[75] PP 1866, XVII, *Report . . . into the Sea Fisheries*, I, Report, p. xiii.

[76] *Ibid.*, p. xii.

[77] For the statistical method see, again, R.G.D. Allen, *Statistics for Economists*, 2nd edn., London, 1951, pp. 143–4. The mean annual deviation from the trend over 1854–67 was: cod, 5.4 per cent; plaice, 6.6 per cent; mackerel (for 1859–67), 5.3 per cent. For vegetables, see above, p. 117 and Chapter V, notes 88, 89.

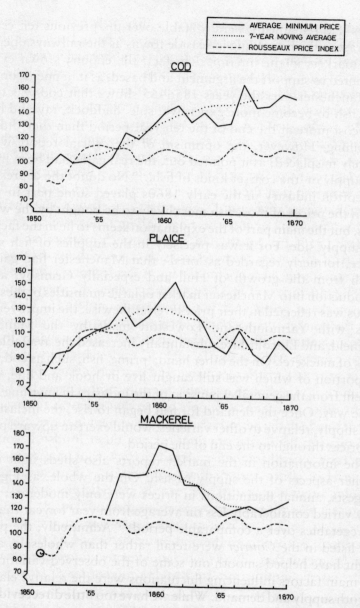

Fig. 6.1 Indices of cod, plaice and mackerel prices in Manchester, 1850–70 (1851–56 = 100)

Source Minimum retail market prices quoted weekly in 'Housewife's Corner' report in *Courier* (see Chapter IV, note 78), reworked to determine annual averages. For the Rousseaux index, see Chapter III, note 109.

the supply side to speculate much further, it is not unreasonable to conclude that this comparative evenness reflected the fact that the demand for fish was very responsive to abnormal price rises. Any tendency for a shortfall in supply to be translated into higher prices was counteracted by a sharp falling-off in demand and a switch to other fish or to different foods. Finding an alternative to plaice, at only 1*d*–2*d* per lb, was not so easy, of course, as choosing one for fish costing two or three times that amount, as did cod and mackerel. Hence, the price of plaice was slightly more volatile, since consumers were less ready, or less able, to look elsewhere. Even so, it might have been expected that the price of a fish such as mackerel would have fluctuated more than it did. In the past, towns like Manchester had received mackerel or fresh herrings only in times of glut. Clearly, by the late 1850s the supply had become much more reliable. Yet the paucity of entries for mackerel in the data source hints that the days of uncertain supply were not far distant. Apart from two short periods in 1851 (7, 14 June and 6, 13 September), when they were undeniably low, mackerel prices were not listed again until 1856. This suggests that the market reports of the early 1850s provide a glimpse of the previous pattern of supply, when mackerel (and probably fresh herrings) came to Manchester in such an unpredictable way that their prices were not worth recording, and that when they did arrive they would be cheap, though available for only a short period of time.[78]

The other aspect of the supply of fish that is worth comment is the extent to which the period saw an improvement in the quality of what was on sale. Perhaps more than for any other foodstuff considered here, taste, as well as income, played an important part in determining the level of consumption. It was sometimes said that there was a popular prejudice against fish, partly on religious grounds, partly because it was alleged to provide an insubstantial meal,[79] but mainly, we suggest, because of well-grounded suspicions that it was likely to be tainted. According to the optimistic views of McCulloch, railway carriage meant that inland towns could expect to receive fish not only in increased quantities but 'fresh and in good order'.[80] However, stray

[78] In passing, it should be noted that the returns of mackerel prices in 1851–56 afford only an unsatisfactory basis for the price movements shown in Figure 6.1. All mackerel prices after 1856 are correspondingly inflated. However, there is nothing that can be done to counteract this.

[79] *A Brief Detail*, pp. 27–8; T. Bernard, 'An account of a supply of fish for the labouring poor with observations', *The Pamphleteer*, I, 1813, p. 440; R.M. Hartwell, 'The rising standard of living in England, 1800–1850', *EcHR*, 2nd ser., XIII, 1961, p. 411.

[80] J.R. McCulloch, *A Descriptive and Statistical Account of the British Empire*, 3rd edn., London, 1847, II, p. 625.

traces of sensitivity on the part of consumers to the quality of what was available can be detected in the seasonal variations in the prices of the different fish as represented in Figure 6.2.[81]

For all three fish, prices were at their lowest during the spring and summer months, though this was especially pronounced for cod and mackerel. As regards mackerel, which was unavailable in the depths of winter, these low prices reflected the highly seasonal nature of the catch. But it is noteworthy that even on a month-by-month examination, there is no evidence of prices plummeting at certain times of the year, as if the market had been overwhelmed by a glut. The system had become too sophisticated for that. However, for cod and plaice, the period of lowest prices was the time when supplies were least plentiful. The heaviest catches of cod, in particular, were in the winter. Quarterly returns of the tonnages of fish forwarded by rail from Hull and Grimsby show a marked drop for the six months from April to September.[82] It is interesting to note that this phenomenon – the lowest prices occurring when supplies were least plentiful – was less pronounced for the cheaper of the two fish. For example, at some point in each summer of the years 1865–69 the price of cod touched a level about 40 per cent below its winter peak; by contrast, the variation for plaice was of the order of 25 per cent. Evidently, consumers in Manchester were wary of purchasing fish in the summer months, being mindful of its natural proclivity to deterioration, which is comparatively rapid even when ice is freely used.[83] The somewhat smaller amplitude of variations observed in the price of plaice cannot be explained by assuming that it arrived in Manchester in better condition than cod in the summer months, since it is not known as a variety that keeps particularly well. Instead, it hints at differing degrees of freedom of choice open to the various income groups. Those buying plaice and other 'offal' fish were less likely, or less able, to worry about any slight deterioration in quality inevitable in the hotter weather; hence, the price of plaice held up rather better than that of cod in the summer months.

To conclude, there is no doubt that, of all the foodstuffs considered

---

[81] Following the method of Allen, *Statistics for Economists*, pp. 144–51.

[82] Stern, 'Fish supply to Billingsgate', pp. 40, 52; PP 1866, XVII, *Report . . . into the Sea Fisheries*, I, Report, Appendix No. 7, p. 12.

[83] C.L. Cutting, 'Fish preservation as a factor in the extension of supply', in Barker and Yudkin (eds.), *Fish in Britain*, p. 24, points out that, for biological reasons, fish in ice will last for only about fourteen to sixteen days, even in favourable conditions, whereas chilled beef from the Argentine can be distributed in edible condition for up to about six weeks after slaughter.

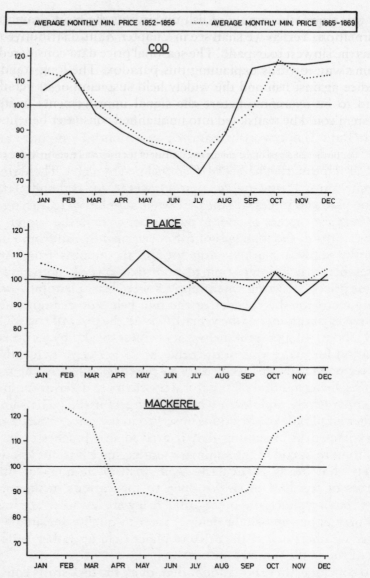

Fig. 6.2 Seasonal variations in cod and plaice prices in Manchester, 1852–56 and 1865–69, and in mackerel prices in Manchester, 1865–69

Source Minimum retail market prices quoted weekly in 'Housewife's Corner' report in *Courier* (see Chapter IV, note 78), reworked to determine monthly averages. Monthly variations are given as ratios to the trend values (= 100) ruling across the two sub-periods chosen for comparison. Note that deliveries of mackerel 1852–56 were too infrequent for quotation.

148

in this study, the supply of fish underwent the most dramatic transformation. Yet, as we shall see in Chapter X, its distributive network was the slowest to expand. The seasonal price data considered here go some way towards explaining this paradox. The long-standing prejudice against fish and the widely held suspicion of its retail trade[84] had to be overcome before the signal improvements in its supply system could be translated into unqualified consumer benefits.

[84] For further evidence of the continuing distrust of the fish retail trade in Manchester, see the correspondence columns of *The Fish Trades Gazette*, 7, 14, 21 July, 1 Sept. 1883.

CHAPTER VII

Market provision, 1770–1870

i. Markets in the manorial era

AT THE BEGINNING of the period, market facilities in the town were already under pressure. The most important location was the traditional Market Place (Plate 4), but lack of space had led to the establishment during the course of the eighteenth century of several smaller and more specialised markets in adjoining streets: for cheese, at Smithy Door and, subsequently, in Hanging Ditch; for potatoes, at Hyde's Cross and, later, in Withy Grove, at the lower end of Shude Hill, where a pig market also made its appearance; for wheat, at the upper end of Market Street Lane; and the fruit or apple market was removed to Fennel Street. Cattle dealing, too, was transferred from the Market Place in 1780 to Hyde's Cross.[1]

These attempts to decentralise and expand the market area were not enough to solve all the problems. In the 1770s the topic of 'the nuisances of the Market Place' found its way into the local newspaper, and in 1783 the author of the town's guidebook remarked on the way in which stalls spread up Smithy Door and beyond into Market Street (Plates 5 and 6), causing the whole district to be filled with 'perpetual throngs'.[2] At the heart of the problem, according to critics, lay a curious and outdated anomaly. Among the many peculiarities of local government in Manchester, touched on in Chapter II, was the fact that its markets were controlled by the Lord of the Manor, a situation that persisted for several years even after the incorporation of the borough in 1838. Manorial rights had been purchased by the Mosley family –

---

[1] MTH, M1/57, History and Situation of the Markets; *Court Leet*, VIII, pp. 125, 212; Redford, I, p. 147.

[2] *Mercury*, 3 Jan. 1775; J. Ogden, *A Description of Manchester by a Native of the Town*, Manchester, 1783, pp. 69–71.

whose seat was at distant Rolleston in Staffordshire – as long ago as 1596, and in the late eighteenth century included: the ownership of markets; the right to regulate them and appoint the various sites where they could be held; the levying of tolls and stallage; and the power to prohibit the selling of goods outside the appropriate market.[3] It is hardly surprising to find these rights facing challenges of one kind or another, to which the Mosleys' responses were mixed. As we shall see, some attempts were made to accommodate the town's needs, but the first priority of the Mosleys was to defend themselves against any erosion of their legal rights.

For example, in 1766 the inhabitants of Salford petitioned for a market of their own on the grounds that facilities in Manchester were insufficient for the increase in population and that a general market in Salford, held on Wednesdays, would be a valuable supplement to those already in existence. A Commission of Inquiry was set up to examine the case for and against and found in favour of the Salford petitioners. However, Sir John Mosley successfully argued for the case to be reopened on the technicality that proper notice had not been given to him of the date and place of the Commission's sitting. This time he was better prepared. A host of affidavits was presented arguing that such a market was not needed and, if it were to be built, the revenue of the Lord of the Manor would inevitably decline, as would the takings of shops located near the existing market sites. Under this bombardment of evidence, the original decision was reversed and Mosley's monopoly was allowed to continue.[4] Another head-on challenge came when two local worthies bought and drained some land off Market Street and erected stalls there, to open as Poolfold Market in July 1781. The ensuing case of *Mosley* v. *Chadwick and Ackers* was argued at length before the King's Bench in 1782, the defendants' case resting on the definition and extent of the manorial rights and the shortage of accommodation. When the Chief Justice, Lord Mansfield, finally delivered a verdict, he ruled that the latter argument was legally irrelevant and, basing himself on the certain reduction in Sir John Parker Mosley's income from stall rents and tolls, and on precedents of actions in other towns, he resolved the case

[3] MTH, M1/57, *Sir John Parker Mosley* v. *Thomas Chadwick and Holland Ackers*, 1782; M1/24/2–28, evidence of James Barnes, Peter Oldham, etc.; PRO, DL 9/50/1, affidavit of Samuel Tennant and John Tonge, 19 Dec. 1767; MCL, Broadside f. 1790/11. For a description of the antecedents of trade restrictions in the markets, see G.H. Tupling, 'Lancashire markets in the sixteenth and seventeenth centuries – II', *TLCAS*, LIX, 1947.
[4] PRO, DL 9/50/1, Papers relating to Salford Market Petition, 1766–69.

in Mosley's favour.[5] Poolfold Market was not, however, closed but purchased by Mosley as an 'official' manorial market, and the unfinished work, giving rise to 144 stalls, was completed under his control.[6]

With dissatisfaction running high, a committee was set up in 1786 at a public meeting of the inhabitants 'to enquire into the Tolls which the Lord of the Manor now levies and how far he is entitled to the same'. The initial aim of this committee was to claim exemption from tolls for all the 'burgesses' of Manchester.[7] The case rested on the interpretation of the 1301 Manorial Charter, but the three counsels whose opinions were sought unanimously agreed that the voluminous evidence collected by the committee showed only that within living memory the town's inhabitants had been accustomed to pay market tolls, and this fact alone would overrule whatever the 1301 Charter intended.[8] Naturally, this advice was not well received. One committee member swore that he would never take a legal opinion in any case again; the counsels had merely pocketed their fees without giving the matter any consideration.[9] However, the committee lowered its sights and turned its attention to a more restricted aspect of the market rights, namely, the right of the Lord of the Manor to toll meal and flour kept in warehouses while in transit through Manchester. Here, they were more successful, and two cases were brought and won against Mosley's tollgatherers for trespass.[10] Although this appeared to be a rather minor part of the manorial rights, it touched on a sensitive area; for corn provided the most obvious example of a trade that had traditionally been conducted in the market but was now moving beyond the reach of the manorial officers. Mosley, therefore, was quick to counter-attack and issued a proclamation making it quite clear that, while it might be legal to keep corn and meal in warehouses on their way through Manchester, it was not permissible on market days to sell them, or any other provisions commonly sold in the markets, either from there or from public houses.[11] The point was emphasised when he brought cases against two flour and meal dealers

[5] MTH, M1/57, *Mosley* v. *Chadwick and Ackers*, 1782.
[6] Ogden, *Description of Manchester*, p. 72.
[7] MTH, M1/24/A; MCL, Broadside f. 1786/1; Redford, I, pp. 192–3. 'Burgesses' were defined as 'all inhabitants of burgages in Manchester whether they own or rent houses from others' (MTH, M1/25/1).
[8] MTH, M1/24/189, 190, 191.
[9] MTH, M1/24/131.
[10] MTH, M1/24/112, 166.
[11] MCL, Broadside f. 1790/11.

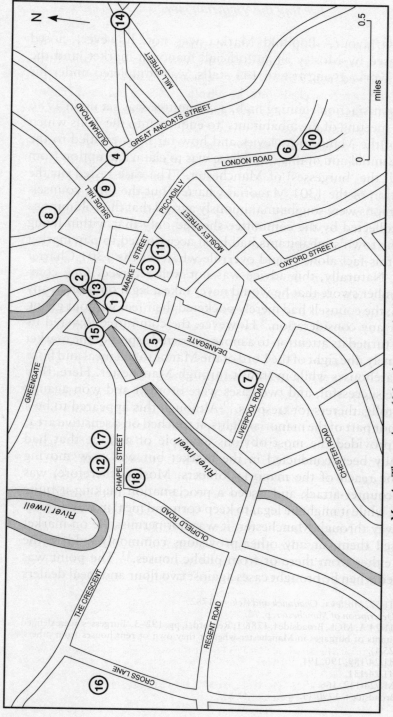

Map 4 The markets of Manchester and Salford, c. 1770–c. 1870

Key: (showing year of opening and closing if appropriate):
1, Market Place including Smithy Door (later called Victoria Market). 2, Fennel Street (1769–1846). 3, Poolfold (1781–1803). 4, New Cross (1802–21). 5, Bridge Street (1803–73). 6, Bank Top (1804–?24). 7, Alport (opens 1804). 8, Miller Street (opens c. 1815). 9, Smithfield (opens 1822). 10, London Road (1824–78). 11, Brown Street (1827–40). 12, Salford Town Hall (1827–48). 13, Fish Market (opens 1828). 14, Bradford Street (c. 1830–46). 15, Salford Trinity (opens c. 1830). 16, Salford Cross Lane (opens 1837). 17, Salford Central (opens 1840). 18, Salford Borough (1848–57).

later in 1790 for exposing flour and oatmeal for sale in a 'private, secret and clandestine way', thus depriving him of his legal tolls. Both cases were resolved in 1791 in Mosley's favour.[12] The committee that had set out so bravely to challenge the whole edifice of manorial rights came to a sad end in July 1792 when each of its members was asked to subscribe £21 to a fund to pay off its debts.[13]

None of this is to suggest that the manorial authorities were completely indifferent to complaints about the markets, and piecemeal adjustments continued, particularly after the death of Sir John Parker Mosley in 1798. Indeed, the early nineteenth century saw unprecedented activity on the part of, or perhaps on behalf of, his youthful successor, Sir Oswald. The year 1803 witnessed the opening of a new shambles in Bridge Street, about a quarter of a mile from the Market Place, though the gain in space was not so great as might have been expected, because the butchers in Poolfold moved over, and Poolfold itself was discontinued.[14] In the following year the potato market was transferred from the congested area at the lower end of Shude Hill to the new St John's Market (better known as Campfield or Alport) in Bridgewater Street. As it turned out, this move was short-lived, because the new market was some 350 yards from the canal wharf, and the farmers' desire to transport their produce just a little further to enjoy the advantages of a more central location was understandable enough.[15] In an effort to keep farmers at Campfield, Mosley instituted several prosecutions for selling potatoes outside the lawful market, but he eventually gave way in July 1809, announcing that the potato market would be re-established at Shude Hill.[16]

Other changes were accomplished with more success and seem to reflect an increasing awareness of the need to provide market facilities outside the immediate vicinity of the town centre. A few shambles were erected at New Cross, by the junction of Great Ancoats Street and Oldham Road, and also at Miller Street, Alport Street and Bank Top.[17] The meal and flour market moved in 1811 from Market Street to a larger building in Nichols's Croft, at the end of the High Street.

[12] MTH, M1/24/169, 199; Redford, I, p. 193.

[13] MTH, M1/24/A.

[14] MTH, M1/25/1, p. 10; J. Aston, *The Manchester Guide*, Manchester, 1804, pp. 264, 266; E. Butterworth, *A Chronological History of Manchester*, Manchester, 1833, p. 18.

[15] W.E.A. Axon (ed.), *The Annals of Manchester*, Manchester, 1886, p. 132; Aston, *Manchester Guide*, pp. 266–7; R.N. Salaman, 'The Oxnoble potato: a study in public house nomenclature', *TLCAS*, LXIV, 1954, p. 77.

[16] MTH, M1/56/1, Broadside, 28 Mar. 1808; M1/56/2, Broadside, 29 July 1809.

[17] MTH, M1/57, History and Situation of the Markets.

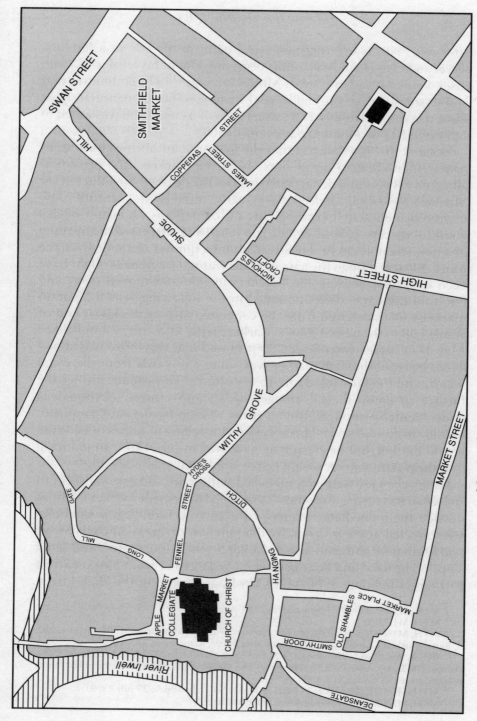

Map 5 The central markets district of Manchester

Here, in what had formerly been a Methodist chapel and was now designated Market House, were also accommodated the assembly-room of the Court Leet and the cheese market, which was moved from Hanging Ditch.[18] Next to migrate was the market for cattle. In 1813 dealers were obliged to move a few hundred yards from Hyde's Cross to the junction of Shude Hill and Swan Street.[19] This new market must have been on the site of what was later to become Smithfield, and the next ten years saw several of the small markets that had grown up in an effort to relieve the congestion of the Market Place coming together in this area. In 1820 the potato market was moved further up Shude Hill to a piece of land that adjoined the cattle market and which had been leased from the Earl of Derby.[20] This entire market site had been levelled and drained by Mosley, who was anxious for it to assume a more general character. Accordingly, the greengrocers and other traders who had collected at the New Cross Shambles were obliged to move into the new market in September 1821. In November the meal and flour market continued on its travels to reach a new warehouse on the site. Officially, the area was given the title of Smithfield Market in May 1822, and it has remained one of the most important markets of Manchester until the present day.[21]

Thus, during the first twenty years of the nineteenth century the markets expanded and changed sites with almost bewildering rapidity, and Mosley appears to have succeeded, for a time, in providing facilities that were more or less adequate. Complaints about overcrowding and poor arrangements ceased to appear in the local newspapers, and it is significant that there was insufficient support for a proposal to purchase the manorial rights from Mosley in 1808. At that time a committee appointed for the purpose at a Town's Meeting came close to an agreement with Mosley, only to founder against the opposition of those who claimed that the exercising of control over the markets by the town could not in itself improve the situation, and that the purchase would entail either more vigorous toll-collection or rising rates: '£70,000 is £70,000, split and divide it as you will'.[22]

[18] MCL, Broadside ff. 1811/2; J. Aston, *Metrical Records of Manchester*, London, 1822, p. 36.

[19] MCL, Broadside ff. 1813/2.

[20] MTH, M1/57, History and Situation of the Markets.

[21] MTH, M1/56/3, Broadside, 21 Aug. 1820; MCL, Broadsides ff. 1821/14; ff. 1821/15; Axon, *Annals*, pp. 162, 165. Smithfield is today Manchester's wholesale fruit and vegetable market.

[22] This episode may be followed through: MTH, M1/21/C; and a series of printed pamphlets in MCL, most notably, C. M'Niven, *An Address to the Inhabitants of Manchester on the*

Plate 4   The Market Place, Manchester, 1823

Plate 5 Smithy Door, looking to Cateaton Street, 1825

Plate 6 Market Street, Manchester, *c.* 1825

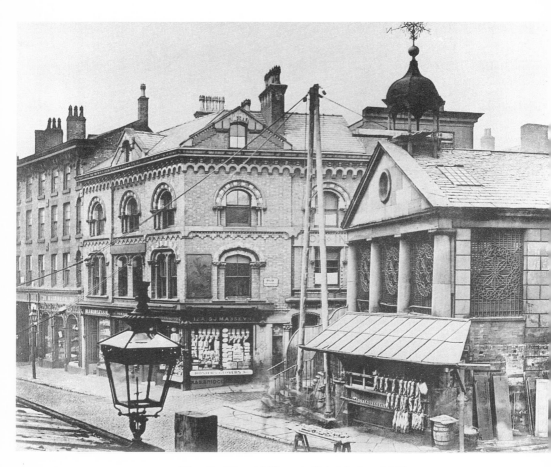

Plate 7   The old Victoria Fish Market, 1860

Plate 8 Smithfield Market, Manchester, 1854

G.R. IV.

Salford Market.

HIS MAJESTY

Having been graciously pleased by His Proclamation, bearing date at Westminster, the Twentieth day of August, One Thousand Eight Hundred and Twenty-five, to declare His Royal Will and Pleasure, that a

MARKET

should be kept, holden, and continued within the Manor and Lordship of Salford, within and upon the Market-Place there, on every

Monday, Wednesday, Thursday, and Saturday,

For the Sale of such Commodities as are usually Bought and Sold in Markets; and furthermore WILLING and COMMANDING that all the Inhabitants of the said Manor and Lordship, and places within or near the same, do repair unto, and frequent the said Market, that the same may be duly kept, frequented, and used as of right, and by the Laws and Statutes of the Realm, the same ought to be kept; and there to Buy, Sell, and Exchange, in as large and ample a manner and form as in any other Market within this realm.

Notice is hereby Given,

That the said Market will be OPENED on SATURDAY, *the 5th day of May next*, and will continue to be there holden on the days above stated, and subject to the Tolls specified in the said Proclamation.

THOMAS HEYWOOD, BOROUGHREEVE.

JOHN RUNCORN, } CONSTABLES.
ISAAC FAULKNER,

THOMAS PEET, CLERK OF THE MARKET.

Police Office, Salford, April 20th, 1827.

PRINTED BY HENRY SMITH, ST. ANN'S-SQUARE.

Plate 9   Broadside announcing the opening of Salford Town Hall Market, 1827

The activity did not come to a total halt with the opening of Smithfield in 1822. Two more markets were established in Manchester, one in London Road in 1824 to serve a more outlying area, the other in Brown Street in 1827 to create extra stalls for butchers. In 1828 the Market Place itself underwent a modest improvement when a fish market was built on the site of the old butchers' shambles, providing covered accommodation for eleven fishmongers (Plate 7).[23] Even so, given that the 1820s were the years of fastest population growth for Manchester and Salford, it is not surprising that long-standing problems re-emerged and, if anything, worsened in this and the ensuing decade. In 1822 Butterworth remarked that the vicinity of the old Market Place was so densely thronged and impassable that he doubted whether women would wish to frequent it,[24] and such issues regularly found their reflection in the proceedings of the Police Commissioners during these years. In their view, the markets did not afford sufficient facility for the disposal of commodities, and two difficulties, in particular, were identified. First, the streets leading to the markets were frequently blocked with porters' and carriers' waggons and carts. The situation had now reached the stage where the Police Commissioners decided in 1826 that it was quite pointless to prosecute offenders.[25] Their general policy seems to have been to turn a blind eye to all but the most blatant obstructions. Nevertheless, complaints continued. An attempt, in 1832, to provide designated stands for carts did little to ease the problem, since vehicles that before had illegally blocked one street now legally blocked another. At the end of the decade a special sub-committee set up specifically to deal with this issue had to admit total failure.[26] The second difficulty was that stalls continued to spill beyond the confines of the appointed sites. In the years 1825–30 the Commissioners ruminated from time to time on the

---

Impolicy of their Purchasing the Manor, Manchester, 1809; J. Aston, *A Reply to Mr M'Niven's 'Address to the Inhabitants of Manchester on the Impolicy of their Purchasing the Manor'*, by *one of the addressed*, Manchester, 1809; F. Philips, *The Murder is Out, or Committee Men Fingering Cash*, Manchester, 1809; Anon., *A Letter to Francis Philips Esq. on his pamphlet entitled 'Murder is Out, etc.'*, *by a native of the parish of Manchester*, Manchester, 1809 (the source of the passage quoted); F. Philips, *Coke upon Lyttleton; or The Rejoinder*, Manchester, 1809.

[23] *Mercury*, 10 Feb. 1824; *Guardian*, 3 Nov. 1827; 20 Dec. 1828.

[24] J. Butterworth, *The Antiquities of the Town, and a Complete History of the Trade of Manchester*, Manchester, 1822, p. 222.

[25] MCLAD, M9/30/1/4, MPC, Mins. of General Committee, 3 Oct. 1821; 8 Feb., 22 Mar. 1826.

[26] *Guardian*, 11 July 1829; MPC, *Fourth Annual Report of Watch, Nuisance and Hackney-Coach Committee*, 1832; *First Annual Report of Hackney-Coach, Porters and Porters' Carts Committee*, 1840.

precise extent of Mosley's market rights, questioning the legality of the use of the surrounding streets for market purposes and of the collecting of tolls from those who traded there, but to little avail.[27] In 1831 it was noted than the manorial officers adhered to no strict bounds and used as much of the streets as was necessary for their purposes. In effect, all idea of limiting the market area had disappeared. The footpaths and carriageways of streets such as Shude Hill, in close proximity to the markets, were cluttered with stalls, many of them occupied, on a daily basis, not by country folk for the disposal of their produce, but by the vendors of 'trifling' articles.[28]

Not surprisingly, this state of affairs was accompanied by renewed criticism of the Lord of the Manor and the way he ran the markets. By this time the corn trade, at least, had slipped beyond the control of the manorial officers and was generally conducted in private warehouses or in the yards of public houses.[29] Indeed, when the Corn Exchange was opened in 1837, what appeared to be a *prima facie* breach of manorial law went unchallenged. But Mosley's powers in other respects remained undiminished, as certain events in the 1820s and 1830s clearly illustrate. Although butchers and fishmongers were forbidden by manorial law to trade outside the market sites in the township of Manchester, in June 1825 John Walker opened a shop for the sale of fish in the Market Place. The affront to the manorial rights could hardly have been more flagrant. Walker had chosen a central position and had persisted in selling fish from his premises despite several warnings from Mosley's solicitor. The case went to law and was heard at the Lancaster Spring Assizes in 1826. Not unexpectedly, in the light of the all-embracing nature of the manorial rights, judgement was given for the Lord of the Manor, but only nominal damages of 1s and costs were awarded against Walker.[30] It was in the sale of meat, however, that Mosley's market rights were being eroded most frequently. At the beginning of the 1820s large numbers of butchers began selling meat outside the markets, but the manorial authorities

[27] MCLAD, M9/30/1/4, MPC, Mins. of General Committee, 13 July 1825; M9/30/1/5, MPC, Mins. of General Committee, 25 July 1827; M9/30/5/1, MPC, Mins. of Watch, Nuisance and Hackney-Coach Committee, 30 Mar. 1829; 8 Mar., 2 Aug. 1830.

[28] MPC, *Third Annual Report of Watch, Nuisance and Hackney-Coach Committee*, 1831; MCLAD, M9/30/4/3, MPC, Mins. of Lamp, Scavenging, Fire-Engine and Nuisance Committee, 23 Sept., 25 Nov. 1835.

[29] MTH, M1/25/3, evidence of tollgatherer, Stock Brown; T. Swindells, *Manchester Streets and Manchester Men*, Manchester, 1906, I, p. 63; J.T. Slugg, *Reminiscences of Manchester Fifty Years Ago*, Manchester, 1881, p. 274.

[30] MTH, M1/50/8, *Sir Oswald Mosley* v. *John Walker*, Brief for Plaintiff, 1826; M1/55/4, 4v.

succeeded in checking the offenders by threatening prosecution.[31] Notwithstanding this intimidation, the practice resumed and by the early 1830s had reached the point where Mosley felt that firm punitive action needed to be taken. In 1832 another major lawsuit began, this time against Jeremiah Hall, a leading butcher in the town. When the case was finally resolved in 1835, once again only nominal damages of 1s were awarded to the Lord of the Manor.[32]

If cases such as these did little to enhance the popularity of the manorial regime, Mosley's attitude to developments in Salford cannot have helped, either. In 1822 the people of Salford again petitioned for their own market on the grounds that it had a large and growing population and, according to the statute book, on Mondays, Wednesdays and Fridays there were no markets nearer than Bolton, Warrington and Stockport respectively.[33] Inevitably, Sir Oswald objected to the petition and complained that the time and place of the Commission of Inquiry set up by the Chancellor of the Duchy of Lancaster to investigate the matter had not been notified to him. In fact, he was obliged to change tactics when it was discovered that Salford had once possessed a market, for the case then became one of the reassertion of ancient right, resulting in the granting of the petition. Mosley immediately made application for the grant of the right to hold the market and, when this strategy failed, objected to the Duchy leasing the rights elsewhere.[34] In the event, his only victory came in opposing the Salford committee's proposal to hold a market on precisely the same days as at Manchester, and even this small triumph was not unqualified. Only three years after the market was opened, in 1827, under the control of the Salford Police Commissioners, the butchers' appeal to the Duchy of Lancaster for exemption from trading restrictions similar to those in Manchester was successful, and the 1830 Salford Improvement Act included a clause to this effect.[35]

Against this background, the situation remained unsatisfactory to all concerned. In 1836 Wheeler spoke for many when he remarked:

[31] MCL, Broadsides ff. 1820/36; ff. 1821/15.

[32] MTH, M1/50/8, *Sir Oswald Mosley* v. *Jeremiah Hall*, Brief for Plaintiff, 1835; PRO, ASSI 55/1, Northern Circuit, Judgement Book, 1810–36, 9 Sept. 1835.

[33] PRO, DL 41/49, Petition to Chancellor of Duchy of Lancaster . . . for a market to be held, 29 July 1822. The argument concerning the proximity of alternative markets was very legalistic because, in practice, Manchester's markets were open every weekday.

[34] PRO, DL 41/49, Mosley to Lord Bexley, 9 July 1823; Mosley to Robert Harper, 23 Nov. 1824.

[35] PRO, DL 41/49, Petition of certain traders . . . in Salford, 28 May 1827; and see 11 Geo. IV, c. 8.

'The markets are not such as a town of great wealth and magnitude might be expected to possess'.[36] Moreover, any marginal improvements were apt to be counterbalanced by new setbacks. In 1839, for example, the Brown Street Market was closed, and its site was occupied by a new central post office; and in 1842 the London Road Market was reduced to a small area of open stalls as a consequence of the extension of the station forming the terminus of the Manchester and Birmingham Railway.[37] For the *Guardian*, the reason why major improvements were unlikely under the existing regime was obvious enough: it could not be expected that 'a gentleman possessing only a life interest in the tolls accruing from this source would, at a necessarily great cost, . . . erect one or more market halls of an extent commensurate with the requirements of the inhabitants'.[38] Meanwhile, for Mosley, the markets must have been becoming more trouble than they were worth. Wheeler suggests that he was not averse to selling his rights to the town even in 1836;[39] after the incorporation of the borough in 1838, this was an increasingly realistic proposition. The annual income from the markets was not inconsiderable, amounting to over £9,000 in the mid-1840s,[40] but Mosley was constantly beset by challenges to his rights. In the circumstances, he must have felt reluctant to spend any more money than was necessary and adopted, instead, a policy of containment by taking a conciliatory line towards regular requests from the Police Commissioners to deal with particularly irksome problems. For example, in 1839 he authorised his steward to accede to an application for the removal of certain stalls deemed specially obstructive in Smithy Door, and the following year agreed to the drawing of a line at the bottom of Shude Hill, beyond which barrels and boxes should not be allowed to stand.[41] But Mosley's concessions would only go so far. In 1841, when the Commissioners took up the case of obstructions occasioned by the placing of stalls on the footpath in Great Ancoats Street, he was reported as being unwilling to give up the right in question and as feeling that his

[36] J. Wheeler, *Manchester: Its Political, Social and Commercial History, Ancient and Modern*, London, 1836, p. 347.

[37] C. Roeder, 'Beginnings of the Manchester post-office', *TLCAS*, XXII, 1904, p. 34; B. Love, *Manchester As It Is*, Manchester, 1839, p. 161; T.W. Freeman, *The Conurbations of Great Britain*, 2nd edn., Manchester, 1966, p. 134.

[38] *Guardian*, 29 Mar. 1845.

[39] Wheeler, *Manchester*, p. 348.

[40] MC, *Proceedings*, 24 Mar. 1845.

[41] MCLAD, M9/30/4/4, MPC, Mins. of Lamp, Scavenging, Fire-Engine and Nuisance Committee, 17 Apr. 1839; 29 Apr. 1840.

desire to co-operate with the authorities 'had not been met in a similar spirit and . . . advantages were continually being taken of any admission on his part'.[42] The preliminary skirmishes in the negotiations to sell the markets had begun.

ii. Markets under municipal control

It was in 1844 and 1846 respectively that the town councils assumed responsibility for their market facilities: first at Salford, as a consequence of the assimilation of the Police Commissioners' powers by the new Corporation; then at Manchester, as a result of the purchase of the market rights from the Mosley family. Such momentous changes seemed to presage the dawn of a new era in the history of the markets, but long-standing problems could not easily be rectified, and some new ones were beginning to appear. For the sake of clarity, it is better to consider developments in Manchester and Salford separately, before drawing some general conclusions.

Manchester's markets

By the 1840s Sir Oswald's asking price for his rights had risen to £200,000. This was thought by many, in retrospect, to have been excessive.[43] He had, however, managed to convince a deputation sent to negotiate with him that he was indifferent as to whether he sold the markets or not, and was content to take his chance on the future increase in their value. The negotiators had also convinced themselves that the terms of payment were favourable to the Council, and the sale had been agreed at Sir Oswald's figure.[44] In his *Family Memoirs*, using the third person to add an air of objectivity, Mosley wrote that 'after many years of unavoidable and anxious litigation in the protection of those manorial rights which he had inherited from his ancestors, he

---

[42] *Ibid.*, 21, 28 July 1841.

[43] See, for example, W. Medcalf, 'On the municipal institutions of the city of Manchester', *Transactions of the Manchester Statistical Society*, 1853–54, pp. 24–5; HLRO, Mins. of Evidence, HL, 1846, XVIII, Manchester Markets Bill, 23 June, p. 23. Evidence of Alderman Thomas Hopkins.

[44] MC, *Proceedings*, 24 Mar. 1845. It was arranged for the Council to pay £5,000 on signing the contract and the rest in instalments of either £4,000 or £6,000 *per annum*, at the option of the Council, at an interest rate of 3¾ per cent. The debt was not finally cleared until 1894, when the total payments amounted to £376,000 (*The Official Handbook of the City of Manchester Markets Department*, London, 1953, p. 15).

had at length the satisfaction of consigning them to hands which alone are capable of managing them'.[45] The Council had gained control over market sites and traders and, in the process, had incurred a sizeable debt. It had also made a firm commitment to improve existing facilities. No longer, as the *Guardian* was quick to point out, could their neglect be blamed on the Lord of the Manor; the inhabitants of Manchester could confidently expect their markets to move out of the Middle Ages into the nineteenth century.[46]

Four problems were especially pressing, all a legacy of the last years of Mosley's control. First, these years had witnessed minimal improvements in the facilities, and it is not surprising that the Council's Markets Committee found them in a neglected and dilapidated state. Indeed, there was more than a hint that Mosley had allowed this to occur in order to exert more pressure on the Council to purchase the markets.[47] Secondly, there was the ever-present problem of streets congested with stalls and carts. To the chairman of the Markets Committee, the removal of these obstructions was the most important reason for purchasing the manorial rights. Shude Hill and Withy Grove were as densely thronged as ever, and only with difficulty was a passage kept open between the stalls. Many of the inhabitants were so accustomed to buying from street traders, it was suggested, that they were unfamiliar with the 'official' market sites.[48] Thirdly, the overcrowding was aggravated by the encroachment into these markets of dealers in old iron, second-hand furniture, shoes and clothing, soft drinks, pies, and the like.[49] How to cope with the spread of these miscellaneous traders was to become a major problem in the future. In the meantime, however, it was to some extent offset by a fourth one, namely, the desire among the butchers to be allowed to trade outside the markets. Mosley had experienced increasing difficulty in restraining them, and the purchase of the manorial rights had encouraged many to think that the new regime would be more tolerant of their breaches of the market law.[50] The Council, for its part, had to choose between taking a growing number of offenders to court, an expensive procedure, and introducing some less restrictive measures.

---

[45] Sir Oswald Mosley, *Family Memoirs*, privately printed, 1849, p. 77.

[46] *Guardian*, 2 Apr. 1845.

[47] MC, *Proceedings*, 20 Oct. 1847; 6 Dec. 1848.

[48] HLRO, Mins. of Evidence, HL, 1846, XVIII, Manchester Markets Bill, 23 June, p. 9; Mins. of Evidence, HC, 1846, CV, Manchester Markets Bill, 8 May, pp. 6–7, 15–16.

[49] *Guardian*, 4 Dec. 1847.

[50] *Courier*, 1 Apr. 1846.

These were the immediate tasks facing the Markets Committee, but underlying them was the need to draw up a concerted plan for the overall development of Manchester's markets. The central markets at Smithfield and around the Market Place were overcrowded and would have to be expanded, but what to do about the markets outside these areas was more difficult to decide. With the exception of Bridge Street, they were not only small but also considered unsavoury in character.[51] The furthest removed from the traditional Market Place was the collection of sixteen stalls erected in the road at the junction of Bradford Street and Beswick Street in Ancoats. 'It is so small', remarked the Markets Committee's chairman, 'that it never arrested my attention'. The London Road Market was not much larger, comprising twenty-six stalls. The Alport Market at Campfield had only twelve stalls, and smallest of all was the Miller Street Market, with its six covered butchers' stalls.[52] The availability of money was crucial to the issue. Contemporaries had not been slow to castigate the Lord of the Manor for failing to provide the necessary finance for new sites, but now the Council was faced with the same difficulty. Land near the centre of Manchester was greatly in demand for commercial interests, and that outside it was scarcely less so for residential purposes. Inevitably, improvements would be expensive.[53]

No-one could dispute the initial enthusiasm of the Markets Committee for the task ahead. Even before the sale of the manorial rights was finalised, a delegation had visited Liverpool to examine its market facilities and had become convinced of the desirability of having one or two large central markets in preference to a number of smaller ones in different parts of the town. The reasoning behind this was that it would be easier to provide smaller markets in the inner suburbs later on, rather than to attempt to find a site for a central market at some future date.[54] Therefore, Smithfield would be extended, and a new site would be developed on the east side of Deansgate, bordered by Brazennose, Bootle and Pool Streets. Into these markets would move all the traders from the Bridge Street Shambles, the Victoria Market

[51] MC, *Proceedings*, 6 Dec. 1848.

[52] HLRO, Mins. of Evidence, HL, 1846, XVIII, Manchester Markets Bill, 23 June, pp. 28–9; MCLAD, M9/40/2/143–5, 1845 Rate Book, pp. 123, 200, 371; and for Miller Street Market, see MTH, M1/41/No. 1A.

[53] D.A. Farnie, 'The commercial development of Manchester in the later nineteenth century', *The Manchester Review*, VII, 1956, pp. 328–9; HLRO, Mins. of Evidence, HL, 1846, XVIII, Manchester Markets Bill, 23 June, p. 8, for comments on the cost of purchasing a new market site and enlarging Smithfield.

[54] MC, *Proceedings*, 28 Jan. 1846; and see *Guardian*, 31 Dec. 1845.

(as the Smithy Door vicinity was now known), the fish market, the street stalls around the Market Place and, as soon as practicable, all other stands and obstructions throughout the town.[55] These were bold plans. The new markets would not be small ones, since future growth and trade needed to be taken into account. Smithfield was to be enlarged to twice its existing size, and the new Deansgate site would be two and a half times as large again. Their positions had been chosen with care. The Council was aware of the risks of changing established market sites, and the proposals would move traders no further than absolutely necessary.[56] Moreover, contrary to opinions expressed in the correspondence columns of one local newspaper, it was claimed that their central positions ensured that one or other of the markets would be within easy walking distance of most of the inhabitants of Manchester, Salford, Hulme and even Chorlton-on-Medlock.[57] As to the rights of butchers and fishmongers to trade freely, whenever and wherever they wished, the Council decided to retain the restrictions so jealously guarded by the Mosleys, though in a modified form. A licence system would be introduced whereby the Council would have discretion to grant traders permission to move out of the markets and open shops.[58]

These principles formed the basis of the Manchester Markets Bill, submitted by the Council to Westminster in 1846. Unfortunately, the master plan soon began to run into difficulties. In the first place, members of the Markets Committee had sadly underestimated the amount of opposition that the continued restrictions on butchers and fishmongers would generate. But even more importantly, they did not foresee the problems that might be encountered in raising the money necessary to extend Smithfield and to buy the new Deansgate site. The crux of the plan was for the Council to be granted a seven-year option on the compulsory purchase of property on the new market site. Some of this land would be developed by the Council with warehouses, offices or shops to be sold to private businesses, and the income so derived would finance the building of the new market on the remainder of the site. Once the older markets had moved into Deansgate or Smithfield, other central sites could be sold, and the

[55] MC, *Proceedings*, 28 Jan. 1846.
[56] *Ibid.*
[57] *Ibid.*; *Courier*, 7 Jan. 1846.
[58] *Courier*, 7 Mar. 1846; *Guardian*, 28 Mar. 1846.

proceeds would go to pay off the original loan.[59] Opposition to the
Bill was widespread and wide-ranging. Some suggested that two new
markets were unnecessary, and that the present facilities, if suitably
renovated, would suffice.[60] But the chief controversies revolved round
the butchers' and fishmongers' licences and the cost to the ratepayers.
Meetings were summoned and addressed by a Mr James Acland,
hot-foot from spending six years in gaol 'for battling with corporate
corruption in Bristol and Hull'.[61] One of the chief contentions was
that the manorial ban respecting meat sales had applied only to
Tuesdays, Thursdays and Saturdays, the market days for meat, and
that the Council was now seeking to extend the prohibition to every
day of the week. There was much justification for this view; for,
whereas the previous market authorities had claimed to hold a fish
market every day, they had indeed specified particular days for the ban
with regard to meat.[62] Once the Corporation had acquired the market
rights, however, this technicality seems to have been quietly dropped,
and the Town Clerk could assert that the ban was total.[63] Acland tried
vainly to re-establish this point, but it tended to get lost in wider
considerations. As the *Courier* put it, he was, in this respect, 'whistling
against the wind'. Even so, the chief target of his attack continued to be
the 'iniquitous monopoly' of the licence scheme, and it was left to
more sober members of the community, namely, those councillors
who had agreed to attend a meeting of ratepayers called to oppose the
Council's plans, to draw attention to their financial implications. The
inhabitants of Manchester were assured that Councillor Naylor, at
least, would oppose any 'useless and extravagant expenditure of the
public money'.[64] At a later meeting 'the crusade to prevent corporate
corruption in Manchester' was taken a step further when the Manchester Free Burgesses' Association was formed to guard against the
Council becoming 'a sink of villainy, vice and corruption'. No doubt
Acland revelled in these emotion-charged meetings, and he rallied
enough support to present Parliament with a petition of opposition

[59] MC, *Proceedings*, 6 Dec. 1848. Interestingly, the full details of this plan were only revealed
two and a half years after its conception. There was no mention at the time in either the Council
minutes or the local press of the plan to develop part of the site for non-market purposes.
[60] *Courier*, 18 Feb. 1846.
[61] *Guardian*, 21, 28 Feb. 1846. For a short account of the remarkable career of James Acland
as a champion of public rights, see F. Boase, *Modern English Biography*, London, 1892, I, p. 10.
[62] MTH, M1/50/8, *Mosley* v. *Walker*, Brief for Plaintiff, 1826; M1/50/8, *Mosley* v. *Hall*, Brief
for Plaintiff, 1835; MCL, Broadside ff. 1821/15.
[63] *Guardian*, 28 Mar. 1846.
[64] *Courier*, 18 Feb., 13 May 1846.

numbering 6,000 signatures and thirty-three yards long.[65] The *Guardian* expressed doubts, chiefly about the fairness of the continued restrictions on butchers and fishmongers, but the *Courier* perceptively focused on what was to prove a more important issue: the powers that the Council was seeking to allow it to purchase the required land, the editorial suggested, were considered by many to be excessive.[66]

Against the background of these keen local controversies, the Markets Bill finally came before a select committee of the House of Commons on 8 May 1846. Acland, bearing his petition, appeared in order to oppose it but achieved little success. As expected, his efforts were directed mainly towards the abolition of licence restrictions on butchers and fishmongers, but the relevant passages in the Bill were accepted by the committee, subject only to a qualifying clause to the effect that the restrictions would cease once the debt to Mosley had been discharged.[67] With minor amendments, the Bill was approved, but its passage through the select committee of the House of Lords was not so smooth. Once again, Acland's petition was presented, though this time Acland himself did not attend. Instead, the main opposition was provided by Edward James, acting as counsel for the owners, lessees and occupiers of the property near Deansgate intended to be purchased compulsorily. It soon transpired that the Lords committee was not so well disposed towards the Council's witnesses, and the questioning assumed a much more rigorous character than in the Commons committee, revealing that the plans were not so far advanced or even so thoroughly thought out as had previously been suggested. As a result of these proceedings, two important alterations were introduced into the Bill. The clause by which the Council sought the option of compulsory purchase of the Deansgate site was severely modified. The length of the option was reduced to three years; if, at the end of that time, the land was not being used for market purposes, the original owners would have the right to repurchase their property at the original price.[68] In addition, the system by which licences were to be granted at the discretion of the Council came in for harsh criticism. To the chairman of the committee, the Duke of Richmond, this part of the Bill was 'a monstrous clause'; no doubt with tongue in cheek, he deemed it 'rather a strong measure to sanction in the year 1846', being

[65] *Guardian*, 28 Feb., 13 May 1846.
[66] *Ibid.*, 28 Mar. 1846; *Courier*, 13 May 1846.
[67] HLRO, Mins. of Evidence, HC, 1846, CV, Manchester Markets Bill, 12 May, p. 2.
[68] HLRO, Mins. of Evidence, HL, 1846, XVIII, Manchester Markets Bill, 23 June, pp. 28, 31, 67, 70–1.

patently out of step with the free trade principles 'so fashionable in Manchester'.[69] In the event, the committee acknowledged the right of the Corporation to receive revenue from this source until the debt had been paid, but the element of discretion in the granting of licences was judged unacceptable. Therefore, a new clause was introduced that obliged the Corporation to grant licences to all who applied for them.[70] With these amendments, the Bill finally received the royal assent on 16 July 1846.[71]

The changes introduced by the Lords select committee had dramatic effects. The butchers' freedom to move out of the markets on payment of a licence fee immediately resulted in a sharp fall in the revenue from Bridge Street, the largest meat market in the town, where, by 1850, two-fifths of the total number of stalls were empty. The exodus from that section of it known as the pork and carcase market was particularly striking, for the number of unoccupied stalls out of the seventy available rose from seven to forty-five between 1845 and 1850.[72] Yet it was the alterations to the compulsory purchase clause that had the more far-reaching consequences. The reduction of the period in which the Corporation could exercise its compulsory purchase powers meant that the implementing of the proposed scheme was suddenly made twice as urgent. However, what really killed the master plan was that the wording of the revised clause effectively restricted the Council to using the land at Deansgate for market purposes only, and not for the sort of speculative development that had been envisaged to finance the scheme. In these circumstances, the only answer was to propose a more limited development of part of the land and to borrow the necessary money against the future sale of the smaller central sites. It was estimated that £100,000 would be needed, and financial undertakings of that kind lay far beyond the range of council members' thinking. The scheme was not formally dropped until October 1848, when it was announced that the option on the compulsory purchase was not to be exercised.[73] But it had been clear for some time that the Council had no intention of pursuing its brainchild. In July 1847 the

---

[69] *Guardian*, 27 June 1846.

[70] HLRO, Mins. of Evidence, HL, 1846, XVIII, Manchester Markets Bill, 23 June, p. 72; 24 June, pp. 8–9. In fact, it was decided not to alter the Bill, but to introduce a new clause as soon as possible and, in the meantime, to act as if the clause was already in operation (MC, *Proceedings*, 29 June 1846).

[71] The Act was passed as 9 & 10 Vict., c. 219.

[72] MC, *Proceedings*, 20 Oct. 1847; MCLAD, M9/40/2/144, 1845 Rate Book, pp. 414–16; M9/40/2/161, 1850 Rate Book, pp. 264–9.

[73] MC, *Proceedings*, 18 Oct., 6 Dec. 1848.

Markets Committee decided to cover in the Victoria Market – one of the first scheduled to be moved in the original scheme – at a cost of £700. No doubt the replacement of 'unsightly wooden erections covered with tattered canvas' by properly constructed stalls under a permanent glazed roof marked an improvement,[74] but it also signalled the resumption of the policy of *ad hoc* adjustments so typical of the manorial era. The grandiose scheme was dead, and the Committee's attentions were henceforth directed mainly towards piecemeal alterations to the existing facilities. In this, as in many aspects of market administration, the problems confronting the Markets Committee were similar to those that had beset the Mosleys, but some were of a different nature, particularly in the years after 1850. The latter were inter-related and comprised: a growth in the importance of wholesale, as against retail, activities; a tendency, within the retail sector, for the purveyors of food to give ground to the sellers of a wider range of articles of popular consumption; and a perceptible diminution in the role of the markets as channels of food distribution.

Wholesaling was not, of course, an entirely novel development. The potato market had been largely wholesale in character from the beginning of the century, but hitherto the division of function between retailer and wholesaler had not been so pronounced as to warrant special attention. Indeed, only rarely were such matters discussed even in 1846 in the lengthy, but ill-focused, debates about market reorganisation.[75] Moreover, the activities of the canal companies in the early 1840s tended to relieve the market authorities of direct responsibility for providing wholesale facilities.[76] By the end of that decade, however, the problem had to be faced more squarely. The provision of wholesale markets by the Lancashire and Yorkshire Railway Company in 1849 and by the Manchester, Sheffield, and Lincolnshire in 1853 at their respective stations was part of the answer.[77] But it was recognised that more facilities were needed, and the development of the Smithfield site took on a greater urgency after the collapse of the scheme to build a new market off Deansgate. An initial obstacle was the length of the lease by which the site was rented from the Earl of Derby, but once that had been extended, the Council

---

[74] *Ibid.*, 14 July 1847; *Guardian*, 15 Jan. 1848.
[75] See, for example, *Courier*, 18 Feb. 1846.
[76] Above, pp. 102–3.
[77] Above, pp. 107, 109.

proceeded with its plan to increase the size of the market by purchasing some land between Coop Street and Oak Street. The extra space was used to reorganise the market traders into more clearly defined wholesale and retail sections. The retailers of fruit and vegetables were obliged to make way for their wholesale counterparts and to move to a smaller area in the market.[78] Significantly, contemporaries began to refer to Smithfield, not simply as a 'market', but as a 'wholesale' one.[79] Further additions were made and extensive improvements carried out in the 1850s, not the least of which was the erection of a massive roof (Plate 8).[80] In a physical sense, Smithfield began to look more and more like a modern wholesale market and, as such, continued to prosper.

Meanwhile, a discernible shift in the character of market retailing was gradually taking place. Stalls selling non-food goods had existed for some time, particularly in the Shude Hill district, but by the late 1840s they had become such a regular feature of the market scene that the Council was reluctant to ban them because of the revenue in tolls and stallage they afforded.[81] Even at Smithfield, despite its concurrent development on the wholesale side, the trend was noticeable. The problem was how to incorporate them within the official market system. In October 1850 the remnants of the old cattle market were transferred from the corner of Swan Street to Campfield, and on the vacated site were accommodated miscellaneous general dealers. Over the next two years their numbers grew to the point where they occupied almost one-third of the available market space.[82] Their presence in the market aroused strong feelings, and at least one acrimonious debate was heard in the council chamber on a resolution that all stalls of non-farming produce should be removed from Smithfield. The Markets Committee firmly refuted its critics, pointing out that they failed to appreciate that the general dealers were allowed to use the market facilities only after wholesalers and farmers had completed their business. It was recognised that the first duty of the Markets Committee was to the sellers of farm produce, but it would be foolish to allow the market to remain empty for the rest of the day when the

[78] MC, *Proceedings*, 23 Oct. 1850; *Manchester Markets By–Laws*, 12 Mar. 1851, Appropriation of Smithfield Market.
[79] For example, H.G. Duffield, *The Stranger's Guide to Manchester*, Manchester, 1850, p. 60.
[80] MC, *Proceedings*, 17 Dec. 1851; 30 Aug. 1854; 31 Oct. 1855.
[81] *Guardian*, 5 Jan. 1848.
[82] MC, *Proceedings*, 26 Feb. 1851; *Guardian*, 7 Aug. 1852.

debt to Sir Oswald Mosley was so large.[83] In fact, this general trade continued to expand to the extent that it was considered worthwhile to provide a special building inside the market for dealers in second-hand clothes and other such articles, and in 1855 a pedlars' market was duly instituted.[84] Moreover, when a new market hall was erected for retailers in 1858, a gallery was specifically reserved for stalls dealing exclusively in artificial flowers, toys, ribbons, trinkets, and the like.[85]

At the equally central Victoria Market, the period of municipal control seemed to begin auspiciously. The glazed roof, begun in 1847, was subsequently extended.[86] Contemporary descriptions of the Christmas scene in the 1850s give every indication of a thriving trade, and a guidebook of the time saw it as the only market, other than Smithfield, worthy of notice in the town.[87] The retailing of fish, in particular, was on a scale which justified the provision, in 1865, of a new market hall specifically for this purpose.[88] Even so, there is a strong suspicion that the years of busiest activity at this site lay in the past. Between 1845 and 1860 the number of designated butchers' stalls fell from thirty-nine to eighteen, and one-third of these were empty. Furthermore, the fishmongers had scarcely settled into the gothic splendour of their new hall before they were agitating to move to Smithfield.[89] Just as significant is the absence of complaints about congestion in the adjacent streets, in sharp contrast to Smithfield where stalls were once again spilling beyond the market area and blocking the approach roads.[90] The site of the Victoria Market was eventually sold in 1874, and all the remaining stall-holders were re-housed in part of the empty fish market.[91]

The decline of the Victoria site hints that Manchester's markets were gradually losing their prime importance for the retail distribution of food during these years. This view is corroborated by the chequered

[83] *Guardian*, 7 Aug. 1852.
[84] MC, *Proceedings*, 30 Aug. 1854; 31 Oct. 1855.
[85] *Guardian*, 22 Jan. 1857; 24 Dec. 1858.
[86] MC, *Proceedings*, 17 Dec. 1851; 30 Aug. 1854; 31 Oct. 1855.
[87] *Guardian*, 24 Dec. 1857; 24 Dec. 1858; [J. Heywood], *The Strangers' Guide to Manchester*, Manchester, 1857, p. 41.
[88] MC, *Proceedings*, 29 Oct. 1862; 7 Oct. 1863; 25 Oct. 1865.
[89] MCLAD, M9/40/2/144, 1845 Rate Book, pp. 305–6; M9/40/2/228, 1860 Rate Book, p. 201; MC, *Proceedings*, 26 Oct. 1870.
[90] MC, *Proceedings*, 3 Jan. 1866.
[91] *Manchester Markets, 1846–1946: The Story of 100 Years' Progress*, Manchester, 1946, p. 13; S.D. Simon, *A Century of City Government: Manchester, 1838–1938*, London, 1938, p. 343.

histories of the town's smaller markets, especially where they were peripheral. On the face of things, this seems paradoxical, for in most cases they seemed well placed to serve large concentrations of population. In the late 1840s the *Guardian* printed a number of letters criticising the centralisation of market facilities and pointing out the inconvenience of travelling in from Hulme, Chorlton-on-Medlock, Greenheys and Stretford.[92] Interest soon waned, however, as the existing smaller markets showed little propensity for growth; indeed, the reverse was the case. As we have already seen, the butchers' shambles in Bridge Street was two-fifths empty as early as 1850; five years on, even though the total number of stalls had been reduced from 178 to 150, less than one-half of these were occupied.[93] Not surprisingly, the Council decided in 1862 to accept an offer for part of the site, retaining only that section which formed the pork and carcase market.[94] Elsewhere, the stalls situated in Ancoats, between Bradford Street and Beswick Street, disappeared as soon as the Council took over the markets.[95] The old apple market in Fennel Street was a casualty of road improvements.[96] The six covered stalls in Miller Street survived until 1890, but no additions or improvements were made in all this time.[97] The story of the Alport Market at Campfield is equally dispiriting. It had never been a large market, and by 1850 only four of the twelve stalls were occupied. A year later the Markets Committee decided to revitalise it by converting half the stalls into shops, and for some time afterwards nurtured a vague idea of developing the site further. However, the expense of acquiring neighbouring properties proved to be a stumbling-block, and the scheme was finally abandoned, leaving the market to continue until the 1870s, though on a scale that was only marginally larger than when the Council took it on.[98]

But perhaps the best illustration of the limited prospects of market sites outside the town centre is provided by the London Road Market. This was the nearest to the fast-growing inner suburbs of Ardwick and

[92] *Guardian*, 12 July 1848; 11 Aug. 1849; 16 Oct., 13 Nov. 1850.
[93] MCLAD, M9/40/2/190, 1855 Rate Book, pp. 151–5, records seventy-nine of the 150 stalls (i.e. 53 per cent) empty.
[94] MC, *Proceedings*, 29 Oct. 1862.
[95] MCLAD, M9/40/2/159, 1850 Rate Book, p. 154, records some property but no stalls at Bradford Street.
[96] MC, *Proceedings*, 21 Jan. 1846.
[97] *Manchester Markets, 1846–1946*, p. 13.
[98] MCLAD, M9/40/2/162, 1850 Rate Book, p. 175; M9/40/2/297, 1870 Rate Book, p. 143; MC, *Proceedings*, 17 Dec. 1851; 26 Oct. 1859.

Chorlton-on-Medlock, and yet, from the time when it was affected by the expansion of the railway station, it did not prosper. The stalls were never more than two-thirds occupied, and its running was the subject of severe criticism. To one councillor, its very presence constituted a 'disgrace to the town',[99] but only in the late 1850s did it become the focus of the Markets Committee's attention. Interestingly, there was no suggestion that such a market had already outlived its usefulness. On the contrary, it was decided to sanction a proposal to build a market hall on the site. After delays at the design and construction stages, the hall was eventually opened in April 1862, with its thirty-four stalls let not only to butchers and greengrocers but also to dealers in second-hand clothing and the like.[100] In the event, the ensuing disappointment was great. Within three years of its opening, the London Road Hall was denounced as a mistake, with 'nothing but bankruptcy and ruin ... before those who occupied the stalls there'.[101] In this instance, the rate books do not give details of the number of stalls occupied, but in 1868 the Markets Committee reported that it had found the area of the market hall too large for the requirements of the locality. As a result, over half of it was leased to other tenants. Ten years later the whole site was sold.[102]

Salford's markets

The new market, which had been opened in May 1827 (Plate 9), was situated at the rear of the Town Hall. It comprised a covered section for meat, fish and vegetables, fronted by a space for open stalls. It was regulated by the Police Commissioners, who bought both the Town Hall and the market from the Duchy of Lancaster for £3,000 in 1834.[103] Unfortunately, the market never met with the success for which its promoters hoped. When developed, it was inappropriately sited on the outskirts of the town and was unpopular with traders and customers alike.[104] Nor had much success been achieved with the more centrally situated Trinity Market, opened in the early 1830s, for between 1835 and 1844 the tolls levied there fell from a mere £24 to

[99] See, for example, MCLAD, M9/40/2/144, 1845 Rate Book, p. 200; M9/40/2/159, 1850 Rate Book, p. 273; M9/40/2/194, 1855 Rate Book, pp. 81–2; *Guardian*, 15 Oct. 1857.
[100] *Guardian*, 24 Dec. 1858; MC, *Proceedings*, 26 Oct. 1859; 2 Oct. 1861; 29 Oct. 1862.
[101] *Guardian*, 6 Apr. 1865.
[102] MC, *Proceedings*, 28 Oct. 1868; *Manchester Markets, 1846–1946*, p. 13.
[103] See A.T. Smith, 'Chronology of Salford', in T. Bergin, D.N. Pearce and S. Shaw (eds.), *Salford, A City and Its Past*, Salford, 1974, p. 146.
[104] PRO, DL 41/49, Petition of certain traders ... in Salford, 28 May 1827.

under £5 *per annum*;[105] nor, for that matter, with the so-called Central Market, established in Chapel Street in 1840, whose name belied both its location and small size.[106]

The problems facing the Salford Council when it assumed responsibility for the town's markets in 1844 were thus quite different from those confronting the Manchester Council. The difficulty lay in establishing the retail markets as viable concerns, rather than in reducing overcrowding and congestion. The Markets Committee sought to improve matters in a number of ways. In 1845 an extension of the municipal buildings necessitated the displacement of some butchers' stalls behind the Town Hall, initially to a site at the corner of Oldfield Road and, subsequently, to the Central Market, 'but with little success'.[107] The tolls accruing from this market and the stalls near Trinity Church continued to fall, and in two successive years, 1847 and 1848, the Markets Committee was obliged to reduce the rent due from their lessee. In the former year it was decided that the stalls fronting the Town Hall, optimistically known as the 'fruit and vegetable market', did insufficient trade to counterbalance the obstruction they caused, and this market was discontinued.[108] Some ambitious plans to develop 'a new and commodious market', under discussion in 1846–48, foundered on the rocks of expense and uncertainty. Instead, it was decided to persevere with the Oldfield Road site, known as the Borough Market from 1848, where eight butchers' stalls were erected and a toll-free vegetable market was established with a view to attracting traders. Even so, the Committee itself recognised that there would be little improvement until the area was covered.[109] In the event, the Borough Market declined and was finally closed in 1857, and it was the Central Market that was covered, though, once again, the success achieved was not spectacular. Here, the returns had 'not yet answered expectations' in 1856, and two years later the tolls were let for a mere £60 *per annum* to a Mr Kirkby, who still paid only £70 for the lease in 1870.[110]

Evidently, the retail markets of Salford were of little consequence and, in view of the various problems they continued to pose, it must

[105] SPC, *An Account of all money received and paid by the Commissioners of Police of Salford, to the Town Hall and Markets Committee, 1833–1845*, includes tolls from Trinity Market from 1834.

[106] According to the *Guardian* (5 Dec. 1855), its area was only about 400 square yards.

[107] SC, *Report of Town Hall and Markets Committee*, 14 Oct. 1846.

[108] *Ibid.*, 28 Sept. 1847; 26 Oct. 1848.

[109] *Ibid.*, 14 Oct. 1846; 28 Sept. 1847; 26 Oct. 1848.

[110] SC, *Proceedings*, 31 Oct. 1855; 28 Oct. 1856; 27 Oct. 1858; 19 Oct. 1871.

have been with a sense of equanimity, not to say relief, that members of the Salford Markets Committee contemplated their other responsibility, the cattle market. This had been opened at Cross Lane by the Police Commissioners in July 1837 but, within less than a month, had been obliged to close owing to lack of support.[111] However, the decision to lease it to two influential cattle dealers, William Higginson and John Nall, worked out well, for they were able to persuade their fellows to transfer their activities from Manchester's Smithfield. The figures for livestock traded at Smithfield show a sharp decline from the end of September, and Cross Lane soon established itself as the major livestock market for the whole area.[112] Here, in the new era of municipal control, the friction and dissent that typified the story of Manchester's markets was largely absent. The practice of leasing the management of Cross Lane continued for most of the period. Consequently, many of the problems of internal organisation were taken out of the hands of the Markets Committee. Of course, a large cattle market created problems in its effects upon the neighbouring area and in the dangers of cattle being driven through the adjacent streets, but a location away from the town centre and the availability of relatively cheap land more than compensated for these.[113] The only major source of conflict in this period was the proposal to change the market day, and the reasons for this have already been discussed. It is worth noting, however, that the Markets Committee, advised by its lessees, based its decision on future developments in the trade and proved itself sensitive to the longer-term interests of the market.[114]

iii. Conclusions: the successes and failures of the markets committees

In general, the record of the Salford Markets Committee was not impressive. In the first place, it failed persistently in its attempts to establish a viable retail market in the borough. Secondly, although its handling of Cross Lane seemed superficially successful, much of the credit was due to the lessees. Furthermore, when the Council itself

[111] SPC, *First Annual Report of Cattle Market Committee*, 1 Nov. 1837.

[112] *Ibid.*; and see *Guardian*, market reports for Smithfield, especially 27 Sept. 1837; 26 May 1838.

[113] For the hazards, see 33 & 34 Vict., c. 129: Salford Improvement Act, 1870, Clause 122. Salford Council acquired almost 27,000 square yards of additional land at Cross Lane in 1862 for an annual rent of only £338 17s 10d (SC, *Proceedings*, 2 July 1862).

[114] SC, *Proceedings*, 18 July 1860; and above, p. 48.

decided to take over the running of the cattle market on the expiry of the lease in 1867, it became clear that the tolls had been let for a figure well under half their true value: Cross Lane was leased for £1,313 *per annum* in 1859–65; this rose to £1,447 in 1865–66; in the first complete year of the Council's management, the tolls amounted to £3,461.[115]

By comparison, the record of the Manchester Markets Committee is more complicated to assess. In the aftermath of the failure of the grandiose master plan, it was frequently accused of putting the collection of tolls before all other considerations, notably in allowing stalls to remain in Shude Hill for the sake of the revenue derived from them.[116] In fact, it was on the initiative of the Improvement Committee, rather than the Markets Committee, that the Council resolved in 1854 to forbid such stalls and to oblige food traders in the streets around Smithfield to move into the 'ample accommodation' in the market itself.[117] The Markets Committee's policy in the 1850s of seeking to accommodate the growing number of non-food retailers was likewise motivated by a desire to reap additional profits.[118] Similarly, an overriding concern with financial return was evinced in 1866 when the Committee congratulated itself on the increase in tolls, while regretting that some trade was still conducted in adjacent streets and thus escaped the attention of the toll collectors.[119]

On the other hand, the long-standing problem of street congestion arising from food sellers' stalls had undoubtedly been mitigated by the late 1850s. On Saturdays, especially in the evening, stalls selling 'every conceivable article of consumption' continued to appear in Shude Hill and Withy Grove, just as stands specialising in chickens, pigeons, rabbits and pets were still a regular feature of trading on that day near the Victoria Market.[120] But these differed from the obstructions complained of earlier, in that they did not represent permanent appendages overflowing into the streets from the official sites. The relative absence of complaints may be taken as evidence of success in this respect, in contrast to the preceding quarter-century. Yet, viewed from another angle, it is apparent that such improvements were

[115] SC, *Abstract of the receipts and expenditure of the Treasurer . . . to the Town Hall and Markets Committee*, 1853–1871.

[116] *Guardian*, 30 Mar. 1850; 21 July 1852; 5 Feb. 1853.

[117] MC, *Proceedings*, 2 Feb. 1853; 25 Oct. 1854.

[118] *Guardian*, 7 Aug. 1852.

[119] MC, *Proceedings*, 3 Jan. 1866.

[120] J.E. and T. Cornish, *Cornishs' Stranger's Guide through Manchester and Salford*, Manchester, 1857, pp. 24–5.

largely due to chance or, at least, to forces over which the Markets Committee could exercise little influence. The happy coincidence of a rise in the number of wholesalers seeking market sites with a decline in demand from food retailers went a long way towards solving the central problem of providing accommodation for all who sought it. In particular, the exodus of butchers from the markets after 1846 released a considerable amount of space. Moreover, the interest shown by the railway companies in developing their own facilities for handling vegetables and fish meant that potential pressure from this quarter was diverted into non-Corporation markets.

Inevitably though, there would come a time when the space created by the decision of some market retailers to open shops and the piecemeal expansion of Smithfield would be overtaken by the development of the wholesale trades. By the early 1860s a familiar refrain was heard again. The streets leading to Smithfield were choked with traffic, and more space was needed within the market. The Council decided to purchase some nearby property and prepared an ambitious plan to build a new road, twenty yards wide, extending from the market to the High Street. Part of the extra space gained would be taken by farmers and market gardeners, but the road would also give a much-needed new approach to the Smithfield site. However, difficulty in acquiring the necessary land meant that even by 1869 only part of the scheme had been completed. The lack of space had by then become urgent, and the Committee was forced to take various short-term measures to help relieve the congestion. An iron roof was placed over some spare land to the south of James Street, and a number of farmers were located on a verandah specially built on to the outside of the market hall.[121] Meanwhile, at Bridge Street, the decision taken in 1862 to sell off much of the site began to look less sensible as the Council came under pressure to expand the facilities available to the wholesale trade, which received an unexpected boost from the restrictions on live cattle movements imposed at the time of the cattle plague in 1866.[122] In the fish trade, too, the Council had to direct its attention for the first time to accommodating wholesalers. The arrangement with the Lancashire and Yorkshire Railway Company was coming to an end, partly because the market had reached the limits of expansion on that site, and partly because the rationale behind the original location in 1856

[121] MC, *Proceedings*, 7 Oct. 1863; 5 Oct. 1864; 2 Oct. 1867; 6 Oct. 1869; HLRO, Mins. of Evidence, HC, 1865, XL, Manchester Improvement Bill, 6 Mar., pp. 3–4.
[122] Below, pp. 185–6.

(that most of the fish traffic to Manchester arrived at the adjacent station) was no longer valid.[123] To the Markets Committee, the only real alternative was to find room in their major site at Smithfield. Such a position would be particularly suitable for dealers from outside Manchester, who could complete all their wholesale purchases within one market. To others on the Council, the reasoning was less compelling in view of its already overcrowded state. As a result, the initial recommendation by the Markets Committee was referred back, and the move was not finally accomplished until 1873.[124]

The policy of selling off parts of some sites and piecemeal adjustments to others was not easy to defend amid the growing pressure from wholesale traders. Only in the provision of a carcase market in Water Street in 1872 could the Markets Committee point to a major addition to the sites purchased from Sir Oswald Mosley.[125] Indeed, the similarity of the 1860s to the manorial period is striking. As soon as complaints began to mount about inadequate facilities, once again resentment was expressed at the system of toll collection.[126] By the early 1870s criticism of the market authorities was as bitter as it had ever been. To those involved in the markets it was obvious that too little of the profits was being used to provide accommodation, and too much was being handed over to the Finance Committee as a contribution to the rates.[127] Moreover, the year 1876 witnessed a dispute which was almost a facsimile of the Chadwick and Ackers case of 1782. Two potato dealers, Peverley and Blakey, were taken to court for letting out part of a warehouse, close to Smithfield, to several fruit and vegetable wholesalers and hence, it was claimed, establishing a rival market and depriving the Corporation of tolls.[128] In the round, there is little doubt that the activities of the Markets Committee, described by one contemporary as the 'sad black sheep' of the Corporation,[129] left much to be desired. However, despite more legal confrontations, it was not until 1884 that the general body of the Council unequivocally pronounced that it was the first duty of its

[123] Above, p. 133.
[124] MC, *Proceedings*, 26 Oct. 1870. The new wholesale fish market was formally opened on 14 Feb. 1873 (Axon, *Annals*, p. 337).
[125] Simon, *City Government*, p. 343.
[126] See, for example, HLRO, Mins. of Evidence, HC, 1865, XL, Manchester Improvement Bill, 6 March, pp. 10–11.
[127] G. Whitworth, *Shudehill Markets Mismanagement*, Manchester, 1875, p. 19.
[128] Redford, III, pp. 57–8.
[129] W.A. Shaw, *Manchester, Old and New*, London, 1896, I, p. 141.

Markets Committee to provide satisfactory and cheap accommodation, rather than to make large profits.[130] Half a century before, the *Guardian* had been saying the same thing about Sir Oswald Mosley.[131]

[130] Redford, III, pp. 66–7.
[131] *Guardian*, 29 Mar. 1845.

CHAPTER VIII

Fresh food marketing

IN THE HISTORY of market institutions through the period 1770–1870, three groups of traders – butchers, fruit and vegetable dealers and fishmongers – figured most prominently. Indeed, the changing scene in the markets was very much a reflection of their evolving needs. However, the fortunes of each trade must be considered individually, both inside and outside the market framework, in order to assess how effectively fresh foods were distributed in the town.

i. The meat trade

The starting point must be to estimate the total number of butchers' outlets – as distinct from businesses or persons describing themselves as butchers – operating at different times. Directories would seem to be an obvious source of such information, but they are, in fact, of limited value for much of the period considered here. Until 1815 they were primarily non-commercial and, even when they changed in character, butchers were listed only twice before 1840 (in 1815 and 1833).[1] In general, their subsequent coverage of this trade improved, though it remained incomplete for many years with respect to market tenants. Fortunately, however, this particular deficiency can in large part be redressed by evidence from the Manchester rate books. As we saw in Chapter VII, throughout the manorial era Manchester's meat trade was conducted almost entirely within the markets, and from

[1] For the changing nature of directories, see above pp. 10–11.

1796 these were registered for rating purposes.[2] Thereafter, the rate books provide a reliable record of the stalls occupied by butchers in the town's principal meat markets, namely, the shambles in the Market Place, Bridge Street (1803) and, after 1822, a designated area in Smithfield. Table 8.1 summarises the number of outlets from directories and rate books for the entire period.

Table 8.1 *Estimates of the number of butchers' retail outlets in Manchester and Salford, 1772–1871*

	1772	1788	1800	1811	1821	1831/33[a]	1840	1850	1861	1871
Directories										
Shops						315	226	518	574	775
	16	33	71	128	Not stated					
Market stalls						115	230	188	45	29
Rate books										
Market stalls	–	–	153	236	222	271	264	207	107	29

Note
(a) 1831 = Rate book; 1833 = Directory.

Sources MCLAD, M9/40/2, Township of Manchester Rate Books; Directories (see Bibliography).

There are numerous discrepancies in these figures, and they cannot be resolved simply by comparing entries in the two sources, since not all the butchers' stalls listed in the rate books have named occupants. However, it is possible to produce a more adequate set of estimates when the underlying strengths and weaknesses of the data sources are examined more closely. In the first place, the directories clearly under-recorded the number of butchers' outlets in 1772 and 1788 because, in principle, they did not seek to include those who traded in Manchester but resided elsewhere. This would apply particularly to surviving farmer–butchers, fattening and slaughtering their stock and bringing the meat to market. Secondly, some butchers occupied more than one stall. For these reasons, the rate books are the better guide for 1800 and 1811. Least satisfactory are the data for 1821, since the directories

[2] MCLAD, M9/40/2/53–292, Township of Manchester Rate Books, Poor Rate Assessments, 1796–1870.

were then at their poorest, and the rate books seem to have been unable to cope with the switching of stalls to Smithfield on the eve of its formal opening. From 1833 there is a basis in the directories for distinguishing between shops and market stalls,[3] although the higher number of butchers' stalls registered in the rate books (except in 1871) suggests that the directories persistently under-recorded these outlets, presumably because some butchers gave to their compilers home addresses only, and not stall numbers. A small compensating factor is that the rate books did not distinguish stalls occupied by butchers in the more general markets, such as Alport and London Road, whereas the directories included the names of a few butchers located there. With these considerations in mind, a further table may be constructed which combines what seem to be the best estimates from the two sources (Table 8.2).

Table 8.2 *Best estimates of the number of butchers' retail outlets in Manchester and Salford, 1772–1871*

1772[a]	1788[a]	1800[b]	1811[b]	1821	1833[a]	1840[c]	1850[c]	1861[c]	1871[c]
16+	33+	153	236	Data inadequate	430	490	725	681	804

Notes
(a) Directory entries.
(b) Rate book entries.
(c) Directories (entries for shops) plus rate books.

Sources   As Table 8.1

Having established the number of outlets, it is possible to gain some indication of their average size. For this purpose the decennial census occupational listings, available from 1841, can be used in conjunction with the number of outlets. Dividing the number of outlets into the occupational totals can give only an approximation,[4] but the data presented in rows (a) and (b) of Table 8.3 leave no doubt that the number of butchers per outlet was small and, as we shall see, among the lowest for all food retailers.[5] Evidently, there must have been a

---

[3] *Pigot and Son's Directory of Manchester and Salford*, 1833.
[4] This is because some of those listed in the census would have worked outside the area covered by directories, and others would have been employed in wholesale establishments. As will be seen below, however, this is not a serious problem with regard to butchers.
[5] Below, pp. 194, 199–200, 209–10, 222–3, and Chapter IX, note 68.

very high proportion of one-man businesses. The inclusion, from 1851, of 'butchers' wives' as a separate category in the census occupational returns has the effect of adding about one-third to the total adult workforce in the butchery trade and can be seen as an acknowledgement of the active role they frequently played in their husbands' businesses. Even so, it does not detract from the impression that the typical outlet was very small.[6] Furthermore, there are indications that the average weekly turnover in the butchery business was low compared to that in other staple food trades. Table 8.4 analyses the results of an enquiry conducted by William Lockett, 'an old and respectable inhabitant of Salford', in the early 1840s at a time when there was widespread concern about the general state of trade in the Manchester area. The figures suggest that butchers were accustomed to operate at a substantially lower level than grocers and provision dealers, though, interestingly, their turnover was subject to only a marginally higher degree of fluctuation when times were bad.

From the evidence already presented, it is apparent that, in the long run, the number of shops increased enormously as against market stalls, although without much effect on the average size of outlets. Within this framework, and using the sources already drawn on to generate Tables 8.1 and 8.2, it is possible to detect the declining importance of farmer–butchers, who were already in a distinct minority before the end of the eighteenth century, and whose role had become peripheral by the 1840s. Of the ninety-eight different stall-holders recorded in the 1800 rate book as occupying butchers'

Table 8.3 *Number of butchers per outlet in Manchester and Salford, 1841–71*

	1841	1851	1861	1871
(a) Adults aged 20 and over	1.7	1.4	1.7	1.6
(b) All	1.9	1.7	2.0	1.9
(c) Including Butchers' Wives	Not given	2.3	2.8	2.7

Sources Census Occupational Abstracts (see Bibliography); Directories (see Bibliography).

[6] Note that the area covered by the 1841 occupational figures (Manchester Borough plus Salford Town) does not correspond perfectly with that adopted for subsequent abstracts (which use parliamentary boroughs), so that the occupational returns for 1841 have been scaled up by 5.9 per cent to improve comparability. Secondly, in the 1871 census, occupational tables for large towns include only those aged 20 and over, necessitating another adjustment to row (b): 1871 'All' = 1871 Adults × 1861 All/1861 Adults.

Table 8.4   *Average weekly takings of certain Salford traders in 1839 and 1841*

Traders	Number of traders covered	Average takings 1839 (£)	Average takings 1841 (£)	% difference 1839–41
Butchers	14	38	24	−37
Grocers	10	123	83	−33
Provision Dealers	13	105	70	−33

Source   J. Adshead, *Distress in Manchester: Evidence of the State of the Labouring Classes in 1840–42*, London, 1842, p. 55.

shambles, sixty-seven can be identified in directories as having a Manchester or Salford address. Of the remaining thirty-one, some had the same surname as those identified and could be related.[7] Thus, at most, fewer than one-third came from outside the town and hence could reasonably be interpreted as farmer–butchers. The 1815 directory happens to record butchers with both their home addresses and stall numbers. Of the 145 listed, only thirty came from outside Manchester and Salford, and none from very far away.[8] An examination of butchers brought before the Court Leet offers corroborative evidence: only thirteen out of fifty-seven offenders in 1770–1800 gave addresses outside the town, and in 1836–46 even fewer, a mere fourteen out of 185.[9]

The emergence of town butchers as the major force in the Manchester meat trade appears to have run well ahead of similar developments in Sheffield.[10] Both cities, however, were slow to evolve a clear distinction between the wholesale and retail sections of the trade. In this respect, a marked contrast can be drawn with London, where the business was divided between carcase (or wholesale) and cutting (or retail) butchers, and where, by the mid nineteenth century, a number of the meat markets had taken on a specialised wholesale role.[11] Interestingly, Jefferys, followed by Perren, has suggested that,

[7] MCLAD, M9/40/2/60. This was the first rate book to name the stall-holders in each of the butchers' shambles.

[8] *Pigot and Deans' Manchester and Salford Directory*, 1815.

[9] See *Court Leet*, VIII, IX, XII.

[10] See J. Blackman, 'The food supply of an industrial town: a study of Sheffield's public markets, 1780–1900', *Business History*, V, 1963, pp. 85–8.

[11] R.B. Westerfield, *Middlemen in English Business, particularly between 1660 and 1760*, New Haven, Conn., 1915, pp. 198–201; and see J. Fletcher, 'Statistical account of the markets of London', *JSSL*, X, 1847, p. 347.

among provincial towns, only Manchester could approach a similar level of development,[12] but this view seems exaggerated, to say the least. Throughout the period no Manchester butcher identified himself as a wholesaler in the directories, and it is significant that the recognition of a need for special wholesale facilities within the market structure came only slowly. It is true that an area of that section of Bridge Street given over to pork butchers contained a number of 'sheds', and these seem to have been the basis for the 1842 guidebook's mention of a 'pork and carcase market' there.[13] But Bridge Street was never described as a wholesale market in the detailed negotiations relating to the sale and reorganisation of the markets in 1846, and it was not until the mid-1860s that attention came to focus on this aspect of the distribution system.

It follows that the typical Manchester butcher was an independent small trader who bought and slaughtered his livestock, then cut up and retailed the meat. However, with modern, and therefore anachronistic, models in mind, it is possible that historians have tried to draw distinctions that are too sharp, especially where provincial towns are concerned. From an early date, Manchester appears to have found a *via media*, embracing an element of wholesale trading on an informal basis, which involved inter-trading between butchers. In the papers of insolvent traders coming before the Court of Quarter Sessions, details of various sums of money owed to debtors, at the point of their bankruptcy, are revealing. In six of the eight cases of Manchester butchers who appeared between 1776 and 1812, money was owed by other Manchester butchers, and the sums listed as outstanding for 'goods sold and delivered' to fellow retailers averaged about one-third of the total amounts due to them.[14] In another case, money had been paid to two other Manchester butchers 'for my use', presumably to buy livestock or meat for the debtor.[15] Through the disposal of surplus meat or particular joints in this way, small traders would have

---

[12] J.B. Jefferys, *Retail Trading in Britain, 1850–1950*, Cambridge, 1954, p. 181; R. Perren, *The Meat Trade in Britain, 1840–1914*, London, 1978, p. 105.

[13] MCLAD, M9/40/2/105, 1831 Rate Book, p. 385; B. Love, *The Handbook of Manchester*, Manchester, 1842, p. 242.

[14] LRO, QJB 45/14 (John Sutcliffe, 1778); QJB 51/5 (Thomas Ashton, 1801); QJB 53/20 (Nathan Edge, 1804); QJB 54/57 (John Taylor, 1806); QJB 57/33 (William Goulden, 1812); QJB 57/43 (John Hopper, 1812).

[15] LRO, QJB 43/9 (William Hudson, 1776).

been able to enter the butchery business without having to commit themselves, from the outset, to actually buying and slaughtering on their own account.

Nevertheless, it was in the nature of the trade that slaughterhouses were ubiquitous. Surveys in 1849 disclosed that the ratio was at least one slaughterhouse to every three butchers, and that it was customary to share, or have access to, another's premises.[16] How to cope with the nuisances to which slaughterhouses gave rise had long been a headache for the town authorities,[17] and in the 1840s, by which time public awareness of health issues had heightened, criticism was freely voiced. Bridge Street was singled out for particular attention, but the numerous other slaughterhouses – typically cramped and squalid, often confined to cellars, and usually located in the most densely populated parts of Manchester and Salford – did not escape censure.[18] By-laws were passed in the late 1840s in an attempt to improve and control them, but it was an uphill struggle. Even by the 1860s little progress had been made. Reports of the Inspector of Nuisances and the Medical Officer of Health of the two councils tell sorry tales, and the notoriety of the town's slaughterhouses had spread well beyond Manchester.[19] Butchers were the strongest opponents of change, and proposals for the provision of public abattoirs were countered by arguments that slaughterhouses needed to be close to shops or stalls.[20]

In turn, the abundance of slaughtering facilities inhibited the development of a formal wholesale sector; as late as 1866 it was claimed that nine out of ten Manchester butchers preferred to buy cattle live.[21] However, the wholesale trade was on the point of receiving an unexpected boost from the regulations imposed at the time of the cattle plague restricting the movement of cattle bought at Cross Lane and requiring them to be slaughtered within four days at licensed premises in Manchester or Salford. These restrictions had far-reaching

[16] The 1850 directory lists 645 butchers for Manchester and Salford. In 1849 a survey for Salford Council (SC, *Report of Nuisance Committee*, 7 Nov. 1849) counted thirty-three slaughterhouses, and a similar survey for Manchester Council (*Guardian*, 8 Dec. 1849) discovered 195, giving a total of 228.

[17] See, for example, *Court Leet*, X, p. 32, 19 Oct. 1807; p. 52, 3 Oct. 1808; p. 133, 20 Apr. 1815; p. 140, 4 Oct. 1815; p. 149, 8 May 1816; XII, pp. 187–8, 30 Sept. 1842.

[18] *Guardian*, 27 Oct., 8 Dec. 1849.

[19] SC, *Reports of Sanitary Committee*, 30 Oct. 1866; 30 Oct. 1867; *Report of General Health Committee*, 20 Oct. 1869; MC, *Proceedings*, 3 Feb. 1869; *PP* 1866, XVI, *Select Committee on Trade in Animals*, Mins. of Evidence, p. 20.

[20] *Guardian*, 8 Dec. 1849; 4 Aug. 1852; 29 June 1853.

[21] *PP* 1866, XVI, *Select Committee on Trade in Animals*, Mins. of Evidence, p. 34.

implications, particularly for butchers from nearby towns, who were now obliged to buy carcases. Special provision was made forthwith at Bridge Street to cope with the demand, but it proved inadequate. At the same time, the Manchester Markets Committee, anxious to exploit the situation, realised that a properly organised wholesale meat market might have considerable potential for future revenue.[22] Similar thoughts had occurred to others, and in 1867 a proposal was made by the Manchester and Salford Abattoir Company to build a dead-meat market on land near Worsley Street and the River Irwell in Salford. The scheme received a sympathetic hearing from the Salford Markets Committee but was finally rejected on sanitary grounds.[23] The seed, however, had been sown, and support continued to grow. Hitherto, pressure for slaughterhouse improvements had come from sanitary reformers, but now the butchers themselves voiced dissatisfaction with the existing facilities. The Manchester and Salford Butchers' Guardian Association began to press for the closure of that 'most inconvenient and incommodious market now held in Bridge Street' and for the building of a public slaughterhouse and market for the exclusive use of wholesale butchers. Needless to say, they also expected the rights of butchers to slaughter privately to remain intact.[24] Even so, on the recommendation of its Markets Committee, the Manchester Council eventually succumbed to the butchers' representations, and an abattoir and carcase market was opened in Water Street in 1872.[25] Meanwhile, the Salford Council came under similar pressure, and in 1870 six public slaughterhouses were provided at Cross Lane.[26]

However, even in the aftermath of the developments prompted by the cattle plague, the meat trade was by no means transformed. It is true that by the early 1870s there existed some substantial businesses such as that of William Brown, who slaughtered between thirty-five and fifty beasts and 150–250 sheep and lambs each week.[27] But there

[22] MC, *Proceedings*, 31 Oct. 1866.

[23] SC, *Proceedings*, 6 Mar. 1867.

[24] MC, *Proceedings*, 4 Aug. 1869.

[25] *Ibid.*, 6 July, 26 Oct. 1870; W.E.A. Axon (ed.), *The Annals of Manchester*, Manchester, 1886, p. 328.

[26] SC, *Report of General Health Committee*, 20 Oct. 1869; *Report of Town Hall and Markets Committee*, 20 Oct. 1870.

[27] PP 1873, XI, *Select Committee on Contagious Diseases (Animals)*, Mins. of Evidence, pp. 552–3.

is much evidence to suggest that the trading practices of most butchers had changed little. A year after their construction, only four of the public slaughterhouses at Cross Lane had been let; even four years on, the number of livestock killed there was insignificant.[28] As late as 1897, according to one authority, there were still about a hundred private slaughterhouses in Manchester, and the typical Edwardian butcher, as recalled by Robert Roberts, bought meat on the hoof and killed his purchases at his own or his neighbour's slaughterhouse.[29]

It is surprising that the preference of butchers to operate independently was so deep-seated and enduring, because the meat trade was a demanding business. It required not only dexterity in slaughtering and cutting, but also a range of expertise, extending from buying in at the right price to disposing of all parts of the carcases, including the profitable utilisation of skins, bones and fat.[30] The history of the co-operatives' endeavours in the trade, which is well documented, gives some indication of the hazards involved. In 1860, a year after its inception, the Failsworth Society established a butchery department, but the experiment lasted only a matter of weeks. The Manchester and Salford Society's first venture, in 1862, while surviving longer, foundered none the less.[31] Many of the problems they encountered could be traced to a lack of expertise and experience on the part of their managing butchers. However, when each society made a second attempt to enter the meat trade in the 1870s, lessons clearly had not been learned, since they were beset by troubles similar to those experienced before.[32] Staffing difficulties were no doubt compounded by the problem of having to dispose of all the cuts of meat within a single branch. One solution might have been the Co-operative Wholesale Society's proposal to purchase livestock on behalf of the

[28] SC, *Reports of Town Hall and Markets Committee*, 19 Oct. 1871; 14 Oct. 1875. An average of six beasts and seventeen sheep per week were slaughtered there in 1875.

[29] W.E. Bear, 'The food supply of Manchester, II, animal produce', *JRASE*, 3rd ser., VIII, 1897, p. 490; R. Roberts, *The Classic Slum*, Manchester, 1971, p. 88.

[30] In 1778 John Sutcliffe had money owing to him from a leather dresser, a chandler and a soap boiler (LRO, QJB 45/14); a hundred years on, the Manchester and Salford Equitable Co-operative Society Ltd, Butchery Department Accounts, 14 Mar. 1874–8 Jan. 1879, show that 8–13 per cent of revenue was derived from this type of sale.

[31] Failsworth Industrial Society Ltd, *Report for quarter ending 31 Dec. 1860*; Manchester and Salford Equitable Co-operative Society Ltd, Mins. of Committee, 28 May, 23 July, 27 Aug., 5 Nov. 1862; 4 Feb. 1863.

[32] The Failsworth Society hired and fired nine butchers over a twenty-eight-month period (Mins. of Committee, 17 Jan., 13 Feb., 4 June, 18 Sept., 23 Oct. 1873; 26 Feb., 9 Apr. 1874; 14 Apr., 10 May 1875); the Manchester and Salford Society employed three successive managers to organise their buying and slaughtering over a seventeen-month period (Mins. of Committee, 23 Feb. 1870; 29 Mar., 19 July 1871).

retail societies, but this was ultimately rejected.[33] The result, to judge from the profit margins ruling in the early 1870s (Table 8.5), was that the financial returns for both societies were disappointing.[34]

The difficulties experienced by the co-operative societies prompt a

Table 8.5   *Profit margins of co-operative butchery departments for selected years in the early 1870s*
(as percentages)

	1870	1871	1873	1874	1875
Manchester and Salford Society					
Gross profit	8.3	12.4	10.8	9.9	8.9
Net profit	–	–	3.4	–	–
Failsworth Society					
Gross profit	–	–	6.9	11.4	8.9
Net profit	–	–	2.6	8.6	6.3

Sources Manchester and Salford Equitable Co-operative Society Ltd, Mins. of Committee, weekly purchases and sales figures, 5 Jan. 1870–20 Dec. 1871; Butchery Department Accounts, 30 Aug. 1873–24 Dec. 1875; Failsworth Industrial Society Ltd, *Quarterly Reports*, 1 Apr. 1873–28 Dec. 1875.

number of questions concerning the viability of the small businesses that made up the greater part of the meat trade in Manchester. It might be assumed that the risks and the constant pressure involved in the weekly cycle of buying, slaughtering, cutting up and selling, together with variations in turnover of the kind indicated in Table 8.4, would have rendered butchers, as a class, particularly vulnerable to exhaustion or to failure. In fact, this does not appear to have been the case. The simple, though laborious, expedient of following up butchery businesses to estimate the proportion still trading after the lapse of a number of years produces impressively high percentages, especially bearing in mind the recording deficiencies of directories,

[33] North of England Co-operative Wholesale Society Ltd, Mins. of Committee, 6, 20 May, 12, 19 Aug. 1871; 17 Feb. 1872; and see *The Co-operator*, 3 June 1871.

[34] In Table 8.5, the calculations follow as closely as possible the conventions used in National Board for Prices and Incomes, Report No. 165, *Prices, Profits and Costs in Food Distribution* (Cmnd. 4645, HMSO, 1971), pp. 65, 79–80, where gross percentage margins = sales – cost of purchases/sales × 100, and the net margins seek to take account of wages and other expenses. For comparison, I have calculated the Manchester and Salford Society's gross margin in its grocery and provision department in 1866 and 1871 to be 30.5 per cent. Note that it is not possible to calculate net profits in every year, or to produce any figures for 1872, owing to gaps in the evidence, usually because figures for overheads, wages, etc. are not given systematically.

which reduce the chances of making successful matches, particularly in the earlier part of the period (Table 8.6).

Table 8.6 *Survival rates of butchers, 1772–1871*

	1772	1788	1800	1811	1815	1833	1840	1850	1861	1871
Number of butchers listed in directory	16	33	71	128	107	421	418	641	576	733
Number of whom listed in next selected directory	8	15	29	49	40	154	175	237	251	–
As a percentage	50	45	41	38	37	37	42	37	44	–

Source Directories (see Bibliography).

Table 8.7 *Number of multiple outlets operated by butchers, 1840–71*

	1840	1850	1861	1871
Number of butchers with				
2 outlets	29	52	39	58
3 outlets	1	3	2	2
4 outlets	–	1	–	–
5 outlets	1	–	–	–
Total number of multiple outlets	66	117	84	122
Total number of outlets[a]	456	706	619	804
Multiple outlets as a % of total	14	17	14	15

Note

(a) From directory listings (see Table 8.1).

Source Directories (see Bibliography).

Further testimony to the stability of the butchery trade is provided by the fact that quite a large number of its members succeeded in establishing businesses with more than one outlet, albeit in some cases in the form of taking on extra market stalls (Table 8.7). The size of these businesses would, of course, have varied considerably. At the meeting which elicited the figures given in Table 8.4, one butcher with a normal weekly turnover of £100, and another who had customers regularly spending £5–£6 per week with him in better times, were each telling their respective tales of woe.[35] Nevertheless, the picture that

[35] *Guardian,* 18 June 1842.

189

emerges clearly from the evidence is that, in Manchester and Salford, the butcher's business was more likely to be a small concern, usually family-run and, perhaps because of this, surprisingly resilient.

ii. The fruit and vegetable trade

Although the various market authorities spent so much of their time debating the vexed question of how to accommodate fruit and vegetable retailers, they remain an elusive quarry for the historian. Documentary evidence on their numbers is scant. The early commercial directories, appearing after 1815, are again manifestly incomplete, and their deficiencies are made all the more striking by the number of traders recorded in the preceding, non-commercial ones. Even the rate books afford little help here. There is no record of the number of stalls specifically designated for dealers in fruit and vegetables because, unlike butchers and fishmongers, they did not require special facilities. Table 8.8, therefore, presents the results of drawing on directories alone to estimate the number of retail outlets.[36]

Table 8.8 *Number of greengrocers' and fruiterers' retail outlets in Manchester and Salford, 1772–1871*

1772	1788	1800[a]	1811[a]	1821	1830	1840	1850	1861	1871
–	5	14	29	4	–	32	85	385	741
Number of which located in markets									
–	3	2	1	–	–	1	32	19	147

Note

(a) Figures for 1800 and 1811 include potato dealers.

Source   Directories (see Bibliography).

The small number of outlets recorded at any date before 1840 is, of course, quite inconsistent with voluminous descriptive evidence of widespread dealing in fruit and vegetables. The most obvious explanation is that these commodities were sold chiefly by producers who had no regular market stall but traded direct with consumers on a casual basis. Certainly, nearly all those brought before the Court Leet for offences involving the selling of fruit and vegetables (mainly apples

---

[36] Wholesalers have been deducted: see Table 8.9.

and potatoes) in the first twenty-five years of the period came from outside Manchester.[37] A survey, in the late 1780s, of the tolls levied by the Lord of the Manor confirms the impression that, within the market framework, this branch of retailing still lacked a permanent core of members. Fruit and vegetable sellers were not usually allocated specific stalls but traded from general areas reserved for 'country people', though there were exceptions. At Smithy Door and in the Market Place, some stalls were set aside for 'gardiners', and these were obviously occupied on a regular basis by local market gardeners.[38] Outside the markets, the few fruiterers and greengrocers operating from shops in the late eighteenth century appear to have catered for a high-class clientele.[39]

However, there were already signs of change, at least as far as potatoes were concerned. Distance from the market was a major consideration for farmers wanting to retail their own produce, and in the late eighteenth century potatoes were already being transported by water from some miles away.[40] Although farmers could bring their produce to the town, they would be reluctant to stay on and retail it through the day as well. Here, therefore, was an obvious area into which middlemen could move, acting as intermediaries between farmers and retailers or consumers. The first case to be brought before the Court Leet involving the sale of potatoes (of short weight) to a retailer came in 1793, and in the highly charged atmosphere surrounding food shortages in the late 1790s, this became an emotive issue. There were numerous cases of regrating (that is, the buying and selling of goods in the same market), and some were on a sizeable scale, involving many loads of potatoes.[41] It is clear that by this time direct transactions between producer and consumer for the purchase of potatoes were becoming increasingly uncommon. James Bentley, a small general shopkeeper, was selling them from his premises in Minshull Street, and the records of his purchases show him usually

[37] In 1770–95, of fourteen offenders whose addresses were specified, twelve were not from the manor of Manchester: they came from Lymm, Altrincham, Stretford, Northwich and Frodsham (*Court Leet*, VIII, IX).

[38] MTH, M1/24/132, Mr Barnes' Book relating to the Tolls, 1787.

[39] See *Mercury*, 4 Jan., 14 Nov. 1780, advertisements of Thomas Revett; 6 Mar. 1804, advertisement of Mary Malham; see also N. Whittock *et al.*, *The Complete Book of Trades*, London, 1837, pp. 239–42.

[40] Above, p. 100.

[41] For example, *Court Leet*, IX, p. 79, 17 Apr. 1793; p. 124, 4 Nov. 1796; p. 134, 27 Oct. 1797; pp. 153–4, 14 Oct. 1799; and see A. Booth, 'Food riots in the north-west of England, 1790–1801', *Past and Present*, No. 77, 1977, pp. 89–90.

buying two loads at a time, often five and, occasionally, as many as ten. In turn, his credit customers regularly bought potatoes from him rather than in the market.[42] Court Leet cases involving false measures provide further examples of general shopkeepers selling potatoes along with more conventional groceries and provisions.[43] This development had two consequences: first, farmers were tempted to complete their transactions outside the markets, though Mosley appears to have been successful in checking this practice; secondly, the official potato market in Shude Hill became recognised as a wholesale one.[44]

The trade in market-garden produce was only a fraction of that in potatoes, and there was far less pressure on growers to surrender their direct links with consumers. It was not feasible, however, even for those farming very close to Manchester to come to market more than once a week, and here, too, the logical step was for conventional retailers to emerge. In fact, after 1800, offenders at the Court Leet charged in connection with the selling of this sort of produce were all residents of Manchester and Salford, describing themselves variously as hucksters, greengrocers or fruiterers.[45] Significantly, in the 1820s, the attention of the authorities began to focus on the allocation of space for greengrocers' and fruiterers' stalls and the attendant difficulties created by them.[46] Even so, the transition to intermediaries came more gradually for other vegetables and fruit than for potatoes. In the recently established markets, such as London Road, trade was firmly in the hands of permanent retailers by the mid-1830s, but elsewhere this was not the case. Producer–retailers still dominated the trading at Smithy Door, and on Saturdays, especially in the summer, both the Market Place and the adjacent streets were 'thronged with farmers and country people' competing for the limited space available.[47]

It was in the 1840s that a shift in the character of the fruit and

---

[42] MCLAD, Misc. 258/1, Accounts for purchase of groceries, 1799–1807.

[43] For example, *Court Leet*, X, p. 39, 18 Apr. 1808; p. 100, 21 Oct. 1812; XI, p. 26, 4 May 1821.

[44] MCL, Broadside ff. 1811/2; J. Aston, *A Picture of Manchester*, Manchester, 1816, p. 217.

[45] For example, *Court Leet*, X, p. 88, 21 Oct. 1811; p. 148, 8 May 1816; XI, p. 95, 13 Oct. 1823.

[46] MCL Broadside ff. 1821/14; MCLAD, M9/30/1/5, MPC, Mins. of General Committee, 10 Oct. 1827; *Courier*, 20 Dec. 1828.

[47] J. Wheeler, *Manchester: Its Political, Social and Commercial History, Ancient and Modern*, London, 1836, p. 347; B. Love, *Manchester As It Is*, Manchester, 1839, p. 160.

vegetable trade became more apparent. The forces of change were not new, but they intensified. On the one hand, by widening the area of supply for the most important commodities, the railways further extended the distance between producer and consumer. On the other hand, as real incomes rose, the weekly trip to market by local farmers was no longer capable of providing an adequate retail service even for market-garden produce. The first sign of change was the growth of the wholesale sector, evidenced in Table 8.9. Among other features, the table demonstrates the importance of the facilities provided by the canal and railway companies. While the agreements between the Council and the companies concerned restricted the goods handled to potatoes and root vegetables,[48] it should be borne in mind that for much of the nineteenth century these formed the major articles of vegetable consumption. For this reason, wholesalers of other products were slower to emerge. At Smithfield, the Council's by-laws of 1851 designated specific areas for retailing and wholesaling, but, as in many of the food trades, a clear division was unrealistic in practice.[49] The 1850 directory does not record a single trader at Smithfield describing himself as a wholesaler; in 1861 four are listed; not until 1871 were a significant number of wholesale dealers operating from there.

Table 8.9 *Wholesale greengrocers, fruiterers and potato merchants in Manchester and Salford, 1840–71*

	1840	*1850*	*1861*	*1871*
Number of businesses	–	30	39	60
Number of outlets located at:				
Castlefield Quay	–	13	5	1
Oldham Road Station	–	4	23	32
Smithfield Market	–	–	4	24
Other addresses	–	14	8	12
Total outlets	–	31	40	69

Source Directories (see Bibliography).

What did decline noticeably was the practice of producers selling direct to consumers. Some market gardeners continued to run regular stalls as they had in the 1780s, and even at the end of the nineteenth century the most tenacious were still resisting pressure to channel their

[48] Above, pp. 107, 109.
[49] MC, *Proceedings*, 12 Mar. 1851; *Guardian*, 15 Mar. 1851.

produce through middlemen.[50] But those wanting to come and pitch their wares on just a few occasions in the spring or summer found this an increasingly difficult proposition. The happy confusion of street trading was now frowned upon, and market space occupied by regular tenants dealing in non-food commodities was not readily relinquished.[51] Moreover, it was not feasible for most growers to trade simultaneously with retailers and consumers. Much of the wholesale trade was conducted very early in the morning, necessitating a midnight start for those driving their carts from a distance; it would have required considerable stamina to retail through the day as well. Some did, but most of the retailing inevitably passed into the hands of full-time urban traders.

For these, the mid-1850s were important years. The decision, in 1854, to clear all stands from the streets around Shude Hill meant that traders were effectively faced with the choice of operating from official market stalls or opening shops.[52] Table 8.8 attests to a very rapid expansion of retail outlets and may well underestimate their numbers, given the tendency of the directories to under-record stall-holders. This impression is confirmed by census occupational returns, showing that the number of adults engaged in the fruit and vegetable trades rose from 269 in 1841 to 767 in 1871.[53] By the 1860s fruit and vegetable retailing had progressed well beyond the casual and chaotic trading of half a century before. Even so, despite its growth, this branch of retailing bore all the hallmarks of a trade that was small in scale and low in status. In the first place, a piece of arithmetic similar to that applied to butchers (Table 8.3), using the occupational data and the number of outlets in 1861 and 1871, produces figures of 1.67 and 1.03 adults per outlet respectively in the fruit and vegetable trade. Secondly, of those adults who described themselves in the census returns as greengrocers or fruiterers, a high proportion (30 per cent in 1861, 29 per cent in 1871) were women, a factor that has tended to be associated with lower-grade occupations. Thirdly, even in 1861 and 1871 no more than 4 per cent of all outlets in this trade were branches of multiples, even if 'multiple' is defined as including businesses with as

[50] G. Whitworth, *Shudehill Markets Mismanagement*, Manchester, 1875, pp. 4–5; W.E. Bear, 'The food supply of Manchester, I, vegetable produce', *JRASE*, 3rd ser., VIII, 1897, pp. 208–9.

[51] *Guardian*, 4 July 1860.

[52] MC, *Proceedings*, 25 Oct. 1854.

[53] Census occupational abstracts (see Bibliography), with a small adjustment to the 1841 census figures as detailed in note 6 above.

few as two addresses.[54] It was observed that 'among shopkeepers, greengrocers stand low in the social scale; . . . no other business can be started with so small a capital, and little skill or knowledge of any kind is required'.[55] These comments relate to London and were made in 1896, but they must have applied with equal force to the Manchester of the 1860s.

iii. The fish trade

We have seen that the distribution networks in both the meat and the fruit and vegetable trades evolved in a piecemeal fashion, in response to changes in the system of supply. This kind of progressive development was more difficult to achieve in the fish trade. Lengthy lines of supply and the absence of producer–retailers might have been expected to favour the early emergence of a wholesale sector, but other factors worked powerfully in the opposite direction. Indeed, an effective distribution network was a prerequisite for an increase in the supply of so perishable a commodity as fish. For many years, however, low levels of consumption discouraged retailers from entering the trade; in turn, this deterred fishermen at the ports from sending large consignments inland; as a result, consumption remained limited. The cycle was self-reinforcing, and it was not until the 1850s that a significant breakthrough occurred.

When Mr Barnes made his survey of the markets in 1787, he counted only one fishmonger – the widow Felton, whose stall stood in solitary splendour – and one seller of cockles and mussels.[56] There had evidently been a decline in consumption since the seventeenth century when fish selling was noticeably more widespread.[57] The continuing paucity of fishmongers at the turn of the century is confirmed by the testimony produced on behalf of both parties in the *Mosley* v. *Walker* lawsuit of 1826. Some of the statements were contradictory, but what stands out in the haze of witnesses' reminiscences is that the two or

[54] Cf. butchers (Table 8.7), and fishmongers (below, note 75).

[55] A. Baxter, 'Grocers, oil and colourmen, etc.', in C. Booth (ed.), *Life and Labour of the People in London*, London, 1896, VII, p. 227.

[56] MTH, M1/24/132, Mr Barnes' Book relating to the Tolls, 1787.

[57] See G.H. Tupling, 'Lancashire markets in the sixteenth and seventeenth centuries – I', *TLCAS*, LVIII, 1945–6, p. 15; J.C. Drummond and A. Wilbraham, *The Englishman's Food*, revised edn., by D.F. Hollingsworth, London, 1957, pp. 63–4; E.H. Phelps Brown and S.V. Hopkins, 'Seven centuries of the prices of consumables, compared with builders' wage-rates', *Economica*, new ser., XXIII, 1956, p. 303.

three regular traders operating twenty-five to thirty years earlier could each be recalled by name.[58]

According to directory evidence, the fish trade in Manchester remained very small in scale until well into the nineteenth century. At no point before 1841 (when the recorded number of fishmongers' outlets was put at twenty-five) did the town directories identify more than three traders. However, since the coverage of the early commercial directories is suspect, and because fishmongers, like butchers, were restricted by manorial law to trading from market sites, the rate books offer a better guide.[59] In this source, there is no specific mention of fish-stalls before 1807, when two were recorded,[60] and subsequent expansion was slow. The market authorities were thus able to contend that provision for fish sellers never failed to meet their requirements. Moreover, although one newspaper questioned the adequacy of the facilities in the new fish market, opened in 1828 and accommodating eleven tenants,[61] there was a noticeable lack of complaint on the part of the fishmongers themselves. Table 8.10 brings together the best estimates of the number of fishmongers' retail outlets operating between 1788 and 1841 and also draws attention to their rapid increase after that date.

From the table it is apparent that the proportion of outlets located in the markets started to fall in the 1840s and continued to decline steadily, although their absolute numbers held up well. Fishmongers had never felt so constrained as butchers by manorial restrictions, and after these had been officially lifted in 1846, there was no precipitate rush to leave the market sites. John Walker's challenge to the manorial rights had been a grand and defiant gesture but an isolated one. The rate books indicate that in the early 1860s the Victoria Fish Market was filled to capacity, and stalls overflowed into the street outside.[62] Indeed, business was so buoyant that it justified the provision, in 1865, of a larger fish hall on the site. By the end of the decade, however, those

---

[58] MTH, M1/50/8, *Sir Oswald Mosley* v. *John Walker*, Brief for Plaintiff, 1826. Note that neither side in the dispute had any interest in understating the number of fish sellers. It was the aim of the Lord of the Manor to show that there had always been sufficient provision of stalls, whereas Walker wished to demonstrate that there had long existed a number of traders selling fish outside the markets.

[59] Apart from Walker's case, no other example has been found of fishmongers challenging the market restrictions. This is confirmed by evidence of George Noton, inspector of markets for Mosley (HLRO, Mins. of Evidence, HC, 1846, CV, Manchester Markets Bill, 8 May, pp. 37–9).

[60] MCLAD, M9/40/2/71, 1807 Rate Book, pp. 305–6.

[61] MTH, M1/50/8, *Mosley* v. *Walker*, Brief for Plaintiff, 1826; *Guardian*, 20 Dec. 1828.

[62] See, for example, MCLAD, M9/40/2/228, 1860 Rate Book, p. 200; MC, *Proceedings*, 29 Oct. 1862.

in the trade no longer considered it a match for a prime position in Smithfield and, by insisting on relocation in the central market, the Victoria fishmongers ensured the continuity of their role in the distribution system for many years to come.[63] Nevertheless, it is clear that the expansion of the trade fell largely outside the established market framework. It is equally certain that the main factor in this progression was the growth of the wholesale sector. For fish, the development of wholesaling was crucial to an improvement in retail provision.

Table 8.10   *Number of fishmongers' retail outlets in Manchester and Salford, 1788–1871*

	1788[a]	1800[a]	1811[a]	1821[b]	1831[b]	1841[a]	1850[a]	1861[a]	1871[a]
Number of outlets	1	2	3	5	11	25	47	80	126
Number of which located in markets	1	2	3	5	11	13	16	17	17
As a percentage	100	100	100	100	100	52	34	21	13

Notes
(a) Directory entries.
(b) Rate book entries.

Sources MCLAD, M9/40/2, Township of Manchester Rate Books; Directories (see Bibliography).

As we saw in Chapter VI, the early railways did not actively encourage the carriage of fish, and it was not until the late 1840s that the benefits of a more rapid means of transport were felt in the trade.[64] Even then, in the lengthy deliberations about the reorganisation of market facilities, accommodation for fish wholesalers was noticeably absent from the agenda of pressing problems. In fact, it was not until the mid-century that the fish trade in Manchester reached that critical threshold at which wholesaling – involving regular and plentiful supplies – became a feasible proposition. In 1852 a wholesaler was allocated some stalls in the poultry section of the Victoria Market, and

[63] Above, p. 170; and see *The Fish Trades Gazette*, 7, 14 July 1883; PP 1890–1, XXXIX, *Royal Commission on Market Rights and Tolls*, XIII, Pt. I, Mins. of Evidence, p. 156.
[64] Above, pp. 130–1.

over the next three years a wholesaling area was allowed to develop informally on the pavement alongside the fish market.[65] Official recognition of the need for proper facilities finally came in 1856 when the Council agreed to a proposal from the Lancashire and Yorkshire Railway Company to establish a wholesale market at the Victoria Station.[66] 'Fish salesmen' were listed for the first time in the 1857 directory and, with the exception of one dealer at the Coleraine Salmon Vaults, all were operating from the new market. Table 8.11 shows how rapidly their numbers grew. Of course, a wholesale depot of the kind provided by the railway company was designed not only to meet the needs of the town itself, but also to supply retailers from the surrounding area.[67] Nevertheless, the rate at which the wholesale sector expanded does seem to indicate that a turning point had been reached, and that fish was no longer considered such a high-risk trade as in the past. The merchant at the port, like Isaac Shutford of Yarmouth, could talk of sending his fish, followed by an invoice, 'in the regular way – to whoever the party is at Manchester',[68] confident that it was the inland wholesaler who would have to bear the loss, if the fish could not be sold.

Table 8.11   *Number of fish wholesalers in Manchester and Salford in 1861 and 1871*

	1861	1871
Fish Salesmen	15	30
(Of whom also have retail outlet	7	10)
(Of whom are also listed as Fish Curers	–	3)
Fish Curers (In addition to above)	–	9
Shellfish Salesmen	6	3
Total	21	42

Source   Directories (see Bibliography).

This review of the history of the fish trade in Manchester contrasts sharply with developments in both the meat and the fruit and vegetable trades. It remained very limited in scale until the mid-century and thereafter expanded rapidly, notably in the wholesale

[65] MC, *Proceedings*, 15 Dec. 1852; *Guardian*, 20 June 1855.
[66] Above, pp. 132–3.
[67] *Guardian*, 27 Oct. 1870.
[68] HLRO, Mins. of Evidence, HC, 1858, XLIV, Manchester, Sheffield, and Lincolnshire and Great Northern Railway Companies Bill, 22 Apr., p. 112.

sector. In general, this picture, with all that it implies in terms of fish consumption, is correct, although there are a few riders that need to be borne in mind. The first is that the seasonal nature of the commodity rendered it particularly suitable for itinerant distribution. How significant this was is an issue that will be addressed in Chapter X.[69] Secondly, it is difficult to assess the role of retailers dealing in shellfish and smoked or salted fish. Shellfish sellers were not accommodated in the fish market that was opened in 1828, and for some years they continued to trade from an area in Smithy Door. Eventually, they were moved into Smithfield, where, in 1850, a special building in Copperas Street, adjoining the main market, was made available for 'the sale of shellfish, herrings and other salted fish'.[70] The whole group cannot have been a large one. Even after this reorganisation, the area they occupied was very limited, and on two consecutive days in 1843 the market lookers arraigned ten traders for selling bad herrings, in what looks suspiciously like a clean sweep.[71] A complicating factor, however, is that smoked and cured fish, unlike shellfish, was often handled by non-specialists; for example, the purchase of the occasional barrel of herrings by shopkeepers and grocers was not an uncommon occurrence.[72] Furthermore, the directories record that in 1836 egg dealers started to include dried fish in their stock and, by 1871, herrings as well.[73]

Finally, the emphasis that has been placed on the relatively small number of outlets, particularly before 1850, does not allow for the fact that the scale on which fishmongers operated (that is, the size of their businesses) tended to be well above the average for other trades, with implications for turnover and consumption. This was certainly recognised by the market authorities, in that from 1828 the accommodation provided for fishmongers was far more substantial than that allocated to butchers and greengrocers: almost half the stalls were double, for 'large dealers', and each had a cellar for storage.[74] A similar exercise to

---

[69] Below, pp. 251–2.

[70] *Courier*, 20 Dec. 1828; MPC, *Tenth Annual Report of Improvement Committee*, 1838; MC, *Proceedings*, 23 Oct. 1850.

[71] MCLAD, M9/40/2/189, 1855 Rate Book, p. 176, gives a gross estimated rental of only £30 for this part of the market; *Court Leet*, XII, pp. 202–5, 10 Oct. 1843.

[72] For example, JRULM, Hibbert-Ware Papers, English MS. 1024, bill from C. Pollit, Importer of . . . Bacon, Hams, Herrings, etc., to Mrs Hibbert, paid 17 Jan. 1812; *The Grocer*, 1, 22 Sept. 1866, advertisements for bloaters; 30 Nov., 14 Dec. 1867, advertisements for 'Finnon Hadies' [*sic*].

[73] *Pigot and Son's Directory of Manchester and Salford*, 1836; *Slater's Directory of Manchester and Salford*, 1871–2.

[74] *Courier*, 20 Dec. 1828.

that performed on butchers and greengrocers, using the occupational data and the number of outlets, adds weight to this view. It is true that the fish trade presents its own peculiar complications in any calculation of the average size of outlets. In 1841, for example, the census category 'fishmonger' must have subsumed fish curers and probably workers in the egg and dried-fish industry, since there are no separate entries for these. Likewise, directory classifications may exaggerate the importance of the trade, in that few fishmongers would have dealt solely in fresh fish: it was recognised that game, poultry and rabbits were part of the fish seller's normal stock-in-trade. In order to circumvent difficulties such as these, it seems prudent to make calculations based on both narrow and broad assumptions about what constituted the fish trade (Table 8.12).

Table 8.12 *Number of fishmongers per outlet in Manchester and Salford, 1841–71*

	1841[a]	1851	1861	1871[a]
(a) *Narrow assumptions* Fishmongers (census)/ Fishmongers' retail outlets – see Table 8.10	4.7	5.2	4.5	3.3
(b) *Broad assumptions* Fishmongers plus Fish Salesmen, Fish Curers, Poulterers, Egg and Dried Fish Dealers (census)/ corresponding outlets in directories	–	3.4	3.5	2.7

Note
(a) Census figures adjusted (see note 6).
Sources Census Occupational Abstracts (see Bibliography); Directories (see Bibliography).

Either approach has its problems, but both sets of figures point to the conclusion that the average size of outlets (and presumably, therefore, turnover) was larger than in the other fresh-food trades.[75] That there should be a marked drop in the average size in 1871 is particularly interesting and highly plausible. For it was in the 1860s, as we

---

[75] Likewise, the number of fishmongers with multiple outlets rose from two in 1850 to nine in 1871, and the proportion of all outlets that were multiple rose from 9 per cent in 1850 to 14 per cent in 1871. For comparisons, see Tables 8.3, 8.7 and pp. 194–5.

shall see in Chapter X, that fishmongers' outlets became more widely dispersed in lower-class districts of the town, and the type of shop being opened would have tended to be decidedly smaller than those previously associated with the trade.

CHAPTER IX

The distribution of groceries, provisions and bread

i. The minor role of the markets

IN CONTRAST to the prominent part played by butchers, fruit and vegetable dealers and fishmongers in the history of market institutions through the period 1770–1870, sellers of other foodstuffs rarely figured. This is not to suggest that the market authorities neglected to provide facilities for dealers in meal, flour, cheese, butter, bread, and the like. Rather, it is an indication of the very early decline of the markets as major channels of distribution for these commodities.

Facilities for meal and flour dealers were available within the markets until the early 1850s: originally in the Market Place, later in Market Street, subsequently at Nichols's Croft and finally in Smithfield.[1] However, in the late eighteenth century most of the trade in meal and flour, like that in corn, was already being conducted illegally outside the markets. This is confirmed by an authorised list of the business addresses of all the wholesale and retail meal, flour and corn dealers in the town, drawn up in 1791 to determine the extent of this unofficial trade.[2]

Cheese dealing cannot have been far behind, since it is recognised as one of the first food trades to have developed a pronounced tripartite structure of producer–wholesaler–retailer.[3] While some large retailers continued to buy direct from farmers, and a few small producers still brought cheese to market themselves, even in the eighteenth century most of the produce from Cheshire was sold off the farm to factors,

[1] MTH, M1/57, History and Situation of the Markets; MCL, Broadside ff. 1821/15; MC, *Proceedings*, 15 Dec. 1852.
[2] MTH, M1/24/133, 'List of wholesale warehouse and shop dealers in Meal, Flour, Corn, etc. in the Town of Manchester', 19 Mar. 1791; and above pp. 152–4.
[3] R.B. Westerfield, *Middlemen in English Business, particularly between 1660 and 1760*, New Haven, Conn., 1915, pp. 204–8.

202

who arranged for it to be shipped to London or taken to Manchester or Stockport to sell to retailers.[4]

On the other hand, the market retained an important retail function for butter until the closing decade of the eighteenth century. The frequent references to butter sellers in the Court Leet records of the 1770s and 1780s signify a thriving trade, comprising mainly producer–retailers, and the same source indicates that some local produce was still being brought to Smithy Door in the 1840s. However, given the increasing quantities of Irish butter reaching Manchester in the 1790s, it is doubtful whether more than a fraction of the total trade was by then conducted in the market.[5] Significantly, when the Smithy Door vicinity underwent some modest improvements in 1839, only five stalls were allocated to butter sellers in the new Victoria Market on the site, and one by one they dwindled away.[6] As was suggested at the time, it would have come as a surprise to most Mancunians to learn that a butter market actually existed there at all.[7]

By the end of the eighteenth century much of the trade in eggs was already conducted by dealers (or higglers), who brought to Manchester the produce of numerous farms, often in distant parts of Lancashire and Cheshire, to sell to retailers.[8] Moreover, the growing traffic in Irish eggs, shipped to Liverpool, then forwarded to Manchester by waterway, had reached such enormous proportions by the mid nineteenth century[9] that it was far beyond the capacity of market stalls.

There is evidence that the market authorities continued to make provision for the sale of bread at Smithy Door until the late eighteenth century. However, the existence of this facility within the market appears to have been closely linked with the Assize of Bread, and the

---

[4] Above, p. 90.

[5] See *Court Leet*, VIII, XII; and above, p. 81.

[6] MCLAD, M9/30/4/4, MPC, Mins. of Lamp, Scavenging, Fire-Engine and Nuisance Committee, 17 Apr. 1839; M9/40/2/144, 1845 Rate Book, p. 306, lists five butter shambles; M9/40/2/228, 1860 Rate Book, p. 201, lists one.

[7] *Guardian*, 11 Dec. 1847.

[8] Holt, p. 185; H. Holland, *General View of the Agriculture of Cheshire*, London, 1808, pp. 293–4.

[9] PP 1826, V, *Select Committee on the Butter Trade of Ireland*, Mins. of Evidence, p. 41; PP 1833, V, *Select Committee on Agriculture*, Mins. of Evidence, p. 175; Mersey and Irwell Navigation Company, Mins. of Committee, 3 July 1835; 15 Oct. 1840. B. Poole, *Statistics of British Commerce*, London, 1852, p. 148, puts the importation of Irish eggs into Liverpool at 90 million *per annum* by 1850.

repeal of this statute in 1815 was largely contemporaneous with the disappearance of bread stalls.[10]

No specific reference has been found to the sale of groceries, such as tea and sugar, from the open market throughout the entire period. Although some market tenants described themselves as hucksters, and might therefore have been dealing in these sorts of commodities, whenever such traders came before the Court Leet, the goods they were selling were invariably fruit or vegetables.[11] The later directories list a few grocery and provision dealers operating from the market hall in Smithfield, but their small numbers only emphasise how peripheral the markets were to the system of distribution associated with these foodstuffs.

ii. The growth of shopkeeping in non-perishable foodstuffs

On the face of things, it should not be difficult to trace the emergence of the shop as the major supplier of commodities in this sphere, using successive directory entries for grocers, tea and coffee dealers, purveyors of bacon and ham, cheesemongers, flour and corn dealers, bakers, confectioners and, of course, those described simply as 'shopkeepers' or 'provision dealers'. In practice, the tabulation of such entries can be very misleading unless the data are scrutinised with great care. One problem is the way in which individual traders might be listed differently in *successive* directories. For example, 23 per cent of the swollen number of flour and corn dealers of 1800 reappeared as shopkeepers in 1811. Yet in 1821 and 1830 the category 'shopkeeper' was omitted, and most of the thirty-four shopkeepers surviving from 1811 who could be traced in the 1821 directory were classified as 'bakers, flour and provision dealers'. Then, there is the more serious problem of multiple entries for individuals in the *same* directory. In 1840, 21 per cent of bakers were also listed as shopkeepers, as were 16 per cent of flour and corn dealers and 13 per cent of grocers. Similarly, in 1871 almost half the tea dealers appeared under other headings, as did all but seven of the forty-four bacon and ham dealers. It should be

[10] MTH, M1/24/132, Mr. Barnes' Book relating to the Tolls, 1787; G.H. Tupling, 'Lancashire markets in the sixteenth and seventeenth centuries – I', *TLCAS*, LVIII, 1945–6, p.15; *idem*, 'Lancashire markets in the sixteenth and seventeenth centuries – II', *TLCAS*, LIX, 1947, pp. 16–17.

[11] See, for example, *Court Leet*, IX, p. 81, 17 Apr. 1793; X, p. 88, 21 Oct. 1811; p. 118, 20 Oct. 1813.

borne in mind, too, that contemporaries often used the terms 'shopkeeper' and 'provision dealer' almost interchangeably, and have been followed in this respect by some modern scholars.[12]

Despite these various difficulties, it is essential to try to measure the aggregate growth of retail outlets for non-perishable foodstuffs, and desirable to offer as detailed a picture of their composition as the sources allow. In arriving at the figures given in Table 9.1, the following steps have been taken:

1. Traders whose businesses appear to have been entirely wholesale have been excluded.[13]
2. The category 'provision dealer' has been reserved for those who were specifically described in the directories as dealing in cheese, butter, bacon and ham.
3. Multiple entries for individuals in the same directory have been eliminated, leaving the retailer in question under the heading that signified the more general pattern of trading.[14] This procedure, though laborious, is essential to avoid double- or even treble-counting.
4. Finally, the lists of traders' names, pruned and adjusted in these ways, have been transformed into outlets, so that retailers with more than one point of sale (rare early on, but increasingly common) have been credited with two, or three, as the case may be.

If we disregard the total figures for 1821 and 1830, which are clearly implausible on account of the omission of the category 'shopkeepers', it is apparent that the aggregate number of outlets of these traders was expanding at a brisk rate in the late eighteenth and early nineteenth centuries. Across the period 1800–71 as a whole, it rose more than sixfold, which was rather more than the growth of the population of Manchester and Salford.[15] More importantly, it is clear that the heavy emphasis given by previous writers to the continuing role of markets, as against fixed shops, in the distribution of non-perishable foodstuffs

---

[12] For example, J. Adshead, *Distress in Manchester: Evidence of the State of the Labouring Classes in 1840–42*, London, 1842, pp. 42, 45. D. Alexander, *Retailing in England during the Industrial Revolution*, London, 1970, p. 99, remarks that 'to some extent, it was arbitrary whether a tradesman was listed as a grocer, provisions dealer or shopkeeper', and refers also to 'compound trading in foodstuffs' (p. 124).

[13] These are covered in Tables 9.5 and 9.6 below.

[14] For this purpose the various categories are arranged in the following order of generality: (1) shopkeeper, (2) grocer, (3) tea and coffee dealer, (4) provision dealer, (5) bacon and ham dealer, (6) cheesemonger, (7) baker, (8) confectioner, (9) flour dealer, (10) corn dealer.

[15] Above p. 19.

Table 9.1 *Number of retail outlets of non-perishable foodstuffs in Manchester and Salford, 1772–1871*

Trade	1772	1788	1800	1811	1821	1830	1840	1850	1861	1871
Shopkeepers	2	125	187	416	–	–	1,027	1,483	2,244[a]	2,729[a]
Grocers and Tea Dealers	30	110	88	134	95	161	235	335	427	516
Provision Dealers[b]	3	4	11	5	18	54	6	17	30	42
Bakers	12	11	58	114	130	93	169	268	350	374
Confectioners	2	10	7	–	18	41	57	119	171	308
Flour and Corn Dealers	16	46	262	66	37	34	38	84	64	67
Total	65	306	613	735	298	383	1,532	2,306	3,286	4,036

Notes
(a) Includes co-operative society branches not listed in directories.
(b) Includes cheesemongers, butter, bacon and ham dealers.

Source Directories (see Bibliography).

is somewhat misplaced.[16] On the contrary, the table indicates that shopkeepers were listed in the earliest directory, that of 1772, and suggests that they accounted for over half of all the retailers of these commodities by 1811. However, the tabulation of directory entries on the lines of Table 9.1 may give a misleading impression in one respect: it does not acknowledge the extent to which a wide variety of foodstuffs were sold by those who were *apparently* specialists in one trade or another, which represents another challenge to received opinion.

iii. The extent of specialisation in the non-perishable food trades

Some have argued that the grocery and provision trades were characterised by a high degree of specialisation. The most obvious examples of the various specialists would be cheesemongers and tea dealers. But even retailers whose range of business was broader had specific areas of trade. Thus, the grocer dealt in foreign produce such as teas, coffees, sugars, spices and dried fruits, and the provision dealer would sell butter, cheese, eggs, bacon, and the like. To Jefferys, this specialisation

[16] See J.B. Jefferys, *Retail Trading in Britain, 1850–1950*, Cambridge, 1954, pp. 3–6; D. Davis, *A History of Shopping*, London, 1966, pp. 253–5.

was central to the structure of the grocery and provision trades in the mid nineteenth century. The presumption was that these specialist shops were directed mainly to the needs of the better-off, leaving the working classes to rely chiefly on markets for their provisions. Moreover, although he conceded that cheesemongers were declining as provision dealers grew in importance, it was not until the last quarter of the nineteenth century that wider changes could be discerned.[17] Already, the evidence of the directories gives the impression that in Manchester, even in the late eighteenth and early nineteenth centuries, these trades did not have such clear lines of demarcation as Jefferys' views might lead us to believe. This suspicion is strongly reinforced by details of what traders actually sold, in so far as information is available.

In this connection, a series of bills received by the Hibbert-Ware family in the early nineteenth century is revealing. The bill-head of Charles Pollit, described as a grocer in the 1811 directory, shows that he dealt in butter, bacon, hams and herrings, as well as the customary sugar and tea, a range of goods almost identical to that carried by Henry Neild, who is listed in the same directory as a mere shopkeeper. Hibbert-Ware dealt with two corn dealers and a flour dealer, all of whom stocked a variety of goods. One, Jonah Twyford, advertised 'butter, cheese, bacon, etc.', in addition to flour and meal; Thomas Moore supplied the family with butter, cheese and pig-meat, as well as rice, meal, bran and flour; and the flour dealer, James Hodkinson, also sold them cheese and butter.[18] Actual trading records of retail outlets are scarce; fortunately, however, some of those kept by James Bentley of Minshull Street, described in the 1800 and 1811 directories as a flour dealer, have survived.[19] In 1799–1802, 44 per cent of his outlay for stock went on flour and meal, 18.5 per cent on butter and cheese, 6.5 per cent on tea and 11 per cent on sugar. Most strikingly of all, the remaining 20 per cent was used to buy in a wide variety of goods, in smaller quantities, including potatoes, bacon, salt, raisins, currants, coffee, treacle, spices, candy, pepper, mustard, rice, and even soap, starch, candles, tobacco and snuff. Nor is there any reason to suppose that the range of Bentley's stock was in any way unusual. Together, the evidence offered by Bentley's accounts and the Hibbert-Ware bills strongly supports the view taken here that the lines of demarcation in

---

[17] Jefferys, *Retail Trading*, pp. 126–30.
[18] JRULM, Hibbert-Ware Papers, English MS. 1024, Tradesmen's Bills, 1802–15.
[19] MCLAD, Misc. 258/1, Accounts for purchase of groceries, 1799–1807.

the grocery and provision trades were very indistinct. Of course, it could be assumed that this was a characteristic of a retailing structure that was only embryonic in the early nineteenth century, and that eventually specialisation would have become more pronounced. Yet it is difficult to be persuaded of this. *The Grocers' Weekly Circular and Price List*, which first appeared in 1846 and was addressed specifically to retail grocers, featured a long price list of commodities that included butter, cheese, ham, pork, eggs and many drysaltery goods.[20] The inaugural issue of *The Grocer*, in 1862, carried a similar list comprising many items that would be classed as provisions rather than groceries.[21]

If the functions of those describing themselves as grocers, provision dealers and shopkeepers were, in practice, very similar, how did the myth of specialisation, reiterated in the work of Jefferys and others, arise? It is probable that the answer lies in the social sphere. Given that the status of shopkeepers in general was always uncertain, it was only to be expected that, as the nineteenth century saw the class divisions of urban society became more pronounced, this would find its reflection in the retail trades. In particular, the title 'grocer' took on a meaning much wider than simply a purveyor of dry goods; rather, it came to refer to someone who dealt with a better class of customer than the humble 'shopkeeper'.[22] Around a search for status developed a mystique and a tradition that, in reality, were based upon the experiences of a very limited section of the trade. Of course, this is not to suggest that the high-class grocer, proud of his skills in processing, sorting and blending, and finding his customers among the upper income groups, had no place in Manchester. Such a grocer was John Fielding at 27, Withy Grove, the issuer, in 1793, of a handsome trade token, which would have served in part as a genteel form of advertising (Plate 12).[23] Another case in point would be Isaac Burgon, whose second cash book, covering the years 1859–62, details deliveries to him of tea, coffee, cocoa, chicory, sugar, sultanas, currants, rice and biscuits – very much the stock-in-trade of the traditional model grocer.[24] Forty years on, John Williams, a leading

---

[20] *The Grocers' Weekly Circular and Price List*, 17 Oct. 1846.

[21] *The Grocer*, 4 Jan. 1862.

[22] For an evocation of this, see J. Aubrey Rees, *The Grocery Trade: Its History and Romance*, London, 1932, II.

[23] H.-C. and L.H. Mui, *Shops and Shopkeeping in Eighteenth-Century England*, Montreal and London, 1989, discuss advertising techniques in chapters 12 and 13.

[24] Isaac Burgon's Cash Book No. 2, 17 Oct. 1859–30 May 1862.

light in the Manchester trade, founded the Grocers' Institute with this class of retailer in mind.[25] But these were not representative figures, for the status of all but the largest traders was ever an ill-defined one. *The Grocer* had not been circulating for very long before it turned its attention to the vexed question of the 'Social Position of Grocers and How to Improve It'. There was no easy answer. Its own advertisers addressed their copy to 'every grocer and shopkeeper', or even 'grocers . . . hawkers and dealers'.[26] When a new magazine, *The Grocer's Journal*, appeared in 1875, it showed a firm grasp of practicalities by pricing itself at one penny, since existing journals for the trade were deemed too expensive.[27] The grocery and provision trade thus encompassed many kinds of retailers, variously described, but distinguished less by the sort of goods they sold than by the social composition of their customers, a fact well recognised by *The Grocer* in more realistic mood.[28]

iv. The scale of businesses

Table 9.2 uses the census occupational data and the number of outlets recorded in directories in the way described in Chapter VIII.[29] For shopkeepers, the results look decidedly bizarre: only in 1841 and 1871 did the number designated as shopkeepers in the censuses correspond to the number of outlets that have been identified in the directories, even if provision dealers and shopkeepers' wives are added in. Undoubtedly, some shopkeepers were either missed or classified in other categories in the censuses, but no reasonable allowance could overturn the conclusion that in the mid nineteenth century the average unit was extremely small. By contrast, the average grocery and tea-dealing outlet appears to have been two or three times as large, though there are no signs of a consistent increase in size here, either.

Calculations of this kind can offer only a very approximate guide; turnover figures are the more direct way of approaching the question of size. Inevitably, though, the level of comparability among the few retailers' account books that have survived is limited, and their

[25] P. Mathias, *Retailing Revolution*, London, 1967, p. 36.
[26] *The Grocer*, 20 Sept. 1862; 3 Jan. 1863.
[27] *The Grocer's Journal*, 3 Dec. 1875.
[28] *The Grocer*, 23 Jan. 1864.
[29] Above, p. 181.

Table 9.2   *Number of shopkeepers, grocers and tea dealers per outlet in Manchester and Salford, 1841–71*

Census designation	1841[a]		1851		1861		1871	
	Adults	All	Adults	All	Adults	All	Adults	All[a]
Shopkeepers	0.96	1.0	0.69	0.72	0.25	0.26	0.44	0.45
Shopkeepers and Provision Dealers	1.12	1.19	–	–	0.77	0.79	0.92	0.96
Above and Shopkeepers' Wives	–	–	0.84	0.87	0.80	0.82	1.00	1.03
Grocers and Tea Dealers	1.97	2.48	2.19	2.87	2.79	3.39	2.31	2.81

Note

(a) Census occupational figures adjusted (see Chapter VIII, note 6).

Sources   Census Occupational Abstracts (see Bibliography); Directories (see Bibliography).

representativeness cannot be taken for granted. In this situation, however, every shred of evidence deserves consideration. At the turn of the century, it is possible to estimate the turnover of James Bentley (Table 9.3). It is interesting to compare the modest levels of weekly takings Bentley endured in the first two years of his business with his subsequent turnover. Prices were rising between 1799 and 1801, but the real growth in his trade is apparent when they began to fall in 1802. As it happens, on an annual basis his sales are not dissimilar to those of Abraham Dent, a Kirkby Stephen shopkeeper, if suitable adjustments are made to take account of an approximate doubling of prices since the 1760s.[30] But it would be unwise to assume that they were typical. For example, Andrew Melrose, an Edinburgh grocer and tea dealer, enjoyed weekly sales of approximately £475 in 1816. It is clear, therefore, that even in this early period there was already a wide range in the size and scope of businesses, as is further evidenced by the diverse bankruptcy cases examined by Alexander.[31]

The first cashbook of Isaac Burgon, later to become one of Manchester's major retailers, suggests, like the Bentley series, that it was

---

[30] T.S. Willan, *An Eighteenth-Century Shopkeeper: Abraham Dent of Kirkby Stephen*, Manchester, 1970, p. 27; and see B.R. Mitchell and P. Deane, *Abstract of British Historical Statistics*, Cambridge, 1962, pp. 469, 471.

[31] In 1816 the turnover of Melrose's two shops amounted to £3,800 per month, an average of £475 each per week (H.-C. and L.H. Mui, 'Andrew Melrose, tea dealer and grocer of Edinburgh, 1812–1833', *Business History*, IX, 1967, p. 34); and see Alexander, *Retailing*, pp. 166–8.

Table 9.3   *Average weekly sales of James Bentley, 1799–1807 (£)*

Year	Average Weekly sales[(a)]	Average Weekly sales[(b)]
1799	6.2	7.8
1800	9.1	10.9
1801	19.5	23.4
1802	29.4	35.3
1807	38.6	46.4

Notes

Bentley's accounts provide figures for most of his wholesale purchases, which have been transformed into average weekly sales, on the basis of assumptions about his gross profit margin, as follows:

(a) A 10 per cent margin (see D. Alexander, *Retailing in England during the Industrial Revolution*, London, 1970, p. 166).

(b) A 25 per cent margin (see T.S. Willan, *An Eighteenth-Century Shopkeeper: Abraham Dent of Kirkby Stephen*, Manchester, 1970, p. 27).

Source   MCLAD, Misc. 258/1, Accounts for purchase of groceries, 1799–1807.

not unusual for a tradesman starting out in business to experience low levels of turnover until he became established. In 1846–47 and 1849–50, Burgon's average weekly receipts were £23 and £29 respectively.[32] The figures produced about this time by William Lockett – again, if typical – denote average weekly takings in the order of £83–£123 for grocers and £70–£105 for provision dealers, according to the state of trade.[33] For the last decade of the period, the evidence of the co-operatives is valuable, even though their typicality cannot be taken for granted. Table 9.4 shows that the Manchester and Salford Society's average weekly sales of groceries and provisions quickly rose above £100 per outlet. Interestingly, however, further success was not channelled into increasing the level of business in each shop but into opening more branches (eleven by 1870), thus keeping the average turnover figures relatively stable.[34] Although the Failsworth Society had more difficulty in establishing its viability, by the late 1860s the weekly turnover in each outlet (five by 1870) was again around

[32] Isaac Burgon's Cash Book No. 1, 1 Aug. 1846–24 Dec. 1863.

[33] Above, p. 182 and Table 8.4.

[34] The summary figures for the Manchester and Salford Society have been reduced by 6 per cent to allow for sales of non-groceries and provisions. See *The Co-operator*, No. 3, July 1860.

£100–£125.[35] The Failsworth Society's early experience is, of course, a reminder that many businesses were operating at a much lower level than this. Overall, however, the receipts of the two co-operatives, together with the figures produced by Lockett, suggest that sales of this order might not be an unreasonable estimate of the turnover of a Manchester retailer, in the middle ranges of the grocery and provision trade, in the period 1840–70.

v. The wholesale function in the grocery and provision trade

Tea-blending and coffee-roasting were central to the status of the specialist grocer, while the provision dealer needed to be expert in assessing the quality of notoriously variable products.[36] In the largest shops, assistants were trained in particular specialities to the point where the young George Heywood, starting out in his own business in 1815, felt uneasy about having to perform a range of tasks in which he was unskilled: 'I find it very strange breaking sugars being unaccustomed to it. I don't know which sorts will do best together.'[37] On the other hand, most small general shopkeepers would have lacked not only the expertise but also the equipment necessary to carry out these tasks, and their viability presupposed the existence of a body of wholesalers to fall back on.

As Table 9.5 demonstrates, very few traders were described unambiguously in the directories as wholesale suppliers of groceries before 1840, but from that point onwards there is a reasonably clear indication of which firms were trading exclusively on that basis. The case of the coffee roasters is an interesting one. In 1830 and 1840 those so described in the directories – with one notable exception – also appeared under other headings, implying that retailers with the necessary expertise offered a service to others less well placed. The exception was the Manchester Coffee Roasting Company, a co-operative venture established in 1823 by 119 signatories to roast the

---

[35] Before 1868, the Failsworth Society figures are for total sales and hence include butchery (for one quarter in 1860) and drapery sales, though these amounts are very small. In 1867 a separate drapery department was opened, and its detailed figures are available from 1868. Groceries and provisions thus account for some 94 per cent of the total sales given in Table 9.4.

[36] See, *inter alia*, Jefferys, *Retail Trading*, pp. 2, 127; Alexander, *Retailing*, pp. 112–15, 123–4; Mui and Mui, 'Andrew Melrose', p. 31; Mathias, *Retailing Revolution*, p. 36.

[37] JRULM, English MS. 703, Diary of George Heywood, p. 62, 7 July 1815.

Table 9.4 *Average weekly sales (groceries and provisions) per outlet of co-operative societies, 1859–70 (to nearest £)*

	1859	1860	1861	1862	1863	1864	1865	1866	1867	1868	1869	1870
Manchester and Salford Society	(a)	118	169	113	88	85	89	100	126	122	117	114
Failsworth Society	33	34	(a)	45	60	61	65	79	100	110	123	126

Note
(a) Figures not available.

Sources Manchester and Salford Equitable Co-operative Society Ltd, summary figures in the *Herald* (magazine of the society), 1860–69; Mins. of Committee, weekly purchases and sales figures, 5 Jan.–28 Dec. 1870; Failsworth Industrial Society Ltd, *Quarterly Reports*, 31 Dec. 1860–3 Jan. 1871. The report for the quarter ending 31 Dec. 1860 provides a summary of sales figures from 1 Apr. 1859.

coffee of members at advantageous rates.[38] The main inference to be drawn from the table, however, is that traders operating exclusively as wholesalers did not begin to emerge in reasonable numbers until about 1840, and even then hardly on a scale commensurate with the needs of the retailers enumerated in Table 9.1.

Table 9.6 presents the results of a similar exercise for the wholesale provision trade. Here, it is somewhat more difficult to decide which traders were wholesalers. 'Factors' and 'merchants' were clearly so, but bacon and ham dealers are an ambiguous case, and a few have had to be included as retailers in Table 9.1 and as wholesalers in Table 9.6.[39] An interesting feature of the provision trade is the early emergence of butter wholesalers, reflecting the importance of Irish supplies. Otherwise, the pattern of development appears to mirror that of the wholesale grocery trade, in that the numbers were small at any point before 1840. One interesting difference is that the trend towards general wholesaling was more noticeable in the provision trade, with an increasing number of traders being listed under two or more headings. However, this must be kept in perspective. The evidence of Tables 9.5 and 9.6 indicates that the lines of demarcation between 'groceries' and 'provisions' were much clearer in the wholesale trade than in the retail sector, and that they became even more pronounced over time. For example, in 1840 seven of the eleven wholesale grocers (Table 9.5) were also listed as butter factors and thus reappear in Table 9.6; in 1850 five out of nineteen were similarly listed; by 1861 only two out of twenty-one were so recorded, and in 1871 only three out of thirty. When, in 1869, the Co-operative Wholesale Society felt that its provision trade would be better served by having its own specialist department, separate from the grocery division,[40] it could be said to be moving with the times.

If taken at face value, the evidence gathered in Tables 9.5 and 9.6 would suggest that wholesale businesses did not emerge in sizeable numbers until after 1840. Yet, as we have seen, retailing in the grocery and provision trades had been expanding long before this, apparently with very little in the way of wholesale support. The explanation lies

---

[38] Manchester Coffee Roasting Company, Articles for regulating and carrying on a Coffee Roasting Concern established in Manchester, 7 Nov. 1823.

[39] To be precise, some bacon and ham dealers, by virtue of also being listed as provision merchants etc., were clearly wholesalers, while others were obviously retailers, in that they were also listed as butchers or shopkeepers. Once these are allocated, the residue appearing in both tables is very small.

[40] North of England Co-operative Wholesale Society Ltd, Mins. of Committee, 6 Feb. 1869.

Table 9.5 *Number of wholesalers in grocery trade, 1772–1871*

	1772	1788	1800	1811	1821	1830	1840	1850	1861	1871
Number listed as										
Wholesale Grocers	–	–	1	4	1	(a)	11	19	21	30
Wholesale Tea and Coffee Dealers	–	–	3	–	1		6	28	–	–
Tea and Coffee Merchants	–	–	–	–	–		–	–	41	77
Coffee Roasters (b)	–	–	–	1	–	8	14	14	6	6
Total	–	–	4	5	2	8+	31	61	68	113
Number of whom listed as										
Wholesale Grocers only	–	–	1	4	1	(a)	8	13	19	21
Wholesale Tea and Coffee Dealers or Merchants only	–	–	3	–	1	–	2	15	36	65
Coffee Roasters only (b)	–	–	–	1	–	8	10	5	3	2
Combination of above	–	–	–	–	–	–	5	14	5	12
Total	–	–	4	5	2	8+	25	47	63	100

Notes

(a) Grocers are listed under the heading 'wholesale and retail' and have been included in Table 9.1.

(b) Includes the Manchester Coffee Roasting Company, omitted in the directories of 1830–61.

Source Directories (see Bibliography).

partly in the role played by 'external' wholesalers, who would not, of course, appear in the Manchester directories, and partly in the wholesale functions discharged by some retail businesses.

There is plenty of evidence to show that wholesalers based outside Manchester came to the town to transact their business. Cheese factors visited the cheese market or the Sawyers' Arms public house, while grocery wholesalers and importers from Liverpool made regular trips to the Old Boar's Head and other public houses.[41] Liverpool, along with London and Bristol, was one of the main centres of the early grocery trade, and large quantities of goods were transported inland from there by the Bridgewater Canal and the Mersey and Irwell Navigation for delivery to Manchester retailers.[42] In the tea trade, London was pre-eminent. Until the East India Company's monopoly ended in 1834, all tea auctions were held in the capital, and provincial wholesalers were thus obliged to play second fiddle to those in London. It was London prices that were quoted in early advertisements, and it was the agents of London dealers who conducted the trade in Manchester before local wholesalers emerged.[43] Although the metropolitan influence was weakened after 1834 as other ports, most notably Liverpool, tried to develop their own trade, even in 1871 seventeen of the tea merchants listed in that year's directory were, in fact, Manchester agents of London firms.[44]

Clearly, the absence of specialist wholesalers in Manchester would have presented few problems for larger grocers and provision dealers. Smaller traders, on the other hand, would have had neither the time nor the business acumen to build up a network of wholesale contacts, and it was in this situation that larger retailers – acting as wholesalers to smaller businesses – played a crucial role. For example, dealers who bought their tea, coffee and chocolate direct from London were able to

[41] E. Baines, *History, Directory and Gazetteer of the County Palatine of Lancaster*, Liverpool, 1825, II, p. 382; E. Allatt, 'The "Ditch": Manchester's provision centre', *The Wholesale Grocer*, Nov. 1954, p. 2.

[42] See, for example, Mersey and Irwell Navigation Company, Mins. of Committee, 5 Nov. 1794; 5 Apr. 1797 (where the consignees are named and can be identified as Manchester grocers); LRO, NCBw 2/2, 13 Aug. 1789; E. Malley, 'The financial administration of the Bridgewater estate, 1780–1800', University of Manchester, M.A., 1929, p. 44; MCL, Parl. f. 385.0942 L1, *Proceedings of the Committee of the House of Commons on the Liverpool and Manchester Railroad Bill*, 1825, pp. 100–12, for evidence of Joseph Harrison, proprietor of the Grocers' Company, about rates charged by the Bridgewater Canal Company.

[43] For example, *Mercury*, 13 Feb. 1770; 19 July 1774; and see Mui and Mui, *Shops and Shopkeeping*, p. 27.

[44] D. Forrest, *Tea for the British*, London, 1973, pp. 118–23; *Slater's Directory of Manchester and Salford*, 1871–2.

Table 9.6 *Number of wholesalers in provision trade, 1772–1871*

	1772	1788	1800	1811	1821	1830	1840	1850	1861	1871
Number listed as										
Provision Merchants	–	–	–	1	–	–	–	12	35	65
Butter Factors	–	–	1	1	–	11	22	28	54	47
Cheese Factors	–	–	–	5	–	–	15	39	53	52
Bacon and Ham Dealers	–	–	–	–	–	–	–	20	38	44
Total	–	–	1	7	–	11	37	99	180	208
Number of whom listed as										
Provision Merchants only	–	–	–	–	–	–	–	7	12	17
Butter Factors only	–	–	–	–	–	11	19	21	21	16
Cheese Factors only	–	–	–	–	–	–	12	26	18	3
Bacon and Ham Dealers only	–	–	–	–	–	–	3	8	10	11
Combination of above	–	–	–	–	–	–	–	16	56	64
Total	–	–	–	7	–	11	34	78	117	111
Number of whom also listed as										
Wholesale Grocers etc. (Table 9.5)	–	–	–	–	–	5	7	5	2	4

Source Directories (see Bibliography).

217

offer quantities for resale to smaller shopkeepers. Such a man was John Currie, listed as a retail tea dealer, who, in the 1770s, advertised these commodities 'wholesale and retail at the very lowest London prices'.[45] About the same time, J. Louthwaite was offering Cumberland butter with 'allowances for a quantity of not less than ten firkins', and Bebbington & Imms drew attention to Cheshire cheese available at their 'shop and warehouse'.[46] It is not difficult to envisage a retailer entering wholesale trading in a small way, for the disposal of goods overbought or acquired astutely, and gradually allowing this aspect of his trade to take precedence over retail transactions. This would have become an increasingly attractive proposition once the problem of storing large consignments had been eased by the practice of waterway carriers, followed by the railways, of offering warehousing free for a time and, subsequently, at low rates.[47] A case in point would be George Southam, described in the directories as a grocer and provision dealer, whose major business in the 1820s was the wholesaling of Irish butter. Another would be William Labrey, ostensibly a retail tea dealer, who supplied no fewer than 2,500 customers with tea, coffee and spices on a wholesale basis.[48]

From the purchasing retailer's point of view, the best evidence of how the system operated is once again provided by the accounts of James Bentley. The sources of his main items of stock over the period 1799–1802 have been analysed to show the proportions bought from dealers with whom he traded once only and those purchased from his main suppliers, and the results are presented in Table 9.7. The picture provided by the figures is a complex one. For tea and sugar, Bentley relied heavily on one or two suppliers. Similarly, much of his cheese came from one dealer, Samuel Swan in Hanging Ditch, though he also did business with a large number of unnamed traders, presumably factors attending the cheese market; occasionally, he specifically mentioned going there, and once even to Stockport market. The way he bought butter is particularly interesting, because the figures disguise the fact that in his first two years of trading he was a regular

[45] See his advertisement in *Mercury*, 17 July 1774.

[46] *Ibid.*, 8 Feb., 30 May 1780.

[47] Mersey and Irwell Navigation Company, Mins. of Committee, 24 Nov. 1834; and see H.B. Wilkinson, *Old Hanging Ditch: Its Trades, Its Traders and Its Renaissance*, London, 1910, p. 84, for the practice of storing butter in railway warehouses in the early 1850s.

[48] PP 1826, V, *Select Committee on the Butter Trade of Ireland*, Mins. of Evidence, pp. 167–74; PP 1833, XXI, *First Report . . . into the Excise Establishment . . . Tea Permits and Surveys*, Appendix No. 54, pp. 168–9.

customer of four dealers whose supplies of Irish produce constituted the major part of his stock. Thereafter, he began to make an increasing number of purchases from unnamed traders, which largely supplanted the supplies from his earlier contacts. Whether this represented a decision to buy less Irish, and more local, butter, or whether he simply felt more competent to make his own assessment of quality, is impossible to know. Rather clearer is the pattern of his trading in flour, the area where one would expect him, as a flour dealer by description, to have had most expertise. At no time did he rely on any individual supplier, nor did he usually deal with unnamed traders. Instead, Bentley dealt with quite a large number of traders, on a regular basis, and often did business with several of them within a short space of time. This was particularly true in 1802 when the price of flour was falling. Furthermore, in this commodity, he had the confidence to deal with suppliers from outside Manchester: one came from Chester, another from Lymm, and there are others who cannot be traced to Manchester addresses. Certainly, with regard to flour, and possibly to butter, Bentley was beginning to shop around for the best buy and to back his own judgement rather than that of his suppliers.

Table 9.7   *Wholesale sources of main items of stock bought by James Bentley, 1799–1802*

Percentage bought from	*Flour*	*Butter*	*Cheese*	*Sugar*	*Tea*
Dealers with whom he traded once only[a]	13	83	72	2	—
His two largest suppliers	31	8	—	69	97
His single largest supplier	(18)	(4)	28	(53)	(59)
Others	56	9	—	29	3
	100	100	100	100	100

Note

(a)   Includes transactions with unnamed suppliers.

Source   MCLAD, Misc. 258/1, Accounts for purchase of groceries, 1799–1807.

In turn, only two of Bentley's major suppliers described themselves as wholesalers. Yet, to judge from Bentley's trade with them, retailers such as Thomas Tebbutt (grocer and tallow chandler), Fogg & Birch, T.S. Fogg, Joseph Owen (all grocers) and J. Clarkson (tea dealer) must have been doing a substantial wholesale trade. For groceries, Bentley also dealt with eleven traders who can be identified as 'flour dealers', like himself, as well as two shopkeepers and six other grocers, in addition to his major suppliers. He did business with a cheesemonger, a cheese and butter dealer, a corn and butter dealer and four corn dealers, none of whom are described in directories as wholesalers. Evidently, by the end of the eighteenth century the grocery and provision trades in Manchester had already evolved a complex structure. Although very few traders described themselves as wholesalers, many larger retailers were acting in this capacity, and numbers of smaller retailers were supplying each other with particular commodities.[49] Accordingly, small shopkeepers would have been able to operate quite successfully long before the growth of the specialist wholesaler.

Table 9.8   *James Bentley's cash and credit payments for wholesale purchases in 1799 and 1802*

Year	By cash at same time	Accounts paid Within 7 days (as a percentage of total)	After more than 7 days
1799	63	7	30
1802	38	24	38

Source   MCLAD, Misc. 258/1, Accounts for purchase of groceries, 1799–1807.

The usefulness of Bentley's accounts does not end here, because they also shed light on the important matter of credit and attest to the caution with which it was extended. Table 9.8 analyses his wholesale purchases in the years 1799 and 1802, based on the dates when he paid the accounts. In his first year of trading, most of Bentley's transactions were on the basis of what he described as 'cash at same time'. Even after three years, much of his stock was paid for either in this way or within seven days. Naturally, dealers with whom he traded once only or infrequently would expect to be paid promptly, but the usual pattern with his larger suppliers, too, was for Bentley to begin on a cash basis and then to be allowed to buy on credit. While the table

[49] Recently, these links have also been remarked on for Cheshire (see I. Mitchell, 'The development of urban retailing, 1700–1815', in P. Clark (ed.), *The Transformation of English Provincial Towns, 1600–1800*, London, 1984, p. 277).

Plate 10 Irish butter on sale at Mr Hyde's shop in Market Street, 1823

Mitchell William, 15 Pall mall
Mycock Thomas, 51 Oxford st, C on M
Nickling James, 47 Boundary st, West.
 Chorlton on Medlock
Parkhurst Henry Francis [and valuer],
 28 Princess st
Pratt James, 73 Great Ducie street, S
Pratt William Henry [& arbitrator], 65
 Faulkner st
Prescott John [& valuer], 73 Princess st
Royle Pookes [& valuer], 52 Princess st
Scully Patrick D. 25 Higher Oswald st,
 Shudehill [nose at
Sheppard Walter [& valuer], 16 Brazen-
 stead & Lomas, 11 Cooper st
Taylor Joseph [and valuer for probate],
 2 Tib lane
Taylor William, 22 Corporation st
Thomas John, 21 Bridge st, Deansgate
Westall Thomas, 13 Bond st
Whittaker Thomas Edward, 55 Cross st
Williamson William, 11 John Dalton st
Wood James [valuer], 9 St. Mary's gate

Axle Tree Makers.

Cary Wm. [spring], Mount st, Red bank
Wagster William, 1 Murray street, and
 Blossom st, Ancoats—*See advert.*

Baby Linen & Ladies' Under-clothing Warehouses.

Atkinson Mountain, 37 Deansgate
Blakey Elizabeth, 5 St. Ann's place
Carter Jos. 157 Gt. Ducie st, Strangeways
Cook Thomas, 11 St. Mary's gate
Cook S. A. & J. 7 King st
Faulkner Rebecca, 70 Deansgate
Forbes Elizabeth, 241 Oxford st, C on M
Griffith Margaret, 275 Oxford st, C on M
Grecott M. A. & L. Old Exchange passage
Hadkinson Jane, 101 Stockport road
Hitchen Winifred, 90 Deansgate
Jewsbury & Crux, 74,76 & 78 Deansgate
Johnson S. L. & E. 205 Oxford st, C on M
Latham Mary, 24 Oxford st, C on M
Massey Elizabeth Martha, 12 Upper
 Brook st, Chorlton on Medlock
Osbaldiston Mary Ann, 102 Oxford st
Peel Thomas, 125 Oldham st
Preen Joseph, 24 Tib st
Reilly James, 285 Oxford st, C on M
Robinson Margaret, 99 Deansgate
Sheldon Mary & Sarah, 182 Stretford rd
Slinn, Abraham, 93 Oxford st, C on M
Southworth Ann, 199 Broad st, Pendleton
Spencer Etty, 3 Ogden st, Piumili brow
Thomas John, 82 & 84, Deansgate
Waring Blanche, 58 Oldham road
Wills John, 23 King st [King st
Withers Phœbe, 6 Old Exchange passage,
Wood Sarah, 170 Stretford road, Hulme

Bacon and Ham Dealers

(*See also Cheese Factors, Provision Dea-
lers, Shopkeepers, and also Pork But-
chers, under Butchers.*)
Allen John, 74 Market st
Allen Peter, 7 Smithy door, Market st
Annacker Peter, 132 & 134 Oxford street
 Chorlton on Medlock—*See advertisment*
Bibby & Norton, 9 Shudehill
Boullen William, 92 Oldham st
Briggs James, 16 Victoria st, Market pl
Broady Thomas & Robert, 23 Shudehill
Brundrett Jeremiah, 65 Shudehill
Clay Francis, 118 Oxford st, C on M
Craven John S. 21 Oxford st, C on M
Cutting Charles, 167a Oxford st, C on M
Darbyshire James,5 Goadsby st,Shudehill
Dixon John (Cumberland), 13 Shudehill
Dobell S. & Co.14 Withy grove
Edwards Thomas 47 Swan, st
Entwistle Mark,5 Swan sr
Hill Henry Geo. 89 Oxford st, C on M
Holmes James, 12 London road
Hope Charles, 63 Shudehill
Hope Thomas, 81 Oxford st, C on M
Iredale Richard, 10 St. Mary's gate
Johnston W. M. & Co. 14 Oak st,Swanst
Jones & Co. 13 Shudehill
Latham Samuel, 358 Stretford road, H
M'Williams John. 1 Goadsby st,Shudehill
Meakin Thomas, 13 Thomas st
Myers Mary, 193 Deansgate
Nesbit John, 9 Goadsby st, Shudehill
Parkinson John, 63 Shudehill
Renshaw George and Ralph, 73 Shudehill
Rider Henry, 51 Shudehill
Rodgers John, 41 Swan st
Sutcliffe Richard, 58 Market st

Swift Matthew, 44 Shudehill
Taylor William, 64 Oldham st
Thompson Wm. 6 Downing st, C on M
Townley John. 52 Shudehill
Wood James, 49a Shudehill

Bag Makers
See Paper Bag Makers.

Bakers and Flour Dealers
(*See also Corn and Flour Dealers.*)
Adderton John, 45 Greengate, Salford
Ainsworth James, 3 Young st, Quay st
Allcock Gregory, 95 Rochdale road
Allsworth Wm. Henry, 161 LongMillgate
Almond James, 344 Oldham road
Anbery Isaac, Crown st, Ashley lane
Andrew James, 32 Thomas st, Shudehill
Ainsworth Ann, 169 Rochdale road
Antrobus William,54 Downing st,,ConM
Arlott David, 65 Hope st, Salford
Armitage Charlotte, 457 Rochdale road
Ashton James, 4 Ashley lane
Avison William, 26 Rochdale road, and
 262 Deansgate
Bailey Abraham, 11 Boond st, Ancoats
Balls William, 33 Greek st, C on M
Barber John, 358 Oldham road
Barber Thomas, 48 Stretford road, H
Barber William, 51 Bury New road
Barlow Thomas, 241 Broad st, Pendleton
Batey Joseph, 290 Deansgate
Batty John, 51 Goulden st, Oldham rd
Baxter Richard, 3 Ellor st, Cross st, S
Beardmore George, 163 Rochdale road
Beaty Thomas, 135 Chester road, Hulme
Beech George, 11 Regent road, Salford
Beeson John, 82 Rochdale road
Belk William, 60 Silk st, Salford
Bell James, 44 Arlington st, Salford
BellHenry(biscuit), 55 Tame st, Ancoats
Bennett Adam, 28 Cross st, Hanover st
Bennett John, 55 Oak st, Swan st
Bennett Peter, 229 Deansgate and 194
 Stretford road, Hulme
Bennison Thomas, 84 Oldham road
Birchall William, 155 Oldfield road, S
Blakeley George, 141 Travis st
Boddy Christopher, 194 Rochdale road &
 Collyhurst
Boden Henry, 68 London road
Bolderson John (and corn dealer), 86 Gt.
 Ducie st, and 74 Oldham st
Bonser Richd. 112 Osborn st, Oldham rd
Booth George, 471 Rochdale road
BoultonThomas, 75 Butler st, Oldham rd
Bowling Thomas, 47 Broad st,Pendleton
Bradley Thomas, 117 Canal st, Ancoats
BradshawJoseph, 90 Upper Mess lane,H
Braithwaite John, 61 Medlock st, Hulme
Brammall Thomas, 91 Chapel st, Salford
Brennan Elizabeth, 11 St.Thomas st
Brierley John, 79 Ridgway st, Butler st,
 and 368 Oldham road
Britton James, 28 Acton st
Britton Robert, 318 Stretford road, H
Brooke James, 100 Medlack st, Hulme
Brooke James S. 154 Warde st, Hulme
Brooke William, Crown Bakery, 77 &
 79 Brook st, C on M, & 53 Portland st
Brownhill John, Ashton Old road, O
Buckley Edward, 22 Sackville st
Buckley James, 26 Lloyd st, Oldham rd
Bullough James, 52 & 128 Stretford rd,H
Bunting Robert, 2-7 Deansgate
Burton Amos, 7 Victoria Bridge st, S
Burton John, 115 L ng Millgate
Burton Thomas J. 20 Oxford st. C on M
Burton William, 184 Chapel st, Salford,
 11 Oldham road, and 13 Albert place,
 Bridge st
Butt John, 34 Chapelfield rd,Union st, A
Butterworth Jas.. Hannah st,Rochdale rd
Calvert Joshua, 29 Butler st, Oldham rd
Capper George, 48 Erskine st, Hulme
Carrington Joseph, 184 Deansgate
Carter Robert, 92 Broughton road S
Chambers & Arnott (biscuit), Strangeways
 st. Adelphi, Salford
Chapman Samuel, 19 Whitecross bank,S
Chester John, 109 Sudell st. Livesey st
Chettle William, 34 Upper Jackson st. H
Clark John, 13 Bank parade, Salford
Clark & Green (fancy bread & biscuit),14
 Medlock st, Hulme, 20 Swan st, and
 38 Market st
Clarke Samuel, 60 Lloyd st, Hulme
Cliffe James, 100 Fairfield st
Cockayne James, 99 Rochdale road
Conrath Philip H. 3 Hornby st,BuryN rd

Connor Samuel, 4 Cross st, Swan st
Cooke George, 85 Broad st. Pendleton
CO-OPERATIVE STORE, 142 Broad st, P
CO-OPERATIVE STORE, 124 Stockport rd
Cooper Mark, 78 Pollard st, Ancoats
Coup William, 16 Rochdale road
Crane John, 294 Oldham road
Crime Joseph, 12 Bradford st,N.Islington
Crompton Ellis, 16 Charles st, C on M
Crompton Henry, 46 Travis st
Crossley Henrv, 81 Chapel st, Salford
Crowther William, 2 Back Ridgefield
Daniels Sarah, 49 Byrom st, Quay st
Davies Edward, 3 Rogers st, Red bank
Davies Edward, 47 Brook st, C on M
Davies John, 76 York st, Hulme
Deane James, Derby pl, 256 Regent rd,S
Deane Philip, 52 Regent road, Salford
Dearden John, 3 Gun st, Ancoats
Dempsey Peter, 23 Bury st, Salford
Diggle Wm. 19 Rusholme road, C on M
Dodd John, 24 Peel st, Pendleton
Downs Edwd. 45 Primrose st
Drinkwater James, 280 Oldham road
Dunn Murdoch and Co. (steam biscuit),
 Blackburn st, Adelphi, Salford
Eaton Edwin, 265 Chapel st, Salford
Edwards John, 49 Camp st, Byrom st
Etchells Issachar, Church st, Newton H
Evans William, 6 Ashley la, L. Millgate
Falkner Joseph, 14 Rochdale road
Farrell John, 18 Booth st West, C on M
Fenton William, Oldham rn, Newton H
Finney Mary, 498 Oldham road
Fisher John (biscuit), Wesley st, C on M
Fitchet Joshua, 8 Sackville st,Portland st
FitzgeraldEdwd.3Tebbutt st,Rochdale rd
Fletcher Richard, 153 Broad st,Pendleton,
 & 34 Arlington st, Salford
Forrest James, 141 Chester road, Hulme
Foster&Duncan, 61 Oxford st,St.Peter's,
 and 47 Market place
Frost Jas 81 Gt. Ducie st, Strangeways
Furness John, 299 Stretford road
Garside George, 39 Great Ancoats st
Garside Thomas, 23 Every st, Ancoats
Gibson Daniel, 176 & 178 Oldham road
Gilbert Samuel, 43 Booth st Wt, C on M
Gleave Ellen, 31 Brook st, C on M
Gleave John, 20 Molyneux st, C on M,
 and 134 Great Ancoats st
Greenwood Edward, 116 Oldham road
Greenwood John, 78 London road and 32
 Oxford st, Chorlton on Medlock
Gregory John, 6 Great Ancoats st
Hatfield George,154 Butler st,Oldham rd
Hailwood Richard, 204 Rochdale road
Handforth Charles Jenkinson 119 Broad
 st, Pendleton
Handforth Daniel, 134 Oldham road
Handforth Thomas, 67 Oldfield road,S
Handforth John William, 31.Bank parade
 and 216 Regent road, Salford
Hargreaves John, 85 Loom st, Poland st
Harrison John, 289 Great Ancoats st
Harrison Samuel, 138 Chester road
Heywood Thomas, 84 Pollard st, Ancoats
Hibbert James, 122 Broughton road, S
Hilditch George. 33 Chancery lane, A
Hodgkinson Frederick, 64 Embden st, G
Holbrook Thomas, 37 Oxford st, C on M
Holehouse George,,57 Long Millgate
Holland George, 114 Red bank and
 48 Oldham road
Holland James, 110 Oldham road
Holland James, 50 Charter st, Shudehill
Holland Joseph, 17 London road, and
 60a Oldham st [Deansgate
Horsfield John, [biscuit] 3 Lad lane,
Horsfield John, Holt's yard, Peter st
Howarth Joseph,.56 Thomas st
Howe Robert, 8 Hope st, Salford
Hughes Daniel, 126 Cheetham hill
Humphreys James, 180 Rochdale road
Huxley James, 60 Fairfield st
Illingworth James [and corn dealer],
 119 London road [Strangeways
Irving Thomas, 71 Great Ducie st,
Jameson Thomas, 51 Clarendon st, H
Iuce William, 4 Elias st,Rochdale rd
Jackson John Henry, 34 Oldham road
Johnson & William, 16 Downing s',
 Chorlton on Medlock
Jenkins William 215 Deansgate
Johnson James, Corporation st
Johnson James, 1 Union terrace, Cheet-
 ham hill [road
Johnson Reuben, 25 Prussia st, Oldham
Johnson Richard, 98 Broughton road, P
Johnson William, 309 Deansgate
Kay Enoch, 195 Chapel st, Salford

Plate 12 Trade token issued in 1793 by John Fielding, grocer, of 27, Withy Grove, Manchester (Diameter of actual token: 2.8cm)

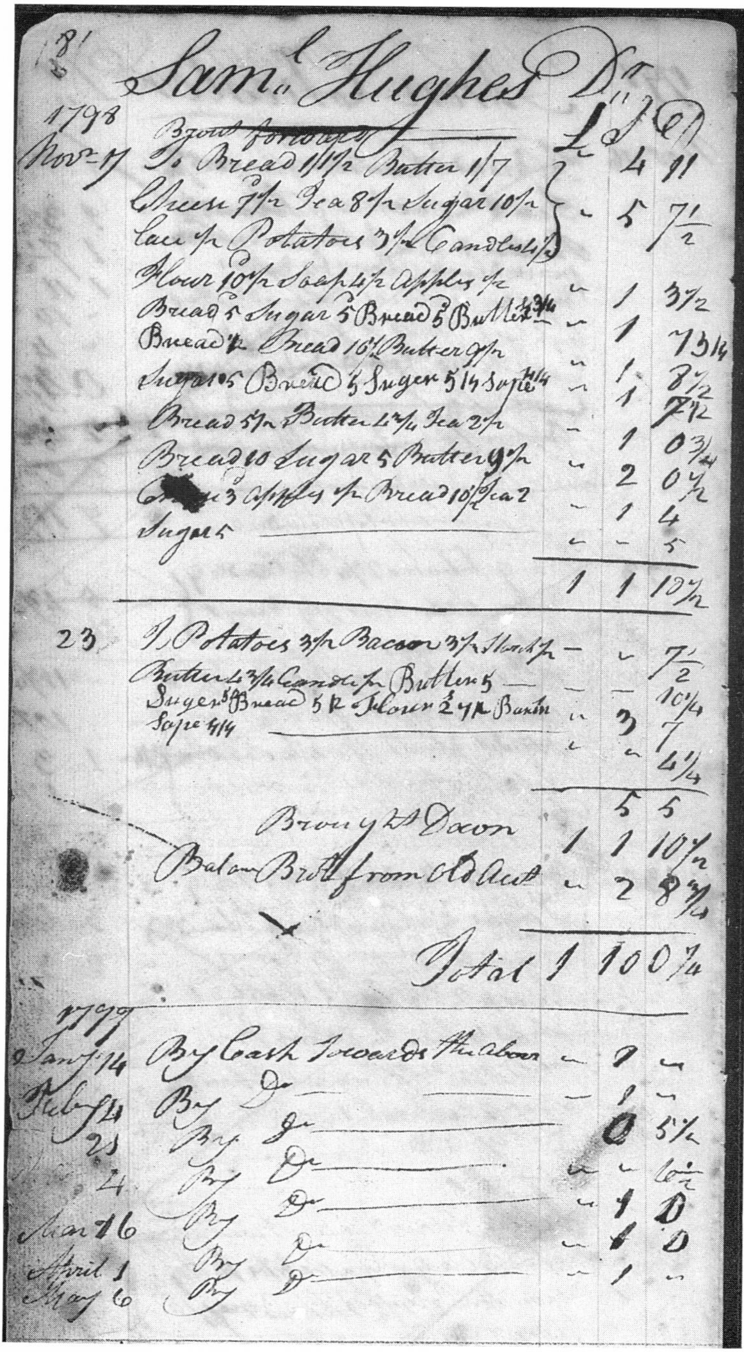

Plate 13 A page of James Bentley's customers' credit ledger, 1798, showing Samuel Hughes's unpaid account

demonstrates Bentley's success in gaining the confidence of his suppliers, it also suggests that credit was not a privilege lightly given.

vi. The case of the bakers

Home baking is often seen as a traditional craft that was an inevitable casualty of town life. It is thought to have lingered in the north longer than in the south partly because of the availability of cheaper fuel, and partly because of the existence of an innate northern pride in home-baked bread, in contrast to the effete southern predilection for the shop-bought variety.[50] In 1817 the Stipendiary Magistrate of Manchester could assert that such skills were widespread and that bread was bought only in households where the wife went out to work.[51] There is some evidence, direct and indirect, to suggest the continuation of the tradition of home bread-making in Manchester, albeit in a modified form. Given that flour and yeast were widely available, and there is no reason to assume otherwise, it was possible to prepare the dough at home and, if desired, to take it elsewhere to be baked. Although it was suggested that the town had no public bakehouses in 1804, there were at least four by 1811, according to that year's directory, and it was about this time when one observer estimated that approximately half the bread eaten in Manchester was baked in this way.[52] An alternative was to use the local baker's oven, for a small charge, a practice that was still common at the end of the nineteenth century.[53]

Even so, it is evident from Table 9.1 that bakers had established themselves as one of the major categories of food retailers by the early nineteenth century, and the growth of outlets continued apace. Moreover, while many bakers sold a range of goods, it is also certain that other retailers sold bread. As early as 1765, 44 per cent of the money

[50] H. Perkin, *The Origins of Modern English Society, 1780–1880*, London, 1969, p. 154.

[51] PP 1818, V, *Report by the Lords' Select Committee on the Poor Laws*, Mins. of Evidence (taken 31 May 1817), p. 249.

[52] J.R. McCulloch, *A Dictionary, Practical, Theoretical and Historical, of Commerce and Commercial Navigation*, new edn., London, 1844, p. 182; *Pigot's Manchester and Salford Directory*, 1811; PP 1814–15, V, *Report from the Committee on Laws relating to the Manufacture, Sale and Assize of Bread*, Appendix No. 8, p. 147.

[53] See, for example, SC, *Proceedings*, 20 Oct. 1864; Failsworth Industrial Society Ltd, Mins. of Committee, 17 Feb. 1868; E.M. Schofield, 'Food and cooking of the working class about 1900', *Transactions of the Historic Society of Lancashire and Cheshire*, CXXIII, 1971, pp. 155–6.

owed to John Moss, a debtor baker, for 'goods sold and delivered' was due from 'shopkeepers'. In 1812, Stephen Burton, a baker in similar straits, was owed large sums of money by two shopkeepers.[54] In both cases, it is reasonable to assume that these debts represented the supply of bread for resale. In the 1790s, all those who bought more than a narrow range of goods on credit from the flour dealer, James Bentley, purchased bread at some time, and most did so regularly. Even in the rural suburb of Didsbury, the sales accounts of the Wood family show that bread was commonly bought by their customers.[55] By 1821 it was recognised that buying 'bread by weight down to a single pound' was the normal practice among the poorer classes in Manchester.[56] In the light of all this evidence, Edward Smith's conclusion, in his survey of the level of nourishment of distressed operatives in Lancashire and Cheshire in 1862–63, that a large proportion of bread was baked at home, seems paradoxical. It should, however, be read as referring to these counties as a whole, because his detailed budgets of Manchester families reveal that, in all but one of the cases, their bread was mainly, and often always, bought from shops. Even the exception was a family turning to home baking as a more economical alternative to its usual practice of buying bread.[57]

The size of the industry that was encouraged by these changing habits was considerable, though it remained technically primitive and is generally reckoned to have been dominated by small businesses. Nationally, bakehouses employed an average of 3.3 persons in 1871,[58] and in Manchester, if anything, the trade was on an even smaller scale. A survey of Salford bakeries in 1864, following the Bakehouse Regulation Act of the preceding year, found that the average establishment employed 1.4 persons.[59] No doubt some employers evaded the net in this first survey, but the small-scale nature of the trade is confirmed by census occupational figures. Unfortunately, the census data do not differentiate between

[54] LRO, QJB 37/30; QJB 57/10.

[55] MCLAD, Misc. 258/1, Accounts for purchase of groceries, 1799–1807; M62/1/1–3, Ledgers of William and Thomas Wood, innkeepers, shopkeepers and farmers of Didsbury, 1767–1838.

[56] PP 1821, V, *Select Committee on the existing Regulations relative to the making and the sale of Bread*, Appendix A, p. 8.

[57] PP 1863, XXV, *Fifth Report of the Medical Officer of the Privy Council*, Appendix V, No. 3, *Economics of Diet*, pp. 346, 375–6, 386–8, 394–5, 397–9.

[58] J.H. Clapham, *An Economic History of Modern Britain*, Cambridge, 1932, II, p. 119.

[59] SC, *Proceedings*, 20 Oct. 1864. There were 162 persons employed in 116 bakehouses in the area.

bakehouse employees and bread retailers, but a simple division of the total number of persons designated as bakers in the census returns, by the total number of bakers' outlets in directory listings, produces a ratio of 2.6 adults per outlet in 1871.[60] Since a good many of the bakehouses and their retail outlets were situated on separate sites, this statistical artefact often had to span two premises. Table 9.9 provides further evidence that the number of bakers operating a business large enough to supply two outlets remained relatively small, despite their long-established presence on the retail scene and the obvious scope for economies of scale in the industry.

Table 9.9 *Number of multiple outlets operated by bakers, 1772–1871*

	1772	1788	1800	1811	1821	1830	1840	1850	1861	1871
Number of bakers	12	11	58	113	128	94	202	293	349	361
Number of whom with										
2 outlets	–	–	–	1	2	3	7	18	24	37
3 outlets	–	–	–	–	–	–	1	–	2	5
4 outlets	–	–	–	–	–	–	–	–	–	–
5 outlets	–	–	–	–	–	–	–	–	–	1
Total number of multiple outlets	–	–	–	2	4	6	17	36	54	94
Total number of outlets	12	11	58	114	130	97	211	311	377	412
Multiple outlets as a % of total				2	3	6	8	12	14	23

Source Directories (see Bibliography).

This is not to say that there were no signs of impending changes. In 1871 two Manchester bakeries were using steam power, and McDougall Brothers had adopted the new, aerated bread process.[61] As to output, the bakery department of the Manchester and Salford Co-operative Society was making great strides. By 1873 it was turning out 11,450 loaves per week, which was eleven to twelve times the quantity produced by the average baker in 1862, according to the

---

[60] If the census figures are adjusted (see Chapter VIII, note 6), the ratio is 3.3 workers per outlet.
[61] *Slater's Directory of Manchester and Salford*, 1871–2.

findings of the factory inspector, H.S. Tremenheere.[62] Moreover, like the Failsworth Society, it had introduced bread-rounds, in addition to supplying its branches.[63] On the other hand, not a single wholesaler is listed in the directories throughout the entire period, and vertical links between millers, corn merchants and bakers were almost non-existent, in sharp contrast to the evidence of horizontal overlapping between retail bakers and other traders.[64] Here, without doubt, was a food trade where the small producer–retailer still stood supreme. For Manchester, as for elsewhere, Tremenheere was correct in suggesting: 'There is probably no branch of trade supplying a vast and constant demand which has so completely remained in the primitive condition of ministering to that demand from a multitude of small and insulated sources as the baking trade'.[65]

It is interesting to consider how far these general conclusions about the bakery industry are applicable to the confectionery trade. Confectioners were established early in Manchester. From the two gingerbread sellers of 1772 their numbers grew steadily to the point where, in 1871, they closely rivalled bakers (see Table 9.1). It might be assumed that they would have developed in close association with bakers, in that their wares ranged from sweets and fruit preserves to pastries, cakes and biscuits.[66] In fact, the Victorian census returns always treated bakers and confectioners as separate categories, and the very small element of overlap in the Manchester directories appears to confirm that the two trades developed along distinct paths.[67] If anything, the confectionery business was conducted on an even smaller scale than the bakery trade: there was a very high proportion of single outlets, and more than half of those engaged in the industry were women.[68] On the other hand, it was becoming

---

[62] Manchester and Salford Equitable Co-operative Society Ltd, Bakery Department Accounts, 16 Aug.–13 Dec. 1873. Tremenheere's figures are given in *PP* 1862, XLVII, *First Report . . . relative to the grievances complained of by the Journeymen Bakers*, pp. xii, lvi.

[63] Failsworth Industrial Society Ltd, Mins. of Committee, 27 Nov. 1871; 15 Jan. 1872; Manchester and Salford Equitable Co-operative Society Ltd, Mins. of Bakery Committee, 15 Oct. 1873; 9 June 1875; 17 July 1878.

[64] From directories listed in the Bibliography, the first vertical overlap was in 1840, 1 baker/miller and 2 baker/corn merchant, miller; 1850, nil; 1861, 4 baker/corn merchant, miller; 1871, 1 baker/miller and 3 baker/corn merchant, miller.

[65] *PP* 1862, XLVII, *First Report . . . relative to the grievances complained of by the Journeymen Bakers*, p. xiii.

[66] See Alexander, *Retailing*, pp. 125–6.

[67] The number of bakers also listed as confectioners in the directories is: 1821, 1; 1830, 1; 1840, 2; 1850, 6; 1861, 5; 1871, 15.

[68] Employees (from 1871 census returns) / outlets (from 1871 directory) = 1.7 adults or 2.0 (all ages) per outlet, when census figures are adjusted (see Chapter VIII, note 6). From directories

considerably more advanced than the bakery trade in some aspects of organisation and production. There were a number of specialist wholesalers in Manchester, six in 1861 and sixteen by 1871.[69] The manufacture of biscuits, in particular, was making significant headway. By the 1850s a number of large biscuit firms were already well established on the national scene, and their products were starting to reach Manchester. In the 1860s Isaac Burgon was taking deliveries direct from Huntley & Palmer of Reading; by the early 1870s other manufacturers, such as Gray, Dunn & Co. of Glasgow, had opened their own retail outlets in the city.[70] It is noteworthy, too, that confectionery was the area which the Co-operative Wholesale Society chose for its first venture into factory production. By 1873 biscuits, currant bread and boiled sweets were being made at its works in Crumpsall in north Manchester.[71]

vii. The role of consumer credit

Credit was a deep-rooted institution in the retail trade. The Hibbert-Ware family was evidently in the habit of running up quite substantial bills over a number of months, and the settling of the credit accounts of this class of customer was a perennial headache for grocers, butchers and fishmongers everywhere.[72] However, it was the prevalence of credit offered by traders catering for the lower end of the market that occasioned most contemporary comment. As early as 1775 the Reverend John Clayton inveighed against the 'shameful extravagance' of the poor of Manchester and their tendency to buy on credit from shopkeepers instead of in the open market, so that their income was

---

listed in the Bibliography, multiple outlets as a percentage of total outlets were: 1840, 2/59 (3%); 1850, 11/131 (8%); 1861, 15/186 (8%); 1871, 36/339 (11%). From census occupational returns, the percentage of female adult confectioners was: 1841, 41%; 1851, 52%; 1861, 56%; 1871, 54%.

[69] *Slater's Directory of Manchester, Liverpool and the Principal Manufacturing Towns in Lancashire*, 1861; *Slater's Directory of Manchester and Salford*, 1871–2.

[70] T.A.B. Corley, 'Nutrition, technology and the growth of the British biscuit industry, 1820–1900', in D.J. Oddy and D.S. Miller (eds.), *The Making of the Modern British Diet*, London, 1976, pp. 18–20; Isaac Burgon's Cash Book No. 2, 17 Oct. 1859–30 May 1862; *Slater's Directory of Manchester and Salford*, 1871–2.

[71] P. Redfern, *The New History of the C.W.S.*, London, 1938, p. 34.

[72] JRULM, Hibbert-Ware Papers, English MS. 1024, Tradesmen's Bills, 1802–15; and see, for example, *The Fish Trades Gazette*, 16 June 1883; Willan, *Abraham Dent*, pp. 26–7; M. Weinstock, *More Dorset Studies*, Dorchester, 1960, p. 89.

'generally spent before it [was] received'.[73] A general shortage of small coinage in the late eighteenth century was another factor encouraging, or perhaps obliging, shopkeepers to allow customers to run up small amounts of debt.[74] This is evidenced in Table 9.10, which analyses the money owed to various traders in Manchester and Salford in the late eighteenth and early nineteenth centuries. As we have already seen, some of the larger debts were owed by fellow retailers, but the rest were clearly customers' unpaid bills, and involved such small sums that they could scarcely have represented the credit accounts of middle-class clients.

It is difficult to be precise about the extent of consumer credit, since contradictory impressions abound. In 1833 it was suggested that in nearby Stockport one-half of the 'commodities purchased for domestic purposes' were bought on credit. In Manchester, according to Neild, credit was 'a very common, if not the general, practice for the working classes', though he was writing in 1841, a year of acute economic depression.[75] When the Failsworth Society opened its first branch in north Manchester in 1859, 'tick' shops were so ubiquitous in the district that the co-operative felt it had no alternative but to conform to the general pattern. Only when the business had become established did it have the confidence to insist on cash-only trading.[76] On the other hand, the practice was not universal. Friedrich Engels claimed that the working class 'sometimes even has to buy on credit'; and, among modern historians, Alexander has contended that cash sales were more common than has generally been acknowledged.[77] Much the firmest evidence is provided by Adshead, whose survey of 651 shopkeepers in four working-class districts of Manchester found that almost one in three of these entertained no credit sales at all and were able to operate on a cash-only basis. By the same token, of course, it follows that the majority of these shopkeepers were giving

[73] See A.P. Wadsworth and J. de L. Mann, *The Cotton Trade and Industrial Lancashire, 1600–1780*, Manchester, 1931, p. 388.

[74] L.S. Pressnell, *Country Banking in the Industrial Revolution*, Oxford, 1956, pp. 14–17; and see P. Mathias, *English Trade Tokens: The Industrial Revolution Illustrated*, London, 1962, pp. 12–17.

[75] *PP* 1833, VI, *Select Committee on Manufactures, Commerce and Shipping*, Mins. of Evidence, pp. 624–5; W. Neild, 'Comparative statement of the income and expenditure of certain families of the working classes in Manchester and Dukinfield in the years 1836 and 1841', *JSSL*, IV, 1841–2, p. 322.

[76] J.H. Ogden, *Failsworth Industrial Society Limited: Jubilee History, 1859–1909*, Manchester, 1909, pp. 22, 28.

[77] F. Engels, *The Condition of the Working Class in England*, translated and edited by W.O. Henderson and W.H. Chaloner, Oxford, 1958, p. 83; Alexander, *Retailing*, p. 184.

Table 9.10 Analysis of money owed to debtor retailers in Manchester and Salford, 1765–1812

Name	Year	Description	Number of debts	Cumulative percentage of debts				Total owed to trader[(a)]		
				under 10s	under £1	under £5	£5 and over	£	s	d
Warhurst	1776	Shopkeeper, Dealer and Chapman	50	48	74	98	100	42	19	0
Ashworth	1800	Shopkeeper	75	47	79	99	100	74	17	5
Bibby	1806	Shopkeeper	15	–	27	87	100	47	3	10
Hadfield	1806	Grocer	105	31	56	94	100	171	17	10½
Batho	1812	Shopkeeper	48	4	33	83	100	152	6	4½
Average			59	32	60	94	100			
Moss	1765	Bread Baker	32	3	25	78	100	117	3	5
Rose	1776	Bread Baker, Dealer and Chapman	25	36	56	100	100	28	14	10
Martin	1794	Baker	32	28	53	94	100	63	12	7¾
Burton	1812	Baker	11	27	55	82	100	20	1	8½
Average			25	22	45	89	100			

Note
(a) Does not include 'money lent' to various people.

Source LRO, Court of Quarter Sessions, Debtors' Insolvency Papers, QJB.

credit, though, as his detailed examples go on to show, only to selected customers.[78] At Didsbury, in the 1780s and 1790s, William Wood kept careful accounts for at least thirty credit customers, all of them humble folk, whose purchases of flour, cheese, treacle, sugar, salt, soap, candles, and the like, ranged from some 5s to £1 10s per month. They came into the shop three or four times a week, occasionally more than once a day. Payments on account were made in round sums and at times took the form of credits for labouring work carried out for Wood, who was also an innkeeper and farmer. Apparently, he kept a close eye on customers whose credit was shaky because, when the accounts were settled after his death, very few bad debts were found.[79] In the town itself, James Bentley, likewise, maintained a careful watch on credit extended as well as that received; even in the difficult years of 1799–1800 he was never tempted to let either get out of hand. He usually owed his creditors the equivalent of up to two weeks' takings, but no more. Although the debts owed to him rose in 1799 to the equivalent of about three-quarters of a week's takings, they were normally a good deal lower than this. Nor were they allowed to run for more than a few weeks without some payment being made. One of Bentley's customers, James Bradshaw, eventually settled his account after nineteen months; another, Ann Chester, brought nothing for eighteen months and then made regular weekly payments of 1s 6d until the debt was finally discharged. In a third case, where the account was never fully paid, the debtor, Samuel Hughes, did not wish, or was not allowed, to give up without a struggle and made contributions ranging from 5½d to 1s over a five-month period (Plate 13).[80] Of course, there were some advantages to the shopkeeper in extending credit. Not only did it inculcate consumer loyalty, but also, as was reported to Adshead, it allowed the tradesman to charge some 2s 6d in the pound more to those who paid weekly rather than with ready cash.[81] Nevertheless, discrimination was needed in assessing the trustworthiness of clients and their ability to pay. In the difficult years of 1840–42 traders were clearly becoming more circumspect in selecting those to whom they extended credit. Shopkeepers, it was said, had 'refused to credit some', while 'W.D. of Prussia Street' had

[78] Adshead, *Distress in Manchester*, p. 43.
[79] MCLAD, M62/1/1–3, Ledgers of William and Thomas Wood, 1767–1838. Mui and Mui, *Shops and Shopkeeping*, pp. 211–15, offers a helpful, extended commentary on Wood's trading practices.
[80] MCLAD, Misc. 258/1, Accounts for purchase of groceries, 1799–1807.
[81] Adshead, *Distress in Manchester*, p. 45.

Table 9.11 *Survival rates of grocers, bakers and shopkeepers, 1772–1871*

	1772	1788	1800	1811	1821	1830	1840	1850	1861	1871
Number of grocers listed in directory	26	42	69	124	75[a]	133	227	319	383	452
Number of whom listed in next selected directory	9	18	35	41	35	62	80	117	160	—
As a percentage	35	43	51	33	47	47	35	37	42	—
Number of bakers listed in directory	14	11	61	112	128	94	202	293	349	361
Number of whom listed in next selected directory	1	3	19	20	28	29	64	90	134	—
As a percentage	7	27	31	18	22	31	32	31	38	—
Number of shopkeepers listed in directory	—	—	—	—	—	—	1,027	1,481	2,226	2,693
Number of whom listed in next selected directory	—	—	—	—	—	—	255	308	452	—
As a percentage	—	—	—	—	—	—	25	21	20	—

Note

(a) Directory source unreliable – see pp. 180–1 above.

Source Directories (see Bibliography).

turned away many of his weekly customers.[82] The implication is that credit was often denied to the very poor, and the reality found its literary reflection in the experience of John Barton, a weaver beset by every kind of misfortune, who soon found that his credit was 'worn out at the little provision shops'.[83] Even sixty years later, in less pressing circumstances, prospective purchasers on credit at the corner shop in which Robert Roberts grew up could expect to receive it only after careful scrutiny and appraisal by his mother.[84]

Although income from the shop was sometimes supplemented by a husband's earnings or a pension,[85] the ultimate survival of the small shopkeeper would depend in large measure on how effectively credit was controlled. Table 9.11 shows that the survival rates of grocers fluctuated within (relatively) narrow limits, while after about 1830 those of bakers firmed up to reach 31–38 per cent. What is particularly striking is the much lower survival rates of 'shopkeepers', once adequate data become available. The services offered by the small establishments that formed most of this group were an essential part of Manchester's evolving distribution system, and the credit they cautiously extended was vital to many members of the working class. But their businesses were nothing if not precarious.

[82] *Ibid.*, pp. 43–4. One of Adshead's informants stated: 'It seems to be the opinion of shopkeepers in general that at least one-third of the money formerly in circulation is withdrawn . . . shopkeepers say they cannot assist them [the poor] as formerly, many of them being almost ruined by giving credit'.

[83] E.C. Gaskell, *Mary Barton*, Everyman's Library edn., London, 1965, p. 22.

[84] R. Roberts, *The Classic Slum*, Manchester, 1971, p. 60.

[85] Adshead, *Distress in Manchester*, pp. 44–5; J. Blackman, 'The development of the retail grocery trade in the nineteenth century', *Business History*, IX, 1967, p. 115.

CHAPTER X

Markets, shops and itinerant traders: an overview

U NTIL THE MIDDLE of the nineteenth century, proposals for new
markets in Manchester and Salford invariably focused on the
need for better facilities for the sale of meat, fish and vegetables.[1] This
seems to accord with the view that, in the nineteenth century, urban
consumers came to look to markets for the weekly or twice-weekly
purchase of perishables and to shops for the everyday buying of
groceries.[2] In reality, the function of the markets in the distribution
system was a good deal more complex than this. In the first place, as
we have seen, the markets played an increasingly important part in
wholesaling activities, though not, it is true, to the same extent as in
London.[3] Secondly, considered in relation to their retailing function,
not all of them prospered. The central markets were always the most
popular.[4] Outlying markets met with only limited success, even
though they were situated closer to the fastest-growing working-class
districts of the town. Obviously, it is difficult to reconcile this fact with
the notion that the working classes saw markets as offering an opportunity to buy perishable commodities more cheaply. Thirdly, the
various groups of traders had different perceptions of the value of
continuing to operate from market outlets. The behaviour of butchers
and fishmongers, both constrained by manorial law to trading from

[1] For example, PRO, DL 41/49, 'Petition . . . for a market to be held', 29 July 1822; SPC,
Report of Town Hall and Markets Committee, 1 Nov. 1840; *Guardian*, 18 Aug. 1849; *Courier*,
19 Oct. 1850.
[2] For argument along these lines, see J. Blackman, 'The food supply of an industrial town: a
study of Sheffield's public markets, 1780–1900', *Business History*, V, 1963, p. 96; D. Alexander,
Retailing in England during the Industrial Revolution, London, 1970, pp. 42, 59–60, 69.
[3] The most comprehensive account for the capital is K.L. Buzzacott, 'London's markets: their
growth, characteristics and functions', University of London, Ph.D., 1972.
[4] Above, pp. 170–2.

market sites until 1846, presents a striking contrast. From the 1820s, some butchers sought to defy these restrictions and to open shops in other parts of the town. When the prohibition was lifted, there was a dramatic fall in the occupancy of butchers' stalls, except those in the central market at Smithfield.[5] Butchers evidently thought that most people, given the choice, would prefer to buy meat at shops rather than at markets. Fishmongers, on the other hand, seemed generally content to trade from market sites; indeed, as late as 1870 some were pressing for additional facilities in Smithfield.[6]

A variation on the argument that markets remained important in nineteenth-century urban society is that they retained an emotional appeal, based on the survival of what Rudé has called the 'ideology of the old English village', with its connotations of a fair wage and a just price, as places where producer and consumer could meet on equal terms.[7] Again, however, the evidence from Manchester lends little support to this view, in that producer–retailers were declining in importance from the last decade of the eighteenth century. Although small quantities of butter and cheese were still brought direct to market by their producers, only fruit and vegetables were retailed on a substantial scale in this way in the nineteenth century. Moreover, by the 1870s all but the most tenacious market gardeners had succumbed to pressure to channel their goods through middlemen.[8]

The trend for market retailing to become a full-time occupation meant that, in order to compete effectively, the trading patterns of market tenants and shopkeepers increasingly converged, the former operating on a daily basis, and the latter staying open for extremely long hours. At Failsworth, in the late 1860s, even the co-operative stores kept open until ten o'clock, 'as long as the private traders' shops'.[9] Furthermore, there is some evidence to show that the relationship between the market trader and his customers was as regular and stable as that between the shopkeeper and his clientele. Table 10.1 presents an analysis of the outstanding bills of various Manchester

[5] Above, p. 167; and see MCLAD, M9/40/2/158, 1850 Rate Book, pp. 151–2, for the occupancy of Smithfield.

[6] MC, *Proceedings*, 26 Oct. 1870.

[7] G. Rudé, 'English rural and urban disturbances, 1830–1831', *Past and Present*, No. 37, 1967, p. 90; and see E.P. Thompson, 'The moral economy of the English crowd in the eighteenth century', *Past and Present*, No. 50, 1971, pp. 76–136.

[8] Above, pp. 193–4.

[9] J.H. Ogden, *Failsworth Industrial Society Limited: Jubilee History, 1859–1909*, Manchester, 1909, pp. 63–4; and see R. Roberts, *The Classic Slum*, Manchester, 1971, p. 60.

Table 10.1 *Analysis of money owed to debtor butchers in Manchester, 1776–1812*

| Name | Year | Number of debts | Cumulative percentage of debts | | | | Total owed to trader[a] | | |
			under 10s	under £1	under £5	£5 and over	£	s	d
White	1776	27	78	89	100	100	12	1	10
Hudson	1776	2	100	100	100	100		6	1½
Sutcliffe	1778	92	62	75	90	100	251	6	11
Ashton	1801	26	46	50	85	100	77	5	1
Edge	1804	17	–	6	59	100	112	1	5½
Taylor	1806	28	21	36	68	100	164	11	1
Goulden	1812	4	25	25	75	100	20	9	7
Hopper	1812	2	–	–	–	100	30	0	0
Average		24.75	50	60	84	100			

Note

(a) Does not include 'money lent' to various people.

Source LRO, Court of Quarter Sessions, Debtors' Insolvency Papers, QJB.

butchers summoned as debtors in the late eighteenth and early nine-teenth centuries.[10] The large number of small debts suggests that market traders were as accustomed as shopkeepers to giving credit, and this implies the same regularity of contact between buyers and sellers as is usually associated with fixed-shop retailing.

i. The locational behaviour of retailers with special reference to *c.* 8,000 traders in 1811, 1850 and 1871

Since there is no compelling evidence to suggest that consumers pre-ferred to shop in markets, or that market and shop retailers operated in ways that were fundamentally dissimilar, other factors must have influenced the decision of some traders to retain a market stall rather than open a shop. It is not without significance that market traders tended to favour a central location. This was evident at the beginning of the nineteenth century when they were reluctant to move away from the Market Place to other, supposedly more convenient, sites. It was equally apparent at the close of the period when Smithfield was filled to capacity while other markets were fast declining.[11] Nor is this difficult to understand. Large central markets can attract more potential customers than a series of smaller ones, and traders gain from clustering in this way.[12]

Then, as now, both market and shop retailers obviously selected sites which they believed would maximise their profits, often going to considerable lengths to determine the optimum location for their activities. When George Heywood, a Manchester grocer, was about to set up in business on his own account, he prudently assessed the position of the shop he was interested in buying and, in particular, took note of its nearest competitors.[13] Mathias has recounted how Thomas Lipton chose the sites for his shops with great care, and this is precisely what one would expect.[14] Yet the contrasting behaviour of butchers and fishmongers in Manchester suggests that retailers in the various trades tended to arrive at different conclusions about their best location, and this was true even within the same trade. In 1871 the

[10] White is described as a butcher and victualler; Hudson as a butcher and innkeeper (LRO, QJB 43/6; QJB 43/9).
[11] Above, pp. 154–6, 170–2.
[12] P. Scott, *Geography and Retailing*, London, 1970, pp. 26–7.
[13] JRULM, English MS. 703, Diary of George Heywood, p. 45, Feb. 1815.
[14] P. Mathias, *Retailing Revolution*, London, 1967, p. 46.

largest multiple grocery retailers in the town were the Manchester and Salford Equitable Co-operative Society, with eleven branches, and Burgon's, Gould's and the Failsworth Industrial Society, with five each. Burgon's shops were concentrated in two main roads, three in Stretford Road and two in Oxford Street, and each shop was no more than two or three minutes' walking distance from the next.[15] The co-operatives, on the other hand, followed quite a different strategy, scattering their branches throughout the city.[16] As the population grew in the working-class districts, so the societies reviewed the need to open new shops, even collecting statistics of the expected amount of trade.[17] It seems clear from their accounts that they sought an optimum level of turnover for each branch. Certainly, the Manchester and Salford Society never entertained the idea of enlarging outlets in the hope of attracting customers from beyond the immediate vicinity. Even their decision, in 1863, to build a 'central store' in Downing Street was accompanied by much heart-searching in view of the thinness of the surrounding population at that time.[18]

How far people were prepared to travel to shop is itself an intriguing question. Mathias has suggested that housewives were prepared to cross a town to save a halfpenny or a farthing,[19] but other evidence indicates that such energetic shopping was far from common. Walking a mile and a half with a heavy basket from Smithfield Market was thought excessive, just as going more than a mile on foot to church was considered almost impossible.[20] Their priorities might have been wrong, but most people thought in terms of yards rather than miles. The records of four traders summoned as debtors in the early nineteenth century include lists of their customers' addresses. An analysis of these addresses shows that, in each case, a high proportion of the trader's customers lived very close to the shop. In one, 70 per cent lived within 400 yards; in another, almost 75 per cent lived within 200 yards.[21] Running to a nearby shop seems to have been more typical

[15] *Slater's Directory of Manchester and Salford*, 1871–2.
[16] *The Co-operator*, No. 1, June 1860.
[17] *Ibid.*, No. 3, July 1860.
[18] Manchester and Salford Equitable Co-operative Society Ltd, Mins. of Committee, 11 Feb. 1863.
[19] Mathias, *Retailing Revolution*, p. 17.
[20] *Guardian*, 11, 18 Aug. 1849; A.D. Gilbert, *Religion and Society in Industrial England*, London, 1976, p. 101.
[21] LRO, QJB 57/5 (Thomas Batho, shopkeeper, 1812); QJB 57/10 (Stephen Burton, baker, 1812). In one of the other two cases, 84 per cent of the customers lived in just two roads (QJB 54/21, Adam Hadfield, grocer, 1806); in the remaining case, 89 per cent lived in four nearby roads (QJB 51/6, Richard Ashworth, shopkeeper, 1801).

than scouring the town for the cheapest bargain.[22]

Random observations of this kind can take us only so far in understanding the pattern of retail provision, and a more systematic
approach is clearly needed. The locational behaviour of retailers is, of
course, a major preoccupation of urban geographers, but one which,
with few exceptions, they have been reluctant to venture back in time
to explore.[23] The central-place theory on which they generally rely is
based, at its simplest, on two premises: first, that any tertiary activity
(in this case, retailing) will be located in the place which maximises the
potential market area; secondly, that provided prices, choice of goods
and general service are comparable, the consumer will utilise his
nearest outlet. There is, however, a tension between these propositions
in that, while the retailer will gain a larger market area by choosing a
central location, the customer may be reluctant to travel any further
than necessary to make a purchase. The concept of a demand
threshold seeks to reconcile this conflict. Assuming that retailers
require a similar level of profitability to be viable, then the larger the
market area needed to attain such a level, the greater the restrictions
will be on suitable locations, and the more marked the tendency to
adopt or remain in town centres. The sorts of commodities sold by
retailers in central sites are classed as 'higher-order' goods and characterised as non-essentials, bought infrequently. Retailers selling 'lower-
order' goods, or daily necessities, can more easily find sites to satisfy
the minimum threshold in less central positions.[24] In the second half of
the twentieth century the theory has required considerable elaboration
in order to cope with major variations in the size of outlets, the cost of
sites, the greater ease of mobility, and so on. Before 1870, however,
these complicating factors ought, in principle, to be less in evidence. As

[22] See Roberts, *Classic Slum*, p. 85; and below, p. 265.

[23] The exceptions are: M.T. Wild and G. Shaw, 'Locational behaviour of urban retailing
during the nineteenth century: the example of Kingston upon Hull', *Transactions of the Institute
of British Geographers*, LXI, 1974; *idem*, 'Population distribution and retail provision: the case
of the Halifax–Calder Valley area of West Yorkshire during the second half of the nineteenth
century', *Journal of Historical Geography*, I, 1975; *idem*, 'Trends in urban retailing: the British
experience during the nineteenth century', *Tijdschrift voor Economische en Sociale Geografie*,
LXX, 1979; G. Shaw, *Processes and Patterns in the Geography of Retail Change, with special
reference to Kingston upon Hull, 1880–1950*, Occasional Papers in Geography, No. 24, University of Hull, 1978. See also the contributions by W.T.R.Pryce and D. Mills to *Aspects of
Historical Geography*, 2, Units 16–17, Course D301, The Open University, Milton Keynes,
1982.

[24] See, for example, the discussions in Scott, *Geography and Retailing*, chapter 1; B.J.L. Berry,
Geography of Market Centers and Retail Distribution, Englewood Cliffs, NJ, 1967, especially
chapter 3; and for a simpler summary, Pryce and Mills, *Aspects of Historical Geography*, pp.
20–2.

we have seen, there are few signs of major changes in the average size of outlets within each of the food trades,[25] and it is generally agreed that it was not until the last quarter of the nineteenth century that fierce price competition, in the modern mode, became more overt. In short, it may be assumed that the size of the catchment area necessary to ensure a viable level of profitability was the overriding factor governing food retailers' locational patterns, and that this, in turn, must have been influenced by the level of consumption of individual foods.

To examine these issues, the locations of six different groups of food retailers – shopkeepers, grocers and tea dealers, bakers, butchers, fishmongers and greengrocers – were traced in the years 1811, 1850 and 1871, using the Manchester and Salford directories and the Manchester rate books. In effect, the dates and retailers chose themselves. The 1811 directory, although unclassified, is the most comprehensive one available for the early part of the century; the 1850 directory should reflect both the enormous growth of the town in the intervening decades and the consequences of the lifting of restrictions on the movement of butchers and fishmongers; by 1871 these retailers, together with confectioners, were the largest groups of food sellers in the town, distributing the most important components of the average diet. At all three points in time, traders described exclusively as wholesalers have been excluded, but not those listed under two or more headings, since the object of the exercise is not an assessment of the total retail provision of any particular area, but a comparison of locational differences between the respective groups. It is therefore better to include in both categories a trader listed separately as, for example, a 'baker' and a 'shopkeeper' when tracing the overall locational pattern of both bakers and shopkeepers. The exercise involved locating almost 8,000 addresses and placing each one into a system of areas and zones, illustrated in Figure 10.1 and spelled out in detail in Appendix B. In all, four zones (A–D) are identified, corresponding approximately to the built-up area as it existed in 1800, 1825, 1850 and 1870. By the last date, these zones contain a total of thirty-seven areas for the purposes of analysis. Zone E, or area 38, is a residual category designed to accommodate any retailers who were included in the Manchester and Salford directories, but whose addresses (usually

---

[25] Above, pp. 182, 194, 200, 210, 222–3. There were, of course, differences in average size between the trades (fishmongers and grocers tending to be somewhat larger), but there is no reason to think that the analysis which follows will be distorted thereby.

of an imprecise nature) lay outside the limits of the built-up area as it existed in 1870.[26]

Using this body of data, the first task is to assess the extent to which different groups of retailers chose to remain in the central parts of the town, and the rate at which they moved out into the growing suburbs. Table 10.2 presents the results of calculating the proportion of each trade in each zone at the selected dates. Measured in this way, the differences in the propensity of the various traders to move away from the centre of the town are quite marked. At all times, shopkeepers were the retailing 'pioneers'. Even in 1811 one-half were already located outside zone A, and by 1871 over one-third were to be found in the most outlying areas (zone E). In 1811 bakers mirrored this behaviour most closely, although in 1850 and 1871 the proportion remaining in what had become central Manchester (zone A) was approximately twice that of shopkeepers. More than three-quarters of grocers and tea dealers were concentrated into zone A in 1811, but by 1850 their tendency to follow shopkeepers and bakers out into the developing areas was surprisingly well pronounced. By contrast, fishmongers and greengrocers were evidently slower to appear in the more peripheral locations. In 1850 almost three-fifths of both groups were still clustered in zone A, and in 1871 approximately one-third. By the second of these dates, however, both trades were quite well represented in all the growing suburban parts of the town. From this it follows, in the language of central-place theory, that in 1850 fish, fruit and vegetables could still be regarded as 'higher-order' goods, though they were losing this status during the next twenty years as outlets spread into zones C, D and E. But even in 1871, a central site, often represented by a market stall, remained an attractive proposition for traders in these commodities. Perhaps the most striking feature of all is the changing locational pattern of butchers. Once freed, in 1846, from the manorial restriction of trading from market sites, they proceeded to open shops, which rapidly spread far and wide. Indeed, by 1871 their locational distribution closely resembled that of shopkeepers. This suggests that butchers had little difficulty in finding sites that would meet their demand threshold in the growing working-class

[26] Deciding in which area a retailer should be placed was normally straightforward, although in that minority of streets which marked boundaries between one area and another it was necessary to proceed with special care, matching street number sequences to contemporary maps. No doubt some misattributions have been made, but any systematic bias is unlikely. Moreover, much of the analysis that follows is conducted on the level of the zone (Table 10.2) or actually uses individual streets (Table 10.3), which clearly minimises the problem.

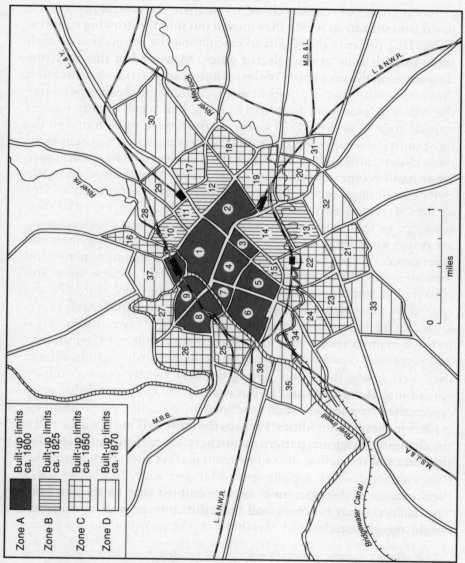

Fig. 10.1 Retail areas and zones in Manchester and Salford, *c.* 1800–*c.* 1870

Table 10.2 *Proportion of food retailers within built-up limits of Manchester and Salford, 1811–71*
(as a percentage)

| | Zone | | | | | |
	A	B	C	D	E	
In 1811						
Shopkeepers	50.4	27.2	12.8	5.9	3.7	(100)
Grocers and Tea Dealers	78.4	6.7	7.5	1.5	6.0	(100)
Bakers	58.9	22.3	11.6	6.3	0.9	(100)
Butchers	98.3	–	1.7	–	–	(100)
Fishmongers	100.0	–	–	–	–	(100)
Greengrocers	69.0	13.8	3.4	13.8	–	(100)
In 1850						
Shopkeepers	14.2	15.1	40.2	17.4	13.1	(100)
Grocers and Tea Dealers	25.4	15.8	31.4	15.0	12.4	(100)
Bakers	28.1	17.1	33.8	14.7	6.4	(100)
Butchers	38.7	9.5	30.3	11.3	10.1	(100)
Fishmongers	57.4	17.0	19.1	6.4	–	(100)
Greengrocers	58.8	16.5	12.9	8.2	3.5	(100)
In 1871						
Shopkeepers	7.5	7.8	27.5	21.6	35.7	(100)
Grocers and Tea Dealers	16.7	8.7	28.0	20.1	26.5	(100)
Bakers	13.3	13.8	32.3	21.4	19.2	(100)
Butchers	12.3	9.3	28.9	18.7	30.8	(100)
Fishmongers	35.7	8.7	25.4	16.7	13.5	(100)
Greengrocers	28.4	8.8	25.6	16.8	21.3	(100)

Notes
Zone A = approximate limit of town in 1800.
Zone B = approximate limit of town in 1825.
Zone C = approximate limit of town in 1850.
Zone D = approximate limit of town in 1870.
Zone E = areas beyond 1870 limits.

Sources MCLAD, M9/40/2, Township of Manchester Rate Books; Directories (see Bibliography).

suburbs. It also implies that, by the mid-century, meat was firmly established among 'lower-order' goods, a finding of considerable social significance.[27]

It is possible to re-analyse the data in such a way as to throw light on the type of location adopted by retailers as they moved away from the town centre. For this purpose, business addresses were divided into

[27] Below, p. 262.

240

Table 10.3 *Location of fixed outlets in Manchester and Salford, 1811–71*
(as a percentage)

	Located in major main roads	Located in minor main roads	Located in other roads and streets	
In 1811				
Shopkeepers	23.7	9.6	66.7	(100)
Grocers and Tea Dealers	43.3	15.7	41.0	(100)
Bakers	31.3	12.5	56.2	(100)
Butchers				
Fishmongers	Not applicable			
Greengrocers				
In 1850				
Shopkeepers	15.3	7.6	77.1	(100)
Grocers and Tea Dealers	52.8	15.6	31.6	(100)
Bakers	41.1	19.1	39.8	(100)
Butchers	37.6	12.0	50.4	(100)
Fishmongers	54.8	19.4	25.8	(100)
Greengrocers	58.5	11.3	30.2	(100)
In 1871				
Shopkeepers	7.7	4.7	87.6	(100)
Grocers and Tea Dealers	46.2	8.0	45.8	(100)
Bakers	43.8	10.6	45.6	(100)
Butchers	39.1	8.3	52.6	(100)
Fishmongers	46.8	13.8	39.4	(100)
Greengrocers	31.3	8.6	60.1	(100)

Source Directories (see Bibliography).

three categories: major main roads, minor main roads, and other roads and streets (see Appendix C). The differences in locational behaviour are analysed in Table 10.3. In finding outlets away from the main thoroughfares, shopkeepers once again led the way. As early as 1811 the small general shop in the back street was already common, with two-thirds of shopkeepers located in the third category. By 1850 half the butchers, too, were to be found in the side streets, and by 1871 the majority of greengrocery outlets as well, though this was clearly a more recent development. But fishmongers remained, even in 1871, fairly firmly wedded to main-road sites. It is reasonable to assume that only those retailers who were sure of being able to generate enough custom in the side streets would have been prepared to accept a position away from a main road. The analysis thus provides strong confirmation of the frequency of meat purchases by 1850 and of the

241

increasingly regular buying of fruit and vegetables by 1871. However, the continuing concentration of fishmongers in main roads implies that they needed a larger catchment area in order to be viable.

The data can be further analysed to determine the extent to which the various groups of retailers spread evenly through the town or, conversely, clustered in particular areas. The most direct and efficient way of describing the retail structure of different areas is by using the local location quotient (LLQ).[28] This expresses the degree of concentration of individual trades in each area in comparison with the overall pattern of retail facilities in that area. It is calculated by dividing the number of, for example, fishmongers' outlets in a particular area, expressed as a percentage of all fishmongers' outlets in the town, by the number of all retail outlets (in this case, those of the six chosen groups of food retailers) in that area, expressed as a percentage of the overall total. Thus, if an area has only 5 per cent of fishmongers, but 10 per cent of all food retailers, the LLQ of fishmongers for that area is 0.5; if fishmongers are as well represented in the area as all food retailers generally, then the quotient is 1.0; if there are more fishmongers in an area relative to other food retailers, the quotient is greater than 1.0. Such a calculation has been performed for each of the six groups of food retailers for the thirty-seven areas, giving rise to 666 individual LLQs. However, to facilitate comparisons, only the areas with extreme quotients, indicating a marked relative paucity or excess of different retail outlets, have been extracted, and these are presented in tabular form for each of the three points in time (Table 10.4).

The high proportion of areas with extreme LLQ values in 1811, 82 per cent or 63 per cent, depending on the limits preferred, suggests that the various groups of retailers were heavily concentrated in a small number of districts. This was obviously true of butchers and fishmongers, who were operating from market sites, but the finding also attests to quite a high degree of clustering among other retailers, most of whom were trading from fixed shops. By 1850 there was a marked fall in the proportion of areas with extreme LLQ values, now only 36 per cent or 33 per cent, according to the limits preferred. Shopkeepers, grocers and bakers were significantly under- or over-represented in only a handful of areas. This was equally true of butchers, contradicting any expectation that they would tend to

[28] See, for example, P.G. Hall, *The Industries of London since 1861*, London, 1962, p. 17; C.H. Lee, *Regional Economic Growth in the United Kingdom since the 1880s*, London, 1971, p. 222.

Table 10.4 Number and percentage of areas with extreme values of local location quotient, 1811–71

Year of observation	Shopkeepers (a)	(b)	Grocers and Tea Dealers (a)	(b)	Bakers (a)	(b)	Butchers (a)	(b)	Fishmongers (a)	(b)	Greengrocers (a)	(b)	Totals Σ(a)+(b)	Total possible(c)	Σ(a)+(b) as a % of total possible(c)
1811 (i) Using all 37 areas	16	9	6	22	11	13	1	34	1	8	8	26	183	222	82
(ii) Using built-up area c. 1800 (areas 1–9)	2	–	1	2	1	3	1	7	1	3	3	4	34	54	63
1850 (i) Using all 37 areas	1	3	1	5	2	6	2	3	11	21	10	15	79	222	36
(ii) Using built-up area c. 1850 (areas 1–27)	–	3	3	2	–	2	2	2	9	11	7	8	54	162	33
1871 Using all 37 areas	–	4	4	7	1	12	2	3	1	11	2	2	51	222	23

Notes
(a) Local location quotient of 1.5 and above.
(b) Local location quotient of 0.5 and below.
(c) Number of areas in observation at each date × 6.

Sources MCLAD, M9/40/2, Township of Manchester Rate Books; Directories (see Bibliography).

cluster in a few better-class areas. The contrast with fishmongers and greengrocers, however, is again quite marked. These were absent or poorly represented in many parts of the town in 1850, and the areas outside the centre where they were more in evidence included some of the most desirable residential districts of Manchester and Salford. By 1871 the provision of retail facilities was even more uniform, in that the proportion of areas with high or low LLQs was only 23 per cent. Greengrocers were established in every area, and there were very few high or low LLQs for this trade. Fishmongers still showed a propensity to cluster in both the central areas and the superior suburbs of the city,[29] but even their under-representation in other areas was much less pronounced than hitherto. The increasingly even distribution of retail facilities, to which Table 10.4 attests, was not merely a reflection of changes in the settlement pattern, but must also be seen as the consequence of a rise in demand for the 'higher-order' commodities to the point where traders were encouraged to locate themselves more widely right across the city.

It could be inferred from this increasingly uniform pattern of retail provision that few areas were either markedly superior or inferior in social and economic terms: indeed, that Manchester was developing as a city characterised by a high degree of social homogeneity. Such a conclusion would, of course, be very much at variance with both contemporary and modern impressions of Manchester, which tend to stress its social divisions along the lines of class, a point discussed in Chapter II.[30] Arguably, however, the thirty-seven areas that have been taken to analyse the distribution of retail facilities are insensitive to variations in social-class composition. It is certainly true that some of these areas were of a mixed character, especially where they comprised substantial housing fronting main roads that was gradually being surrounded by working-class dwellings.[31] It is, however, possible to select for further analysis those areas which were more or less 'pure' in type. Drawing selectively from among the 666 LLQs originally calculated (see Appendix D), one may note that in 1850 a highly desirable residential district (area 37) in Salford, extending towards Cheetham Hill and Lower Broughton, showed a relatively large representation of 'higher-order' retailers, whereas these were either non-

---

[29] In 1871 the LLQs of fishmongers were particularly high in areas 1, 2, 3, 4, 7, 8, 9, 15, 27, 35, 37.
[30] Above, pp. 30–4.
[31] For example, areas 10, 13, 20, 22 (see Appendix B).

existent or sparse in a band of working-class districts (areas 16, 17, 18, 29, 30 and 31) around the northern and eastern periphery of Manchester. By contrast, these latter areas were comparatively well served by 'lower-order' retailers, especially shopkeepers, and this is consistent with contemporary observations of the different social complexions of the areas.[32] Similarly, in 1871 it is possible to pick out some striking instances of areas where a relatively meagre representation of 'higher-order' retailers was associated with poor-quality working-class housing, such as those along the banks of the River Medlock, to the south of central Manchester, and including the notorious Little Ireland.[33] But these examples can be counterbalanced by others, showing that areas which contained some of the worst slums in the city at that time, like those to the north of Miller Street and Swan Street and those on either side of Deansgate,[34] possessed retail facilities which compared favourably with other, more respectable districts. Perhaps the most graphic illustration of the lack of congruity between housing and retail patterns is provided by a segment of the city stretching northwards from Miller Street and Swan Street (areas 10 and 11, and 28 and 29). Starting at the centre of the city, there was a classic formation of concentric rings of different sorts of housing, with some of the worst back-to-back houses giving way to rather better working-class dwellings, and they, in turn, to the houses of artisans and clerks. Yet the range of retail provision was better in the inner districts than in the more outlying areas.[35] Finally, in a separate exercise, special attention has been paid to zone E and to six enclaves within it of unquestionably high social status, namely, Lower Broughton, Cheetham, Fallowfield, Rusholme, Greenheys and Harpurhey. Among these, in 1850, only Lower Broughton possessed retail facilities remotely approaching its distinctly middle-class profile. For the rest, butchers, fishmongers and greengrocers were on the whole under-represented, though grocers were usually better represented than bakers and shopkeepers. The balance improved by 1871, but no more so than in other areas.[36]

[32] See particularly F. Engels, *The Condition of the Working Class in England*, translated and edited by W.O. Henderson and W.H. Chaloner, Oxford, 1958, pp. 55, 68–70; G.R. Catt, *The Pictorial History of Manchester*, London, 1844, p. 23.

[33] Areas 13, 22, 34 (see Appendices B and D).

[34] Areas 5, 6, 10, 11 (see Appendices B and D).

[35] See Appendices B and D.

[36] See H.B. Rodgers, 'The suburban growth of Victorian Manchester', *Journal of the Manchester Geographical Society*, LVIII, 1961–62, pp. 3–6; and see Appendix D.

Evidently, the social map of Manchester and that of its retail facilities failed to coincide in any obvious way, and there are several reasons why this was so.[37] In the first place, partially overriding the influence of social composition and income level in any area was the reluctance of 'higher-order' retailers to leave a central site or a busy main thoroughfare, such as Oldham Road or Rochdale Road, even if it was flanked by working-class districts. Similarly, many middle-class suburbanites would not have welcomed the establishment of retail outlets in their neighbourhood.[38] The third reason follows from both of these and relates to customers' willingness to travel long distances to retail outlets. Theoretically, their behaviour is supposed to reflect not only comparative costs but also the time available, and the effort required, to make such journeys. That the better-off were less sensitive to higher costs is obvious, but time and effort were also of less significance to this group, since it was not their time and effort that were being expended. Servants could be sent to central shops, or the household could afford to deal with those retailers who collected orders and made deliveries. Such services were expected 'without stint', lamented *The Fish Trades Gazette*; nor were these expectations to be disappointed if the retailer wished to stay in business.[39]

ii. The role of itinerant traders

Although the invocation of theory and simple measuring techniques have much to tell us about the locational behaviour of the majority of fixed retailers, they are of little avail as regards itinerant traders because of the very nature of their activities. Analysis has always been complicated by the fact that they ranged from those selling a few articles from the hand to quite substantial tradesmen, such as the pot-seller, with his cartload of wares, whose appearance in the 1880s at the Oxfordshire hamlet of Juniper Hill so excited Flora Thompson.[40] Nor are matters helped by the contemporary habit of using the terms 'hawker' and 'huckster' almost interchangeably and

[37] Apart, that is, from the general difficulties always associated with defining social areas in spatial terms. See pp. 32–4.

[38] See D.J. Olsen, *The Growth of Victorian London*, London, 1976, pp. 127–8, 242, 263–4, for examples of suburbs where the absence of shops was seen as one of the criteria for an area to be judged socially acceptable.

[39] *The Fish Trades Gazette*, 16 June 1883.

[40] F. Thompson, *Lark Rise to Candleford*, Penguin edn., Harmondsworth, 1974, pp. 130–3.

sometimes extending the latter to include stall-holders or even small shopkeepers.[41] The general view is that the early nineteenth century saw the demise of the regular hawkers or pedlars who travelled from village to village with their wares, usually manufactured goods. The growth of shops and transport facilities meant that their days were numbered in all but the most isolated rural communities.[42] On the other hand, it has been suggested that, in towns, itinerant traders performed an important function in this period by bridging the gap that appeared in the interval between the development of residential suburbs and the growth of suburban shops. Indeed, according to Alexander, the pedlar's trade was developing into a distinctly urban, rather than a rural, occupation. This development, it is thought, was most apparent in the selling of foodstuffs. Eighteenth-century legislation requiring hawkers to be licensed had specifically exempted sellers of food. However, policies varied widely from place to place, since local by-laws, enacted under pressure from shopkeepers or market authorities, served as an alternative form of constraint. In general, it was smaller towns that were more restrictive, while more tolerance was shown to street traders in large cities.[43]

This was certainly the case in Manchester. It is true that a by-law was passed by the Police Commissioners in 1838 prohibiting the sale of fruit, vegetables and other merchandise in the street.[44] But this measure has to be viewed in the context of the Police Commissioners' efforts to prevent Mosley's markets from spilling beyond their traditional sites, and the targets were potential stall-holders rather than itinerant traders. When the Council assumed control over the markets, hawking was prohibited within their precincts but allowed outside them, provided the goods were carried in the hand.[45] The limitation seems to have been liberally interpreted, with only the blatant obstruction of footpaths incurring the authorities' wrath. Indeed, by

[41] For example, *Court Leet*, X, p. 88, 21 Oct. 1811; XII, p. 39, 6 Oct. 1834; *PP* 1833, VI, *Select Committee on Manufactures, Commerce and Shipping*, Mins. of Evidence, pp. 624–5; W. Cooke Taylor, *Notes of a Tour in the Manufacturing Districts of Lancashire*, 2nd edn., London, 1842, p. 176.

[42] J.H. Clapham, *An Economic History of Modern Britain*, Cambridge, 1926, I, pp. 220–4; Alexander, *Retailing*, p. 84.

[43] Alexander, *Retailing*, pp. 65–8, 84.

[44] MCLAD, M9/30/4/4, MPC, Instructions and Regulations for the Nuisance Department of the Commissioners of the Manchester Police, 1838, p. 10.

[45] 9 & 10 Vict., c. 219: Manchester Markets Act, 1846, Clause 53; and see F. Folio, *The Hawkers and Street Dealers of Manchester*, Manchester, 1858, p. 15.

1890 this *de facto* situation had become the official position.[46]

The market authorities in Salford were less tolerant of hawkers, and a licensing system was still in operation there in the last decade of the century.[47] Earlier, their policy had entailed prosecution and fines, and Table 10.5 shows the number of cases brought against hawkers of 'fish, fruit, vegetables and other commodities' in the period for which statistics are documented. The Salford authorities' more restrictive measures must, however, be viewed in the context of their failure to establish viable retail markets in the borough. Traders who had been persuaded to rent stalls felt a natural sense of grievance against hawkers. The Markets Committee came under strong pressure to limit street trading, but it openly declared its reluctance to become involved. Even when it did take action, the magistrates tended to deal leniently with offenders, either issuing cautions or imposing only nominal fines.[48] The question obviously arises whether the transgressors recorded in Table 10.5 were merely token victims drawn from among

Table 10.5 *Number of cases of hawking in Salford, 1848–62*

Year	Number of cases	Year	Number of cases	Year	Number of cases
1848	93	1853	208	1858	91
1849	42	1854	117	1859	107
1850	131	1855	63	1860	119
1851	192	1856	42	1861	121
1852	151	1857	98	1862	83

Sources SC, *Annual Reports of Nuisance Committee*, 1848–52; *Annual Reports of Sanitary and Nuisance Committee*, 1853–62.

much larger numbers of hawkers. Given the background to the Salford Council's policy, it is difficult to believe that this was so. Moreover, the fact that the number of cases shows no tendency to rise in line with the growth of population is a further indication that those prosecuted were not simply the tip of an iceberg.

Legal statistics are, of course, notoriously difficult to interpret. In

[46] *Guardian*, 10 Feb. 1849; *PP* 1890–1, XXXVII, *Royal Commission on Market Rights and Tolls*, VII, Mins. of Evidence, p. 356.

[47] PP 1890–1, XXXVII, *Royal Commission on Market Rights and Tolls*, VII, Mins. of Evidence, pp. 577, 582.

[48] SC, *Reports of Town Hall and Markets Committee*, 26 Oct. 1848; 31 Oct. 1853. The fines ranged from 1s to upwards of 5s, presumably for the more persistent offenders.

our quest for numbers, we may turn, instead, to the data from successive census returns. Unfortunately, these figures, too, are shot through with problems. Hawking was in some measure both casual and seasonal; many would drift into and out of the activity and not figure in the censuses, taken in early June in 1841 and in late March or early April in 1851–71.[49] This was a problem confronted by Mayhew, who considered that, in London, the true number of hawkers was fifteen to twenty times higher than the figure stated in the 1841 census. However, it is clear that, to achieve this rather astonishing multiplier, Mayhew took a very broad view of what constituted street trading. In his eyes, the costermonger played a distinct role in the itinerant selling of fruit, vegetables and fish. But, for the rest, his account of street sellers covers a bewildering range of itinerant traders and even market stall-holders, the majority of whom dealt in commodities other than food.[50] John Page, the superintendent of the Manchester markets, writing in 1858 under the pen-name of Felix Folio, seems to have been rather more ready than Mayhew to accept census evidence, but his survey of hawkers and street dealers likewise comprised a wide range of traders.[51] For what they are worth, the local census figures are given in Table 10.6. All that can safely be said is that between 1851 and 1871 there was no evident propensity for the number of street traders to rise in line with the growth of population or shops. Furthermore, if

Table 10.6 *Number of hawkers etc. in Manchester and Salford, 1841–71*

Census description	1841	1851	1861	1871
Hawker, Huckster, Pedlar	613[a]	–	–	–
Hawker, Pedlar	–	1,979	1,302	2,027[a]
General Dealer, Costermonger	–	–	159	–
Huckster, Costermonger	–	–	–	27[a]
Fruit, Flower Vendor	–	–	127	–

Note
(a) If figures are adjusted as per Chapter VIII, note 6, they read respectively: 1841 = 649; 1871 = 2,295 and 29.

Source Census Occupational Abstracts (see Bibliography).

[49] See the useful discussion of data problems in D.R. Green, 'Street trading in London: a case study of casual labour, 1830–60', in J.H. Johnson and C.G. Pooley (eds.), *The Structure of Nineteenth Century Cities*, London, 1982, where it is stressed that the decennial censuses are apt to miss 'the day-to-day fluidity of lower-class life' (p. 135).
[50] H. Mayhew, *London Labour and the London Poor*, London, 1861, I, pp. 3–7.
[51] Folio, *Hawkers*, pp. 13, 32, 72.

we follow Mayhew in equating costermongers with itinerant fruit and vegetable sellers, the figures for 1861 (159 plus 127, but allowing for the fact that they include Salford) are not altogether at odds with an estimate given in a council debate in 1849 that some 200 hawkers sold fruit and vegetables from barrows in the streets of Manchester.[52]

Clearly, numbers are always going to be elusive, though a little more can be said about the potential function of hawkers in the distributive network. As far as non-perishable foodstuffs are concerned, it is difficult to envisage a role for hawkers in filling the gap between high-class retailers and working-class markets in the way that some commentators have suggested. The prevalence of small general shops meant that such a gap did not exist in Manchester and Salford. Consequently, the function of the hawker was only marginal. An exception to this generalisation could be the selling of tea. The Muis have suggested that the hawking of tea was common in Lancashire in 1818, although the evidence of a parliamentary enquiry in 1833 shows that, by this date at least, the amount involved was negligible.[53] Even so, the practice obviously lingered on, and *The Grocer* was fearful that, with the advent of packet tea, it would spread. Indeed, a Manchester retailer was moved to write that their worst fears were being confirmed: some 'second-class' grocers in the town were not above employing hawkers to take packets about the streets.[54]

However, it was in the area of perishable foodstuffs that the itinerant retailer might, if anywhere, have continued to play a significant role. This was certainly the case with milk, which, of course, is still largely distributed on this basis today. The commercial directories, which appeared from 1815, eschewed any mention of milk sellers or dairies, but the pattern of distribution is reasonably clear. In the late eighteenth century, the farmer delivered his milk to the retailer's milk house in the town, and the customer bought direct from there. As the town grew, milk was sold through either small general shops or itinerant milkmen.[55] For the working classes, the local shop would have been the usual source, but for consumers in more distant suburbs,

[52] *Guardian*, 10 Feb. 1849.

[53] H.-C. and L.H. Mui, 'Andrew Melrose, tea dealer and grocer of Edinburgh, 1812–1833', *Business History*, IX, 1967, p. 40; *PP* 1833, XXI, *First Report . . . into the Excise Establishment . . . Tea Permits and Surveys*, Appendix No. 11, p. 63.

[54] *The Grocer*, 14 Aug. 1869. See also Mayhew, *London Labour*, I, pp. 455–7.

[55] Holt, p. 154; Aikin, p. 204; S. Bamford, *Early Days*, new edn., W.H. Chaloner (ed.), London, 1967, pp. 101–2. See also *Court Leet*, IX, X, XI, XII: the milk sellers appearing before the Court Leet were accused of using false measures at their shops; their disappearance from the records after 1823 could be explained by an increasing itinerant trade.

milk was carried through the streets by men with yokes across their shoulders.[56] After the mid-century two or three wheeled milk-carts or perambulators appeared and, on the better-class rounds, horse-drawn carts, with boys acting as runners between cart and houses. Neither, however, had displaced the familiar men with yokes by the 1870s.[57]

The role of the itinerant seller of fruit and vegetables or fish is less clearly discernible. According to Mayhew, the far-flung suburbs of the metropolis were supplied by hawkers who obtained their goods from large wholesale markets.[58] But London was not a typical case. It was exceptional because of the precocious development of its wholesale facilities, the vast extent of its suburbs and the existence of a large pool of casual labour, flexible enough to switch between the different commodities available, and mobile enough to cover huge catchment areas.[59] In Manchester, conditions were different. In the first half of the nineteenth century, there existed neither wholesale markets nor suburban developments on a scale commensurate with those of London. Demand for these sorts of foodstuffs could be catered for by producer–retailers or market traders. Consequently, in Manchester, the role of the hawker was limited to dealing in the occasional glut of perishable foods – there being always the possibility of an imbalance between what producers sent to market and what retailers thought they could sell – or the disposal of stale goods bought from retailers to the poorer classes. In so far as both Engels and Folio emphasise the latter aspect,[60] there is a striking contrast between the role of the hawker in Manchester and the more central one claimed by Mayhew for his counterpart in London.

But even in Manchester itinerant trading varied to some degree both between and within the different commodities. In the milk trade, where a pattern of 'rounds' was probably most clearly defined, the regular sellers, like those in London no doubt, had to meet a certain amount of unwelcome competition from casual vendors taking advantage of the falling wholesale prices occasioned annually by the

---

[56] See E.C. Gaskell, *Mary Barton*, Everyman's Library edn., London, 1965, p. 13; *The Dairyman*, 2 Dec. 1878; L.M. Hayes, *Reminiscences of Manchester and some of its Local Surroundings from the Year 1840*, London, 1905, pp. 94–5; and see P.J. Atkins, 'The milk trade of London, *c.* 1790–1914', University of Cambridge, Ph.D., 1977, p. 268.

[57] Hayes, *Reminiscences*, p. 94; *The Co-operator*, 6 June 1868; T.B. Titterton, *A Brief History, 1875–1961: J. Titterton & Sons Ltd.*, Stockport, 1961, p. 9.

[58] Mayhew, *London Labour*, I, pp. 5, 7.

[59] Green, 'Street trading in London', pp. 131–4, 137, 147.

[60] Engels, *Condition of the Working Class*, p. 80; Folio, *Hawkers*, pp. 34, 130.

summer 'flush' of supplies.[61] In the fish trade, the development of a wholesale sector in the late 1850s might conceivably have led to the emergence of a Mayhew-style class of itinerant vendors. In practice, however, the selling of fish remained decidedly centralised, and the hawker's function continued to be the handling of either occasional gluts or stale fish that could not be disposed of through the conventional retail channels.[62] The fruit and vegetable trade was a different case again. Here, a distinct role was played by men and women known as 'dollopers', who bought 'dollops', or small quantities, of whatever inferior goods were left over at the end of the wholesale market's normal business.[63] But the trade also included itinerant vendors of a superior status, who endeavoured to build up a regular round by switching from one commodity in season to the next.[64] It might be supposed that the role of these itinerants would have been upheld by the relatively small number of fixed retail outlets for fruit and vegetables, especially in the developing suburbs, throughout much of the period. However, the itinerant vendor's share in this trade should not be exaggerated, because potential demand bore closely upon the mobility of retailers. In the very outer suburbs, where greengrocery outlets were particularly slow to become established, most consumers had the means to avail themselves of delivery services or to employ servants to fetch and carry, rather than deal with the itinerant class of tradesman.

It was no doubt true, as Folio contended, that almost anything could be bought on the streets of Manchester.[65] Even so, the role of hawkers in the food distribution system of the town was clearly much more marginal than in London. 'The itinerant vendor', observed Hardy, 'plays a part in the life of London which has no parallel in any other city with which I am acquainted.'[66] John Page, writing in 1880, unwittingly put his finger on the difference when he noted that costermongers, 'so long in vogue in London', were becoming more

---

[61] See E.H. Whetham, 'The London milk trade, 1860–1900', *EcHR*, 2nd ser., XVII, 1964, pp. 372–3; Mayhew, *London Labour*, I, p. 192.

[62] MC, *Proceedings*, 26 Oct. 1870; Folio, *Hawkers*, p. 34.

[63] Folio, *Hawkers*, pp. 130–1; W. Tomlinson, *Bye-ways of Manchester Life*, Manchester, 1887, pp. 56–7.

[64] Tomlinson, *Manchester Life*, p. 56; Folio, *Hawkers*, pp. 11, 132.

[65] Folio, *Hawkers*, p. 10.

[66] H. Hardy, 'Costers and street sellers', in C. Booth (ed.), *Life and Labour of the People in London*, London, 1896, VII, p. 260. For interesting comments along these lines about Liverpool, see *PP* 1890–1, XXXVII, *Royal Commission on Market Rights and Tolls*, VII, Mins. of Evidence, p. 348.

common in provincial towns but, in the same breath, pointed to the opening of greengrocers' shops in almost every street.[67] For the development of wholesale markets and the suburban spread of provincial towns were accompanied by rising real wages. As a result, small retailers were encouraged to move into the newer parts of towns to satisfy the demand for higher-quality foods. In places such as Manchester, the itinerant trader might share to some extent in the gains to be derived from the general increase in the consumption of milk, fish, fruit and vegetables, but regular retailers would be the greater beneficiaries. The hawker remained on the periphery of the distribution system, his standing, in the popular eye, scarcely above that of the rag and bone man.[68]

[67] J. Page, 'The sources of supply of the Manchester fruit and vegetable markets', *JRASE*, 2nd ser., XVI, 1880, p. 485.
[68] Roberts, *Classic Slum*, p. 8.

CHAPTER XI
Conclusions

THE STUDY of urban food supply is nothing if not an eclectic topic, and a simple recapitulation of the chief findings on a chapter-by-chapter basis would scarcely be adequate. The opportunity will be taken to discuss their relevance to our understanding of the distribution system and to the wider debate on standards of living during the period.

i. Sources of supply, food markets and food shops

While these researches have been in progress, agricultural historians have evinced much more interest in the marketing of farm produce, although, naturally, from the point of view of the farmer. On the whole, it is the early modern period which has received most attention,[1] but the late eighteenth and nineteenth centuries have not been neglected. In addition to various specialised studies, which have been mentioned at appropriate points in the text, Howell has offered a valuable sketch of changes in the marketing of Welsh agricultural produce, and Perren has brought together and developed almost all

---

[1] See especially J.A. Chartres, 'Markets and marketing in metropolitan western England in the late seventeenth and eighteenth centuries', in M. Havinden (ed.), *Husbandry and Marketing in the South-West, 1500–1800*, Exeter, 1973; D. Baker, 'The marketing of corn in the first half of the eighteenth century: north-east Kent', *Agricultural History Review*, 2nd ser., XVIII, 1970; A. Everitt, 'The marketing of agricultural produce', in J. Thirsk (ed.), *The Agrarian History of England and Wales*, IV, *1500–1640*, Cambridge, 1967; and J.A. Chartres, 'The marketing of agricultural produce', in J. Thirsk (ed.), *The Agrarian History of England and Wales*, V(II), *1640–1750*, Cambridge, 1985.

that is known about the subject on a broader canvas.[2] Some aspects of the present study bear directly on these issues. For example, Chapter V might be read as a response to Minchinton's plea, in 1977, for 'a study of the changing supply of vegetables to the newly-industrialized areas of Britain',[3] while numerous illustrations have been given of the responses of food producers, locally and further afield, to increasing demand and to improvements in transport facilities, showing that the precise relationships were rarely quite so simple as might be supposed.[4] It is perhaps fair to claim that, as a result, more is known about the sources of Manchester's food supplies than of any other provincial town. However, it is changes in the system of distribution within the town itself which will be stressed here.

The passing of Manchester's markets from manorial to municipal control is an interesting story in its own right, and from time to time the changing functions of the markets have been touched upon. It is clear that, throughout the period, producer–retailers were in a minority among market traders and by 1870 they were confined, in the main, to a few market gardeners.[5] On the other hand, the evolution of a distinct wholesale sector was comparatively slow. Although potatoes and cheese were handled on this basis from an early date, it was not until about 1850 that specialist wholesalers in root and green vegetables, fish, groceries and other provisions could be traced in significant numbers, while in the meat trade they had made little headway even by 1870.[6] In short, wholesale facilities in Manchester's markets were nowhere near so fully developed as in London, which is not to say that the wholesale function did not exist. On the contrary, there is ample evidence of inter-trading between dealers who were primarily retailers, and this practice, with its associated web of credit, seems to have served Manchester's needs reasonably effectively for the greater part of the period considered here.[7] It follows that much of the business transacted in the markets remained retail, and their association with freshness and cheapness, particularly in the case of highly perishable foods, is no doubt a partial explanation. By the Victorian

[2] D.W. Howell, *Land and People in Nineteenth-Century Wales*, London, 1977, chapter 7; R. Perren, 'Markets and marketing', in G.E. Mingay (ed.), *The Agrarian History of England and Wales*, VI, *1750–1850*, Cambridge, 1989.
[3] W. Minchinton, review of D. Oddy and D. Miller (eds.), *The Making of the Modern British Diet*, London, 1976, in *EcHR*, 2nd ser., XXX, 1977, p. 194.
[4] Above, pp. 44, 45–6, 49, 55–7, 74–5, 79, 85, 88–9, 96, 97–8, 104–5, 107–8, 109, 120–1.
[5] Above, pp. 193–4.
[6] Above, pp. 183–4, 185, 191–2, 193, 197, 202–3, 212, 214.
[7] Above, pp. 184, 214–18, 219–21.

period, however, perhaps the major factor in their continuing retail function was the attraction of the general market atmosphere. The covering of the markets, the provision of gas lighting and attempts by the market authorities to control rowdyism, combined with the increasing number of general dealers, sellers of drinks, hot sausages and pies – so bitterly criticised when they first appeared – all played their part.[8] '90 per cent shopping and 10 per cent buying' was increasingly the order of the day, as going to the market on a Saturday became a recognised leisure pursuit.[9]

However, the major finding concerns the early proliferation of fixed shops in Manchester. Small general shops existed in large numbers as early as 1788 and were well dispersed throughout the town, including its numerous back streets, by 1811, and much the same was true of bakers' outlets. Butchers followed suit once the manorial restrictions on their trading locations had been lifted, as did grocers and tea dealers by 1850, although the trend was slower to emerge with greengrocers and fishmongers.[10] This evidence reinforces the view, now emerging, that the role of fixed shops in the early industrial town has been grossly underestimated. As was explained in the Introduction, at the time when these researches began, the prevailing opinion, based largely on the work of Jefferys and Davis, emphasised the slowness of the distribution system to adapt itself to the economic and social challenges posed by nineteenth-century urbanisation. It was generally assumed that most food, until at least the middle of the nineteenth century, was sold through markets or market halls, and that such shops as existed catered chiefly for the better-off. Only the pioneering article of Janet Blackman called this into question, although Burnett, too, had voiced his suspicions that small general shops were more common in the early industrial town than the conventional wisdom allowed.[11]

More recently, the role of shopkeepers as the vital link between producers and consumers has been increasingly acknowledged. One of the most important studies is that of Winstanley, though he is

[8] Above, pp. 162, 168, 169; and see *Guardian*, 17 Dec. 1853; 24 Dec. 1857.

[9] See T. Wright, *The Great Unwashed*, London, 1868, pp. 205–16. The rise in the recreational importance of Saturdays is discussed in D.A. Reid, 'The decline of Saint Monday, 1766–1876', *Past and Present*, No. 71, 1976, pp. 99–100; and the phrase '90 per cent shopping etc.' appears in J.W. Wingate and A. Corbin (eds.), *Changing Patterns in Retailing*, Homewood, Ill., 1956, p. 133. Much of this paragraph is taken from R. Scola, 'Food markets and shops in Manchester, 1770–1870', *Journal of Historical Geography*, I, 1975, pp. 166–7.

[10] Above, pp. 205–6, 238–41.

[11] Above, pp. 5–6.

primarily concerned with shopkeepers' social and political identities and with the post-1890 period, where he can draw on oral sources.[12] More germane to the issues raised in this book – the place of shopkeeping within the distributive network as a whole – is Alexander's work, which provides a broad overview of retailing at a rather earlier period, though food distribution is but one part of his study. While he upheld the view that markets occupied a central position in the first half of the nineteenth century, Alexander's conclusions in other respects aligned more closely with Blackman's rather than with those of Jefferys and Davis: most market traders were no longer producer–retailers, but ordinary retailers selling mainly perishable foods.[13] Hard on the heels of Alexander's book came a case study of Kingston upon Hull, the work of two historical geographers. In a useful investigation of the locational behaviour of fixed-shop outlets – they did not study market provision or itinerant traders – Wild and Shaw drew attention to the 'early origin' of these. Their starting point was a directory of 1823 and, between then and 1851, they traced a relative shift in the distribution of shops, especially food-retailing outlets, away from the Old Town towards the developing suburbs, notably those which could be said to have had a working-class flavour.[14] The implication of their work, taken together with that of Blackman and Alexander, was to push back the time-scale of changes, once thought to have occurred in the later nineteenth century, as far as the 1820s and 1830s. Subsequently, they extended their range to cover many more Yorkshire towns,[15] and also moved further back in time by taking advantage of the existence of a directory for 1798.[16] It was discovered that, even at this early date when the

[12] M.J. Winstanley, *The Shopkeeper's World, 1830–1914*, Manchester, 1983. See also G. Crossick and H.-G. Haupt (eds.), *Shopkeepers and Master Artisans in Nineteenth-Century Europe*, London, 1984, esp. chapters 1, 3 and 11.

[13] D. Alexander, *Retailing in England during the Industrial Revolution*, London, 1970, pp. 42, 59–60, 110–11, 127–8.

[14] M.T. Wild and G. Shaw, 'Locational behaviour of urban retailing during the nineteenth century: the example of Kingston upon Hull', *Transactions of the Institute of British Geographers*, LXI, 1974, pp. 102, 108, 113, 115.

[15] M.T. Wild and G. Shaw, 'Population distribution and retail provision: the case of the Halifax–Calder Valley area of West Yorkshire during the second half of the nineteenth century', *Journal of Historical Geography*, I, 1975, pp. 193–210. Here the authors drew attention to a 'sharp increase in shop provision from 1830 to 1853' and to the high proportion of food shops (pp. 202–3).

[16] M.T. Wild and G. Shaw, 'Trends in urban retailing: the British experience during the nineteenth century', *Tijdschrift voor Economische en Sociale Geografie*, LXX, 1979, pp. 35–44. They do not give a precise reference for this directory, although it is presumably a 'national' one and thus likely to err on the side of under-counting (p. 38).

market place was still the dominant focus of retail trading, Hull, York and Leeds were already showing signs of developing outlying shopping clusters in response to embryonic suburbanisation. This trend later became even more pronounced. In 1798 some 62 per cent of shops recorded in the three towns already mentioned and in two others, Beverley and Wakefield, were within 200 metres of their respective market places, but the proportion fell successively to 51 per cent in 1823, 23 per cent in 1851 and 12 per cent in 1881. The trend is seen as a response to growing congestion in some of the central streets and greater competition for space within them, coupled with the increasing pull of the suburbs. It is pointed out by the two authors that the food trades were generally able to operate within relatively limited neighbourhoods and were much more inconvenienced than other trades by the problems of central districts. Accordingly, they showed a preference for suburban locations and hence played a significant part in the decentralisation of retailing.

Meanwhile, as historical geographers have cautiously inched their way back in time, historians have not stood still. However, they have shown a marked predilection for an approach to the subject of retailing from the other direction, that is to say, from the eighteenth century. One important contribution focuses on Cheshire and has drawn attention to the complementary nature of markets and shops, particularly with respect to the purchasing of necessities such as foodstuffs; to increasing concern about attempts by traders (including itinerant dealers) to avoid operating through the markets; and to the development of fixed-shop retailing during the second half of the eighteenth century, which gave rise to growing numbers of provision shops, butchers and the like in rapidly expanding industrialised towns such as Macclesfield and Stockport.[17] The most recent substantial publication is *Shops and Shopkeeping in Eighteenth-Century England* by Hoh-Cheung and Lorna Mui. They choose to operate on a national canvas, and their work centres upon the manipulation of revenue accounts, which show that by the second half of the eighteenth century fixed shops were to be found virtually everywhere, although the geographical spread was uneven.[18] They also make use of national directories – rather than local ones, which, in principle, might be

[17] I. Mitchell, 'The development of urban retailing, 1700–1815', in P. Clark (ed.), *The Transformation of English Provincial Towns, 1600–1800*, London, 1984, pp. 265–6, 270–2.

[18] H.-C. and L.H. Mui, *Shops and Shopkeeping in Eighteenth-Century England*, Montreal and London, 1989, esp. chapters 2 and 5.

preferred[19] – to show an expansion of 'major shop trades' between 1783 and 1822. One of their tables happens to include Manchester and indicates a 475 per cent increase for the food trades in this town.[20]

It is fascinating to compare the approaches of recent studies, including the present volume, and to note how, despite their different starting points and sources of evidence, they converge on the conclusion that fixed-shop retailing developed much earlier than was commonly assumed only a generation ago. Mitchell and the Muis start from the eighteenth century and peer forward into the nineteenth, whereas the work of the historical geographers and this book are rooted in the nineteenth century and look back to its predecessor, making extensive use of local directories. The main thrust of the Muis' analysis, given the nature of their main sources, is cross-sectional, affording an insight into the distribution of shops in communities of different kinds, and the same is true of the work of Wild and Shaw. While it is not suggested that these authorities are unconcerned with temporal change,[21] this dimension is central to the present study, focused as it is on a particular place. The growth of shopkeeping can thus be examined in the context of the development of the distribution system as a whole. That the Muis have failed to do this, by ignoring markets, is a just criticism of their highly commendable book.[22] As we have seen, a further advantage of the case-study approach is that it offers better opportunities to explore the emergence of the specialised function of wholesaling. But, most importantly of all, concentrating on a particular place enables the observed changes in the distribution system to be related much more closely to prevailing economic and social conditions, and the remainder of this chapter will dwell upon their significance for the people of Manchester during these years.

ii. Rising consumption standards

The aggregate demand for food in Manchester was driven on by substantial increases in population and, in the long term, by rising

---

[19] See the review of the Muis' work by J. Hoppit in *The Times Higher Education Supplement*, 8 Sept. 1989.

[20] Mui and Mui, *Shops and Shopkeeping*, p. 67.

[21] Wild and Shaw do, of course, deal with long-term changes, although, as geographers, their research emphasises spatial variations. The Muis consider a wide range of issues including the politics of shopkeeping and changing retail practices, particularly in the tea trade.

[22] Hoppit, review (see note 19).

incomes. The first of these forces has already been fully documented,[23] and it has not been possible to produce and justify a new real wage series for Manchester, which would require a book to itself. Still, it would not do to proceed without giving some indication of how the phasing of real wage gains might be envisaged in the light of existing evidence. The dates given are, of course, approximate.

1770–92

The likelihood is that Manchester's wage-earners were securing real wage gains in this period. This impression is based on the conclusions of Elizabeth Gilboy, that there was a comparatively swift rise in money wages in Lancashire and the North and West Ridings of Yorkshire, which was not accompanied by corresponding price increases for oats or wheat.[24] Recently, her view has been endorsed by Hunt and Botham, who provide some new wage data for Staffordshire,[25] and it accords with various indications of economic buoyancy in Manchester, such as booming marriage rates and the proliferation of buildings.[26] Aspects of the present study which afford indirect supporting evidence include observations on increases in demand for meat and Irish butter, and testimony that by 1800 fixed-shop outlets were very numerous.[27]

1793–1819

Local evidence, in the form of Ashton's Oldham-based indices of the cost of diet, draws attention to the prevalence of high and dramatically fluctuating prices, with variations ranging between 92 (spring 1799) and 253 (January 1801) down to 1809 (1791 = 100), and between 86 (1816) and 129 (1812) for 1810–19 (1810 = 100).[28] Some workers may have achieved wage rises of the size required to cope. The indications are that spinners' wages may have increased to the extent necessary to uphold consumption levels, and the same may have been

[23] Above, pp. 16–20.

[24] E.W. Gilboy, *Wages in Eighteenth Century England*, Cambridge, Mass., 1934, p. 214.

[25] E.H. Hunt and F.W. Botham, 'Wages in Britain during the industrial revolution', *EcHR*, 2nd ser., XL, 1987, esp. pp. 382, 394, 397–8.

[26] Above, p. 17; and on buildings, see Aikin, pp. 192–3.

[27] Above, pp. 42, 81, 205–6.

[28] T.S. Ashton, 'The standard of life of the workers in England, 1790–1830', in F.A. Hayek (ed.), *Capitalism and the Historians*, London, 1954, pp. 153, 155. The figures were drawn from an unpublished manuscript by W. Rowbottam, and from the *Mercury*, 18 Jan. 1820.

true of stone masons, tailors and whitesmiths, but handloom weavers' wages were already in headlong decline, whether expressed in terms of money, flour, oatmeal or meat equivalents.[29] Given the underlying growth of population and the congestion of the markets, the expansion of small shopkeeping might be expected to have continued and apparently did so.[30] On the other hand, it is doubtful whether meat consumption kept pace with population growth.[31] Overall, it seems improbable that the forward momentum characteristic of the 1770–92 period was sustained.

1820–50

Recent work at the national level points to very substantial real wage gains during this period.[32] For Lancashire, Fleischman has produced a table showing significant, though highly variable, wage increases between the 1820s and 1840s, while, within the cotton industry, pressure on spinners' piece-rates was offset by higher productivity, leaving wages fairly stable.[33] However, for the most part, real wage gains were underpinned by moderate prices – even low ones, if the war years are taken as the yardstick[34] – and an abundant supply of foodstuffs. We have noted, *inter alia*, ample supplies of potatoes and carrots, at low prices, in 1827–42; and substantial increases in the importation of Irish butter, bacon and ham, as well as livestock after 1829.[35] The growth of the meat supply seems to have surpassed that of population by the mid-1830s, and the prices obtaining for cattle

[29] R.K. Fleischman, *Conditions of Life among the Cotton Workers of Southeastern Lancashire, 1780–1850*, New York and London, 1985, pp. 102–3, 114–15, 189.

[30] Above, p. 206.

[31] Above, p. 57.

[32] P.H. Lindert and J.G. Williamson, 'English workers' living standards during the industrial revolution: a new look', *EcHR*, 2nd ser., XXXVI, 1983, pp. 11, 13. N.F.R. Crafts, *British Economic Growth during the Industrial Revolution*, Oxford, 1985, pp. 99–103, suspects that Lindert and Williamson exaggerate in claiming a near doubling of real wages, but his own figures also attest to considerable gains.

[33] Fleischman, *Conditions of Life*, pp. 160–1, 188–9.

[34] According to Lindert and Williamson, 'English workers' living standards', p. 11, there was a reduction in the cost of living from 183 (1819) to 100 (1850). Crafts, *British Economic Growth*, p. 101, while stressing that no cost-of-living index can be very reliable, sees the cost of living as falling from 136 (1820) to 121 (1830) and to 100 (1850).

[35] Above, pp. 46, 63, 81–2, 113. B. Thomas, 'Escaping from constraints: the industrial revolution in a Malthusian context', in R.I. Rotberg and T.K. Rabb (eds.), *Population and History: From the Traditional to the Modern World*, Cambridge, 1986, pp. 181–5, gives particular emphasis to imports from Ireland, concluding that 'the supply of grains, butter, meat and livestock would have been smaller by at least one-sixth in the 1830s and early 1840s had it not been for imports'.

tended to drift downwards through 1825–33, and again in 1842–50.[36] In short, the Manchester evidence seems to lend support to the more optimistic view of living standards in these years.

1851–70

Traditionally, these years are thought to have seen a significant increase in real wages,[37] although it is clear that much of the improvement was concentrated into the 1860s and that the position must have varied greatly across the country.[38] It is worth pointing out that the more the image of the 1820–50 period is rehabilitated, the less scope there remains for inferring major gains in 1851–70. However, from the fragmentary wage data available it would appear that Manchester's engineering workers improved their money wages by around 10 per cent, while textile operatives did rather better (upwards of 20 per cent) and building workers fared particularly well (33 per cent for joiners, 23 per cent for bricklayers, 21 per cent for labourers).[39] There are various indications that consumption standards were rising. The *per capita* consumption of meat certainly ran ahead of anything known before 1840, causing prices to rise somewhat despite increases in supply, and much the same applied to fish. Likewise, there are signs of an extension in the social range of the market for butter, while the rapid expansion of greengrocers' outlets and their spread through the suburbs appears to attest to higher levels of vegetable consumption.[40] Moreover, there is no doubt that in this period consumers benefited substantially from developments in the railway network, which, by extending the range of sources for a variety of foodstuffs, assured better supplies and tended to reduce annual and seasonal variations, if not necessarily prices.[41]

Such is the likely phasing of the standard of living in Manchester, judged by movements in real wages and some corresponding evidence

[36] Above, p. 58, and Figure 3.2.
[37] This impression is based largely on G.H. Wood's index of real wages, reprinted in B.R. Mitchell and P. Deane, *Abstract of British Historical Statistics*, Cambridge, 1962, p. 343, which suggests an improvement of around 16 per cent, if we simply compare the years 1850 and 1870.
[38] See R.A. Church, *The Great Victorian Boom, 1850–1873*, London, 1975, pp. 71–3.
[39] Based upon the statements given for 1850 (or 1851) and 1870 in A.L. Bowley, *Wages in the United Kingdom in the Nineteenth Century*, Cambridge, 1900, p. 62 and tables facing pp. 119, 123.
[40] Above, pp. 59, 86, 143, 190.
[41] Above, pp. 68–70, 114–20, 142, 143–6.

from this book. However, if in the last analysis we are looking for links between earning power and the evolution of Manchester's food supply and distribution channels, it is at least as important to consider comparative *levels* of pay, and to bear in mind the question of family incomes in the round. By contemporary standards, Manchester was always a high-wage economy, and the reasons for this are not far to seek.

By the 1790s industrialisation was exercising a marked effect on agricultural wages in the northern counties, and those put forward by Bowley for Lancashire (13s 6d in 1795, 12s 6d in 1824, 13s 6d in 1851) were, respectively, 50, 31 and 42 per cent above the ruling national averages.[42] Since agricultural wages were everywhere a kind of base line, or a reference point by which others fixed their position, this suggests that higher wages would have prevailed across the board. The average wage earned by male adult spinners in Lancashire in the first half of the nineteenth century was of the order of 24s, more than double what a southern farm worker could expect to receive, and in Manchester itself the figure was regularly around 3s–4s higher again.[43] A comparison of general factory wages for Manchester (forty-three mills in 1835) with 151 Lancashire mills in 1833, likewise shows marginally higher wages in the town, when the data are compared by age and sex.[44] According to the foremost historian of regional wage differentials, the levels of wages prevailing in Lancashire, Cheshire and the West Riding in 1850 'owed much to the unusually buoyant labour requirements of the late eighteenth century and the first half of the nineteenth century'.[45] In the years that followed, a decline – only relative – in textile employment signified that the region was no longer a focal point of economic change, but it continued to exhibit comparatively high wage levels. In 1860 the hourly rates of building craftsmen were 7d an hour in Manchester and, as such, higher than in Newport (3½d), Birmingham and Glasgow (5d), Bristol (5¼d), Newcastle (5½d) and – allegedly – even London (6¾d). The last figure may strain credulity a little, and the relative position of building workers is perhaps more plausibly summed up in Hunt's figures for 1886: London 9d, Manchester 8d and Taunton

---

[42] Calculated from the figures given in Bowley, *Wages in the United Kingdom*, table facing p. 144.

[43] Fleischman, *Conditions of Life*, pp. 159–60.

[44] *Ibid.*, p. 179.

[45] E.H. Hunt, *Regional Wage Variations in Britain, 1850–1914*, Oxford, 1973, p. 164.

$5d.$[46] However, there is no gainsaying his general verdict. The three counties showed:

Wages ... high by contemporary standards ... and in many occupations among the highest in Britain. ... Compared with other areas, and particularly with the rural south of England, the chief characteristic of labour in the industrial north was its high wages and long term prosperity.[47]

Another feature of northern industrial society that was particularly evident in Lancashire was the high level of economic activity among females and young persons. For example, in 1806–33 virtually all card-room hands were females, with an earning capacity of around $9s$ a week, while in 1833 the earnings of reelers were put at $8s$, and in the 1820s and 1830s women powerloom weavers could reckon on earning $10s$–$11s$. The cotton textile industry likewise provided opportunities for children (typically aged ten to twelve) to earn $3s$–$3s$ $6d$ a week as scavengers and piecers, about $4s$ $6d$ at fourteen and $8s$–$9s$ in their later teens, as spinning assistants.[48] Hunt has used the censuses to demonstrate, with respect to the proportion of females in employment, that Lancashire stood third among all English counties in 1851,[49] while Table 2.1 shows that in 1871 the proportion of females occupied (at all ages) was 36.5 per cent, which was about one-third above the average for England and Wales and twice the level observed in Sheffield, a metal-working town, ten years earlier.[50] It is one of the ironies of the nineteenth-century wage structure that opportunities for females and adolescents were more extensive in precisely those regions where male earnings were highest,[51] and several informed commentators have made the point that, potentially, aggregate family incomes in Lancashire were high by contemporary standards. We must, of course, remember that a sum which might be a very useful supplement to a family's income when brought in by a working wife, might be little more than a pittance for a single woman, and that there were costs involved to qualify the gains. For example, Manchester

[46] *Ibid.*, pp. 68–9, 101, 167–8.
[47] *Ibid.*, pp. 37, 39.
[48] Fleischman, *Conditions of Life*, pp. 162, 164–5, 177, 234.
[49] Hunt, *Regional Wage Variations*, p. 127. The two counties which exceeded the Lancashire female activity rate (47 per cent for those aged fifteen and over) were Bedfordshire (57 per cent) and Buckinghamshire (48 per cent), both having extensive domestic outwork industries.
[50] Above, p. 25; and for the national and Sheffield figures, see W.A. Armstrong, 'The use of information about occupation', in E.A. Wrigley (ed.), *Nineteenth-Century Society. Essays in the use of quantitative methods for the study of social data*, Cambridge, 1972, pp. 250, 280–1.
[51] Hunt, *Regional Wage Variations*, pp. 112, 126.

appears to have been particularly notorious for the inadequacy of its schooling, at least in the 1830s.[52] Likewise, factory wives were frequently condemned for their alleged domestic inadequacies, in an age which came close to sanctifying the home. Whether or not such charges were valid or fair is a moot point, and we have some sympathy with Margaret Hewitt's views on this matter.[53] However, the link with the theme of this book is an obvious one. Where a significant proportion of women were employed full-time, this must have provided more money and simultaneously reduced the time available for running a home. It is difficult to imagine a formula more calculated to hurry on the development of conventional shopkeeping and a reliance on shops for the nineteenth-century equivalent of convenience foods:

Run, Mary dear, just round the corner, and get some fresh eggs at Tipping's ... and see if he has any nice ham cut ... and Mary ... you must get a pennyworth of milk and a loaf of bread – mind you get it fresh and new ... No, its not all. .... Thou must get six-pennyworth of rum, to warm the tea; thou'll get it at the 'Grapes'.[54]

It is frequently remarked that the first Industrial Revolution was not a foreseeable event, nor did any significant element of planning enter into the process of urbanisation that accompanied it. The environmental conditions ruling in many British towns at the beginning of Victoria's reign have often been criticised, and it is commonly observed that the lessons took two or three generations to digest and even longer to prompt effective action. Against this background, it might appear that in the area of food supply and distribution, at least, considerable success was achieved. Redford has observed that in the middle of the eighteenth century 'a growing town like Manchester might be reduced from a state of tolerable sufficiency to one of semi-starvation merely by a week of severe weather, or any other factor causing a temporary dislocation of local communications'.[55] By contrast, the Manchester of 1870 drew from far and wide for its

---

[52] In 1834 a report of the Manchester Statistical Society suggested that 20,000 attended day and evening or Sunday schools, 23,000 Sunday schools only, and 17,000 no institution whatsoever. See A.P. Wadsworth, 'The first Manchester Sunday schools', in M.W. Flinn and T.C. Smout (eds.), *Essays in Social History*, Oxford, 1974, pp. 116–17.

[53] M. Hewitt, *Wives and Mothers in Victorian Industry*, London, 1958, esp. pp. 77, 81, 83–4.

[54] E.C. Gaskell, *Mary Barton*, Everyman's Library edn., London, 1965, p. 13.

[55] Redford, I, p. 141. In passing, it appears that Redford may have been tempted to exaggerate the threat of food scarcity and dearth in Manchester 'for nearly a century' after 1753, perhaps because he attached particular importance to the establishment of free trade and the role of Manchester men in achieving this (see pp. 142, 149).

supplies and had evolved a comparatively sophisticated and flexible system of distribution. The possibility of famine had long since been removed and, after 1812, occasional food riots ceased to take place.[56] Market forces had responded not only to the ever-increasing numbers of potential consumers, but also to rising incomes. What better illustration could we have of the operation of Adam Smith's invisible hand? There is a great deal of justification for such a view, but it sits uneasily alongside the impression, powerfully entrenched in the public mind, that the period we have surveyed was a time of misery. A balanced conclusion requires that various qualifying factors should be discussed. These concern the quality of food, the element of uncertainty introduced by short-term fluctuations, and an apparent failure of the imputed higher consumption standards to seriously improve the state of health prevailing in Manchester.

iii. The quality of food

In the main body of the text little attention has been paid to this important matter, although variations in the quality of foodstuffs clearly had far-reaching social, economic and medical consequences, as Burnett has pointed out.[57] Examples of petty dishonesty, the substitution of bad products for good and so on can be found in any age. In 1845 Engels inveighed against the deceit practised 'in the sale of all articles offered for sale to the workers', instancing potatoes which were shrivelled and bad, stale cheese, rancid bacon and meat which was old, tough and partially tainted. To round off his criticisms, small shopkeepers were accused of generally using false weights and measures.[58] In addition, large-scale urbanisation is commonly assumed to have vastly extended opportunities for the adulteration of food. It seems sensible to concentrate upon the period after 1850

---

[56] J. Bohstedt, *Riots and Community Politics in England and Wales, 1790–1810*, Cambridge, Mass., 1983. He attributes their demise to increases in the number of shops (which made face-to-face confrontation between producers and consumers practically impossible and morally pointless); to the fact that a town as precociously 'modern' as Manchester soon developed alternative means of pursuing grievances (industrial action, including strikes); and he notes also that food crises were ceasing to be 'as acute and as general as they had been before. . . . And the system of marketing food evened out its distribution.' (See esp. pp. 86–9, 91–2, 100, 213.)

[57] J. Burnett, *Plenty and Want: A Social History of Diet in England from 1815 to the Present Day*, London, 1966, p. 72.

[58] F. Engels, *The Condition of the Working Class in England*, translated and edited by W.O. Henderson and W.H. Chaloner, Oxford, 1958, pp. 80–5.

when, as Burnett points out, there is reason to believe that adulteration reached its height and when public concern was beginning to mount, leading eventually to the Acts of 1872 and 1875, which are thought to have been conducive to major improvements and, indeed, form the basis of the present laws relating to food quality.[59] Although the illustrative evidence is abundant, no-one has ever been able to quantify the extent to which food offered for sale was bad, stale or adulterated, and there is no prospect of being able to measure this in Manchester. However, some statements of probability can be made, commodity by commodity.

Flour and bread

As the Webbs have observed, the use of alum in flour and bread was commonplace in the mid eighteenth century.[60] In fact, this was considered a highly justifiable form of adulteration. *The Grocer*, in 1862, could still defend the practice, arguing that it counteracted the excess gluten sometimes found in British wheat, helped to make bread whiter and firmer, and allowed it to keep better.[61] While there is no doubt of its widespread use in Manchester, a local report of 1863 suggests that alum was usually added at the stage of bread manufacture, rather than to flour. The same source suggests that the augmentation of flour and sweetmeats with sulphate of lime had once been the practice, but had recently disappeared. Otherwise, there is evidence of the addition of potato starch and maize to wheaten flour, and of rice and maize to oatmeal, though these practices were not seriously prejudicial to health.[62]

Milk and butter

The most common form of adulteration of milk, in Manchester as elsewhere, was simply the addition of water. For his 1863 report, Dr Angus Smith had no specimens to test, yet personally recalled instances where milk had been diluted by the addition of from four to

---

[59] Burnett, *Plenty and Want*, pp. 72, 78, 197–200, 205–7.
[60] S. and B. Webb, 'The assize of bread', *The Economic Journal*, XIV, 1904, p. 203.
[61] *The Grocer*, 1, 8 Mar. 1862.
[62] Manchester and Salford Sanitary Association, *Report of the Sub-Committee upon the Adulteration of Food* (signed by Dr R. Angus Smith), Manchester, 1863, pp. 4, 12 (MCL, 614.06 M1); *PP* 1856, VIII, *Select Committee on Adulteration of Food etc.*, Mins. of Evidence, pp. 131, 134.

six times its volume, before being sold. This would certainly have starved children dependent on cow's milk for nourishment, but it seems probable that the usual addition was of the order of 10–15 per cent. Still, the practice was widespread. As late as 1875–89, 23 per cent of milk samples taken in Manchester were adulterated, according to an article in *The Lancet*.[63] With butter, deception usually took the form of mixing salted with fresh butter, the pure article being some-what 'difficult to get'.[64]

Vegetables

For obvious reasons, these were not capable of being adulterated, but, as we have seen, there were various channels for the disposal of produce that was likely to be stale and consequently of reduced nutritional value.[65] Otherwise, the chief threat to the customer was the giving of short weight. There is evidence that, in the era of manorial control, the market authorities' assaults on this sort of offence were only sporadic; for example, eight greengrocers were apprehended on 5 September 1835, and four on 24 August 1839, all in Smithfield Market; and four potato dealers were caught in one week in March 1837 practising similar deceits.[66]

Coffee and tea

With respect to coffee, the addition of roasted corn or ground crusts of bread was not unknown, but the most common adulterant was chicory.[67] That this was.a normal practice in Manchester is strongly suggested by the Manchester Coffee Roasting Company's decision in 1845 to install a 'granulating machine' to prepare chicory for its members, and thereafter the company prepared and packaged it on a regular basis.[68] A cash book of Isaac Burgon, a prominent grocer in

[63] Manchester and Salford Sanitary Association, *Report . . . upon the Adulteration of Food*, p. 11; *PP* 1856, VIII, *Select Committee on Adulteration of Food etc.*, Mins. of Evidence, p. 133; and article quoted in F.B. Smith, *The People's Health, 1830–1910*, London, 1979, p. 214.

[64] Manchester and Salford Sanitary Association, *Report . . . upon the Adulteration of Food*, p. 10.

[65] Above, p. 252.

[66] *Court Leet*, XII, pp. 52–5, 12 Oct. 1835; pp. 81, 84, 88, 91, 14 Apr. 1837; pp. 128–30, 17 Oct. 1839.

[67] Burnett, *Plenty and Want*, pp. 79, 88.

[68] Manchester Coffee Roasting Company, Mins. of Committee of Proprietors, 6 Mar. 1845; 10 Oct. 1852; 28 Nov. 1854; 27 Nov. 1855.

the town, likewise indicates regular purchases of chicory.[69] As to tea, it was notorious that an amazing variety of adulterants was applied, both in the countries of origin and by blenders and merchants once the imports had reached England. When sold by itinerant vendors – a practice complained of by Manchester grocers and reputable tea dealers in 1818 – teas of reasonable quality were highly likely to be mixed with lower grades, for the further the habit of tea-drinking moved down the social scale, the cheaper the product had to be.[70] Whether or not the problem was any worse in Manchester than elsewhere is unclear, although two witnesses giving evidence in 1874 to the Select Committee on the Adulteration of Food Act implied that this might have been so. Sir Henry Peek, MP, and Thomas Davy, a Sheffield grocer and tea dealer, spoke of tea that would have been seized by analysts in other towns in the north of England and the Midlands being disposed of with impunity in Manchester.[71]

Fish

Attention has been drawn to the difficulty of keeping fish in fresh condition.[72] It was a matter to which the officers of the Court Leet addressed themselves from time to time. For example, ten fishmongers were fined in October 1843, all for selling 'diseased' herrings, and two were charged in October 1844, one of them in respect of fifty unwholesome salmon.[73] The advent of rail-borne fish by no means solved this problem. At Salford, for 1855–70, there is a record of fish seized in amounts varying from 56 lb to as much as 3 tons 12 cwt (1862).[74] However, it is impossible to determine a trend, because the absence of any comparable figures for four of these years suggests that the authorities' attention to this matter was subject to vagaries. Again, this was a product that was likely to be sold outside the normal retail channels once it had reached the stage of incipient or actual decay.[75]

---

[69] Isaac Burgon's Cash Book No. 2, 17 Oct. 1859–30 May 1862, see, for example, entries for 4, 23, 31 Jan. 1861.
[70] Burnett, *Plenty and Want*, pp. 75–6; Mui and Mui, *Shops and Shopkeeping*, p. 280.
[71] *PP* 1874, VI, *Select Committee on the Adulteration of Food Act (1872)*, Mins. of Evidence, pp. 47, 104.
[72] Above, pp. 127–8.
[73] Above, p. 199; *Court Leet*, XII, p. 233, 15 Oct. 1844.
[74] SC, *Reports of Sanitary and Nuisance Committee*, 1855–70.
[75] Above, p. 252.

Meat

The selling of bad meat likewise received the sporadic attention of the officers of the Court Leet. Three cases were heard at Easter and four at Michaelmas in 1777, and five at Easter in 1783, and in the remaining years of manorial control of the markets the indictments gradually increased in number and frequency. Even so, inspection was not systematic and consisted, rather, of periodic purges, which meant that cases usually came in batches, although the sole offender arraigned at Easter in 1821 may have been exceptional in his audacity in offering 90 lb of liver from his stall in a 'deceased [*sic*] and unwholesome state'.[76] The fines levied were generally lenient, to say the least, and the problem of bad meat does not appear to have been an area of priority for the Manchester Council when it assumed responsibility for the markets in 1846, although Salford, to its credit, appointed a meat inspector in 1852.[77] It is, of course, necessary to bear in mind that if, as Perren has contended, up to 25 per cent of farm livestock in the 1850s and 1860s suffered from some kind of disease, a considerable shortfall in meat supply, and hence higher prices, would have been inevitable had it been possible to control the trade.[78] While there is no reason to think that the position in Manchester was worse than elsewhere, there is some direct evidence on the diseased meat trade, given before the Select Committee on the Adulteration of Food (1856) by Reginald John Richardson, officer of the Local Board of Health for Newton Heath, a district on the north-eastern outskirts of the town. Here, there were sixteen slaughterhouses, including two known to kill and prepare diseased animals, and one that specialised exclusively in them. The meat obtained from these animals was described locally as 'slinked' beef. The firmer parts of the flesh were sold on stalls as joints, the rest found its way into sausages, polonies, saveloys and brawn. Similarly, 'slinked' veal was used in sausages to tone down their colour – otherwise too red – as was a certain amount of horseflesh.[79] In Charles Dickens's *Hard Times*, the successful manufacturer, Mr

[76] *Court Leet*, VIII, pp. 181–2, 21 Apr. 1777; p. 188, 15 Oct. 1777; pp. 229–30, 7 May 1783; XI, p. 29, 4 May 1821. The three offenders prosecuted at Easter 1777 were apprehended within four days in April; three of the four at Michaelmas 1777, within seven days in May; and the five at Easter 1783, within seven days in April.

[77] See a letter to the editor of the *Guardian*, 19 Aug. 1846, from a butcher claiming that, until a few years ago, the seizure of bad meat had been common. For Salford, see *Guardian*, 8 May 1852.

[78] R. Perren, *The Meat Trade in Britain, 1840–1914*, London, 1978, p. 60.

[79] *PP* 1856, VIII, *Select Committee on Adulteration of Food etc.*, Mins. of Evidence, pp. 137–41.

Bounderby, claimed to have consumed the equivalent of at least three horses in his youth, under the guise of polonies and the like, and there was still an extensive trade in 'horse-beef' in the poorer districts of Manchester and Salford as late as 1888.[80]

The evidence discussed above could be extended considerably, but without clarifying the issues very much further. Dr Angus Smith, in the local enquiry of 1863, was not unduly perturbed. Although the purchases subjected to analysis had been made only in an inferior class of shops (and thus represented the food of 'the poorer part of the inhabitants'), he concluded that dangerous adulteration involving pernicious substances was 'not extensively practised in Manchester'. He did, however, concede that deceit in connection with food was common.[81] In view of what we now know, this may have been a somewhat complacent verdict. As Perren has pointed out, some of the pathological conditions affecting livestock were transmissible to man, certainly animal parasites and anthrax. Moreover, as Burnett has emphasised, any lowering of the nutritional value of food, especially of basic articles of diet, could seriously affect public health. In particular, children reared on a diet of adulterated bread and diluted milk were ill-equipped to resist the infectious diseases and gastric complaints that took such a heavy toll of infant life.[82]

iv. The effects of short-term fluctuations on diets and nutritional standards

It is the historian's privilege to engage in the analysis of long-term changes, and even the identification of medium-term trends, lasting some twenty to thirty years (above, pp. 259–62), is necessarily a retrospective exercise. It goes without saying that the people of Manchester would have made little sense of what has been said so far; indeed, very few of them would have lived through even two such complete trend periods. What would have been more real, in terms of their own experience, were short-term economic fluctuations, resulting in 'good' or, alternatively, 'lean' years.

[80] Charles Dickens, *Hard Times*, Everyman's Library edn., London, 1966, p. 117; *The Meat Trades Journal*, 19 May 1888.
[81] Manchester and Salford Sanitary Association, *Report . . . upon the Adulteration of Food*, pp. 3, 11–12.
[82] Perren, *Meat Trade*, p. 63; Burnett, *Plenty and Want*, pp. 88–9.

271

So far as fluctuations in food prices are concerned, it is possible to envisage two sharply contrasting situations: one in which most of the food requirements are produced locally and, as such, are prone for natural reasons to years of plenty and years of dearth; and another, characteristic of the present day, in which the majority of people – unless in the farming business – are blissfully unaware of, say, the state of harvests over the last five years. There are many signs in this book that during the period 1770–1870 Manchester, with its ever-widening range of potential sources of supply, and enhanced scope for choice, was moving away from the first of these abstract models towards the second. However, this is not to say that fluctuations in food prices were not keenly felt, and long after the extreme variations experienced during the Napoleonic Wars. This was bound to be the case at a time when families devoted a far higher proportion of their incomes to the purchase of foodstuffs than today. Moreover, at any time of rising prices, those burdened by large numbers of young children, or headed by a widow, or afflicted by the incapacity of the main wage-earner, whether arising from accident, illness or old age, would undoubtedly have felt the pinch. Yet it is likely that fluctuations in employment were more significant than food prices *per se* in extending or contracting the range and depth of social or nutritional privations. In general, people could cope with high prices if fully employed, but a moderate or even low price climate would avail them little in situations where many were unemployed or on short-time.

There were, of course, close connections between harvests and economic fluctuations. Bad harvests affected the economy through their effects on internal purchasing power, and any importation required was likely to have an adverse influence on the balance of payments and so cause interest rates to rise. However, a second main contributory factor was the vicissitudes of foreign trade, and a third, of increasing importance, was the investment cycle.[83] The correspondence between the cost of subsistence (as measured by wheat prices) and cyclical fluctuations affecting employment was not, therefore, quite so close as is sometimes assumed.[84] It is possible to identify years in which food prices, measured by this yardstick, were high, but when unemployment, by implication, was happily low: these included

[83] P. Mathias, *The First Industrial Nation: An Economic History of Britain, 1700–1914*, 2nd edn., London, 1983, pp. 207–16, explains these relationships with exceptional clarity.
[84] The following observations are based on a scrutiny of the annual data given in W.W. Rostow, *British Economy of the Nineteenth Century*, Oxford, 1948, pp. 124–5.

1800, 1810, 1818 and 1824–25. Conversely, downswings or low points in food prices were sometimes accompanied by adverse business conditions, for example in 1793, 1797–98, 1803 and 1821–22. On this basis, the years that were positively roseate – in that brisk business conditions and plentiful employment were accompanied by low or declining prices – were 1791–92, 1802 and 1845. On the other hand, the cruellest years, those in which high cereal prices and increasing unemployment coincided in a devastating way, were 1811–12, 1819, 1826, 1829–30, 1832, 1840–42 and 1848.

No attempt can be made to trace in detail the impact on food consumption of every variation in prices or in unemployment levels in Manchester. However, we are fortunate to have some very detailed information on the privations endured in the town in the early 1840s. Joseph Adshead's *Distress in Manchester* has already been drawn upon to a limited extent in order to illustrate fluctuations in the turnover of shopkeepers.[85] The political context in which it was written should be borne in mind, although there is no suggestion that his observations were other than reliable.[86] In addition, William Neild, then Mayor of Manchester, undertook a small-scale survey of the income and expenditure of families in Manchester and nearby Dukinfield, and it has since proved possible to re-analyse his material to illuminate the impact of the depression on their diets.

Adshead started from a close study of the distribution of bedding and clothing by a charitable relief society. About 12,000 families were considered, constituting perhaps one-third of the township of Manchester, and the available funds ran to assisting 10,132. Of these, 43 per cent were Irish, 15 per cent were headed by handloom weavers, and 23 per cent by widows or 'persons past labour'. To a large extent, then, it was the 'more indigent' population that came under review. Certainly, one gains the impression that in this part of his report Adshead was looking primarily at the ordinary bedrock of Manchester's poverty, especially since the returns relate to April–June 1840, before the industrial depression had reached its nadir.[87] As it deepened, increasing short-time and unemployment were noted by Manchester's Town Missionaries, drawn from various religious

---

[85] Above, p. 182.

[86] Adshead and Neild (see below) were both members of the council of the Manchester Anti-Corn-Law Association. See A. Prentice, *History of the Anti-Corn-Law League*, London, 1853, I, p. 105.

[87] J. Adshead, *Distress in Manchester: Evidence of the State of the Labouring Classes in 1840–42*, London, 1842, pp. v, 10–13.

denominations. By August 1841 they were reporting as follows: 'One-third . . . unemployed at present' (Charlestown); 'Nearly one-half . . . are in distress through want of employment. Several decent families have been obliged to part with their furniture' (St Mary's); 'Nearly one-half . . . are working short-time, and perhaps one-fourth are altogether unemployed' (Peter Street); 'Hundreds have no work, nor the least prospect of any' (Travis Street); 'Nearly one-fourth are out of regular employment, and many of those in work are on short-time' (Pollard Street).[88] One of Manchester's numerous pawnbrokers, commenting in November 1841 on the fact that he and his fellows had never held such large stocks before, stated: 'In consequence of the working people being not more than four days a week employed, [they] . . . have had great difficulty in paying interest on goods pledged . . . and, in a great many cases, they have lost them altogether'.[89] Another feature 'strongly marking the increase of poverty, and its extension to a superior class' was the admission, as patients, to various public institutions of 'those who have evidently been in better circumstances, and who have not heretofore been accustomed to depend on charity for medical attendance' (Dr R.B. Howard, January 1842).[90] Tradesmen suffered, as we have seen, and in the months that followed the amount of relief expended on the poor increased further. Including the voluntary charitable contributions, the index of expenditure provided a barometer of this depression: on the base 1838–39 = 100, the figures were 131 (1839–40), 138 (1840–41) and 164 (1841–42).[91]

Adshead did not comment on diets directly, and this is where Neild's enquiry is useful. The nineteen families discussed comprised twelve from Manchester, 'selected because they were of sober and industrious habits', who were not, in the early months of 1841, experiencing unemployment. By contrast, the seven Dukinfield families had seen their wages fall 'in common with those of the generality of the working classes in the cotton trade', although they had 'suffered much less from reduced hours of labour than many

---

[88] *Ibid.*, pp. 25–34.

[89] *Ibid.*, p. 22. Note that pledging, which seems indicative of deep poverty in modern eyes, was regarded as a respectable source of credit among the working classes (and to some extent those above them) in the nineteenth century, and was regularly resorted to in good times as well as bad. The fact that Manchester possessed 248 pawnshops in 1870 and was the largest centre of concentration outside London is not, therefore, in itself evidence of large-scale poverty. See M. Tebbutt, *Making Ends Meet: Pawnbroking and Working-Class Credit*, Leicester, 1983, esp. pp. 2, 18, 23, 135, 166.

[90] Adshead, *Distress in Manchester*, p. 47.

[91] *Ibid.*, p. 41.

similarly employed'. The incomes of the families in question ranged from 14s (a washer with only one dependant) to £4 10s (a millwright with nine) in Manchester, and from 8s 8d (a card-room hand with two dependants) to £1 4s (a dresser with five) in Dukinfield.[92] McKenzie has analysed the diets of these two rather differently situated groups, leading to the following conclusions:

(i) In both Manchester and Dukinfield, families spent about the same proportion of their incomes on bread, flour, potatoes, meat, butter and sugar. However, since the average incomes of the Dukinfield families were significantly lower – a disadvantage not altogether offset by the fact that their families were also, on average, smaller – their *per capita* intake of all foodstuffs other than sugar was depressed, compared to that of the Manchester families.

(ii) The average calorific intake per head was 2,600 in the Manchester families, but only 1,900 in those at Dukinfield, against modern recommendations of about 2,500 calories.

(iii) In the Manchester families, the *per capita* intake of protein slightly exceeded modern recommended allowances, but fell well short of them in those at Dukinfield. Iron requirements appear to have been fully met, and those for vitamin C amply exceeded, especially in Manchester.

(iv) Among the Dukinfield families, six out of seven were receiving a diet so deficient in calories and protein as to be serious. McKenzie suggests that 'this diet would have some immediate effect upon health and ability to resist disease'.[93]

The studies by Neild and McKenzie on the one hand, and by Adshead on the other, complement each other very effectively. Obviously, the impression of a universal catastrophe, to which a casual reading of Adshead might give rise, is not altogether warranted, since there were numerous wage-earners who held on to their employment and would have been able to ride these difficult years. But the example of the Dukinfield families shows the extent to which even a partial loss of earnings could affect dietary standards, well before the large numbers of desperate cases which feature so prominently in Adshead's account are reached. In fact, this depression was probably

[92] W. Neild, 'Comparative statement of the income and expenditure of certain families of the working classes in Manchester and Dukinfield in the years 1836 and 1841', *JSSL*, IV, 1841–2, pp. 321, 323–34.

[93] J.C. McKenzie, 'The composition and nutritional value of diets in Manchester and Dukinfield in 1841', *TLCAS*, LXXII, 1962, pp. 128–9, 131–3, 137–9.

as dire a situation as existed at any time in the nineteenth century. 'The universal testimony is, that there never was any distress equal to that which exists at present – that all other seasons of distress were trifling in comparison.'[94] But the privations of the time, though on a larger scale, cannot have been much different in kind from those encountered in other dismal years, such as 1819 and 1826, and they were to recur, to a greater or lesser extent, in the cyclical troughs of 1848, 1858, 1862 and 1868.

Among these later phases of distress, one is of particular interest in the present context, for it is linked with the so-called Cotton Famine. Contrary to the impression given by its name, this depression in the Lancashire cotton industry did not originate in a shortage of raw cotton arising from the American Civil War; rather, it reflected a crisis of over-production induced by falling sales abroad, including the United States.[95] By November 1861 numerous mills had stopped or were working short-time, and the cotton districts saw major unemployment, perhaps reaching a total of as many as 458,000 persons (22 per cent of the population) out of work in December 1862. Some signs of recovery were visible in the following spring. Yet in the June of that year a large proportion of Manchester's population (13.6 per cent) still required relief, although the corresponding figures were frequently much higher in other, less diversified towns (Glossop 33.1 per cent, Preston 23.3 per cent, Prestwich 18.0 per cent, Stockport 17.4 per cent, etc.), and a full recovery was not achieved until 1865.[96] At no time was there an absolute shortage of food.[97] Thus, the particular interest of this episode, in the present context, is the further light it throws on the effects of trade depressions on diets. For it was during December 1862 and January 1863 that Dr Edward Smith was sent by the Privy Council to report on the diet of cotton operatives in six towns, including Manchester. His report covered thirty-six single persons and forty-four families. In sixteen cases – seven single women and nine families – he was able to obtain details of their pre-famine diets as well, thus making it possible to trace the dietary adjustments necessitated by unemployment and reduced incomes. Oddy has

[94] Adshead, *Distress in Manchester*, pp. 37–8. This view is generally accepted by modern historians. See, for example, Mathias, *First Industrial Nation*, p. 214; E.J. Hobsbawm, *Labouring Men*, London, 1964, p. 74.

[95] D.A. Farnie, *The English Cotton Industry and the World Market, 1815–1896*, Oxford, 1979, pp. 138–45.

[96] D.J. Oddy, 'Urban famine in nineteenth-century Britain: the effect of the Lancashire cotton famine on working-class diet and health', *EcHR*, 2nd ser., XXXVI, 1983, pp. 72–3, 81.

[97] Farnie, *Cotton Industry*, p. 157.

analysed this material, indicating an average reduction of food expenditure of some 57 per cent for single females and 33–37 per cent for families, and he shows that interesting variations occurred in various articles of diet. Among the single women, consumption of meat and potatoes fell most (−83 per cent and −64 per cent respectively); bread consumption declined by far less (−33 per cent); sugar intake decreased least of all (−25 per cent). This suggests that these women were tending to adopt a diet of tea, bread and perhaps butter or treacle. The families, likewise, economised on meat and potatoes, but their bread consumption fell by less than that of single women (−17 per cent), and they consumed more oatmeal (+43 per cent), probably eaten as porridge in conjunction with milk (−33 per cent) and either sugar (no change) or treacle. In the round, these figures suggest a shift away from cooked meals towards the eating of bread and treacle, with a heavy reliance on oatmeal porridge and tea.[98] Oddy points out that these reduced diets still provided 2,000–2,500 calories a day and were 'certainly not starvation diets'. Indeed, they were not dissimilar in terms of calorific and nutrient content to those of a range of relatively low-paid indoor domestic workers whom Smith went on to study in more sizeable numbers later in 1863.[99]

v. Patterns of health and mortality

There are no sources that enable us to study the extent of sickness and ill-health in any systematic way for eighteenth- and nineteenth-century cities. For a surrogate measure, it is necessary to rely upon changes in death rates, including – after the establishment of civil registration in 1837 – those associated with specific diseases. For Manchester, there is, at best, only a modest improvement in general levels of mortality to report. As we have seen, Percival calculated a high rate of mortality – 35 per 1,000 at risk – for the 1780s.[100] This was principally due to the child (0–4) death rate, which was still accounting for 40–50 per cent of all deaths in the second half of the

[98] Oddy, 'Urban famine', pp. 76–9.
[99] *Ibid.*, pp. 79–80. It is in this context that a written comment from Lord Stanley to Disraeli should be understood: 'The truth is the operatives living on two-thirds of their former wages are better off than the average English labourers' (Farnie, *Cotton Industry*, p. 157).
[100] Above, p. 17.

nineteenth century.[101] Set in any comparative context, Manchester was without doubt an unhealthy place. In a fairly detailed analysis, covering 105 registration districts for 1848–54, Manchester's death rate from all causes (at 33.0 per 1,000) was found to be some 50 per cent above the national average (22.0) and exceeded only in Liverpool. The Salford and Chorlton districts, though better (28.0 and 25.0 respectively), were 27 per cent and 13 per cent above the average.[102] Moreover, the centre–periphery contrasts hinted at in these registration district statistics have been confirmed by a more detailed analysis at the sub-district level. In the 1860s crude mortality rates of 34 or higher still ruled in the pre-nineteenth-century core of the city, adjacent to the central business district, while the rest of Manchester Township, together with most of Hulme and parts of Chorlton-on-Medlock, yielded rates of 27 or higher, in contrast to outer suburban areas where mortality rarely exceeded 21 per 1,000.[103]

This, it must be said, is a dismal record. If it is true, as one authority has contended, that the long-term amelioration in British mortality has owed far more to better standards of nutrition than to the efforts of medical men or to autonomous variations in the virulence of diseases,[104] then the failure of Manchester's death rates to improve significantly might appear to cast doubts on any idea that the population of Manchester was benefiting to any great extent from rising real wages or higher levels of nutrition, at least during the period covered by this book. Indeed, the Pooleys have suggested that it was not until the 'cycle of structural poverty' was broken and medical knowledge advanced in the post-1870 period that the health of Manchester's working-class population substantially improved. Among the factors upholding high mortality levels, the two authors refer specifically to 'unsuitable and contaminated food', and they seek to associate mortality peaks with trade depressions in the cotton industry – in effect, the issues to which we have drawn attention in sections iii and iv of this chapter.[105]

Clearly, the interaction of income fluctuations, nutrition, health and

[101] M.E. and C.G. Pooley, 'Health, society and environment in nineteenth-century Manchester', in R. Woods and J. Woodward (eds.), *Urban Disease and Mortality in Nineteenth-Century England*, London, 1984, p. 155.

[102] E.H. Greenhow, *Papers Relating to the Sanitary State of the People of England*, London, 1858, pp. 162–4.

[103] Pooley and Pooley, 'Health, society and environment', pp. 163–5.

[104] T. McKeown, *The Modern Rise of Population*, London, 1976, pp. 65–6, 128–42; and see Chapter I, note 2.

[105] Pooley and Pooley, 'Health, society and environment', pp. 155, 160, 175.

mortality is a complex area of investigation, and one that raises many interesting questions. High among these is the possibility of starvation in the more difficult years. Was the man quoted by Adshead who claimed to have 'long been out of work and . . . almost "clemmed" to death' exaggerating? Did 'Jones of Great Mount Street', a shoemaker by trade and 'for want of nourishment unable to work', actually succumb to the fate foretold for him by Missionary E.H., who declared that Jones had 'death printed in his countenance'?[106] The fact is that crude mortality rates did *not* rise in Manchester in response to the distress of 1840–42. Moreover, for 1860–62, Oddy has shown that Lancashire's death rates actually stood below the decadal average, and he observes that 'death by starvation was extremely rare, if it occurred at all'.[107] Perhaps these findings are rather less surprising than would have been the case a generation ago, for work on earlier periods has shown that, in England, there had been no close correlation between mortality variations and either corn prices or real wages ever since the early seventeenth century.[108] This was not obvious to contemporaries, and one is reminded of an interesting, if inconclusive, debate between the statistician, William Farr, and the Secretary of the Poor Law Commissioners, Edwin Chadwick, in 1839–40. Chadwick took great exception to a statement in the *First Annual Report of the Registrar-General* to the effect that sixty-three persons had died of starvation during the first half-year of civil registration, since, if true, this would have reflected badly on the operation of the Poor Law. Much turned on the meaning of the word 'starvation', and Glass has concluded that, in so far as some of the details were concerned, Farr was wrong. However, his general instinct to link poverty with mortality was sound. Whereas Chadwick's criticisms reflected a narrower view of the factors affecting mortality, Farr's comments were those of a pioneer of social medicine.[109]

In fact, this is the line taken by most modern authorities. Oddy allows that the more monotonous diets of 1861–62 produced a hunger for something different, well expressed by a girl who 'had na had a taste o' grease for a long time', and that the effects of a restricted

[106] Adshead, *Distress in Manchester*, pp. 28, 51.

[107] Pooley and Pooley, 'Health, society and environment', Figure 7.2, p. 155; Oddy, 'Urban famine', pp. 82, 84.

[108] J.D. Chambers, *Population, Economy and Society in Pre-Industrial England*, Oxford, 1972, pp. 87–96; E.A. Wrigley and R.S. Schofield, *The Population History of England, 1541–1871: A Reconstruction*, London, 1981, pp. 413–17; N.L. Tranter, *Population and Society, 1750–1940*, London, 1985, p. 84.

[109] D.V. Glass, *Numbering the People*, Farnborough, Hants., 1973, pp. 146–7, 150–67.

diet began to show over time in terms of lowered physical status. People became thin, especially mothers who bore the brunt of the attempt to eke out food supplies. Furthermore, there were signs of nutritional deficiency diseases such as scurvy, and the presence of infectious diseases in epidemic form – most obviously typhus, which struck Manchester severely in the summer of 1862 – and references to the presence of chicken-pox, whooping-cough and scarlet fever. Of course, it is impossible to disentangle the various influences at work, but there can be little doubt that there was some connection with the Cotton Famine, since it is generally acknowledged by modern nutritionists that people with low nutritional status are less resistant to infection.[110] Likewise, the Pooleys believe that their postulated link between trade depressions and mortality peaks is likely to have been through falling living standards and reduced resistance to disease. While refraining from any comment on the puzzling lack of correspondence in 1841–42, they instance the way in which high mortality in the late 1840s – which saw epidemics of typhus, influenza, diarrhoea and cholera – coincided with an industrial recession, but add that the Irish potato famine and the large-scale immigration associated with it was another, significant contributory factor.[111]

Certainly, Manchester's mortality could never be described as low, even in the most propitious years. Some diseases were of an endemic nature, the most obvious case in point being tuberculosis, which, in Manchester as elsewhere, was the single most important agent of mortality, and one on which dietary standards had a direct bearing.[112] More generally, the Pooleys have drawn attention to the way in which chest and throat diseases, like many others, featured as causes of death to a much greater extent in the poorer central areas than in the outlying suburbs.[113] Throughout the period, we may safely assume, there was a substantial – though perhaps slowly diminishing – class of Mancunians whose incomes, even at the best of times, would not have run to diets calculated to keep them in good health.[114] Moreover, as we have seen, a fair proportion of the food available was likely to be

---

[110] Oddy, 'Urban famine', pp. 81–4, 86.

[111] Pooley and Pooley, 'Health, society and environment', p. 155.

[112] *Ibid.*, pp. 158–9; G. Cronjé, 'Tuberculosis and mortality decline in England and Wales, 1851–1910', in Woods and Woodward (eds.), *Urban Disease and Mortality*, p. 79.

[113] Pooley and Pooley, 'Health, society and environment', pp. 165–6.

[114] For example, those afflicted by adverse family circumstances – sickness, widowhood, large families and old age. See B.S. Rowntree, *Poverty: A Study of Town Life*, 2nd edn., London, 1902, chapter V; J.H. Treble, *Urban Poverty in Britain, 1830–1914*, London, 1979, chapters III and V, esp. p. 152.

either past its best or even contaminated, and this hazard was not confined to consumers who, because of their limited means, were obliged to shop as cheaply as possible. The case of milk is especially intriguing. On the face of things, an increased availability of milk looks like an unqualified improvement, but this was not necessarily so. In the first place, if adulterated with water, its food value was considerably reduced. In Lancashire, the fall in infant mortality that coincided with the Cotton Famine has been attributed to greater home care and longer breast-feeding by unemployed mothers.[115] More seriously, raw milk is an almost perfect carrier of infection. Prominent among the numerous pathogens it can transmit is the tubercle bacillus in its bovine form. As late as 1896–1907, 8.7 per cent of samples taken from Manchester's milk supply, and 10 per cent from Salford's, showed evidence of the presence of tuberculosis.[116] The Pooleys have added another interesting observation. Milk can also carry scarlet fever, and they note that the incidence of this infection was nearly as high in the outlying districts of Manchester as in the poorer central areas.[117] This raises the possibility – though it can only be a conjecture – that, if mothers in these districts, generally characterised by higher incomes, were pioneers in moving away from breast-feeding, they may have unwittingly placed their children at greater risk of infection.

As the subject matter of this book demands, special attention has been paid to links between nutrition and health, although there were, of course, many other factors bearing on the explanation of Manchester's high mortality rates. There is no need to do more than summarise them briefly. As the Pooleys point out, one factor was immigration. It is probable that migrants from rural areas would have had little chance to develop resistance to the endemic and epidemic

---

[115] Hewitt, *Wives and Mothers*, pp. 104, 118. However, the argument is a controversial one, partly because the year-by-year fluctuations for the country as a whole were similar through 1855–63, and partly because it was realised that 'nursing in straitened circumstances may be better for children than fulness of good cheer without it; but when hard times are prolonged . . . the greatest amount of parental attention will not expel physical decline' (Registrar-General, *Twenty-Fifth Annual Report*, quoted in Oddy, 'Urban famine', p. 84).

[116] *PP* 1909, XXIX, *Thirty-Eighth Annual Report of the Local Government Board, 1908–9*, Appendix B 5, *Report by A.S. Delépine on Investigations in the Public Health Laboratory of the University of Manchester upon the Prevalence and Sources of the Tubercle Bacilli in Cows' Milk*, p. 401. However, higher proportions were recorded at Derby and Burton-on-Trent. This reference was kindly supplied by Dr P.J. Atkins. Note that when the national infant mortality rate began its long-delayed decline in the early twentieth century, one explanation stresses the introduction of pathogen-free milk in the form of pasteurised, dried or condensed supplies. See M.W. Beaver, 'Population, infant mortality and milk', *Population Studies*, XXVII, 1973, pp. 244, 252–4.

[117] Pooley and Pooley, 'Health, society and environment', pp. 165–7.

diseases of large urban areas. In the case of the Irish, they were blamed for introducing disease and were themselves particularly susceptible.[118] Another factor was overcrowding and low housing standards. Manchester was notorious for its numerous cellar dwellings, and by and large (saving the central business district) the density of both housing and population declined fairly evenly with distance from the centre.[119] It is well known that tuberculosis is linked with overcrowding as well as with dietary deficiencies and, as Cronjé has observed, housing standards were 'not nearly as responsive to changes in prosperity as was diet'.[120] Then there is the question of sanitary deficiencies. Suffice it to say that, when an attempt was made to clear Manchester's privy middens in 1845, the task involved the removal of 70,000 tons of excrement, and that in 1869 Manchester still possessed 38,000 middens, outnumbering water closets by four to one.[121] Such conditions were liable to promote the faecal contamination of both food and water; not surprisingly, diarrhoea, dysentery and cholera, together with typhoid, accounted for many deaths. The air was visibly impure, with upwards of 500 factory chimneys discharging masses of dense smoke, while the Irwell was so silted up by the 1860s that its bed was said to be rising by two to three inches a year.[122] And Manchester's record in tackling these problems was patchy, to say the least. On the credit side, it was the first town to prohibit the construction of back-to-backs (1845), and the second to appoint a public analyst, though not until 1873. On the other hand, as matters stood in 1865, there were no public baths or wash-houses, even though they had already been provided by many other municipalities such as Birmingham and Liverpool, and even Maidstone and Durham. Although Manchester possessed a strong body of concerned and knowledgeable medical men, it did not appoint a Medical Officer of Health until 1868, and on grounds of expense it was particularly slow to order slum clearance, nothing of any consequence being achieved before 1891.[123] For the sake of convenience, all these factors may be grouped under the heading 'environmental influences', and they were bound to have a profound effect on mortality in Manchester, however abundant

[118] *Ibid.*, p. 149.
[119] *Ibid.*, pp. 167–9. The estimated number of cellar dwellers in 1843 was 18,000, i.e. some 12 per cent of the population, a problem which was not tackled effectively until 1868. See A.S. Wohl, *Endangered Lives. Public Health in Victorian Britain*, London, 1983, pp. 297–8.
[120] Cronjé, 'Tuberculosis and mortality decline', pp. 98, 101.
[121] Wohl, *Endangered Lives*, pp. 96–7.
[122] *Ibid.*, pp. 208–9, 234–5.
[123] *Ibid.*, pp. 54, 74, 181, 295, 316–17.

the supply of food might be, and however good its quality on arrival.

Perhaps we have reached the point at which this study should be brought to a final conclusion, for it is not obvious, in the present state of our knowledge, that much more can be said. Many instances have been given in these pages of the dynamic nature of free enterprise, in the spheres of production, transportation and distribution. The history of Manchester's food supply undoubtedly attests to the ability of the capitalist system to deliver the goods, once the opportunity for profit has been perceived. It is only fair to acknowledge this, in 1989–90, when, to the satisfaction of many in the West, the centrally-planned economies of Eastern Europe are visibly collapsing, largely on account of their failure to do just this. But our applause should be qualified: it is a question of two cheers rather than three. Clearly, from the standpoint of the consumer, the mechanisms through which food was supplied to the town worked in only a rough and ready way. Quality might be compromised and deceit might flourish, while an overall improvement, even a transformation, of food supply could co-exist with endemic hunger and misery among the less fortunate elements of Mancunian society. This is only to be expected, for in the last analysis free enterprise ministers to effective demand rather than to human needs. It was not until the Edwardian period that the British state began to make headway with the kind of welfare measures that might redress the more obvious inequities in society, but progress in this respect was real, if frequently hesitant and faltering, until 1979. The electorate then chose to return a government bent on reversing the tide of collectivism – indeed, one which talked in terms of restoring Victorian values. Were these objectives to be fully realised, they would certainly usher in a world far more uncomfortable than that which most of us have been used to. The history of Manchester's food supply in an era of unfettered individualism has some lessons that are relevant today. It recalls both the advantages and drawbacks of leaving everything to market forces, and is a timely reminder of the value of a mixed system: one that tempers the undoubted vitality of free enterprise with a generous measure of public responsibility in those areas where it is apt to be found wanting, namely, care and compassion.

APPENDIX A

Tonnages carried on the Bridgewater Canal

The estimates given in Chapter V, Tables 5.1, 5.2 and 5.3 require a more detailed explanation than can be given in the main text.

Table 5.1 (1770–86)

These tonnages are calculated from the cash receipts entered in the Bridgewater Canal Company's General Accounts, 1764–90 (LRO, NCBw 6/1), for the carriage of 'market goods' between Lymm, Altrincham and Manchester. The company was charging 4s and 3s per ton respectively to carry these goods to Manchester in 1770 (LRO, NCBw 1/1, Day Book of Matthias Shelvoke, 3, 9 July 1770), and these rates seem to have prevailed until the 1790s (E. Malley, 'The financial administration of the Bridgewater estate, 1780–1800', University of Manchester, M.A., 1929, pp. 65–7). The tonnages have been obtained by dividing the receipts by the rate of 4s or 3s, as the case may be. In principle, the calculation is straightforward, but note:

(i) It cannot be carried forward beyond 1786, because during the following year the 'market goods' accounts were subsumed into a general traffic account.

(ii) The fall in the tonnages recorded for Altrincham in the 1770s must be seen against the background of the extension of the canal and the opening of more stations. Unfortunately, it is not possible, from the accounts, to trace the extent to which these new stations carried market goods.

(iii) The receipts represent the carriage of goods on the company's own boats only. However, there is reason to believe that, in this period, independent carriers were more concerned with long-distance traffic (Malley, thesis, pp. 38–9; C. Hadfield and G. Biddle, *The Canals of North West England*, Newton Abbot, 1970, I, pp. 36, 90–2).

(iv) The figures may include some market goods passing in the opposite

284

direction, i.e. from Manchester to Lymm and Altrincham. However, according to entries in the Shelvoke Day Book, this could represent only a very small proportion of the traffic in market goods. Entries for 1769–70 show that traffic from Manchester to Lymm amounted to only 2.6 per cent of the total, and from Manchester to Altrincham, 5.3 per cent.

(v) If anything, Table 5.1 could underestimate the tonnages involved. The entries in the General Accounts have had an allowance deducted for the cost of 'land carriage from Castlefield', the company's terminus in Manchester. I have assumed that this was charged in addition to the standard 4s or 3s freight rate. This may not have been so. An examination of the weekly entries for this traffic in Shelvoke's Day Book for 1769–70 shows that gross receipts total 30 per cent more than the entry for the corresponding period in the annual General Account. Moreover, some tonnage figures given, in addition to cash receipts, in the General Account for part of the year 1787 produce a rate per ton 20 per cent lower than the standard freight rates of 4s and 3s. Both pieces of evidence suggest that the freight rate charged to customers included an element for wharfage, land carriage, etc., and that, for accounting purposes, this was deducted from the receipts before the final figures for water carriage were entered into the General Accounts. If this was so, the cash receipts should be divided by smaller figures representing the true rate per ton, rather than the 4s or 3s which I have used. The effect of this would be to raise the annual tonnages given in Table 5.1 by about a quarter throughout the period covered, but would not affect the conclusions drawn in the text.

Tables 5.2 and 5.3

General Accounts for the Bridgewater Trust exist for 1844–50, 1855, 1860, 1864–65, 1868 and 1871, but the amount of detail provided varies considerably in accordance with changes in accounting procedures. See F.C. Mather, *After the Canal Duke*, Oxford, 1970, pp. 360–1. [The accounts for 1849–50, which form the basis of Table 5.2, were consulted at the Lancashire Record Office (NCBw 6/3), and the contents of those for 1855 and 1860 were kindly made available to the author by Professor Mather many years ago. The originals were subsequently returned to their private owner, the Duke of Sutherland.] It is only for the years 1849, 1850, 1855 and 1860 that the data can be disaggregated sufficiently for a comparison to be made with 1770–86. The figures quoted are stated tonnages, but note:

(i) No distinction can be made, as was possible in Table 5.1, between 'market' and 'non-market' goods.
(ii) The figures for tonnages conveyed by independent carriers are those recorded *from* the various stations, but not all need be going to Manchester.

(iii) The 1849 figures for traffic carried by the Trustees' own boats are for tonnages carried *between* the stations and Manchester, and therefore a certain proportion could be coming *from* Manchester. However, in 1850 the accounting procedure changed to recording tonnages *from* the different stations, bringing the figures into line with (ii). Hence, the 1849 figures for the Trustees' own trade are adjusted totals taking this into account.

Despite these various caveats, descriptive evidence and other traffic details in the accounts suggest that the general picture will not be heavily distorted. It is clear from comparisons of the three tables that this stretch of the canal was much more heavily used in 1849–50 than in 1770–86, but that it lost much of its traffic to the railways in the 1850s.

APPENDIX B

Explanation and description of retail areas and zones

I

The determination of economic and social boundaries is a perennial problem for the student of the nineteenth-century city. Descriptions of the character of districts that caught the attention of contemporaries abound, but they typically focus on extreme conditions (of squalor or salubrity), are distinguished more for their eloquence than for objective factual observation, and almost always fail to spell out the precise spatial limits to which their comments apply. Administrative divisions offer another possibility, but in the present study census enumeration districts have been judged to offer too fine, and registration sub-districts too coarse, a mesh to be suitable as they stand. They are, in any case, administrative artefacts. A third option, the use of grid squares, seemed even more artificial. There is the further consideration that it is necessary to devise a scheme which can accommodate the outward spread of the town over time.

II

The essence of the method is to start from the heart of Manchester, adopting areas according as closely as possible with the boundaries of the sanitary districts identified by the Officer of Health (*Report of the Officer of Health for Manchester*, 1 Jan. 1881), which, in turn, are sub-divisions of the registration sub-districts of Market Street, London Road, Deansgate, St George's and Ancoats. This gives rise to a total of twenty areas (on Figure 10.1, they are numbered 1–7, 10–12, 14–19, 28–30, 37). Another ten areas (13, 20–4, 31–4) lie mainly or entirely to the south of the River Medlock, i.e. in the registration districts of Chorlton-on-Medlock and Hulme. The sub-divisions adopted by the Officer of Health for Manchester are shown on a

287

map accompanying his Report for 1887 (published May 1888). Again, the areas used respect as far as possible the boundaries of his sanitary districts, either singly or in combination. Since no comparable material exists for Salford, the seven areas identified to the west of the River Irwell (8, 9, 25–7, 35, 36) have had to be drawn more arbitrarily. Finally, area 38 has a 'catch-all' character; it has no specific boundaries and is simply used to accommodate all traders who were listed in the Manchester directories, usually with imprecise addresses, but who were located outside areas 1–37.

III

The thirty-seven areas thus identified are arranged into zones corresponding approximately to the extent of the built-up limits *c.* 1800, *c.* 1825, *c.* 1850 and *c.* 1870, which can be followed on a succession of maps:

(i) Bancks and Thornton, *Plan of Manchester and Salford*, 1800.
(ii) Bancks and Co., *Plan of Manchester and Salford*, 1828.
(iii) Folding plan of Manchester and Salford in *Slater's Directory of Manchester and Salford*, 1850.
(iv) Kelly, *Post Office Map of Manchester and Salford*, 1873.

Zone A corresponds to the built-up limits *c.* 1800 (areas 1–9).
Zone B represents the additions by *c.* 1825 (areas 10–15).
Zone C shows further extensions by *c.* 1850 (areas 16–27).
Zone D brings in further accretions by *c.* 1870 (areas 28–37).
Zone E (area 38) is residual.

IV

There follows a description of the boundaries of each of the thirty-seven areas, zone by zone. The street names used for this purpose are those of 1873. In addition, a brief profile of each area is given, using the following sources and abbreviations:

(i) *Report of the Officer of Health for Manchester*, 1 Jan. 1881 (OH). His comments on sanitary districts (SD), are annotated as MS 1 (Market St, No. 1) *et seq.*, and similarly for London Road (LR), Deansgate (DG), St George's (SG) and Ancoats (AN). Likewise, HU (with numbers as appropriate) stands for Hulme, CM for Chorlton-on-Medlock, AR for Ardwick (part of the Chorlton-on-Medlock registration district) and CH for Cheetham. Unless otherwise specified, all comments derive from this source.
(ii) Maps (as listed under III above).
(iii) J. Aston, *A Picture of Manchester*, Manchester, 1816. (Aston)

(iv) J.P. Kay, *The Moral and Physical Condition of the Working Classes Employed in the Cotton Manufacture in Manchester*, 2nd edn., London, 1832. (Kay)

(v) R.B. Howard, 'On the prevalence of diseases arising from . . . physical causes amongst the labouring classes in Manchester', Poor Law Commissioners, *Sanitary Enquiry. England. Local Reports*, pp. 294–335. *PP* 1842 (HL), XXVII. (Howard)

(vi) P.H. Holland, Replies to Questions, Chorlton-upon-Medlock, *First Report of the Commissioners appointed to inquire into the State of Large Towns and Populous Districts*, Appendix, *Special Reports*, pp. 58–70. *PP* 1844, XVII. (Holland)

(vii) F. Engels, *The Condition of the Working Class in England*, translated and edited by W.O. Henderson and W.H. Chaloner, Oxford, 1958. (Engels)

(viii) D.A. Farnie, 'The commercial development of Manchester in the later nineteenth century', *The Manchester Review*, VII, 1956. (Farnie)

(ix) H.B. Rodgers, 'The suburban growth of Victorian Manchester', *Journal of the Manchester Geographical Society*, LVIII, 1961–62. (Rodgers)

(x) R.L. Greenall, 'The making of the borough of Salford, 1830–53', in S.P. Bell (ed.), *Victorian Lancashire*, Newton Abbot, 1974. (Greenall).

V. Areas and profiles

Zone A

1. *Bounded by*: Swan St, Oldham St, Market St, Blackfriars St, River Irwell, New Bridge St, Ducie Bridge, Miller St.
Comments: Engels (pp. 56–60) criticises courts and alleys between Long Millgate and River Irk – coal-black and stinking. Even the better streets (e.g. Todd St, Withy Grove) tortuous. OHSD MS 2, 3: considerable number of houses used for business purposes. Dwellings generally old, poor condition. Some back-to-backs. Considerable number work at markets (Smithfield, Shude Hill).

2. *Bounded by*: Great Ancoats St, Store St, London Rd, Piccadilly, Oldham St.
Comments: Levers Row neighbourhood once middle-class (Rodgers, p. 2). OHSD LR 2: generally old property, pre-1830, and most are back-to-backs, frequently damp. Streets fairly good condition. Varied working-class population including some hawkers.

3. *Bounded by*: Piccadilly, Portland St, Bond St, Mosley St.
Comments: Once fashionable neighbourhood but changing by 1840s

(Rodgers, p. 2). Becoming a warehouse district by 1850s (Farnie, p. 329). Part of OHSD MS 4: very few dwelling houses remain – shops, warehouses, offices.

4. *Bounded by*: Market St, Mosley St, Princess St, Brazennose St, Deansgate.
Comments: As area 3 (Rodgers; Farnie). Part of OHSD MS 4: buildings mainly substantial business premises.

5. *Bounded by*: Brazennose St, Princess St, Mosley St, Lower Mosley St, Great Bridgewater St, Deansgate.
Comments: OHSD DG 2: nearly half the land covered by pre-1830 housing, including back-to-backs. Remainder is business property, including Central Station. Many small streets occupied by people with no settled occupation.

6. *Bounded by*: Deansgate, Liverpool Rd, River Irwell, Bridge St (but not including it – see area 7).
Comments: Close courts, loathsome streets – prostitutes and thieves – e.g. Cumberland St, Wood St (Kay, p. 36). OHSD DG 3, 4: to north of Quay St, all dwellings pre-1830, mostly back-to-back. South of Quay St, poor housing, extensive railway yards, canal wharves. Many tramps.

7. *Bounded by*: Deansgate, Bridge St, River Irwell.
Comments: Area includes Bridge Street Market. Part of OHSD MS 4: very few dwelling houses remain, but those on banks of Irwell and in Back Bridge St severely censured.

8. *Bounded by*: Blackfriars St, River Irwell, New Bailey St, Chapel St, St Stephen's St, Blackfriars Rd.
Comments: Part of borough of Salford, representing south-western side as far as developed by *c.* 1800 (map). Area between Blackfriars St and New Bailey St very confined, densely populated (Howard, p. 314).

9. *Bounded by*: Greengate, New Bridge St, River Irwell, Blackfriars St, Blackfriars Rd.
Comments: See area 8. North-eastern side of Salford *c.* 1800. Eastern end particularly squalid. Removal of some of filthiest streets as a result of construction of railway to Liverpool, but still a dirty district. Narrow side streets and courts off Chapel St, Greengate, Gravel Lane, never cleaned since built (Engels, p. 74).

Zone B

10. *Bounded by*: Rochdale Rd, Miller St, Long Millgate, Red Bank, Roger St, Gould St.

Comments: Miller St 'reasonably decent' but flanked by alleys – many pigs; south of St Michael's Church, rather more evidence of planning (Engels, pp. 62–3). OHSD SG 6: mostly pre-1830, many back-to-backs. Population consists of lowest orders, but boundary along Rochdale Rd occupied by shopkeepers.

11. *Bounded by*: Oldham Rd, Swan St, Rochdale Rd, Lees St.
Comments: OHSD SG 5: housing similar to area 10. Population includes many working as wholesale cabinet manufacturers, or in cotton-waste warehouses.

12. *Bounded by*: Bradford Rd, Mill St, Great Ancoats St, Oldham Rd, German St, Bradford St.
Comments: OHSD AN 1, 5: nearly all housing pre-1830, many back-to-backs. West of Union St, nearly all poor people except in Oldham Rd and Great Ancoats St. Hawkers and hurdy-gurdy players.

13. *Bounded by*: London Rd, Downing St, Grosvenor St, Oxford St, Charles St, Granby Row.
Comments: Mostly south of River Medlock. Howard (p. 316) saw district of Chorlton-on-Medlock as freer from accumulations of filth than other parts of Manchester, and labouring classes as 'less commonly indigent or destitute'. Holland (pp. 59–60) noted two-thirds had own 'necessaries' and distinguished between streets that were paved, sewered, cleaned (Oxford St, Greek St, York St); intermediate ones, tolerably clean (Cross St, Stafford St); and a third class, often little better than courts (Mark Lane, Back Temple St, Billington St). Area corresponds approximately to OHSD CM 1, 2.

14. *Bounded by*: Piccadilly, London Rd, Granby Row, Charles St, Oxford St, Portland St.
Comments: OHSD LR 1: numerous courts of back-to-backs, mostly built before 1830 and damp. (These were built to south and east of Portland St, once fashionable but in transition in 1840s – Rodgers, p. 4.) Area bisected by Rochdale Canal; works and warehouses between canal and River Medlock (map, 1850).

15. *Bounded by*: Bond St, Portland St, Great Bridgewater St, Lower Mosley St, Mosley St.
Comments: Part of OHSD DG 1: all houses pre-1830, some back-to-backs. Various works and warehouses adjacent to canal (map, 1850).

Zone C

16. *Bounded by*: North St, Red Bank, Long Millgate, Ducie Bridge, York St.
Comments: OHSD MS 1: homes in northern part of district well-built, somewhat elevated, healthy. In lower part (n.b., crossed by River Irk), houses small, crowded, poorly drained. Many Jewish tailors. Engels (p. 61) remarks on alleys, courts, stenches above Ducie Bridge and to west of Long Millgate.

17. *Bounded by*: Oldham Rd, Butler St, Bradford St, German St.
Comments: OHSD AN 2, 12: some pre-1830 housing, rest mainly 1830–50. Shopkeepers occupy Oldham Rd. Many employed in factories, glass works, boiler works.

18. *Bounded by*: Mill St, Beswick St, Every St, Great Ancoats St.
Comments: OHSD AN 6, 7, 8, 9: north-western end mostly pre-1830. Back-to-backs, many dilapidated, occupied by mill-workers. North-eastern corner and over half the southern end built since 1830; few back-to-backs; housing mill and iron works' operatives, but some artisans, warehousemen, clerks working in the city.

19. *Bounded by*: Great Ancoats St, Pin Mill Brow, Ogden St, Fairfield St, Birmingham St, London Rd, Store St.
Comments: Large working-class quarter growing up south of Great Ancoats St on bare, hilly stretch of land – irregularly built rows and courts, interspersed with muddy tracts. Area crossed by Manchester and Birmingham Railway is worst part of district (Engels, p. 71). Part of OHSD LR 3: half of houses old, pre-1830. Most inhabitants 'of the industrial order', including many employed on railways, with extensive depots in district.

20. *Bounded by*: Fairfield St, Union St, Higher Ardwick, Ardwick Green, Downing St, London Rd, Birmingham St.
Comments: Corner to north-west of River Medlock contains many back-to-backs (Kay, p. 37, describes vicinity as 'extremely wretched'). Most of area, south of Medlock, is OHSD AR 1, 2, including one of earliest suburbs, Ardwick Green, which was surrounded and invaded by poor housing by 1840s (Rodgers, p. 8).

21. *Bounded by*: Oxford St, Coupland St, Hall St, Vine St, Stretford Rd, Cavendish St.
Comments: OHSD CM 3, HU 10: Chorlton part, between Boundary Lane and Oxford St, already fairly spaciously developed by 1850 (map), and just over junction of Oxford St and Coupland St, appeared Owens College (1851). Hulme part, to south and west of Boundary Lane, two-thirds developed by 1850, but infilled in next twenty years (maps, 1850, 1873).

22. *Bounded by*: Great Bridgewater St, Oxford St, Cavendish St, Stretford Rd, Medlock St, Albion St.
Comments: Partly in OHSD DG 1 (north-west of River Medlock). Mostly warehouses by Rochdale Canal. Here is notorious Little Ireland (Engels, p. 72). Rest, south of river, corresponds to OHSD CM 1 and resembles area 13. At south-east corner lies Grosvenor Square, laid out as nucleus of fashionable district *c*. 1800, but never made it. Engulfed, as were older terraces on Oxford St (Rodgers, p. 4).

23. *Bounded by*: Medlock St, Stretford Rd, Lower Moss Lane, City Rd.
Comments: Hulme seen as 'really one big working-class quarter', like Ancoats. In some parts, cottages packed closely, others less densely crowded, but most surrounded by filth. Dampness, back alleys, cellar dwellings (Engels, p. 73). Area corresponds to OHSD HU 5, 6.

24. *Bounded by*: Great Bridgewater St, Albion St, City Rd, Lower Moss Lane, Chester Rd, Deansgate.
Comments: North of River Medlock, corresponds to OHSD DG 2 – see area 5. Most lies to south of river and corresponds to OHSD HU 3, 4 – see Engels's description of area 23. Fully developed by 1850 (map).

25. *Bounded by*: River Irwell, Hampson St, Oldfield Rd, Chapel St, New Bailey St.
Comments: Includes Islington Grove and surrounding streets in proximity to Bolton Railway – dwellings in which it is impossible to live in cleanliness and comfort (Engels, p. 75). Howard (p. 314) critical of Barrow St. Contains New Bailey Prison, 1787, extended 1814, 'such is the increase of depravity' (Aston, p. 194).

26. *Bounded by*: Chapel St, River Irwell, Broughton Rd, St Stephen's St.
Comments: Various works, e.g. print, copper, and timber yards front river *c*. 1850 (map). Appears more spaciously laid out than areas 8, 9, but some infilling by 1873 (map).

27. *Bounded by*: River Irwell, New Bridge St, Greengate, Broughton Rd.
Comments: Fairly densely packed streets in 1850, having developed considerably since 1828 (maps). Streets between Broughton Rd, Greengate and river furnish many fever patients (Howard, p. 315).

Zone D

28. *Bounded by*: Red Bank, Cheetham St, Collyhurst Rd, Gorton St, Rochdale Rd, Gould St, Roger St.

Comments: Mostly OHSD SG 7, 8 (to south of River Irk). Three-quarters of this part built-up by 1850. Apart from shopkeepers (Rochdale Rd), occupied by poor class of people – porters, labourers. Engels (p. 65) refers to single rows, but much filth, pigs; does not give impression of being part of a big city. Middle band of area largely built since 1850 – thrifty people. Northernmost part (OHSD CH 1) little developed even in 1873 (map).

29. *Bounded by*: Rochdale Rd, Osborne St, Oldham Rd, Lees St.
Comments: OHSD SG 3, 4: most housing erected since 1850. Many improvements – old houses once fronting Oldham Rd replaced by churches, schools, business premises. Most inhabitants work for railway (extensive sidings) or in engineering and iron works.

30. *Bounded by*: Oldham Rd, Hulme Hall Lane, Bradford Rd, Butler St.
Comments: OHSD AN 3, 4: south-western part of this area developed steadily through period – one-third pre-1830, one-third 1830–70, rest still developing around steel and chemical works at Miles Platting. Workmen's houses. Some warehousemen and clerks.

31. *Bounded by*: Chancery Lane, Summer Place, Hyde Rd, Higher Ardwick, Union St, Ogden St.
Comments: OHSD AR 2, 3: map (1850) suggests that the part north of London and North Western Railway is similar to north of area 20. To south of railway, much less developed and still so in 1873 (map), though a large area occupied by Ardwick Cemetery.

32. *Bounded by*: Downing St, Ardwick Green, Brunswick St, Oxford St, Grosvenor St.
Comments: OHSD CM 4, 5: map (1850) shows northern and north-western parts resemble area 13, which it adjoins. Rest largely infilled by 1873 (map), but not to same level of density.

33. *Bounded by*: Stretford Rd, Vine St, Embden St, Moss Lane West, Chorlton Rd.
Comments: OHSD HU 8, 9, 11: probably that area of Hulme identified by Engels (p. 73) as less densely populated part of district – houses of more modern construction, more open to fresh air, but still plenty of filth. Some infilling by 1873 (map), but southern extremities evidently more spacious than most of Hulme.

34. *Bounded by*: Liverpool Rd, Deansgate, Chester Rd, Cornbrook, River Irwell.
Comments: Traversed by Bridgewater Canal ('foul and offensive' – Holland,

p. 58). Altrincham Railway and chemical works at Cornbrook. Comparison of 1850 and 1873 maps shows infilling between Bridgewater Canal and Chester Rd. OHSD HU 1, 2.

35. *Bounded by*: Regent Rd, River Irwell, Hulton St, Gloucester Terrace.
Comments: Only area to immediate south of Regent Rd developed *c.* 1850 (map), but a major mill (Sunny Side) adjacent to Irwell and dye works downstream. Considerable infilling by 1873 (map).

36. *Bounded by*: Hampson St, River Irwell, Regent Rd, Oldfield Rd.
Comments: An 'outlying' district of Salford (Engels, p. 75), but in dwellings along Regent Rd it is impossible to live in cleanliness and comfort. Oldfield Rd, Regent Rd, etc. unpaved, unsoughed and filthy; inhabitants generally poor (Howard, p. 314).

37. *Bounded by*: York St, New Bridge St, River Irwell, Sherborne St, Exchange St.
Comments: Area bisected by Great Ducie St and Bury New Rd, flanked in 1850 by dwellings built to reasonably regular plan (map). Rest of area largely developed on similar lines by 1873 (map). Includes Strangeways Prison.

Zone E

38. Boundaries indeterminate.
Comments: Area encircles Manchester and Salford, defined by 1–37 above. While containing the most salubrious suburbs, it should not be thought of as exclusively upper-middle class.

Salford side of River Irwell
Between Oldfield Rd and Cross Lane, divided by Hope St, is a working-class area (Engels, p. 75), and cattle market is situated at junction of Cross Lane and High St. At Pendleton, industrial settlements at Douglas Green and Charlestown, where population is in coal-mining, textiles (Greenall, p. 37). On the other hand, large houses – even mansions – along Eccles Rd (Greenall, p. 37) and The Crescent (Rodgers, p. 5). These, however, though remaining desirable, came to be backed by railway and canal and to view (across Irwell) bleach and dye works (map, 1850).

Manchester side of River Irwell
Here, area 38 includes Holt Town (mills) and Beswick, poised in 1871 to grow rapidly, reaching 10,000 inhabitants by 1886, housed in respectable cottages – no back-to-backs (*Report of the Officer of Health for Manchester for 1886*, p. 39). However, note Cheetham Hill, Higher and Lower

Broughton ('breezy heights' – Engels, p. 55); Greenheys (to immediate south and west of area 21); Plymouth Grove (where Mrs Gaskell lived); Victoria Park (first developed in the 1830s, subsequently gated and locked – Rodgers, p. 8); and, further out, suburbanised villages of Fallowfield, Withington and Didsbury.

APPENDIX C
Classification of business addresses

Major main roads
Bank Parade
Bank Top
Brook Street
Broughton Road
Chapel Street
Chester Road
City Road
Deansgate
Downing Street
Great Ancoats Street
Great Ducie Street
Greengate
Hyde Road
Knott Mill
Levers Row
London Road
Market Street
Miller Street
Oldfield Road
Oldham Road
Oxford Street
Paradise
Piccadilly
Pin Mill Brow
Regent Road
Rochdale Road (St George's Road)
St Mary's Gate
Shooters Brow

Minor main roads
Bond Street
Bridge Street (Manchester)
Butler Street
Cannon Street
Cavendish Street
Corporation Street
Cross Lane
David Street
Gravel Lane
Great Bridgewater Street
Great Jackson Street
Grosvenor Street
Hanging Ditch
High Street
John Dalton Street
King Street
Liverpool Road
Long Millgate
Lower Mosley Street
Medlock Street
Mill Street
Mosley Street
New Bailey Street
New Bridge Street
North Street
Oldham Street
Ordsall Lane
Peter Street

297

Major main roads (contd.)
Stockport Road
Stretford Road
Swan Street
The Crescent
Upper Brook Street
White Cross Bank
York Street

Minor main roads (contd.)
Plymouth Grove
Pollard Street
Portland Street
Princess Street
Quay Street
Red Bank
St Stephen's Street
Shude Hill
Victoria Street
Water Street

All other business addresses are included in the category 'Other roads and streets' in Table 10.3.

APPENDIX D

Selected local location quotients in 1850 and 1871

A. Within the 37 areas of analysis

		Shopkeepers	Grocers and Tea Dealers	Bakers	Butchers	Fish-mongers	Green-grocers
1850							
	AREA						
	16	1.01	0.69	1.90	0.94	–	–
	17	1.10	0.94	1.39	0.84	–	–
	18	1.34	0.61	0.85	0.73	–	–
	29	1.18	0.92	1.28	0.71	–	–
	30	1.63	0.21	0.89	0.33	–	–
	31	1.36	0.89	0.84	0.55	–	–
	37	0.54	2.00	1.47	1.02	1.88	2.07
1871							
	5	0.69	1.30	2.04	1.40	–	0.95
	6	0.91	1.23	1.30	0.82	0.46	1.23
	10	0.88	1.04	1.50	1.01	1.46	1.01
	11	0.52	1.62	2.10	1.27	1.12	1.28
	13	0.93	1.03	1.68	0.95	0.54	0.95
	22	1.22	0.73	0.87	0.86	1.02	0.62
	28	0.82	1.11	1.80	1.11	0.58	1.02
	29	1.31	0.55	1.12	0.58	0.51	0.68
	34	1.03	1.10	1.22	0.95	–	0.92

B. Within zone E (area 38): specified suburbs

	Shopkeepers	Grocers and Tea Dealers	Bakers	Butchers	Fish-mongers	Green-grocers
1850						
Lower Broughton	0.71	2.04	1.45	1.04	–	–
Cheetham	1.50	1.31	0.78	1.01	–	–
Fallowfield	2.33	–	–	–	–	–
Rusholme	1.20	1.37	0.80	0.71	–	–
Greenheys	1.30	2.07	–	–	–	4.37
Harpurhey	1.25	0.51	–	1.31	–	–
1871						
Lower Broughton	0.92	0.96	0.69	1.22	1.79	1.10
Cheetham	1.34	1.04	0.68	0.70	0.54	0.38
Fallowfield	1.18	1.73	0.76	0.76	–	0.42
Rusholme	0.95	1.16	0.60	0.93	0.96	1.35
Greenheys	1.13	1.42	–	1.31	–	0.65
Harpurhey	1.12	1.44	0.74	0.97	–	0.64

Bibliography

MANUSCRIPT SOURCES

HOUSE OF LORDS RECORD OFFICE, LONDON

Minutes of Evidence on Private Bills taken before Select Committees of the House of Commons and the House of Lords, 1836–65

JOHN RYLANDS UNIVERSITY LIBRARY OF MANCHESTER

English MS. 703	Diary of George Heywood, grocer, 1788–1840
English MS. 1024	Hibbert-Ware Papers, Tradesmen's Bills, 1802–15

LANCASHIRE COUNTY RECORD OFFICE, PRESTON

Bridgewater Collieries Papers:

NCBw 1/1	Day Book of Matthias Shelvoke, 1769–70
1/2–3	Day Books of Robert Lansdale, 1772–79
2/1–6	Cash Books of Robert Lansdale, 1776–1820
2/9	Book of receipts, 1840–41
2/11	Book of payments, 1842–44
6/1	Book of General Accounts, 1764–90
6/3	Bridgewater Trust General Accounts, 1844–50

Court of Quarter Sessions:

QJB 37–57	Debtors' Insolvency Papers, 1765–1812

MANCHESTER CENTRAL LIBRARY, ARCHIVES DEPARTMENT

M9/30/1/4–5	Minute Books of the General Committee of the Manchester Police Commissioners, 1819–28
M9/30/4/3–4	Minute Books of the Lamp, Scavenging, Fire-Engine and Nuisance Committee of the Manchester Police Commissioners, 1833–43

M9/30/5/1	Minute Book of the Watch, Nuisance and Hackney-Coach Committee of the Manchester Police Commissioners, 1828–31
M9/40/2/53–292	Township of Manchester Rate Books, Poor Rate Assessments, 1796–1870
M10/23/6/7	Township of Rusholme, Minutes of Local Board of Health, 1869–75
M62/1/1–3	Ledgers of William and Thomas Wood, innkeepers, shopkeepers and farmers of Didsbury, 1767–1838
M126/2/2,4	Manchester and Salford Sanitary Association, Visiting Committee's Reports, 1853–54
Misc. 41	Three bills for fish etc. bought from John Walker, fishmonger, Market Place, Manchester, 1821
Misc. 258/1	Accounts for purchase of groceries, James Bentley, flour dealer, 1799–1807
MS. F. 942.73912 J15	S.C. Johnson (fl. 1915–47), 'Manchester Corn and Produce Exchange: Memoirs of Persons and Streets in the Eighteen Nineties', n.d.

MANCHESTER TOWN HALL, MUNIMENTS ROOM

Records of the Manor of Manchester:

M1/21/C	Report of the Select Committee appointed at a Meeting on the Twenty-Second Day of June 1808 for the Purpose of corresponding and conferring with the Lord of the Manor of Manchester respecting the Purchase of the Manor, 28 Sept. 1808
M1/24/A	Report of a Committee appointed at a Town's Meeting, held on the Sixth Day of December 1786, and dissolved on the Ninth Day of July 1792, 2 Jan. 1793
M1/24/1–221	Sundry Law Papers principally connected with the Manorial Rights, 1787–91
M1/25/1–19	Further Papers connected with the Manorial Rights, 1787–91
M1/41/No. 1A	Agreement between Sir Oswald Mosley, Bart. and the Mayor, Aldermen and the Burgesses of the Borough of Manchester, 24 June 1845
M1/50/1–8	Miscellaneous Papers connected with the Manorial Rights, c. 1825–c. 1835
M1/55/4,4v	Record of *Mosley Bart.* v. *Walker*, 17 Mar. 1826,

| | with judgement in case on verso, 7 Aug. 1827 |
| M1/57 | MS. Book 'Market Actions and Tolls etc.', n.d., covers *c*. 1767–*c*. 1837 |

PUBLIC RECORD OFFICE, LONDON

British Transport Historical Records:

RAIL 343	Lancashire and Yorkshire Railway Company
/484	Working Expenses Sub-Committee Minutes, 1852
/493–505	Traffic Committee Minutes, 1848–56
RAIL 371	Liverpool and Manchester Railway Company
/1–6	Board Minutes, 1830–43
/8	Management Committee Minutes, 1831–32
/9	Finance Committee Minutes, 1831
/10–11	Traffic Sub-Committee Minutes, 1834–43
RAIL 410	London and North Western Railway Company
/87	Special Committee Minutes, 1865
/140	Road and Traffic Committee (London) Minutes, 1852–53
/150–2	Road and Traffic Committee (Northern Division) Minutes, 1852–54
/153	Road and Traffic Committee (Manchester Division) Minutes, 1850
/155	Road and Traffic Committee (North-Eastern Division) Minutes, 1852
/159	Road and Traffic Committee (Liverpool Division) Minutes, 1850–54
/167	Northern Sub-Committee Minutes, 1861
/172–5	General Traffic Committee Minutes, 1864–69
/516	Northern Committee Minutes, 1867
/719	Reports on the Merchandise Traffic of the Town and Port of Liverpool, 1853
RAIL 458	Manchester, Bolton, and Bury Canal Navigation and Railway Company
/15	Book of Claims, 1846–47
RAIL 463	Manchester, Sheffield, and Lincolnshire Railway Company
/1–9	Board of Directors Minutes, 1851–66
/2–5	Reports of the Directors to the Meetings of the Proprietors, 1855–60
/288	Traffic Ledger No. 2, 1851–56
RAIL 465	Manchester, South Junction, and Altrincham

	Railway Company
/3	Board of Directors Minutes, 1855–56
RAIL 846	Leeds and Liverpool Canal Company
/9	Committee of Company of Proprietors Minutes, 1818

Records of the Clerks of Assize:
ASSI 55/1   Northern Circuit, Judgement Book, 1810–36

Records of the Duchy of Lancaster:
DL 9   Affidavits, Reports, Orders, Petitions
DL 41   Miscellanea

RECORDS IN PRIVATE HANDS

Bridgewater Trust Papers, General Account Books for the years 1855 and 1860: Mertoun, St Boswell's, Roxburghshire

Failsworth Industrial Society Ltd, Committee Minutes, 1868–75: Norwest Co-operative Society, Chestergate Store, Stockport

Isaac Burgon's Cash Books, No. 1, 1846–63; No. 2, 1859–62: Consulted at T. Seymour Mead & Co. Ltd, Houldsworth Square, Reddish, Stockport (Sadly, recent enquiries to the Argyll Group PLC, which acquired Seymour Mead & Co., strongly suggest that these records have not been preserved)

Manchester Coffee Roasting Company Ltd, Articles for regulating and carrying on a Coffee Roasting Concern established in Manchester, 7 Nov. 1823; Committee of Proprietors Minutes, 1845–55: Consulted at Plantation House, Thomas Street, Middleton, Greater Manchester (The company was dissolved on 31 Dec. 1981. Its records do not appear to have been deposited in any public archives)

Manchester and Salford Equitable Co-operative Society Ltd, Bakery Committee Minutes, 1873–78; Bakery Department Accounts, 1873; Butchery Department Accounts, 1873–79; Committee Minutes, 1862–71: Norwest Co-operative Society, Chestergate Store, Stockport

Mersey and Irwell Navigation Company, Orders of the Board of Directors, Books for the years 1779–1844: Manchester Ship Canal Company, Property Division, Dock Office, Trafford Road, Salford

North of England Co-operative Wholesale Society Ltd, Committee Minutes, 1865–71; Grocery and Provisions Sub-Committee Minutes, 1874–75: New Century House, Balloon Street, Manchester

Bibliography

PRINTED PRIMARY SOURCES

BROADSIDES

In Manchester Central Library, Local History Library
f. 1786/1   *Meeting in Manchester*, 2 Dec. 1786
f. 1790/11   *Manchester Market, c. 1790*
ff. 1811/2   *Manor of Manchester*, 20 Sept. 1811
f. 1812/18   *For the Improvement of Fruit*, 3 Aug. 1812
ff. 1813/2   *Market for the Buying and Selling of Horned Cattle*, 6 Aug. 1813
ff. 1820/36   *Manchester Markets*, 1 Sept. 1820
ff. 1821/14   *Stalls and Standings for Greengrocers and other vendors of marketable commodities*, 22 Aug. 1821
ff. 1821/15   *New Warehouse for the sale of Flour and Meal*, 26 Oct. 1821
                             Notice to Butchers, 27 Oct. 1821

In Manchester Town Hall, Muniments Room
M1/56/1   *Potato Market, Manor of Manchester*, 28 Mar. 1808
M1/56/2   *Manchester*, 29 July 1809
M1/56/3   *New Market, Shudehill, Manchester*, 21 Aug. 1820

DIRECTORIES

E. Raffald, *The Manchester Directory for the Year 1772*
E. Raffald, *Manchester and Salford Directory for 1781*
Lewis's Directory of Manchester and Salford, 1788
Bancks' Manchester and Salford Directory, 1800
Pigot's Manchester and Salford Directory, 1811
Pigot and Deans' Manchester and Salford Directory, 1815
Pigot and Deans' New Directory of Manchester and Salford, 1821–2
Pigot and Son's General Directory of Manchester and Salford, 1830
Pigot and Son's General and Classified Directory of Manchester and Salford, 1833
Pigot and Son's General and Classified Directory of Manchester and Salford, 1836
Pigot and Slater's General and Classified Directory of Manchester and Salford, 1840
Pigot and Slater's General and Classified Directory of Manchester and Salford, May edn., 1841

Pigot and Slater's General and Classified Directory of Manchester and Salford, 1843

Slater's General and Classified Directory of Manchester and Salford, 1845

Slater's General and Classified Directory of Manchester and Salford, 1850

Slater's Royal National Commercial Directory of Manchester, Liverpool and the Principal Manufacturing Towns in Lancashire, 1861

Slater's General and Classified Directory of Manchester and Salford, 1871–2

GOVERNMENT PUBLICATIONS

Parliamentary Papers:

1785, Third Report from the Select Committee on the State of the British Fisheries in Reports from Committees of the House of Commons, X, 1803

1798, Second Report from the Select Committee on the State of the British Herring Fisheries in Reports from Committees of the House of Commons, X, 1803

1800, Sixth Report from the Select Committee on the State of the British Herring Fisheries in Reports from Committees of the House of Commons, X, 1803

1801 (174) II, Second Report from the Select Committee appointed to consider of the Present High Price of Provisions

1814–15 (186) V, Report from the Committee on Laws relating to the Manufacture, Sale and Assize of Bread

1818 (400) V, Report by the Lords' Select Committee on the Poor Laws

1820 (255) II, Report from the Select Committee on Petitions complaining of Agricultural Distress

1821 (426) V, Report from the Select Committee on the existing Regulations relative to the making and the sale of Bread

1821 (668) IX, Report from the Select Committee to whom the several Petitions . . . complaining of the depressed state of the Agriculture of the United Kingdom were referred

1825, Proceedings of the Committee of the House of Commons on the Liverpool and Manchester Railway Bill. Sessions, 1825

1826 (406) V, Report from the Select Committee on the Butter Trade of Ireland

1833 (612) V, Report from the Select Committee on Agriculture

1833 (690) VI, Report from the Select Committee on Manufactures, Commerce and Shipping

1833 (676) XIV, Report from the Select Committee on British Channel Fisheries

1833 (417) XXI, First Report of the Commissioners of Inquiry into the Excise Establishment . . . Tea Permits and Surveys

1836 (189) VIII–Pt. I, Second Report from the Select Committee on the State

306

of Agriculture

1837 (464) V, *Report from the Select Committee of the House of Lords on the State of Agriculture in England and Wales*

1839 (398) VIII, *Report from the Select Committee on the Fresh Fruit Trade*

1840 (474) XIII, *Fifth Report from the Select Committee on Railway Communication*

1842 (HL) XXVII, Poor Law Commissioners, *Sanitary Enquiry. England. Local Reports*

1842 (184) XXXIX, *An Account of the Quantities of Cheese Imported into the Several Ports of Great Britain for the years 1840 and 1841*

1842 (414) XL, *Return of the Quantities of Wheat sold . . . in 1836, 1839, and 1842 etc.*

1843 (373) LII, *An Account . . . of Cheese Imported . . . for the year 1842*

1844 [572] XVII, *First Report of the Commissioners appointed to inquire into the State of Large Towns and Populous Districts*

1844 [587] XXVII, *Census of Great Britain, 1841. Occupation Abstract: Pt. I*

1844 (203) XLV, *An Account . . . of Cheese Imported . . . for the year 1843*

1845 (614) XXXIX, *Railway Tolls: Return of the Various Charges*

1846 (489) XIII, *Report by the Lords' Select Committee on the best means of enforcing one uniform system of Management of Railroads*

1847–8 [937] LXIII, *Railway Commission: Return of the Passenger and Goods Traffic on each Railway . . . for the Two Years ending 30 June 1846 and 30 June 1847*

1852–3 [1632] LXXXVI, *Census of Great Britain, 1851. Population Tables, Pt. I, Numbers of the Inhabitants in the Years 1801, 1811, 1821, 1831, 1841, and 1851, II*

1852–3 [1691–II] LXXXVIII–Pt. II, *Census of Great Britain, 1851. Population Tables, Pt. II, Ages, Civil Condition, Occupations, etc., II*

1856 (379) VIII, *Report from the Select Committee on Adulteration of Food etc.*

1862 [3027] XLVII, *First Report (by Mr Tremenheere) to the Home Secretary relative to the grievances complained of by the Journeymen Bakers*

1862 [3056] L, *Census of England and Wales, 1861. Population Tables, I, Numbers and Distribution*

1863 (161) XXV, *Fifth Report of the Medical Officer of the Privy Council, Appendix V, No. 3, Report of Dr E. Smith, Economics of Diet*

1863 [3221] LIII–Pt. I, *Census of England and Wales, 1861. Population Tables, II, Ages, Civil Condition, Occupations, etc.*

1866 (427) XVI, *Report from the Select Committee on Trade in Animals*

1866 [3596] XVII; [3596–I] XVIII, *Report of the Commissioners appointed to inquire into the Sea Fisheries of the United Kingdom*

1866 [3591] XXII, *First Report of the Commissioners appointed to inquire into the Origin and Nature etc. of the Cattle Plague*

1866 [3600] XXII, *Second Report of the Commissioners appointed to inquire into the Origin and Nature etc. of the Cattle Plague*

1867 [3844–I] XXXVIII, *Report of the Royal Commission on Railways*

1867 [3941] LXXI, *Agricultural Returns for Great Britain . . . for 1867*

1867–8 [4060] XVIII, *Report on the Cattle Plague in Great Britain, during the years 1865, 1866, and 1867*

1870 [C. 116] LXI, *Report from the Committee . . . on the Transit of Animals by Sea and Land*

1870 [C. 223] LXVIII, *Agricultural Returns of Great Britain . . . for 1870*

1872 [C. 676] LXVI–Pt. I, *Census of England and Wales, 1871. Population Tables: Areas, Houses and Inhabitants*, I, *Counties*

1873 (353) XI, *Report from the Select Committee on Contagious Diseases (Animals)*

1873 [C. 872] LXXI–Pt. I, *Census of England and Wales, 1871. Population Tables: Areas, Houses and Inhabitants*, III, *Population Abstracts: Ages, Civil Condition, Occupations, etc.*

1874 (262) VI, *Report from the Select Committee on the Adulteration of Food Act (1872)*

1877 (362) IX, *Report from the Select Committee on the Cattle Plague and Importation of Livestock*

1878–9 (406) LXV, *Return of the Quantity of Fish conveyed inland by Railway from each of the principal Fishing Ports of England and Wales in the year 1878*

1881 (374) XIII; (374–I) XIV, *Report from the Select Committee on Railways*

1881 [C. 3096–II] XVII, *Royal Commission on Agriculture*

1882 [C. 3375–V] XV, *Royal Commission on Agriculture. Reports of Assistant Commissioners*

1882 (318) LXIV, *Return of the Quantity of Fish conveyed inland by Railway from each of the principal Fishing Ports of England and Wales, Scotland and Ireland, for each year since 1878*

1890–1 [C. 6268–I] XXXVII; [C. 6268–III] XXXVIII; [C. 6268–VI] XXXIX, *Royal Commission on Market Rights and Tolls*

1909 [Cd. 4928] XXIX, *Thirty-Eighth Annual Report of the Local Government Board, 1908–9*

1971 [Cmnd. 4645], National Board for Prices and Incomes, Report No. 165, *Prices, Profits and Costs in Food Distribution*

Local Acts of Parliament:

11 Geo. IV, c. 8: Salford Improvement Act, 1830

9 & 10 Vict., c. 219: Manchester Markets Act, 1846

33 & 34 Vict., c. 129: Salford Improvement Act, 1870

Bibliography

Parliamentary Debates:
Hansard, *Parliamentary Debates*, 3rd ser., LXXVIII, 1845

LOCAL GOVERNMENT RECORDS

The Court Leet Records of the Manor of Manchester, J.P. Earwaker (ed.),
   VIII–XII, 1756–1846, Manchester, 1888–90
Manchester Police Commissioners' Annual Reports, 1829–42
Manchester Borough/City Council Proceedings, 1844–70
Reports of the Officer of Health for Manchester, 1881, 1886, 1887
Salford Police Commissioners' Reports, 1831–45
Salford Borough Council Reports, 1844–52
Salford Borough Council Proceedings, 1853–79

MAPS and PLANS

Bancks and Thornton, *Plan of Manchester and Salford*, 1800
Bancks and Co., *Plan of Manchester and Salford*, 1828
Folding plan of Manchester and Salford in *Slater's Directory of Manchester
   and Salford*, 1850
Kelly, *Post Office Map of Manchester and Salford*, 1873

NEWSPAPERS, MAGAZINES and TRADE JOURNALS

The Co-operative News
The Co-operator
The Dairyman
The Farmer's Magazine
The Fish Trades Gazette
The Grocer
The Grocer's Journal
The Grocers' Weekly Circular and Price List
The Manchester Courier
The Manchester Guardian
The Manchester Mercury
The Manchester and Salford Advertiser
The Manchester and Salford Co-operative Herald
The Meat Trades Journal

BOOKS, ESSAYS, PAMPHLETS and REPORTS

Adshead, J., *Distress in Manchester: Evidence of the State of the Labouring
   Classes in 1840–42*, London, 1842

Aikin, J., *A Description of the Country from Thirty to Forty Miles round Manchester*, London, 1795

Anon., *A Brief Detail of the Home Fishery from Early Times*, London, 1763

Anon., *The History of Inland Navigations*, London, 1766

Anon., *An Account of the Land-Carriage Fish-Undertaking continued by Grant and Company*, London, 1768

Anon., 'Fishponds', *Annals of Agriculture*, XXXIII, 1799

Anon., 'A rural sketch of the county of Lancaster', *The Farmer's Magazine*, I, 1800

Anon., 'Some notes on poultry and fish', *Annals of Agriculture*, XXXIX, 1803

Anon., *A Letter to Francis Philips Esq. on his pamphlet entitled 'Murder is Out, etc.', by a native of the parish of Manchester*, Manchester, 1809

Anon., *The New Manchester Guide*, Manchester, 1815

Anon., *A Treatise on Milk*, London, 1825

Anon., 'Recollections of Manchester, 1808–30', in J. Harland (ed.), *Collectanea relating to Manchester and its neighbourhood, at various periods – II*, Chetham Society Publications, 1st ser., LXXII, Manchester, 1867

Anon., 'The proletariat on a false scent', *The Quarterly Review*, CXXXII, 1872

Aston, J., *The Manchester Guide*, Manchester, 1804

Aston, J., *A Reply to Mr M'Niven's 'Address to the Inhabitants of Manchester on the Impolicy of their Purchasing the Manor', by one of the addressed*, Manchester, 1809

Aston, J., *A Picture of Manchester*, Manchester, 1816

Aston, J., *Metrical Records of Manchester*, London, 1822

Axon, W.E.A. (ed.), *The Annals of Manchester*, Manchester, 1886

Bailey, J. and Culley, G., *General View of the Agriculture of the Counties of Northumberland, Cumberland and Westmoreland*, 3rd edn., London, 1813

Baines, E., *History, Directory and Gazetteer of the County Palatine of Lancaster*, 2 vols., Liverpool, 1824–25

Baines, E., *History of the County Palatine and Duchy of Lancaster*, 4 vols., London, 1836

Baines, T., *Lancashire and Cheshire, Past and Present*, 2 vols., London, 1867

Baker, H., 'On the growth of the commercial centre of Manchester: movement of population and pressure of habitation, 1861–71', *Transactions of the Manchester Statistical Society*, 1871–72

Bamford, S., *Early Days*, new edn., W.H. Chaloner (ed.), London, 1967

Bankes, J., 'On fish ponds', *Annals of Agriculture*, XL, 1804

Baxter, A., 'Grocers, oil and colourmen, etc.', in C. Booth (ed.), *Life and Labour of the People in London*, VII, London, 1896

Bear, W.E., 'The food supply of Manchester, I, vegetable produce', *JRASE*,

3rd ser., VIII, 1897

Bear, W.E., 'The food supply of Manchester, II, animal produce', *JRASE*, 3rd ser., VIII, 1897

Beesley, G., *A Report of the State of Agriculture in Lancashire*, Preston, 1849

Bernard, T., 'An account of a supply of fish for the labouring poor with observations', *The Pamphleteer*, I, 1813

Binns, J., *Notes on the Agriculture of Lancashire with Suggestions for its Improvement*, Preston, 1851

Board of Agriculture, *Agricultural State of the Kingdom*, London, 1816

Butterworth, E., *A Chronological History of Manchester*, Manchester, 1833

Butterworth, J., *The Antiquities of the Town, and a Complete History of the Trade of Manchester*, Manchester, 1822

Caird, J., *English Agriculture in 1850–51*, London, 1852

Campbell, J.H., 'Answers to queries relating to the agriculture of Lancashire', *Annals of Agriculture*, XX, 1793

Catt, G.R., *The Pictorial History of Manchester*, London, 1844

Chamberlaine, J., 'Account of making Cheshire cheese etc.', *Annals of Agriculture*, XVII, 1792

Cheshire Junction Railway, *Extracts from the Minutes of Evidence given in support of the Cheshire Junction Railway Bill before the Committee of the House of Lords in the session of 1836*, Manchester, 1836

Clarke, J.A., 'Farming of Lincolnshire', *JRASE*, 1st ser., XII, 1851

Cobbett, W., *Rural Rides*, G.D.H. and M. Cole (eds.), 3 vols., London, 1930

Cooke, G.A., *Topographical and Statistical Description of the County of Chester*, London, 1810

Co-operative Wholesale Society Ltd, *Co-operative Wholesale Society Limited: Annual for the year 1884*, Manchester, 1884

Cornish, J.E. and Cornish, T., *Cornishs' Stranger's Guide through Manchester and Salford*, Manchester, 1857

Defoe, D., *A Tour through the Whole Island of Great Britain*, Penguin edn., Harmondsworth, 1971

Dickens, Charles, *Hard Times*, Everyman's Library edn., London, 1966

Dickson, R.W., *General View of the Agriculture of Lancashire*, London, 1815

Disraeli, B., *Coningsby*, Everyman's Library edn., London, 1911

Dodd, G., *The Food of London*, London, 1856

Duffield, H.G., *The Stranger's Guide to Manchester*, Manchester, 1850

Eccleston, T., 'Remarkable culture of potatoes', *Annals of Agriculture*, XXXVII, 1801

Eden, F.M., *The State of the Poor*, 3 vols., London, 1797

Engels, F., *The Condition of the Working Class in England*, translated and edited by W.O. Henderson and W.H. Chaloner, Oxford, 1958

Failsworth Industrial Society Ltd, *Quarterly Reports*, Failsworth, 1860–75

Faucher, L., *Manchester in 1844: Its Present Condition and Future Prospects*, London, 1844

Fletcher, J., 'Statistical account of the markets of London', *JSSL*, X, 1847

Folio, F., *The Hawkers and Street Dealers of Manchester*, Manchester, 1858

Garnett, W.J., 'Farming of Lancashire', *JRASE*, 1st ser., X, 1849

Gaskell, E.C., *Mary Barton*, Everyman's Library edn., London, 1965

Gaskell, E.C., *North and South*, Everyman's Library edn., London, 1967

Gaskell, P., *Artisans and Machinery*, London, 1836

Graham, W.A., 'Adaptation of official returns of railway traffic to the general purposes of statistical inquiry', *JSSL*, VIII, 1845

Greenhow, E.H., *Papers Relating to the Sanitary State of the People of England*, London, 1858

Harding, W., 'Facts bearing on the progress of the railway system', *JSSL*, XI, 1848

Hardy, H., 'Costers and street sellers', in C. Booth (ed.), *Life and Labour of the People in London*, VII, London, 1896

Hayes, L.M., *Reminiscences of Manchester and some of its Local Surroundings from the Year 1840*, London, 1905

Herbert, R., 'Statistics of live stock and dead meat for consumption in the metropolis', *JRASE*, 1st ser., XX, 1859

[Heywood, J.], *The Strangers' Guide to Manchester*, Manchester, 1857

Holland, H., *General View of the Agriculture of Cheshire*, London, 1808

Holt, J., *General View of the Agriculture of the County of Lancaster*, London, 1795

Jenkins, H.M., 'Report on Cheshire dairy-farming', *JRASE*, 2nd ser., VI, 1870

Kay, J.P., *The Moral and Physical Condition of the Working Classes Employed in the Cotton Manufacture in Manchester*, 2nd edn., London, 1832

Kirkpatrick, H., *An Account of the Manner in which Potatoes are cultivated and preserved and the uses to which they are applied in the counties of Lancaster and Chester*, Warrington, 1796

Loudon, J.C., *An Encyclopaedia of Agriculture*, 5th edn., London, 1844

Love, B., *Manchester As It Is*, Manchester, 1839

Love, B., *The Handbook of Manchester*, Manchester, 1842

McConnel, W., 'An attempt to ascertain the quantity of butchers' meat consumed in Manchester in 1836', *Collection of Miscellaneous Reports and Papers read before the Manchester Statistical Society*, London and Manchester, 1838

McCulloch, J.R., *A Dictionary, Practical, Theoretical, and Historical, of Commerce and Commercial Navigation*, new edn., London, 1844; new edn., London, 1852; new edn., London, 1869

McCulloch, J.R., *A Descriptive and Statistical Account of the British Empire*,

Bibliography

3rd edn., 2 vols., London, 1847

McCulloch, J.R., *A Dictionary, Geographical, Statistical, and Historical, of the Various Countries, Places and Principal Natural Objects in the World*, new edn., 2 vols., London, 1852

MacGregor, J., *Commercial Statistics*, 5 vols., London, 1843–50

M'Niven, C., *An Address to the Inhabitants of Manchester on the Impolicy of their Purchasing the Manor*, Manchester, 1809

Manby, E.F., 'Cultivation of early potatoes', *JRASE*, 1st ser., XVIII, 1857

Manchester and Salford Sanitary Association, *Report of the Sub-Committee upon the Adulteration of Food*, Manchester, 1863

Marshall, W., *The Rural Economy of the Midland Counties*, 2 vols., London, 1790

Marshall, W., *The Review and Abstract of the County Reports to the Board of Agriculture*, 5 vols., York, 1818

Mayhew, H., *London Labour and the London Poor*, 4 vols., London, 1861–62

Medcalf, W., 'On the municipal institutions of the city of Manchester', *Transactions of the Manchester Statistical Society*, 1853–54

Morton, J.C., 'Town milk', *JRASE*, 2nd ser., IV, 1868

Morton, J.C., 'Report on the Liverpool prize-farm competition, 1877 – dairy and stock farms', *JRASE*, 2nd ser., XIII, 1877

Mosley, Sir Oswald, *Family Memoirs*, privately printed, 1849

Neild, W., 'Comparative statement of the income and expenditure of certain families of the working classes in Manchester and Dukinfield in the years 1836 and 1841', *JSSL*, IV, 1841–2

North, R., 'A discourse on fish and fish ponds', *Annals of Agriculture*, XXXVIII, 1802

Ogden, J., *A Description of Manchester by a Native of the Town*, Manchester, 1783

Page, J., 'The sources of supply of the Manchester fruit and vegetable markets', *JRASE*, 2nd ser., XVI, 1880

Palin, W., 'The farming of Cheshire', *JRASE*, 1st ser., V, 1844

Percival, T., 'Observations on the state of population in Manchester', (1789 edn.), reprinted in *Population and Disease in Early Industrial England*, Pioneers of Demography Series, Farnborough, Hants., 1973

Philips, F., *The Murder is Out, or Committee Men Fingering Cash*, Manchester, 1809

Philips, F., *Coke upon Lyttleton; or The Rejoinder*, Manchester, 1809

Plymley, J., *General View of the Agriculture of Shropshire*, London, 1803

Pomeroy, W.T., *General View of the Agriculture of the County of Worcester*, London, 1794

Poole, B., *Statistics of British Commerce*, London, 1852

Poole, B., *The Commerce of Liverpool*, London, 1854

Prentice, A., *History of the Anti-Corn-Law League*, 2 vols., London, 1853

Pringle, A., *General View of the Agriculture of Westmoreland*, London, 1794

Redhead, W., Laing, R. and Marshall, W., *Observations on the Different Breeds of Sheep and the State of Sheep Farming in Some of the Principal Counties of England*, Edinburgh, 1792

Rennie, G.B., Brown, R. and Shirreff, J., *General View of the Agriculture of the West Riding of Yorkshire*, London, 1794

Roberton, J., *Are the laws and customs of England, which interfere with the partition of landed property amongst children, and with the free disposal of it as a marketable commodity, beneficial or injurious to society?*, Manchester, 1852

Rothwell, W., *Report of the Agriculture of the County of Lancaster*, London, 1850

Salt, S., *Statistics and Calculations essentially necessary to Persons connected with Railways or Canals*, Manchester, 1845

Salt, S., *Facts and Figures, principally relating to Railways and Commerce*, London, 1848

Sandars, J., *A Letter on the Subject of the Projected Railroad between Liverpool and Manchester*, 5th edn., Liverpool, 1825

Shaw, W.A., *Manchester, Old and New*, 3 vols., London, 1896

Sheldon, J.P., *Dairy Farming*, London, 1881

Shirriff, S.D., 'Report upon the Liverpool prize-farm competition in Lancashire, Cheshire and North Wales, 1877 – arable farms', *JRASE*, 2nd ser., XIII, 1877

Sidney, S., *Railways and Agriculture in North Lincolnshire*, London, 1848

Slugg, J.T., *Reminiscences of Manchester Fifty Years Ago*, Manchester, 1881

Taylor, W. Cooke, *Notes of a Tour in the Manufacturing Districts of Lancashire*, 2nd edn., London, 1842

Tomlinson, W., *Bye-ways of Manchester Life*, Manchester, 1887

Tuke, J., *General View of the Agriculture of the North Riding of Yorkshire*, London, 1800

Wedge, T., *General View of the Agriculture of the County Palatine of Chester*, London, 1794

Wheeler, J., *Manchester: Its Political, Social and Commercial History, Ancient and Modern*, London, 1836

White, H., 'A detailed account of the making of Cheshire cheese', *JRASE*, 1st ser., VI, 1845

Whitehead, C., 'The cultivation of hops, fruit, and vegetables', *JRASE*, 2nd ser., XIV, 1878

Whittock, N. *et al.*, *The Complete Book of Trades*, London, 1837

Whitworth, G., *Shudehill Markets Mismanagement*, Manchester, 1875

Wilbraham, G., 'System in which potatoes are rendered beneficial to the poor in Cheshire', *Annals of Agriculture*, XXXV, 1800

Bibliography

Williams, J.B., 'On the principles of railway management', *JSSL*, IX, 1846
Wright, T., *The Great Unwashed*, London, 1868
Wright, W., 'On the improvements in the farming of Yorkshire since the date of the last reports in this journal', *JRASE*, 1st ser., XXII, 1861
Young, A., *A Six Months Tour Through the North of England*, 2nd edn., 4 vols., London, 1771
Young, A., 'Excursion to Yorkshire', *Annals of Agriculture*, XXVII, 1796
Young, A., *General View of the Agriculture of Lincolnshire*, 2nd edn., London, 1813

SECONDARY SOURCES

Albert, W., *The Turnpike Road System in England, 1663–1840*, Cambridge, 1972
Alexander, D., *Retailing in England during the Industrial Revolution*, London, 1970
Allatt, E., 'The "Ditch": Manchester's provision centre', *The Wholesale Grocer*, Nov. 1954
Allen, R.G.D., *Statistics for Economists*, 2nd edn., London, 1951
Anderson, G., *Victorian Clerks*, Manchester, 1976
Anderson, M., *Family Structure in Nineteenth Century Lancashire*, Cambridge, 1971
Armstrong, W.A., 'The use of information about occupation', in E.A. Wrigley (ed.), *Nineteenth-Century Society. Essays in the use of quantitative methods for the study of social data*, Cambridge, 1972
Armstrong, A., *Stability and Change in an English County Town: A Social Study of York, 1801–51*, Cambridge, 1974
Ashton, T.S., 'The standard of life of the workers in England, 1790–1830', in F.A. Hayek (ed.), *Capitalism and the Historians*, London, 1954
Atkins, P.J., 'London's intra-urban milk supply, *circa* 1790–1914, *Transactions of the Institute of British Geographers*, new ser., II, 1977
Atkins, P.J., 'The growth of London's railway milk trade, *c.* 1845–1914', *Journal of Transport History*, new ser., IV, 1978
Baker, D., 'The marketing of corn in the first half of the eighteenth century: north-east Kent', *Agricultural History Review*, 2nd ser., XVIII, 1970
Barker, T.C., 'Nineteenth century diet; some twentieth century questions', in T.C. Barker, J.C. McKenzie and J. Yudkin (eds.), *Our Changing Fare*, London, 1966
Barker, T.C., Oddy, D.J. and Yudkin, J., *The Dietary Surveys of Dr Edward Smith 1862–3: A New Assessment*, Occasional Paper No. 1, Department of Nutrition, Queen Elizabeth College, London, 1970
Beaver, M.W., 'Population, infant mortality and milk', *Population Studies*,

XXVII, 1973

Beavington, F., 'Early market gardening in Bedfordshire', *Transactions of the Institute of British Geographers*, XXXVII, 1965

Beavington, F., 'The development of market gardening in Bedfordshire, 1799–1939', *Agricultural History Review*, XXIII, 1975

Berry, B.J.L., *Geography of Market Centers and Retail Distribution*, Englewood Cliffs, NJ, 1967

Blackman, J., 'The food supply of an industrial town: a study of Sheffield's public markets, 1780–1900', *Business History*, V, 1963

Blackman, J., 'Changing marketing methods and food consumption', in T.C. Barker, J.C. McKenzie and J. Yudkin (eds.), *Our Changing Fare*, London, 1966

Blackman, J., 'The development of the retail grocery trade in the nineteenth century', *Business History*, IX, 1967

Blackman, J., 'The cattle trade and agrarian change on the eve of the railway age', *Agricultural History Review*, XXIII, 1975

Boase, F., *Modern English Biography*, 6 vols., London, 1892–1921

Bohstedt, J., *Riots and Community Politics in England and Wales, 1790–1810*, Cambridge, Mass., 1983

Bonser, K.J., *The Drovers*, London, 1970

Booth, A., 'Food riots in the north-west of England, 1790–1801', *Past and Present*, No. 77, 1977

Borsay, P., 'The English urban renaissance: the development of provincial urban culture, *c.* 1680-*c.* 1760', *Social History*, II, 1977

Bowley, A.L., *Wages in the United Kingdom in the Nineteenth Century*, Cambridge, 1900

Briggs, A., *Victorian Cities*, London, 1963

Burnett, J., *Plenty and Want: A Social History of Diet in England from 1815 to the Present Day*, London, 1966

Cannadine, D., 'Victorian cities. How different?', *Social History*, II, 1977

Carter, E.F., *An Historical Geography of the Railways of the British Isles*, London, 1959

Chalklin, C.W., *The Provincial Towns of Georgian England: A Study of the Building Process, 1740–1820*, London, 1974

Chaloner, W.H., 'The birth of modern Manchester', in British Association for the Advancement of Science, *Manchester and Its Region*, Manchester, 1962

Chaloner, W.H., 'Trends in fish consumption', in T.C. Barker, J.C. McKenzie and J. Yudkin (eds.), *Our Changing Fare*, London, 1966

Chambers, J.D., *Population, Economy and Society in Pre-Industrial England*, Oxford, 1972

Chambers, J.D. and Mingay, G.E., *The Agricultural Revolution, 1750–1880*, London, 1966

Channon, G., 'The Aberdeenshire beef trade with London: a study in steamship and railway competition, 1850–69', *Transport History*, II, 1969

Chartres, J.A., 'Markets and marketing in metropolitan western England in the late seventeenth and eighteenth centuries', in M. Havinden (ed.), *Husbandry and Marketing in the South-West, 1500–1800*, Exeter, 1973

Chartres, J.A., 'The marketing of agricultural produce', in J. Thirsk (ed.), *The Agrarian History of England and Wales*, V (II), *1640–1750*, Cambridge, 1985

Church, R.A., *The Great Victorian Boom, 1850–1873*, London, 1975

Clapham, J.H., *An Economic History of Modern Britain*, 3 vols., Cambridge, 1926–38

Corley, T.A.B., 'Nutrition, technology and the growth of the British biscuit industry, 1820–1900', in D.J. Oddy and D.S. Miller (eds.), *The Making of the Modern British Diet*, London, 1976

Crafts, N.F.R., *British Economic Growth during the Industrial Revolution*, Oxford, 1985

Cronjé, G., 'Tuberculosis and mortality decline in England and Wales, 1851–1910', in R. Woods and J. Woodward (eds.), *Urban Disease and Mortality in Nineteenth-Century England*, London, 1984

Crossick, G. and Haupt, H.-G. (eds.), *Shopkeepers and Master Artisans in Nineteenth-Century Europe*, London, 1984

Cullen, L.M., *Anglo-Irish Trade, 1660–1800*, Manchester, 1968

Cutting, C.L., *Fish Saving*, London, 1955

Cutting, C.L., 'Fish preservation as a factor in the extension of supply', in T.C. Barker and J. Yudkin (eds.), *Fish in Britain*, Occasional Paper No. 2, Department of Nutrition, Queen Elizabeth College, London, 1971

Davies, W.K.D., Giggs, J.A. and Herbert, D.T., 'Directories, rate books and the commercial structure of towns', *Geography*, LIII, 1969

Davis, D., *A History of Shopping*, London, 1966

Delépine, S., 'The Manchester milk supply from a public health point of view', *Transactions of the Manchester Statistical Society*, 1909–10

Dennis, R., *English Industrial Cities of the Nineteenth Century. A Social Geography*, Cambridge, 1984

Dodd, J.P., 'South Lancashire in transition: a study of the crop returns for 1795–1801', *Transactions of the Historic Society of Lancashire and Cheshire*, CXVII, 1965

Dow, G., *Great Central*, 3 vols., London, 1959–65

Drummond, J.C. and Wilbraham, A., *The Englishman's Food*, revised edn., by D.F. Hollingsworth, London, 1957

Edwards, M.M., *The Growth of the British Cotton Trade, 1780–1815*, Manchester, 1967

Ernle, Lord, *English Farming, Past and Present*, 6th edn., London, 1961

Everitt, A., 'The marketing of agricultural produce', in J. Thirsk (ed.), *The*

Agrarian History of England and Wales, IV, *1500–1640*, Cambridge, 1967

Farnie, D.A., 'The commercial development of Manchester in the later nineteenth century', *The Manchester Review*, VII, 1956

Farnie, D.A., *The English Cotton Industry and the World Market, 1815–1896*, Oxford, 1979

Fisher, F.J., 'The development of the London food market, 1540–1640', *EcHR*, 1st ser., V, 1934–5

Fleischman, R.K., *Conditions of Life among the Cotton Workers of Southeastern Lancashire, 1780–1850*, New York and London, 1985

Fletcher, T.W., 'Lancashire livestock farming during the great depression', *Agricultural History Review*, IX, 1961

Fletcher, T.W., 'The agrarian revolution in arable Lancashire', *TLCAS*, LXXII, 1962

Forrest, D., *Tea for the British*, London, 1973

Frangopulo, N.J. (ed.), *Rich Inheritance*, Manchester, 1962

Freeman, T.W., *The Conurbations of Great Britain*, 2nd edn., Manchester, 1966

Fussell, G.E., 'The London cheesemongers of the eighteenth century', *Economic History*, I, 1926–29

Fussell, G.E., 'The early days of railway milk transport – I', *Dairy Engineering*, LXXIII, 1956

Fussell, G.E., *The English Dairy Farmer, 1500–1900*, London, 1966

Fussell, G.E. and Goodman, C., 'Eighteenth-century traffic in livestock', *Economic History*, III, 1934–37

Fussell, G.E. and Goodman, C., 'The eighteenth-century traffic in milk products', *Economic History*, III, 1934–37

Fussell, G.E. and Goodman, C., 'Traffic in farm produce in eighteenth-century England; except livestock and livestock products', *Agricultural History*, XII, 1938

Garrard, J., *Leadership and Power in Victorian Industrial Towns, 1830–80*, Manchester, 1983

Gatrell, V.A.C., 'Labour, power, and the size of firms in Lancashire cotton in the second quarter of the nineteenth century', *EcHR*, 2nd ser., XXX, 1977

Gatrell, V.A.C., 'Incorporation and the pursuit of liberal hegemony in Manchester, 1790–1839', in D. Fraser (ed.), *Municipal Reform and the Industrial City*, Leicester, 1982

Gilbert, A.D., *Religion and Society in Industrial England*, London, 1976

Gilboy, E.W., *Wages in Eighteenth Century England*, Cambridge, Mass., 1934

Glass, D.V., *Numbering the People*, Farnborough, Hants., 1973

Gourvish, T.R., *Mark Huish and the London and North Western Railway*, Leicester, 1972

Granger, C.W.J. and Elliott, C.M., 'A fresh look at wheat prices and markets in the eighteenth century', *EcHR*, 2nd ser., XX, 1967

Green, D.R., 'Street trading in London: a case study of casual labour, 1830–60', in J.H. Johnson and C.G. Pooley (eds.), *The Structure of Nineteenth Century Cities*, London, 1982

Greenall, R.L., 'The making of the borough of Salford, 1830–1853', in S.P. Bell (ed.), *Victorian Lancashire*, Newton Abbot, 1974

Grinling, C.H., *The History of the Great Northern Railway, 1845–1922*, revised edn., London, 1966

Hadfield, C. and Biddle, G., *The Canals of North West England*, 2 vols., Newton Abbot,1970

Haldane, A.R.B., *The Drove Roads of Scotland*, London, 1952

Hall, P.G., *The Industries of London since 1861*, London, 1962

Hartwell, R.M., 'The rising standard of living in England, 1800–1850', *EcHR*, 2nd ser., XIII, 1961

Hawke, G.R., *Railways and Economic Growth in England and Wales, 1840–1870*, Oxford, 1970

Henstock, A., 'Cheese manufacture and marketing in Derbyshire and north Staffordshire, 1670–1870', *Derbyshire Archaeological Journal*, LXXXIX, 1969

Hewitt, M., *Wives and Mothers in Victorian Industry*, London, 1958

Hobsbawm, E.J., 'The British standard of living, 1790–1850', *EcHR*, 2nd ser., X, 1957

Hobsbawm, E.J., *Labouring Men*, London, 1964

Hobsbawm, E.J. and Hartwell, R.M., 'The standard of living during the industrial revolution: a discussion', *EcHR*, 2nd ser., XVI, 1963

Holderness, B.A., 'Prices, productivity and output', in G.E. Mingay (ed.), *The Agrarian History of England and Wales*, VI, *1750–1850*, Cambridge, 1989

Holmes, R.S., 'Ownership and migration from a study of rate books', *Area*, V, 1973

Holt, G.O., *A Regional History of the Railways of Great Britain*, X, *The North West*, Newton Abbot, 1978

Hoole, K., *A Regional History of the Railways of Great Britain*, IV, *North East England*, Dawlish, 1965

Howell, D.W., *Land and People in Nineteenth-Century Wales*, London, 1977

Hunt, E.H., *Regional Wage Variations in Britain, 1850–1914*, Oxford, 1973

Hunt, E.H. and Botham, F.W., 'Wages in Britain during the industrial revolution', *EcHR*, 2nd ser., XL, 1987

Jefferys, J.B., *Retail Trading in Britain, 1850–1950*, Cambridge, 1954

John, A.H., 'Aspects of English economic growth in the first half of the eighteenth century', *Economica*, new ser., XXVIII, 1961

Jones, B.C., 'Inventories of goods and chattels', *Amateur Historian*, II, 1954–5

Jones, E.L., 'The changing basis of English agricultural prosperity, 1853–73', *Agricultural History Review*, X, 1962

Jones, E.L. and Mingay, G.E. (eds.), *Land, Labour and Population in the Industrial Revolution*, London, 1967

Kellett, J.R., *The Impact of Railways on Victorian Cities*, London, 1969

Kidd, A.J., 'The middle class in nineteenth-century Manchester', in A.J. Kidd and K.W. Roberts (eds.), *City, Class and Culture: Studies of Social Policy and Cultural Production in Victorian Manchester*, Manchester, 1985

Kidd, A.J., ' "Outcast Manchester": voluntary charity, poor relief and the casual poor, 1860–1905', in A.J. Kidd and K.W. Roberts (eds.), *City, Class and Culture: Studies of Social Policy and Cultural Production in Victorian Manchester*, Manchester, 1985

Langton, J. and Laxton, P., 'Parish registers and urban structure: the example of late-eighteenth-century Liverpool', *Urban History Yearbook*, 1978

Lawton, R. and Pooley, C.G., 'David Brindley's Liverpool: an aspect of urban society in the 1880s', *Transactions of the Historic Society of Lancashire and Cheshire*, CXXV, 1974

Lee, C.H., *Regional Economic Growth in the United Kingdom since the 1880s*, London, 1971

Lindert, P.H. and Williamson, J.G., 'English workers' living standards during the industrial revolution: a new look', *EcHR*, 2nd ser., XXXVI, 1983

Lloyd-Jones, R. and Le Roux, A.A., 'The size of firms in the cotton industry: Manchester, 1815–41', *EcHR*, 2nd ser., XXXIII, 1980

Lloyd-Jones, R. and Lewis, M.J., *Manchester and the Age of the Factory*, London, 1988

McKenzie, J.C., 'The composition and nutritional value of diets in Manchester and Dukinfield in 1841', *TLCAS*, LXXII, 1962

McKeown, T., *The Modern Rise of Population*, London, 1976

McKeown, T. and Brown, R.G., 'Medical evidence related to English population changes in the eighteenth century', *Population Studies*, IX, 1955

McKeown, T. and Record, R.G., 'Reasons for the decline of mortality in England and Wales during the nineteenth century', *Population Studies*, XVI, 1962

Manchester Corporation Markets Department, *Manchester Markets, 1846–1946. The Story of 100 Years' Progress*, Manchester, 1946

Manchester Corporation Markets Department, *The Official Handbook of the City of Manchester Markets Department*, London, 1953

Marshall, J., *The Lancashire and Yorkshire Railway*, 3 vols., Newton Abbot, 1969–72

Mather, F.C., *After the Canal Duke: A Study of the Industrial Estates administered by the Trustees of the Third Duke of Bridgewater in the Age*

320

of Railway Building, 1825–1872, Oxford, 1970

Mathias, P., *English Trade Tokens: The Industrial Revolution Illustrated*, London, 1962

Mathias, P., *Retailing Revolution*, London, 1967

Mathias, P., *The First Industrial Nation: An Economic History of Britain, 1700–1914*, 2nd edn., London, 1983

Mercer, W.B., 'Two centuries of Cheshire cheese farming', *JRASE*, XCVIII, 1937

Mercer, W.B., *A Survey of the Agriculture of Cheshire*, London, 1963

Mitchell, B.R. and Deane, P., *Abstract of British Historical Statistics*, Cambridge, 1962

Mitchell, I., 'The development of urban retailing, 1700–1815', in P. Clark (ed.), *The Transformation of English Provincial Towns, 1600–1800*, London, 1984

Mui, H.-C. and Mui, L.H., 'Andrew Melrose, tea dealer and grocer of Edinburgh, 1812–1833', *Business History*, IX, 1967

Mui, H.-C. and Mui, L.H., *Shops and Shopkeeping in Eighteenth-Century England*, Montreal and London, 1989

Musson, A.E. and Robinson, E., *Science and Technology in the Industrial Revolution*, Manchester, 1969

Norton, J.E., *Guide to the National and Provincial Directories of England and Wales, excluding London, published before 1856*, London, 1950

Oddy, D.J., 'Urban famine in nineteenth-century Britain: the effect of the Lancashire cotton famine on working-class diet and health', *EcHR*, 2nd ser., XXXVI, 1983

O'Donovan, J., *The Economic History of Live Stock in Ireland*, Dublin, 1940

Ogden, J.H., *Failsworth Industrial Society Limited: Jubilee History, 1859–1909*, Manchester, 1909

Ó Gráda, C., 'The beginnings of the Irish creamery system, 1880–1914', *EcHR*, 2nd ser., XXX, 1977

Olsen, D.J., *The Growth of Victorian London*, London, 1976

Orwin, C.S. and Whetham, E.H., *History of British Agriculture, 1846–1914*, London, 1964

O'Tuathaigh, M.A.G., 'The Irish in nineteenth-century Britain: problems of integration', *Transactions of the Royal Historical Society*, 5th ser., XXXI, 1981

Pawson, E., *Transport and Economy: The Turnpike Roads of Eighteenth Century Britain*, London, 1977

Pelling, H., *Social Geography of British Elections, 1885–1910*, London, 1967

Perkin, H., *The Origins of Modern English Society, 1780–1880*, London, 1969

Perren, R., *The Meat Trade in Britain, 1840–1914*, London, 1978

Perren, R., 'Markets and marketing', in G.E. Mingay (ed.), *The Agrarian History of England and Wales*, VI, *1750–1850*, Cambridge, 1989

Phelps Brown, E.H. and Hopkins, S.V., 'Seven centuries of the prices of consumables, compared with builders' wage-rates', *Economica*, new ser., XXIII, 1956

Pooley, M.E. and Pooley, C.G., 'Health, society and environment in nineteenth-century Manchester', in R. Woods and J. Woodward (eds.), *Urban Disease and Mortality in Nineteenth-Century England*, London, 1984

Porter, G.R., *The Progress of the Nation*, revised edn., by F.W. Hirst, London, 1912

Porter, R.E., 'The marketing of agricultural produce in Cheshire during the nineteenth century', *Transactions of the Historic Society of Lancashire and Cheshire*, CXXVI, 1977

Porter, R.E., 'The value of farm notebooks: a new example from Cheshire', *The Local Historian*, XIII, 1979

Potter, J., 'Atlantic economy, 1815–60: the U.S.A. and the industrial revolution in Britain', in L.S. Pressnell (ed.), *Studies in the Industrial Revolution*, London, 1960

Pressnell, L.S., *Country Banking in the Industrial Revolution*, Oxford, 1956

Pryce, W.T.R. and Mills, D., *Aspects of Historical Geography*, 2, Units 16–17, Course D301, The Open University, Milton Keynes, 1982

Redfern, P., *The New History of the C.W.S.*, London, 1938

Redford, A., *Labour Migration in England, 1800–1850*, 2nd edn., Manchester, 1964

Redford, A. and Russell, I.S., *The History of Local Government in Manchester*, 3 vols., London, 1939–40

Rees, J. Aubrey, *The Grocery Trade: Its History and Romance*, 2 vols., London, 1932

Reid, D.A., 'The decline of Saint Monday, 1766–1876', *Past and Present*, No. 71, 1976

Roberts, B., 'Agrarian organization and urban development', in J.D. Wirth and R.L. Jones (eds.), *Manchester and São Paulo. Problems of Rapid Urban Growth*, Stanford, Calif., 1978

Roberts, R., *The Classic Slum*, Manchester, 1971

Rodgers, H.B., 'The suburban growth of Victorian Manchester', *Journal of the Manchester Geographical Society*, LVIII, 1961–62

Roeder, C., 'Beginnings of the Manchester post-office', *TLCAS*, XXII, 1904

Rostow, W.W., *British Economy of the Nineteenth Century*, Oxford, 1948

Rowntree, B.S., *Poverty: A Study of Town Life*, 2nd edn., London, 1902

Rudé, G., 'English rural and urban disturbances, 1830–1831', *Past and Present*, No. 37, 1967

Salaman, R.N., *The History and Social Influence of the Potato*, Cambridge, 1949

Bibliography

Salaman, R.N., 'The Oxnoble potato: a study in public house nomenclature', *TLCAS*, LXIV, 1954

Samuel, R., 'The workshop of the world: steam power and hand technology in mid-Victorian Britain, *History Workshop*, No. 3, 1977

Schofield, E.M., 'Food and cooking of the working class about 1900', *Transactions of the Historic Society of Lancashire and Cheshire*, CXXIII, 1971

Scola, R., 'Food markets and shops in Manchester, 1770–1870', *Journal of Historical Geography*, I, 1975

Scola, R., 'Retailing in the nineteenth-century town: some problems and possibilities', in J.H. Johnson and C.G. Pooley (eds.), *The Structure of Nineteenth Century Cities*, London, 1982

Scott, P., *Geography and Retailing*, London, 1970

Sharpless, J.B., 'Intercity development and dependency: Liverpool and Manchester', in J.D. Wirth and R.L. Jones (eds.), *Manchester and São Paulo. Problems of Rapid Urban Growth*, Stanford, Calif., 1978

Shaw, G., *Processes and Patterns in the Geography of Retail Change, with special reference to Kingston upon Hull, 1880–1950*, Occasional Papers in Geography, No. 24, University of Hull, 1978

Shirley, R.W., 'Legal institutions and early industrial growth', in J.D. Wirth and R.L. Jones (eds.), *Manchester and São Paulo. Problems of Rapid Urban Growth*, Stanford, Calif., 1978

Simon, S.D., *A Century of City Government: Manchester, 1838–1938*, London, 1938

Skeel, C., 'The cattle trade between Wales and England from the fifteenth to the nineteenth centuries', *Transactions of the Royal Historical Society*, 4th ser., IX, 1926

Smith, A.T., 'Chronology of Salford', in T. Bergin, D.N. Pearce and S. Shaw (eds.),*Salford, A City and Its Past*, Salford, 1974

Smith, F.B., *The People's Health, 1830–1910*, London, 1979

Smith, J.H., 'The cattle trade of Aberdeenshire in the nineteenth century', *Agricultural History Review*, III, 1955

Smith, R., 'Manchester as a centre for the manufacture and merchanting of cotton goods, 1820–30', *University of Birmingham Historical Journal*, IV, 1953–4

Steel, W.L., *The History of the London and North Western Railway*, London, 1914

Stern, W.M., 'Fish supplies for London in the 1760s: an experiment in overland transport – I', *Journal of the Royal Society of Arts*, May, 1970

Stern, W.M., 'Fish supplies for London in the 1760s: an experiment in overland transport – II', *Journal of the Royal Society of Arts*, June, 1970

Stern, W.M., 'The fish supply to Billingsgate from the nineteenth century to the Second World War', in T.C. Barker and J. Yudkin (eds.), *Fish in Britain*, Occasional Paper No. 2, Department of Nutrition, Queen

Elizabeth College, London, 1971

Swindells, T., *Manchester Streets and Manchester Men*, 5 vols., Manchester, 1906–8

Tait, J. (ed.), *The Court Leet or Portmoot Records of Salford, 1735–1738*, Chetham Society Publications, new ser., XCIV, Manchester, 1935

Taylor, D., 'London's milk supply, 1850–1900: a reinterpretation', *Agricultural History*, XLV, 1971

Taylor, D., 'The English dairy industry, 1860–1930', *EcHR*, 2nd ser., XXIX, 1976

Tebbutt, M., *Making Ends Meet: Pawnbroking and Working-Class Credit*, Leicester, 1983

Thomas, B., 'Escaping from constraints: the industrial revolution in a Malthusian context', in R.I. Rotberg and T.K. Rabb (eds.), *Population and History: From the Traditional to the Modern World*, Cambridge, 1986

Thomas, W.J. and Perkins, R.J., 'Land utilization and agriculture in the north-west', in British Association for the Advancement of Science, *Manchester and Its Region*, Manchester, 1962

Thompson, E.P., 'The moral economy of the English crowd in the eighteenth century', *Past and Present*, No. 50, 1971

Thompson, F., *Lark Rise to Candleford*, Penguin edn., Harmondsworth, 1974

Titterton, T.B., *A Brief History, 1875–1961: J. Titterton & Sons Ltd.*, Stockport, 1961

Tomlinson, V.I., 'Salford activities connected with the Bridgewater Canal', *TLCAS*, LXVI, 1956

Tomlinson, V.I., 'The Manchester, Bolton, and Bury Canal Navigation and Railway Company, 1790–1845, I, the canal', *TLCAS*, LXXV–LXXVI, 1965–6

Tomlinson, W.W., *The North-Eastern Railway*, 2nd edn., Newton Abbot, 1967

Torode, A., 'Trends in fruit consumption', in T.C. Barker, J.C. McKenzie and J. Yudkin (eds.), *Our Changing Fare*, London, 1966

Tranter, N.L., *Population and Society, 1750–1940*, London, 1985

Treble, J.H., *Urban Poverty in Britain, 1830–1914*, London, 1979

Trow-Smith, R., *English Husbandry: From the Earliest Times to the Present Day*, London, 1951

Tupling, G.H., 'Lancashire markets in the sixteenth and seventeenth centuries – I', *TLCAS*, LVIII, 1945–6

Tupling, G.H., 'Lancashire markets in the sixteenth and seventeenth centuries – II', *TLCAS*, LIX, 1947

Tupling, G.H., *Lancashire Directories, 1684–1957*, revised edn., by S. Horrocks, Manchester, 1968

Unwin, G., *Samuel Oldknow and the Arkwrights*, Manchester, 1924

Bibliography

Vigier, F., *Change and Apathy. Liverpool and Manchester during the Industrial Revolution*, Cambridge, Mass., 1970

Wadsworth, A.P., 'The first Manchester Sunday schools', in M.W. Flinn and T.C. Smout (eds.), *Essays in Social History*, Oxford, 1974

Wadsworth, A.P. and Mann, J. de L., *The Cotton Trade and Industrial Lancashire, 1600–1780*, Manchester, 1931

Walton, J.K., *Lancashire. A Social History, 1558–1939*, Manchester, 1987

Ward, D., 'Victorian cities. How modern?', *Journal of Historical Geography*, I, 1975

Webb, S. and Webb, B., 'The assize of bread', *The Economic Journal*, XIV, 1904

Webb, S. and Webb, B., *English Local Government*, IV, *Statutory Authorities for Special Purposes*, London, 1922

Weinstock, M., *More Dorset Studies*, Dorchester, 1960

Werly, J.M., 'The Irish in Manchester, 1832–49', *Irish Historical Studies*, XVIII, 1972–3

Westerfield, R.B., *Middlemen in English Business, particularly between 1660 and 1760*, New Haven, Conn., 1915

Whetham, E.H., 'The London milk trade, 1860–1900', *EcHR*, 2nd ser., XVII, 1964

Wild, M.T. and Shaw, G., 'Locational behaviour of urban retailing during the nineteenth century: the example of Kingston upon Hull', *Transactions of the Institute of British Geographers*, LXI, 1974

Wild, M.T. and Shaw, G., 'Population distribution and retail provision: the case of the Halifax–Calder Valley area of West Yorkshire during the second half of the nineteenth century', *Journal of Historical Geography*, I, 1975

Wild, M.T. and Shaw, G., 'Trends in urban retailing: the British experience during the nineteenth century', *Tijdschrift voor Economische en Sociale Geografie*, LXX, 1979

Wilkinson, H.B., *Old Hanging Ditch: Its Trades, Its Traders and Its Renaissance*, London, 1910

Willan, T.S., *An Eighteenth-Century Shopkeeper: Abraham Dent of Kirkby Stephen*, Manchester, 1970

Wilson, C., 'Economy and society in late Victorian Britain', *EcHR*, 2nd ser., XVIII, 1965

Wingate, J.W. and Corbin, A. (eds.), *Changing Patterns in Retailing*, Homewood, Ill., 1956

Winstanley, M.J., *The Shopkeeper's World, 1830–1914*, Manchester, 1983

Wohl, A.S., *Endangered Lives. Public Health in Victorian Britain*, London, 1983

Wrigley, E.A., 'Men on the land and men in the countryside: employment in agriculture in early-nineteenth-century England', in L. Bonfield, R.M.

Smith and K. Wrightson (eds.), *The World We Have Gained: Histories of Population and Social Structure*, Oxford, 1986

Wrigley, E.A. and Schofield, R.S., *The Population History of England, 1541–1871: A Reconstruction*, London, 1981

Wyke, T.J., 'Nineteenth century Manchester: a preliminary bibliography', in A.J. Kidd and K.W. Roberts (eds.), *City, Class and Culture: Studies of Social Policy and Cultural Production in Victorian Manchester*, Manchester, 1985

Yudkin, J., 'History and the nutritionist', in T.C. Barker, J.C. McKenzie and J. Yudkin (eds.), *Our Changing Fare*, London, 1966

UNPUBLISHED SECONDARY SOURCES

Atkins, P.J., 'The milk trade of London, *c.* 1790–1914', University of Cambridge, Ph.D., 1977

Battersby, R.J., 'The development of market gardening in England, 1850–1914', University of London, Ph.D., 1960

Bellamy, J.M., 'Some aspects of the economy of Hull in the nineteenth century with special reference to business history', University of Hull, Ph.D., 1965

Buzzacott, K.L., 'London's markets: their growth, characteristics and functions', University of London, Ph.D., 1972

Davies, C.S., 'The agricultural history of Cheshire, 1750–1850', University of Manchester,Ph.D., 1953

McGrath, P.V., 'The marketing of food, fodder and livestock in the London area in the seventeenth century, with some reference to the sources of supply', University of London, M.A., 1948

Malley, E., 'The financial administration of the Bridgewater estate, 1780–1800', University of Manchester, M.A., 1929

Mitchell, S.I., 'Urban markets and retail distribution 1730–1815, with particular reference to Macclesfield, Stockport and Chester', University of Oxford, D.Phil., 1974

Porter, R.E., 'Agricultural change in Cheshire during the nineteenth century', University of Liverpool, Ph.D., 1974

Sutton, J.H., 'Early Fleetwood, 1835–1847', University of Lancaster, M.Litt., 1968

Index

Index

Index

mortality rates, 278
sugar
consumption, 275, 277
retail distribution channels, 206, 207, 208, 228
wholesale sources of James Bentley's stock, 218, *219*
sulphate of lime, adulterant in flour and sweetmeats, 267
Sutcliffe, John, butcher, 187 n. 30
Swan, Samuel, cheesemonger, 218
Swan Street, Manchester, *155*, 156, 169
sweets, retail distribution channels, 207, 224

Taylor, D., 71–2
tea
adulteration, 269
consumption, 277
retail trade in shops, 206, 207, 208
retail trade, itinerant, 250, 269
wholesale sources of James Bentley's stock, 218, *219*
wholesale trade, *215*, 216–18
tea dealers, retail, 204, 206
Tebbutt, Thomas, grocer and tallow chandler, 219
telegraph system, effect on livestock trade, 68
tench, 129
Thompson, Flora, 246
Timperley, Cheshire, 99
transport of vegetables by road from, 105 n. 48, 112
Tipperary, Ireland, Co-operative Wholesale Society's Irish butter buyers based in, 83
Tocqueville, Alexis de, 21
tolls
Bridgewater Canal, 111
markets in Manchester, 151–60 *passim*, 169, 175, 177
markets in Salford, 172–3, 174–5
payments in lieu of, by railway companies, to Manchester Corporation, 107, 108, 109–10
Toryism, in Manchester, 26–8
Town Clerk of Manchester, *see* Heron, Sir Joseph
trade cycle, 15
see also economic fluctuations; trade depressions
trade depressions, 273–6
and mortality rates, 278–80
effects on diet, 274–5, 276–7
trade journals, value as source, 12
trade tokens, 208, Plate 12
trading records, scarcity of, value as source, 12–13, 209–10
treacle

consumption, 277
retail distribution channels, 207, 228
Tremenheere, H.S., factory inspector, 223–4
Trent, River, traffic in Cheshire cheese, 90
trout, 129
price, 130
tuberculosis, 280, 281, 282
turbot, 127, 128
turnips
as livestock fodder, 96, 116
consumption, 193
increase in cultivation in Lancashire and Cheshire, 114, 116
prices, 113–20
seasonal availability, 117–18, *119*
sources of supply, 96–8, 109–10
turnover of retailers
Abraham Dent, 210
Andrew Melrose, 210
butchers, 182, *183*, 189
Failsworth Industrial Society, grocery and provision departments, 211–12, *213*
grocers, 182, *183*, 211, 212
Isaac Burgon, 210–11
James Bentley, 210, *211*
Manchester and Salford Equitable Co-operative Society, grocery and provision departments, 211, 212, *213*
provision dealers, 182, *183*, 211, 212
turnpikes, 8–9
Twyford, Jonah, corn dealer, 207
typhoid, 282
typhus, 280

unemployment (and/or short-time)
and price movements of foodstuffs, 272–3
effects on diet, 272, 273, 274–5, 276–7
United States of America
and Cotton Famine, 276
apple imports from, 121, 123
bacon and ham imports from, 63
butter imports from, 81 n. 57
cheese imports from, 92
salt-pork imports from, 64

veal
'slinked', 270
supplies from Lancashire and Cheshire, 38, 61–2
see also calves
vegetables, 2, 3
consumption, 116, 193, 238, 241–2, 244, 253, 262
cultivation in Lancashire and Cheshire, 93–8, 114–16
imports, 118

345